The
Maine
COAST
GUIDE

for small boats

MAINE COAST GUIDE

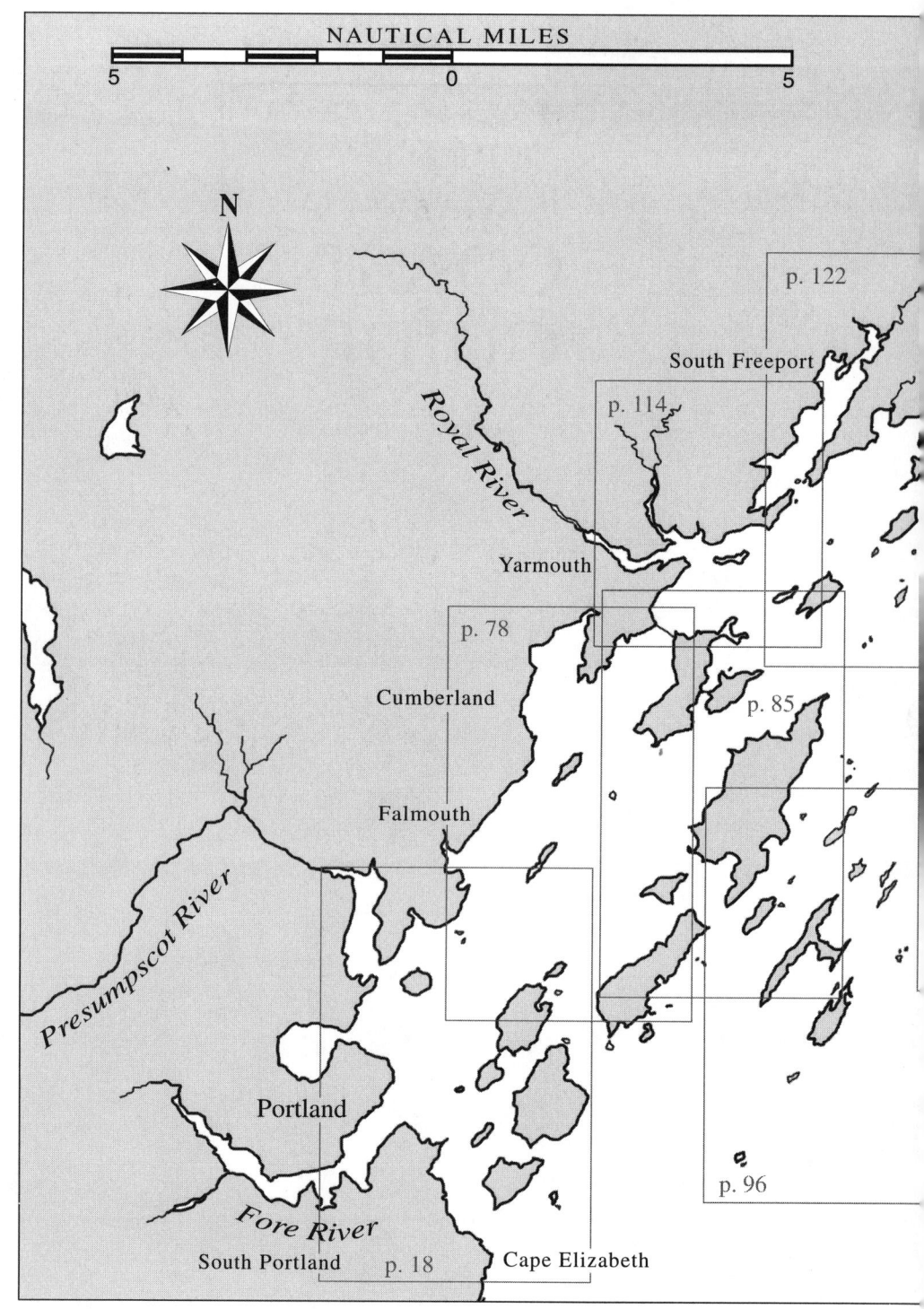

Index chart

CASCO BAY

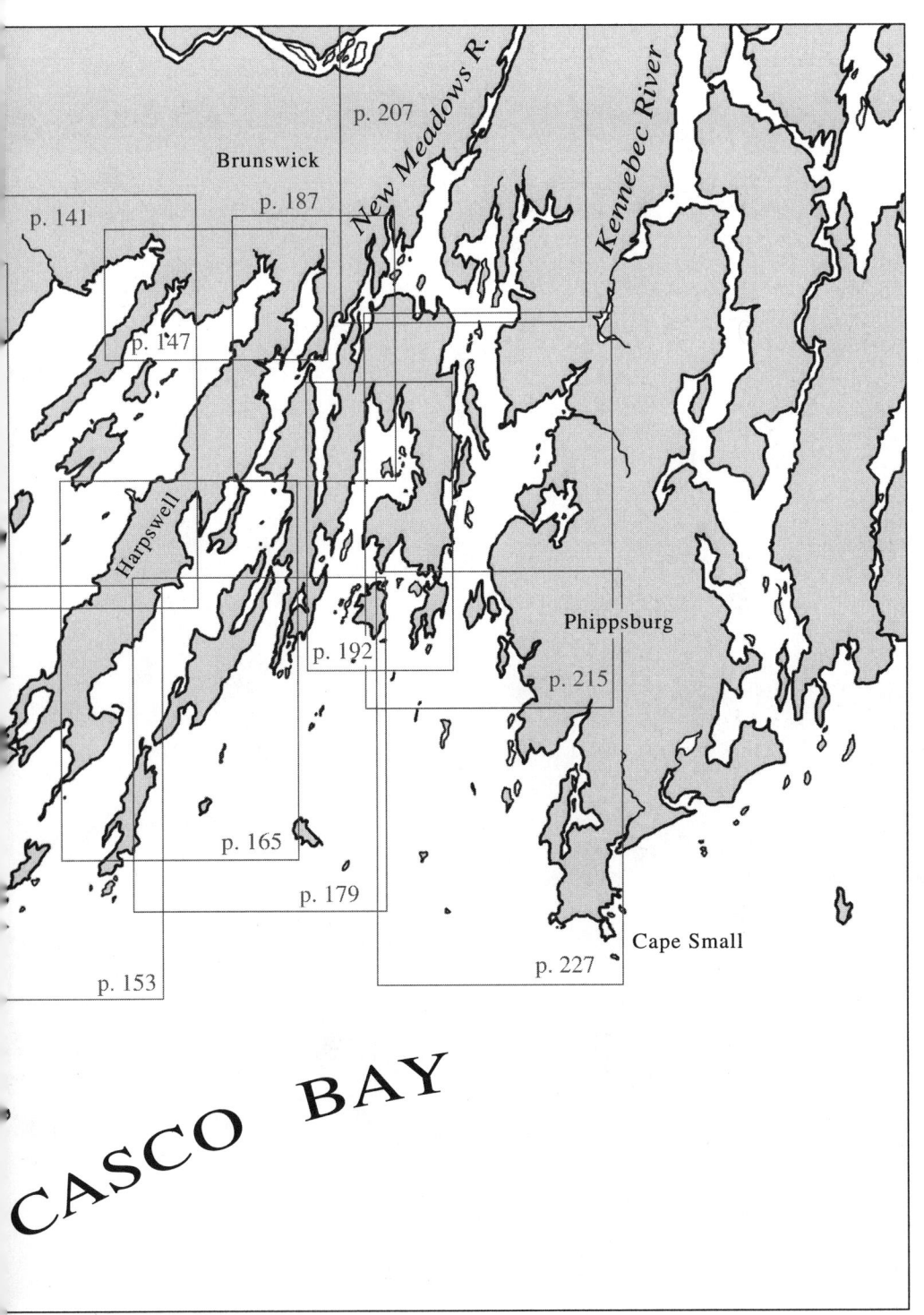

Index chart

The Maine
COAST
GUIDE

for small boats

———— CASCO BAY ————

Curtis Rindlaub

Published by Diamond Pass Publishing, Inc.
Printed in the United States of America

Copyright © 2000 by Curtis C. Rindlaub

All Rights reserved. No part of this book may be reproduced or transmitted in any form or by any means, electronic or mechanical, including photocopying, recording, or any information and storage retrieval system without prior permission in writing from the publisher.

"Diamond Pass Publishing" and "Maine Coast Guide" are registered trademarks.

> The entries from the diary of Jeremiah P. Applegate, pages 36-37, were discovered by the Deering High School Creative Writing Class of 1938 and published in their *Stroudwater Sketches*, Portland, Maine.
>
> Excerpt on page 42 originally published in *Island Journal*; reprinted with permission from the Island Institute.
>
> Excerpts on pages 185, 212, and 232 from *Yankee Coast*, by Robert P. Tristram Coffin. Copyright 1947 by Robert P. Tristram Coffin. Copyright renewed © 1975 by Richard N. Coffin, Mary Alice Westcott, and Robert P.T. Coffin, Jr.. Excerpts used with permission of Scribner, a Division of Simon and Schuster.

> While every effort has been made to assure the accuracy of this book, it is not a substitute for careful judgment, prudent seamanship, and common sense. Neither the publishers nor the authors assume any liability for any errors or omissions or for how this book or its contents are used or interpreted or for any consequences resulting directly or indirectly from the use of this book.

Questions, comments, and suggestions are greatly appreciated.
Please address them to:

Diamond Pass Publishing, Inc.　　　　　　　　　　207-766-2337
19 Brook Lane　　　　　　　　　　　　　　diamondpass@gwi.net
Peaks Island, Maine 04108　　　　　http://www.gwi.net/diamondpass

Library of Congress Catalogue Card Number:
ISBN: 0-9649246-2-5

Where hillside oaks and beeches
Overlook the long, blue reaches,
Silver coves, and pebbled beaches
And green isles of Casco Bay.

John Greenleaf Whittier

CONTENTS

Index chart *ii*
Preface *xii*
How to use this book *xiv*
Small Boating in Maine *3-15*

Portland and the City Islands *19*
Portland Head *19*
Fore River *32*
Portland *38*
The Portland Islands *49-68*

The Western Shore *69*
Presumpscot River *69*
Falmouth *77*
Cousins Island *84*
Little John *87*

Chebeague and Vicinity *89*
Great Chebeague *89*
Little Chebeague *92*

The Outer Islands of Western Casco Bay *99*
Cliff *99*
Jewell *103*
Halfway Rock *111*

Western Rivers and Islands *115*
Royal River *115*
Cousins River *118*
Harraseeket River *124*
Wolfe's Neck *134*
Bustins and the Silver Islands *136*

The Central Bays *140*
Maquoit Bay *140*
Wharton Point *142*
Middle Bay *144*
Merepoint *144*
Birch Island *145*
Middle Bay Cove *146*
Lookout Point *148*
The Goslings *150*
Whaleboat Island *154*

Potts Harbor and Broad Sound *155*
Basin Cove *156*
Haskell Island *159*
Broad Sound *161*
Eagle Island *161*

Harpswell and Merriconeag Sounds *164*
Orrs Island *166*
Bailey Island *170*
Wills Gut *172*

Eastern Casco Bay *178*
Sebascodegan Island *184*
Inside Passage *186*
Quahog Bay *192*
Ridley Cove *197*

Eastern Outer Islands *201*
Ragged Island *201*
Mark Island *204*

New Meadows River *205*
New Meadows Lake *205*
Sawyer Park *209*
The Gurnet *211*
Winnegance Bay *216*
The Basin *220*
Cundys Harbor *221*

The Eastern Shore *225*
Sebasco Harbor *228*
West Point *230*
Cape Small Harbor *234*
Hermit Island *237*
Small Point *240*

Appendixes *242*
Emergency numbers *242*
Environmental organizations *244*
Boat rentals *247*
Public transportation *248*
Saltwater fishing *249-252*
Launching ramps *253*
Fuel Services *254*
Dining by boat *255*

CHARTS

Index Chart *ii*

Overview charts
Portland Harbor *18*
Fore River *33*
Presumpscot River *70*
Hussey Anchorage *78*
Chebeague Island and vicinity *85*
Outer Islands of Casco Bay *96*
Royal and Cousins River *114*
Harraseeket River and Flying Point *122*
Maquoit and Middle Bay *141*
Upper Middle Bay *147*
Potts Harbor and Broad Sound *153*
Harpswell and Merriconeag Sound *165*
Eastern Casco Bay *179*
Inside Passage *187*
Quahog Bay and Ridley Cove *192*
Upper New Meadows River *207*
Lower New Meadows River *215*
Small Point and Cape Small *227*

Detail Charts
Portland Head *20*
Ram Island *22*
Danford Cove *25*
Simonton Cove, Willard Beach *26*
Spring Point *27*
Bug Light, South Portland Boat Ramp *29*
Sunset Marina, Centerboard Yacht Club *31*
South Port Marine *32*
Stroudwater *35*
Portland waterfront *39*
Portland Yacht Services, Fish Point *44*
East End Beach *46*
Back Cove *47*
Fort Gorges, Diamond Island Ledge *49*

House Island *51*
Cushing Point *54*
Peaks Island *55*
Whitehead Passage *58*
Little Diamond Island *60*
Great Diamond Island, Diamond Cove *62*
Hussey Sound *64*
Big Sandy Beach, Vaill Island *67*
Gilsland Farm, Mile Pond *73*
Presumpscot Falls *74*
Mackworth Island *75*
Falmouth Foreside *79*
Broad Cove *82*
Prince Point *83*
Basket Island *84*
Doyle Point, Cousins Island *84*
Sandy Point, Cousins Island *86*
Littlejohn Island *88*
Chebeague Island *89*
Little Chebeague Island *93*
Crow Island, Long Island *94*
Chandler Cove, Chebeague Island *95*
Sand Island *97*
Crow Island, Chebeague I. Boat Yard *98*
Cliff Island *99*
Outer Green Island *101*
Inner Green Island *102*
Jewell Island *105*
West Brown Cow, Broken Cove *110*
Halfway Rock *111*
Bangs Island *112*
Bates, Ministerial, and Stave Island *113*
Royal River *116*
Cousins River *118*
Upper Cousins River, Pratts Brook *120*
Winslow Memorial Park *121*
Lanes Island, Fogg Point *121*

Moshier, Little Moshier Island *123*
South Freeport, Harraseeket River *125*
Porter Landing, Harraseeket River *128*
Mast Landing *131*
Wolfe's Neck State Park *134*
Little River, Recompence Shore *135*
Bustins Island *137*
The Silver Islands *139*
Little Flying Point *140*
Wharton Point *142*
Merepoint Bay *144*
Simpsons Point *146*
Middle Bay Cove, Carrying Place *147*
Lookout Point *148*
Upper Goose Island *149*
The Goslings *150*
Little Whaleboat Island *152*
Whaleboat Island *154*
Potts Harbor *155*
Basin Cove *156*
Potts Point *158*
Upper Flag Island *159*
Haskell Island *160*
Eagle Island *161*
Little Mark Island, Great Mark I. *163*
Strawberry Creek Island *164*
Long Cove, Lumbos hole *167*
Reed Cove, Beals Cove, Orrs I. *169*
Stover Cove *170*
Wills Gut *173*
Mackerel Cove, Bailey Island *175*
Lands End, Bailey Island *176*
Little Harbor, Giant's Steps *180*
Water Cove *181*
Lowell Cove *182*
Pond Island *183*
Ram Island *184*

Ewin Narrows *188*
Prince Gurnet, Doughty Island *188*
Buttermilk Cove, Theg Gurnet *189*
Gun Point Cove, Long Point Cove *190*
Cedar Ledges *191*
Orrs Cove, Great Island Boat Yard *193*
Snow, Little Snow Island *194*
Card Cove, Pole Island *195*
Raspberry Island *195*
Bethel Point, Yarmouth Island *196*
Ridley Cove *197*
Jenny Island *199*
Two Bush, Elm Islands *199*
Ragged Island *201*
Round Rock, Saddleback Ledge *202*
New Meadows Lake *206*
New Meadows Marina, Sawyer Park *209*
Thomas Bay *210*
The Gurnet, Coombs Islands *211*
Back Cove, Hamilton Sanctuary *213*
Mill Cove, Sabino *214*
Three Islands *216*
Brighams Cove *217*
Painted Point Ramp *217*
Long Island Harbor *218*
Dingley Island, Dingley Cove *219*
The Basin *220*
Cundys Harbor *221*
Fort Point, Sandy Cove *222*
Malaga Island, Sebasco *225*
Sebasco Harbor *229*
West Point *230*
Tottman Cove *233*
Cape Small Harbor *235*
Head Beach, Hermit Island *238*
Bald Head *239*
Small Point *240*

PREFACE

FEW people are lucky enough to have explored the magnificent coast of Maine from the perspective of a small boat, tucking in and out of creeks and rivers, discovering secluded pocket beaches, or venturing out to offshore islands. The *Maine Coast Guides* detail coastal small-boat exploration opportunities throughout Maine, region by region. Whether you are a kayaker, canoeist, cruising sailor, or sports fisherman—whether you operate a sport boat, a skiff, a punt, a pocket-cruiser, or an inflatable—these guides will help you discover the thin band of the Maine coast that ebbs and flows between sea and land, between air and water, between man and nature, between the past and the future.

The *Maine Coast Guides* are intended both for boaters unfamiliar with the coast of Maine—or with particular parts of it—and for veteran Maine boaters. With meticulous attention to detail, these guides pinpoint all areas of public access to Maine's waters—where to launch your boats and where to land them and where to park your cars while you take to the water. They suggest places to explore, from winding tidal creeks and rivers to remote offshore islands. They locate hikes and pocket beaches, life-giving marshes behind barrier islands and rugged coasts battered by crashing waves.

The *Maine Coast Guides* will help you plan your explorations prudently. They include hundreds of overview charts and detailed sketch charts with clear piloting descriptions by land and by sea. They depict outfitters, boat services, boat rental and touring opportunities, and small-boat events along the coast. They will steer you toward restaurants on the water and to nearby campgrounds and lodgings, so you can extend your visit.

On the water, the Guides alert you to possible dangers and help you plan for them or avoid them altogether. They discuss tides, currents, fog, and small-boat coastal navigation. They describe areas of protection from the winds and the seas and safe passages when the weather turns foul. And, in the event that you should need them, they contain complete listings of emergency numbers.

The *Maine Coast Guides* follow the natural geographic divisions of the coast into six distinct regions, each with its own guidebook. This keeps each guide small enough for use aboard small boats yet big enough to contain in-depth detail of the region. Each Guide will introduce you to a new area or help broaden your understanding of your familiar summer waters by steering you toward new gunkholes, tickles, and picnic spots or by helping you discover something new about the ecology or history of these magic places.

Mostly, these Guides are meant to inspire. The *Maine Coast Guides* focus on the coast more intimately than any other previous source. Hopefully, they will entice you to strap the kayak or skiff to the top of the car and head for the coast. Or they will encourage you to take on a little more fuel for that summer picnic and head for more distant horizons. Or perhaps they will tempt you to row the dinghy past your anchored yacht and up the quiet waters of a nearby estuary. Most importantly, we hope they will help you appreciate the tempestuous beauty, the miraculous fragility, and the staunch ruggedness of this beguiling coast.

Few places on earth are as magnificent as the Maine coast, and all it takes to discover it is a fair sky and a small boat.

Enjoy.

HOW TO USE THIS BOOK

This Maine Coast Guide is designed to be used both as a stand-alone reference for trip planning or general interest and as a working tool on the water to be used in conjunction with standard nautical charts.

General Information

"Small Boating in Maine" details the joys and challenges of exploring the Maine coast in a small boat—the boating seasons, Maine's weather, tides and currents, fog, safe preparation and navigation, and environmental concerns. Please read this section first.

Geography

Maine's geography does not lend itself easily to being lined up in a certain order. The Coast Guides presume that a small-boat voyage begins on the mainland and radiates outwards to nearby offshore destinations. These hub-and-spoke areas are covered with an index chart, overview charts, detail charts, and text entries, beginning from the southwest and working toward the northeast.

Index chart

An index chart at the beginning of this guide shows the entire region and the geographic and page-number location of each overview chart.

Overview charts

Full-page overview charts cover general areas of the region. Each chart is referenced by the index chart and the chart list at the beginning of this book. They provide a general lay of the land: its coast, its prominent features, and nearby landmarks.

Overview charts pinpoint the location of each numbered text entry in this guide. These numbers should be copied to your navigational charts for quick reference on the water. General courses and their headings are also shown. All charts in the Casco Bay volume are based on NOAA chart 13290 or, where necessary, on USGS topographic maps.

Overview and detail charts are for illustration and orientation only and should not be used for navigation.

Detail charts

Over a hundred detail charts provide a close-up look at many of this guide's entries. They illustrate the specifics of the location—parking, launching, approaches, offshore dangers, landing areas, beaches.

Entries

Numbered text entries describe anything of interest to boaters—launching ramps, put-ins, picnic beaches, tackle shops and chandleries, danger spots, locations of historical significance, areas of shallow-draft exploration, fuel docks and waterfront restaurants, hiking trails, and areas of significant natural history. The location of each entry is shown on the nearby overview chart. Please note: many entries describe private property for historical or general interest and for the sake of completeness. *An entry included in this book does not in anyway constitute permission to land on private property.* Individual entries may be preceded by the following symbols depicting available facilities:

🗼	lighthouse
🛥	launching ramp
🛶	portable boat put-in
⚓	moorings and dockage
⚓	anchorage
J	fishing spot, supplies
⛺	camping
⛽	fuel, gas or diesel
🚰	fresh water
🔧	mechanic
	pump-out station
🚽	toilet
🚿	showers
🛒	groceries
🍴	restaurant
	laundromat
☎	telephone
👣	hiking trails

xv

SMALL BOATING IN MAINE

People have been navigating the coast of Maine in small boats for thousands of years. Mainland natives traveled regularly by canoe to offshore summer settlements for hunting, clamming, fishing, and feasting. Island settlers piloted small boats to neighboring islands and the mainland, and lighthouse keepers often rowed small dories or skiffs great distances to get supplies for their isolated outposts.

Today, boaters are again discovering the joys and challenges of exploring in small boats of all kinds. Small boats enable us to live away from the water, yet still enjoy it. They give us the freedom to explore different areas of the coast by traveling between them by land rather than making an arduous sea passage. Their slight build and draft allow us to squeeze into the tightest gunkholes or ghost up the shallowest inlets. But most importantly, small boats bring us closer to the coast in both body and spirit by letting us feel the tug of the current, the lift of the swell, or the shift of wind across our bows. They let us breathe the briny air and taste the salt on our lips. If we were any closer to the surface of the sea, we'd be in it.

The Maine coast is ideal for exploration by small boat. It offers an unlimited variety of coastline, from ancient salt-marshes and sandy beaches to craggy rockbound shores. Its thousands of islands beg to be discovered, and they calm the waters in their lees. Rivers minute and majestic scrawl through the mainland to the sea, branching and bending around granite outcrops as benign trickles or as exhilarating tidal rapids or reversing falls. Scenic lighthouses pepper the coast, and wildlife is abundant.

Modern small boats have developed into rugged, reliable and safe vehicles for exploring this coast. Sea kayaks often have built-in bulkheads, flotation, and bilge pumps. Small outboard engines have become quieter, cleaner, and more fuel efficient. Rowing dories and skiffs are often equipped with sliding seats and featherweight oars. VHF marine radios and Global Positioning System receivers can now fit in the palm of your hand. Fabrics for inflatables have become evermore scuff and puncture resistant. Sails and sail rigs are lighter and simpler than ever before, and even sailing kites are now common equipment on many small craft.

Yet any mariner will tell you that a coast is the most dangerous part of an ocean, and Maine is no exception. If anything, Maine's coast is more dangerous than most, with its large tides, swirling currents, icy waters, unforgiving rocks, and thick fogs. Add to this the inherent dangers of the remoteness of many sections of the coast, where an ankle twisted on the slippery rocks could mean a long, painful journey home, or worse. Maine, probably more than any other coast, deserves the respect and care of mariners, particularly those in small boats.

This book presumes that anyone who plans to explore the Maine coast in a small boat is already thoroughly familiar with the safe operation of his or her craft in most types of weather and sea conditions and familiar with the limitations of both their boat and themselves. Boaters using this guide should also have a working knowledge of coastal navigation and navigational charts and tools and have plans for self-rescue in the event of emergencies.

MAINE COAST GUIDE

When to come

Small boats ply Maine waters almost year round. Hardy souls can explore the sheltered waters in tidal rivers and estuaries in the dead of winter, and windsurfers can catch the strong autumn winds late into the fall. But for the most part, recreational boating along the coast of Maine occurs in the summer months when the air and water are at their warmest. This guide will help steer you to those off-season destinations, but it generally assumes that you will be exploring during the late spring, summer, or early fall.

Maine's spring doesn't really begin until May or June, when the first warm fronts bring warm, moist air to the coast. But the fronts are just as likely to bring cold and rain. Some years, the second half of June is glorious; in others, it might as well be March. Most facilities are not in full swing until July.

The typical boating season lasts from the beginning of July until Labor Day. The days are warm, the nights are cool, and the winds are typically light to moderate from the southwest. The water, however, is still quite cool, and it often condenses any moist air moving in from the southeast to form Maine's notorious fog.

By September, the water has warmed enough to lessen the probability of fog and the days can be sparkling. This can be some of the best boating of the year. But by late October, the winds—particularly those from the north—carry an arctic nip that gets increasingly hard to ignore.

Where to go

The geography of Maine divides the coast into six distinct regions, each divided from the other by a bold headland or cape, each with its own distinct geology and feel. This series of guides follows those natural divisions, dedicating a volume to each region.

The Southern Coast begins at the mighty Piscataqua River and its tributaries and offshore at the remote Isles of Shoals. It includes historic York and Kennebunk rivers, and the sandy shores of the mainland to Cape Elizabeth. You can wend your way up the Aschusset River through the Wells Estuary, visit the artist community of Ogunquit, or bask on Maine's great beaches—Wells, Moody, Old Orchard, Scarborough and Crescent. In the next region, you can explore island-studded Casco Bay. Here is Maine's busiest port and largest harbor, Portland, with its famous lighthouse at Portland Head. Yet the fishing communities of Sebasco and West Point on its eastern shore are as remote as any Down East. The midcoast and Muscongus Bay come next, serrated by Maine's great rivers—the Kennebec, the Sheepscot, the Damariscotta, and the St. George—and punctuated offshore by Monhegan, the artists' island.

Another great river, the Penobscot, forms the next region, Penobscot Bay. From the Camden Hills to elegant Castine to remote Matinicus, this is some of Maine's most spectacular cruising ground. Island destinations include Islesboro, North Haven, and Vinalhaven. Mount Desert Island, crowned by Cadillac Mountain, defines the next region. Blue Hill Bay sprawls to the west until it breaks apart among the myriad islands of Merchant Row and Jericho Bay. Frenchman Bay lies to the east, cradled by the rugged arm of Schoodic Point.

The last region stretches beyond Schoodic, along the rugged "Bold Coast" and into Passamaquoddy Bay. This remote territory seethes with tides and often hides in the thickest fogs, yet it rewards the boater with unmatched beauty and grandeur.

Ocean access

The Maine coast is rich in public access to coastal waters. Most coastal communities have public launching sites that are available to residents and non-residents alike. Many have public parks on the waterfront where portable boats can be launched. And most have commercial facilities such as marinas and boatyards where permission to launch can be arranged, usually for a small fee.

A rarer commodity is coastal parking. The limited parking near most public ramps is usually crowded, and overnight parking is often not permitted. You may have to make long-term parking arrangements with local authorities or through local businesses. These guides will highlight both waterfront access and parking options.

Islands and private property

Few things are as alluring—or as tempting to explore—as a remote island floating on the horizon. Yet in Maine, there is a good chance that that island is private, and landing is not allowed. The same is true along the thousands of miles of Maine's mainland coast.

This guidebook details all the points along both island and mainland shores where the general public *is* permitted to launch or land. It will urge you to visit these treasures not just for a warm beach or a good camping site, but to become familiar with the fragile sense of each place, each unique, and how you, the visitor, fit into it.

Of equal importance, this book outlines where *not* to land, because the land is private or ecologically sensitive. You can still explore many of these places by water, where the only trace you will leave is a ripple.

More than 3,000 islands dot the coast of Maine, and almost half again as many ledges and rocks. About half of these are owned by public agencies, but most are very small. Of the islands larger than one acre in size, about 860 are in private hands. Of those, 600 are owned by individuals. About 170 islands are inhabited, and 14 support year-round communities.

In terms of acreage, 95% of the Maine islands are private, one of the highest concentrations of private ownership in the country. While at first glance this figure seems to smack of exclusivity, boaters along the coast should always remember that it has been the careful stewardship by these island owners that has protected most of these islands from the pressures of development and preserved their rugged beauty. Ninety percent of the private islands are undeveloped, and this has done much to keep Maine as beautiful as it is. We owe a great debt to their owners, and we can show it by respecting their privacy. Often, island owners are incredibly generous in sharing their offshore treasures. Many have quietly allowed several generations of the general public to explore their islands, though such unbounded generosity has become rarer with increased use.

Do not land on private islands or land without permission to do so. This book in no way constitutes that permission.

In addition to private landowners, many conservation organizations have worked to ensure protection of Maine's islands and coastline. Property owned by these groups or protected by their conservation easements is noted in this book, both for what you can explore and what should be avoided. Appendix C lists these dedicated groups. Please support them if you can.

For extended exploration or camping, we highly recommend joining the Maine Island Trail Association, which works in a unique partnership with island owners to exchange user-stewardship with access to certain privately owned islands (see "Camping," p. 12, or Appendix C, p. 246).

Of the Maine islands that are public, many can be reached by public transportation. Another 30 can be explored by small boat. The remaining rocks and ledges and nesting islands should be left to the birds and the seals.

Weather

Maine weather, above all, is changeable. A classic Maine line is "If you don't like the weather, wait a minute." This is because Maine's weather is influenced by a number of factors, each affecting the others. General weather patterns, effects of ocean temperatures and offshore winds, and local conditions such as a bay, a landmass, or a warm river current can dramatically change the weather in the immediate vicinity.

Wind. On a typical fair-weather summer day, morning winds are light. As the sun rises and warms the air over coastal landmasses, the wind gradually fills from the southwest, and by mid-afternoon it can reach 15 or 20 knots, though often less, before weakening by sunset. The force of these afternoon sea breezes should not be underestimated. Lobstermen begin hauling their traps at dawn to avoid the chop of the afternoon. Skippers of small boats should do the same, planning their most exposed roundings or passages before noon and stopping early.

If the sea breezes should veer slightly to the southeast or east, they will pass over the cold currents from the north, which will condense the moisture they carry into thick fog. This transformation can happen in a matter of minutes, not hours, so have a "fog plan" in the back of your mind at all times to help you decide where to run when you can't see anything (see "Fog" below).

Northwest winds carry little or no moisture and are generally clearing winds associated with cold fronts. They bring sparkling weather, but often gusty conditions. The strongest gusts blow just after the cold front has passed, after which they tend to taper off and shift to the southwest.

The shape of coastal landmasses can affect wind in many different ways. They can physically redirect or block the wind, create a sheltered lee, or funnel the wind and accelerate it through constrictions, a phenomenon known as the Venturi effect. Landmasses can also produce aerodynamic effects like downdrafts, where wind passing over a land is deflected down the lee side of the landmass, or wind wrap, where wind may change direction at a point by wrapping around it.

Landmasses can also affect the wind thermally. When a warming landmass heats the air over it, the rising hot air can interrupt the windflow over the land, or the rising air can create a wind of its own as cooler wind rushes in to fill the vacuum it has left.

The result of all these landmass effects is that wind will always have a strong local influence. One bay or cove may be windy while another is calm, or the wind direction or strength in one place may be quite different than its direction or strength in another place nearby. Boaters must remember that calm winds at the launching site do not mean that it will be calm off nearby points or offshore.

Above all, boaters should consider the wind's effect on the water. The greater the distance the wind travels over the water, called "fetch," the larger the waves it creates. Likewise, the shallower the water, the steeper the chop. And if the wind is opposing any current, the waves will be even steeper (see "Tides and tidal currents," below).

Fog. Fog is a fact of boating life in Maine. Southeasterly or easterly winds are typically moisture-laden, having picked up their wet cargo as they crossed the warm Gulf Stream. Once they encounter the cold waters in the Gulf of Maine, their moisture condenses into thick fog. Fog generally is most prevalent during mid-July, then it tapers off toward September as the Maine waters warm.

Fog does not need to be intimidating, but it warrants careful coastal navigation and planning by boaters (see "Navigation," p. 10). Often, small boats can escape the fog on warmer bodies of water such as shallow or protected bays and coves or rivers.

Gales. The strongest winds during the spring and summer are produced by fronts and thunderstorms, often from the south and southwest. These can reach 20 or 30 knots or more, and they can build quite suddenly. If you see disturbances in the skies to the south and southwest, make plans to avoid being on the water, or be ready for a prompt landing in a protected area.

Hurricanes. Hurricane season along the entire Atlantic coast runs from June through October. Historically most hurricanes that have hit Maine arrived in late August or September, and they have often lost some of their strength by the time they arrive. Hurricanes are tracked from their inception in the Gulf of Mexico and the Caribbean, so generally they will be forecasted several days ahead of their arrival.

Forecasts. Weather-watching is a universal preoccupation with Mainers, and Maine's forecasting infrastructure is excellent on both local and network TV and radio. National Ocean and Atmospheric Administration broadcasts updated forecasts 24 hours a day on VHF channels 01, 02, and 03 and by phone at 207-688-3210. These forecasts paint excellent pictures of large-scale weather patterns, but they often will not accurately reflect local conditions, which may be more benign or more dangerous. Use the forecasts as guidelines only, weighing them against your local observations of weather conditions and change.

Tides and tidal currents

Maine's tides are large. The tides themselves and their associated tidal currents are of vital importance to boaters on this coast. Average tidal ranges run from about 8.7 feet along the southern coast to 20 feet or more in Passamaquoddy Bay. The changing water depth can create a beautiful bay out of a mud flat or change an easy landing into an arduous trek over slippery rocks.

Tidal currents generally flood in a northeasterly direction and ebb to the southwest, but coastal geography determines their ultimate direction. Currents in east-west passages vary in direction all along the coast.

Tidal currents are subject to physical landmass influences similar to those of the wind. Constrictions tend to increase the force of the current; more expansive shorelines will slow them. And near points or headlands, the directions of the currents may change. Boaters can often use these currents to boost their speed or progress. Adverse currents can be avoided by keeping close to shore, where the shoreline slows the movement of the water or where the current actually reverses itself in a back-current that can help push the boat along.

The currents, however, can be dangerous, especially when wind opposes the current. This opposition can set up steep standing or breaking waves that can present real hazards to small boats. And since the currents are tidal, these waves may appear at certain points in the tide cycle yet be completely absent at other times.

Two rules help estimate the height of tide and its associated currents at different stages of the tide cycle. The "Rule of Twelfths" estimates tide heights between high and low water. Over the six-hour period between any high and low tide, 1/12 of the volume of water will move in the first hour, 2/12 will move in the second hour, 3/12 will move in the third hour, 3/12 will move in the fourth hour, 2/12 will move in the fifth hour, and the last 1/12 will move in the sixth hour. For example, if the tide rises 1.25 feet in the first hour after low tide, the water will be 2.5 feet deeper in the next hour and the total tide range will be about 15 feet.

The "50-90 rule" estimates current speeds between slack water and maximum flow. Divide the time between slack water and maximum ebb or flood into thirds. In the first third, the current will increase to 50% of its maximum. In the second third it will reach 90%. And in the last third, it only increases the last 10%.

The complexities of Maine's convoluted coast make charting its currents a daunting task. Current tables are available, but their information is often too general for the boater dealing with the eddies and counter currents close inshore. Wherever possible, we have included current information in our text. Maine is also blessed with a perfect way to estimate the strength and direction of tidal currents almost anywhere along the coast—lobster buoys. These ubiquitous floating telltales stream back in any current, and the ripples around them easily show the current's strength. Remeber, *never haul a lobster trap*, even out of curiosity—these are owned by the lobstermen who fish them, and few things are considered more sacred in Maine.

Rivers and river currents

River currents, unlike tidal currents, flow ceaselessly toward the sea. However, where the rivers empty into the sea, they are influenced by the rise and fall of the tides, sometimes for great distances inland. Here, the "Rule of Twelfths" does not apply. Rising tides and flooding currents slow the river current or even reverse it, forcing water to flow upriver. Likewise as the tide falls, ebb currents add to the force of the river current. Some boaters deliberately seek the challenges and thrills of this combined current in places where the shoreline constricts it into boiling whitewater. How much influence the tide has over the river current depends upon such factors as the strength and volume of the river current, the tidal range, and the geography of the river.

Again, boaters can use these currents to their advantage when going with them, or they can seek out back-currents or eddies close to the river banks when the current is adverse. Beware, however, of standing waves, which are often formed during the ebb, when the combined river and ebb currents are opposed by a wind blowing upriver.

Other dangers lurk in especially narrow constrictions. For example, Upper and Lower Hells Gate, between the Kennebec and Sheepscot River, squeeze the currents to six or eight knots. Rocky bottoms redirect the current upwards into upwellings or boils that fan out at the surface—often with enough force to send a small boat rocketing sideways—and the eddyline can be pocked with whirlpools.

Preparations

Boat. The *Maine Coast Guides* are written for all types of small craft—windsurfers, kayaks, skiffs, inflatables, sport boats, small sailboats, kayaks, canoes, and others. It is not within the scope of these books to describe boat maintenance or safe handling. However, your boat—no matter what type of boat it is—should be well maintained and well equipped. Ideally it should contain some type of positive flotation and be able to be bailed or pumped dry rapidly. It should have more than one means of propulsion, such as extra paddles for a kayak or extra oars for an outboard-powered skiff or small sailboat. It should have all the required safety gear such as lights, flares, a horn, anchors, and lifejackets. We recommend flares, even when they are not required, on small boats such as kayaks since such low-lying vessels are very difficult to see from any distance at all, even in perfect visibility. If your boat is engine-driven and operated by a single person, the engine should be equipped with a kill-switch mechanism, and the kill switch should be used in the event that the operator falls overboard.

If your boat is too large to be beached, it should be equipped with adequate anchoring or mooring ground tackle and lines and some method of gauging depth. Even if you are in a dinghy or a kayak, some form of an anchor with plenty of line is a good idea. It might keep you from getting carried away by a contrary wind or current, or it might simply allow you to rest a moment to take in the beauty or have a snack. Spare parts for your boat, depending on type, might include patch kits, a small tool kit, shear pins, etc..

If possible, a radar reflector should be mounted to your boat, as high as possible. This inexpensive, lightweight device produces a bright blip on radar screens of nearby boats, and the margin of safety it provides is well worth the slight additional windage it creates. If your boat has no mast, we suggest mounting a pole or antenna or similar device to support the reflector aloft. If you have the opportunity, ask someone with radar if they pick your boat up on their screen.

Safety supplies. In addition to the safety equipment associated with your boat and basic navigational supplies (see p. 10), you should carry certain basic safety supplies.

Bring along raingear and a change of dry clothing in a watertight bag. Maine's water is cold, only reaching a temperature of 60-62°F in the height of summer, and wet clothing is a leading cause of hypothermia. If you are in a particularly wet boat such as a kayak, you should consider wearing or bringing a wetsuit or a drysuit.

Matches or a lighter should be included in the drybag, as well a knife and a signaling mirror, insect repellent, sunscreen, and a small first-aid kit. At a minimum the first-aid kit should include bandages, antibiotic ointment, an Ace bandage, and an anti-itch lotion such as Calamine or Benadryl. Boaters planning extensive voyages should be familiar with wilderness medicine and carry a good medical reference.

Food and drink should be stowed aboard in quantities relative to the length of your planned trip, with extra for contingencies. Water should be brought with you. Remember, alcohol and small-boat handling do not mix.

Hand-held VHF marine radios have become quite inexpensive relative to the degree of safety they can provide. They enable a small boat in distress to contact other boats on channel 09 or the Coast Guard on channel 16. They also receive NOAA's continual marine weather forecasts broadcast on channels 01, 02, and 03, which in addition to weather reports include updates about fire dangers (see "Fires," p. 12). If you do not plan to carry a VHF radio, a small, lightweight weather radio available from boating or electronics stores will enable you to receive the same NOAA forecasts. While cellular phone systems also cover coastal Maine with a fair degree of reliability, they are not helpful in contacting other boats in emergencies, since you won't know what number to dial.

And even though the air may be cool in Maine, do not underestimate the power of the sun, particularly when it is reflected off the water. Bring dark sunglasses and hats with visors, and use strong sunscreen.

Companions. Few experiences in life are as awe-inspiring as being alone on a big ocean in a small boat. Yet there is safety in numbers. Companions—in your boat or in their own—can exponentially increase your chances of survival or rescue in emergency situations. It can be fun to have friends around, too.

On this fragile coast, however, you can have too much of a good thing. Large groups can't help but have an adverse impact when they land, explore, and camp. The Maine Island Trail Association recommends limiting your group size to four or fewer.

Float plan. A float plan is nothing more than letting someone responsible know where you will be, what you will be doing, and when you expect to be back. It serves the obvious purpose of alerting rescuers in the event that you do not come back, and it gives them a starting point for their search.

The float plan does not need to be more elaborate than a note on the kitchen table to your family describing your short outing and when you plan to return, or it can be as detailed as a day-by-day itinerary. It should, however, be as specific as possible and be written down. Its recipient should read it and know who to call in the event that you do not return as planned.

Anticipation and humility. Nothing will steer you clear of danger more consistently than careful observation and anticipation, the hallmark of great leaders and explorers. Try to anticipate situations before they develop into dangers—the shift of the wind, the sky becoming more overcast, the tiring of your companion, the slightly different pitch of the outboard. Consider "what-if" scenarios to force yourself to plan how you would respond to various crises.

Next to anticipation, being humble is your most vital survival tool. Some risk is inherent in voyaging by small boat, but don't be foolish. If you feel a pit in your stomach, a lump in your throat, or the pang of fear, take heed. This is your early-warning system sensing danger. The action you should take is the action that will alleviate those feelings. Under the vast sky, floating tentatively on the looming ocean, following an age-old coastline, we are small and insignificant. Our wills, our pride, our plans, our hopes, and our dreams, which loom so large in our everyday lives, are reduced by this grand perspective to almost nothing. And this, perhaps, is the very reason we are here in a small boat on a big ocean.

Navigation

These Guides assume a thorough knowledge of coastal navigation. A complete discussion on this subject is beyond the scope of this book. However, we offer the following suggestions.

Official, up-to-date coastal charts are an absolute necessity. They are published by NOAA or packaged in Chart Kits by Better Boating Association or as coated charts by Waterproof Charts, Inc.. They are available at most boat chandleries. Do not navigate by road maps, post cards, place mats, souvenir tee-shirts, or even by the charts in this book. Any reference in this guide to "the chart" refers to NOAA chart 13290 of Casco Bay at a scale of 1:40,000. You should also carry tide tables, parallel rules (or similar) for plotting courses, and a compass for following them. Ideally, your compass should be mounted in such a way that you can steer by it and use it to take bearings. If not, you should carry a smaller, hand-bearing compass.

Binoculars will help you find distant marks and landmarks. Binoculars with an internal compass can be used as a hand-bearing compass, either by aiming them where a mark should be or by reading the bearing to a mark that is visible. They also can help you track your drift when you take successive bearings to a particular landmark.

When running a compass course, try to take into account any cross-currents (often indicated by lobster buoys) or cross-winds. Deliberately steer slightly to one side of your course or the other. That way, if you don't know exactly where you are when you make landfall, you will know which way to run down that coast. For example, if you steer slightly to the left of your course to a small pocket beach on a distant shore, when you make landfall, you'll know to run along the coast toward the right until you find the beach.

Navigational electronics have recently become so small and affordable that they can be used on even the smallest vessels. They are particularly useful in Maine, where visibility is often reduced by fog. Hand-held GPS units now have enough memory that waypoints can be plotted and stored before you take to the water, and some can even graphically plot your progress and store your routes. Be thoroughly familiar with the use and the limitations of your receiver before you rely on it in fog, and remember that the time you need to use your GPS is not the time you will want to be calculating your waypoints from the chart, particularly in a small boat. Prepare your navigation before the morning leg or the day in advance.

For the sake of accuracy, we do not recommend using somebody else's waypoints, waypoint lists, or waypoints published on charts such as BBA's Chart Kits, and none are included in this guide. Either determine your waypoints from the chart, or record them at their location ahead of time, and *check them against the chart before you use them*. To minimize mistakes in taking waypoints off the chart or in entering them into your receiver, a good practice is to also measure the bearings and distances between waypoints on the chart and compare them to the bearings and distances calculated by the receiver. If they differ greatly, something is wrong.

Avoidance. Your navigation is wedded to the navigation of other boats. Try to anticipate where they may be, and plan your navigation to keep you away from them, particularly in the fog. Small boats can avoid the entrances to busy harbors and obvious coastal routes by staying well out of the main channels. But in Maine, where lobsterboats work close inshore in erratic circles, anticipation may be difficult. Try to increase your visibilty by wearing brightly-colored or reflective clothing, especially hats, or even by mounting high flags on your boat. Radar reflectors mounted as high as possible can make even the smallest boat appear like a ship on another boat's screen. And in the fog, sound your horn regularly and listen for others.

Respect for the environment

Fires. The foremost threat to coastal ecology is the threat of fire. Most of the spruce-studded islands in Maine have become wooded only in the last 60 years when island farming became economically impractical. The invading spruce sprang up in dense stands, growing top-heavy and unstable as they competed for sunlight. Now as they get older, winter storms fell whole swaths of trees, and the forest floor is thick with the tinder of smaller trees that have died from lack of sunlight. This inherent danger of fire is exacerbated by remote coastal locations, fragile coastal ecology, and exposure to sea breezes.

Fires are prohibited on many islands, and in dry spells open fires may be prohibited everywhere. Permits are required for all open fires. NOAA's weather forecasts (VHF Ch. 01, 02, 03; 207-688-3210) will include fire information. Camp stoves are highly recommended as an alternative.

If you absolutely must have an open fire, use extreme care. Please leave your ax at home. Build the fire below the high-tide line with driftwood only, but do not use lumber from old lobster traps which is often treated with toxic preservative. Do not scour the forests for fuel. The deadwood supports local wildlife, and it will eventually replenish the island's soil. Be sure to have a bucket or pot filled with water nearby to extinguish wayward sparks.

The Maine Forest Service issues permits at the following locations: Augusta 207-287-2275, Gray 207-657-3552, Jefferson 207-549-3802, Old Town 207-827-6191, Jonesboro 207-434-2621, Cherryfield 207-546-2346. If you plan on having your fire on a private island, you may need to present written permission from the land owner before the permit will be issued.

Camping. If you plan to camp in an area other than a designated campground, *it is imperative that you have permission to do so*, either directly from the owner of the property or by joining an organization such as the Maine Island Trail Association (MITA), which promotes careful stewardship, low-impact camping, and public access to both publicly and privately owned islands. Join by calling Rockland 207-596-6456 or Portland 207-761-8225.

Your equipment should include tents with fine mesh screening and all support stakes and poles (don't cut these from tree limbs), warm sleeping bags, ample food and water, and a cookstove and utensils. Make camp on grassy sites where the earth is stabilized by the grass roots rather than on the more easily eroded soils under pine needle ground cover. Arrange your camp in such a way that repeated walking on vegetation can be avoided, trying instead to walk on rocks.

Soils. Tread lightly. Coastal soils are thin and easily eroded. Stay on marked paths, beaches, or rock ledges and avoid wet areas and steep embankments. Along the southern beaches, stay off dunes and dune grasses.

One plant that seems perfectly adapted to these thin soils is poison ivy, and some islands seem as if they grow little else. Know how to identify poison ivy by its three shiny leaves, because in Maine it can grow in forms ranging from ground cover to shoulder-high bushes.

Bugs. Mosquitoes and "no-see-um" midges, on the other hand, are anything but endangered. They are ubiquitous along the entire coast but tend to be concentrated in areas of low-lying wet or marshy areas. They swarm at dusk, but nightfall usually brings temperatures cool enough to moderate this menace. Carry effective repellents at all times. If you are camping, choose sites where a breeze might keep insects at bay, and consider packing an inexpensive head net as insurance. Spring outbreaks of black flies are, fortunately, much less prevalent along the coast than inland.

Many of Maine's islands support high populations of deer, which often have become quite tame through their forced proximity with humans. Please do not feed these deer or any other wildlife. The deer carry with them a new cause for concern, the deer tick, which in rare instances can transmit Lyme disease to humans. The deer tick is much smaller than the common dog tick, ranging in size from 1/32 inch to 1/8 inch. General precautions for avoiding them should include leaving as little skin exposed as possible and spraying clothes with insect repellent before exploring on land. You should examine yourself for ticks regularly. If you find what you suspect to be a deer tick, remove it by gently pulling it upwards with tweezers, without squeezing it too hard, until it lets go, and save it in alcohol or tape for identification. Contact the Maine Lyme Disease Project at 207-761-9777 if you have questions or concerns.

Brown-tailed moth caterpillars have recently become an irritating pest on some islands and coastal locations in Casco Bay and along the southern coast. The fine hairs of these caterpillars contain a toxin that can produce an itchy rash upon contact with skin. Unfortunately, their hairs are easily airborne, so you can get the rash without actually touching the caterpillars. The caterpillar larvae winter in web nests in the branches of deciduous trees, favoring oaks and sumacs, until they hatch in the spring. They are brown with two parallel lines of white dots down their backs, and two orange dots in the center, near the tail. By August, they metamorphose into white moths with fuzzy brown tails. Lotions like Calamine and Benadryl can alleviate the irritation of the rash. For more on brown-tailed moths, see Vaill Island, p. 68.

Trash. All trash should be packed out and disposed of properly on the mainland, not on islands. (Even inhabited islands have trash problems. Don't add to them.) Do not throw anything overboard that didn't originate in the sea—not even biodegradable items like banana peels or apple cores. Fish parts or shellfish shells can be returned from whence they came, but they should be disposed of well below the low-tide line so that rank remains aren't washed back ashore. Maine has a bottle deposit. Please recycle. Along the wrack line, you will, doubtless, see trash that has floated ashore. If you have the space, you can leave the coast a better place by picking some of it up and packing it with you.

Human waste. This is becoming an increasingly odious (and odorous) problem as more and more people take to the coast in small boats. The best policy for day trips is to go before you go. But plan for the inevitable. Bring toilet paper and Ziploc bags to pack it out along with the rest of your trash. And bring a small container with a bomb-proof, water-tight lid and lime or kitty litter to pack the rest of the mess for proper disposal. Or, if you have the room, bring a portable head on your boat. Federal law prohibits discharging untreated waste into waters within three miles of the coast, so if your boat is large enough to be equipped with a permanent head, it is mandatory that some form of holding tank be installed. Please use it. Overboard discharge increases the bacteria and lowers the dissolved oxygen content in the water. Holding tank pump-out stations are listed in Appenidx B.

Foraging. Berries, mushrooms, and many edible plants can be found along the coast, along with clams, mussels, crabs, periwinkles, sea urchins, and even seaweed. Always be sure to identify your food, particularly mushrooms, before eating. Never take shellfish from areas affected by **red tide**, which can led to paralytic shellfish poisoning in humans. Call the Red Tide Hotline at 1-800-232-4733 to determine which areas are closed due to red tide. Be aware that many coastal cottages are still "grandfathered" to allow "overboard" waste systems, which usually consist of little more than a long pipe to the water. If you see a pipe running from a cottage over the rocks and down to the sea, choose a different area to pick your mussels.

Birds. Maine's coastal islands are vital nesting habitat for colonial seabirds and waterfowl from early spring through the summer. They prefer to nest on the ground on small, isolated, treeless islands. Disturbing the parents can sometimes lead them to abandon their nests or young or expose them to predators. *State and Federally owned islands are closed to visitors between April 1 and mid to late August,* but avoid all nesting areas during that period. Stay at least 100 yards away from nesting shores. If birds are flushed from their nests or they dive you in alarm, you are much too close.

Bald eagles have been making a strong comeback in Maine since they were thinned nearly to extinction by the ravages of DDT. However these magnificent birds are easily disturbed by human presence.

Ospreys have adapted to man more easily. They often make their nests right on navigational buoys or in trees along the shoreline, using the same nests year after year, one generation after the next. One nest on Shipstern Island is over 100 years old. Still, human disturbance can cause nesting ospreys undue stress. Please keep well away from eagle or osprey nests.

The Migratory Bird Treaty Act makes it unlawful to disturb migratory birds or their nests. The presence of nesting birds may be posted on some state-owned islands, but look for signs from the birds themselves—warning calls and screeches, aggressive flying and dive-bombing, or diversionary tactics such as feigned injury. If you inadvertently find yourself among nesting birds, retrace your steps or your route quietly and carefully.

Marine mammals. Seals love to bask on ledges and rocks, and it is tempting to try to bring small boats within very close range of them. However, recent research shows that disturbances from small boats can be very stressful and disruptive to the seals. Curiously, kayaks tend to be more alarm to seals more than larger boats. Please observe seals from minimum distance of 100 yards, especially during pupping season in May and June. If you see seals getting restless or beginning to slip in to the water, you are too close.

Porpoises, dolphins, and whales also visit the waters of Maine. The great whales—finback, humpback, minke, and pilot whales—don't usually come as close inshore as they once did. If, however, you should be near one in your small boat, use extreme care not to get too close to these powerful and unpredictable creatures.

Fish. The coastal waters of Maine and the rivers flowing into them are rich in fish, both saltwater and anadromous species that go up rivers to spawn. The runs of mackerel keep young boys on the docks with rods and jigs for most of the summer. And the recent rebound of stripped bass populations has put Maine on the map for big fighting fish, particularly on rivers such as the Kennebec where sections are known to boil in feeding frenzies. No licenses are required for salt-water fishing except for Atlantic Salmon, but size and bag limits do apply to striped bass. Currently anglers can keep one fish per day between 20 and 26 inches and one fish per day 40 inches or greater. For more information, see Appendix F or contact the Maine Department of Marine Resources 207-624-6550 or 207-633-9500. For information about Atlantic Salmon, contact the Department of Inland Fisheries and Wildlife at 1-800-321-0184.

Oil and fuel. This beautiful coast will only stay that way if you leave it that way. If your boat is powered, keep your engine well-tuned to limit its emissions and boost its efficiency, and use exceptional care in avoiding fuel and oil spills. As little as *one ounce* of engine oil spilled into *31,250 gallons* of seawater can kill half of the crab larvae in that water. All powered boats should have inexpensive oil-absorbent pads or socks in the bilge, and they should be disposed of properly. Detergents and soaps should not be used to disperse an accidental spill. While they make the oil disappear, they actually help mix it into the water column where it affects more marine life, and the detergents themselves reduce the amount of available oxygen in the water. Report spills to 1-800-424-8802.

Archaeology. Modern small boats follow in the wake of the first discoverers of the Maine coast who paddled these waters in dugouts and birch-bark canoes. Recent archeological finds have confirmed that natives camped, dug clams, hunted, and fished on these shores as long as 5,000 years ago. Evidence of more recent encampments in the form of middens, shell heaps from generations of feasting, are numerous along the coast. Many of the oldest sites are now submerged under a rising ocean, but by conservative estimates, there are still over 1,000 prehistoric shell heaps along the coast.

Unfortunately the thought of shell heaps seems to trigger the same response in some people as the image of gold mines, and over the years the middens have been wantonly plundered in search of arrowheads and pottery shards. Such pilfering, however, disturbs the natural stratification of the midden and scrambles any archeological record it may hold. Also, the shells neutralize Maine's naturally acidic soil, thereby preserving bones and bone tools that would otherwise have decomposed, and any disturbance accelerates that process. For these reasons, this book deliberately does not mention the location of Indian middens except in the most obvious cases. Please, do not disturb any middens you may discover. Unauthorized digging of any archeological site should be reported to the local police department as listed in Appendix A.

Diving. Casco Bay is the graveyard to innumerable wrecks and countless ledges teaming with underwater wildlife. This guide mentions prominent wrecks, many of which attract intrepid sport divers. Commercial divers harvest urchins and scallops. The water, however, can be cold and murky, the currents can be swift, and entanglement in potwarp, monofilament, or kelp is an ever-present danger. Divers should be properly trained, well-equipped, and above all, careful.

In addition, divers should recognize the archaeological significance of historic wrecks and be fully aware of laws regarding them. In Maine, all wrecks in territorial waters belong to the state. Any wreck over fifty years old is considered historic, and taking anything from them is prohibited. For more information, contact the Maine State Museum in Augusta at 207-287-2301.

CASCO BAY

CASCO BAY is where the great rocky coast of Maine begins. At Cape Elizabeth the sandy shores of the southern coast give way to high bluffs and rocky ledges. Strings of islands, like pearls on a necklace, drape across the bay. Behind the islands lie deep, protected harbors and rivers large and small running to the sea. This is a bay of contrasts, from the raw open ocean to the still, warm waters of the upper estuaries, from the deep ledge-strewn channels to vast clam flats and pocket marshes, from the tranquillity of a lone island to the hustle and bustle of Maine's largest port and city.

When Giovanni da Verrazzano mapped Casco Bay in 1524, he named it "The Land of the Bad People" after the savages who wore skins and jeered and mooned the white men. The Abenakis themselves called this place Aucocisco (or Uh-ko-sis-co, pronounced like San Francisco) with the poetic meaning of "Place of the Flying Cranes" or the more pragmatic meaning of "Marshy Place" or "Place of the Slimy Mud," depending on who you talk to. White men quickly shortened and Anglicized it to Casco. An alternate theory is that when Spanish explorer Estevan Gomez sailed into Casco Bay in 1525, he thought the bay looked like a helmet, or *casco* in Spanish, and christened it *Bahia de Casco*, Bay of Helmets.

The early settlers were quick to recognize the advantages of Casco Bay. The offshore islands were perfect toeholds for settlement, relatively safe from attack from mainland Indians, large enough to clear and farm, close to fishing grounds, and blessed with protected anchorages in their lee. There were so many islands that when Colonel W. Romer made a quick trip to Casco Bay in 1700 as His Britannic Majesty's Chief Engineer for the Colonies, he couldn't survey them all. He wrote back to London, "Said Casco Bay has a multitude of islands, these being reported as many islands as there are days in the year." Soon they were known as the Calendar Islands—a name that stuck even though the actual count only reached 222, of which only about 138 are large enough to be considered "real" islands.

The larger rivers that cut into the mainland were perfect for promoting trade with the Indians and for harvesting the new country's natural bounty, growing tall and true—masts. Eventually, the rivers proved to be perfect places for mainland settlements and shipbuilding. The mouth of the Fore River was the most navigable of these rivers, deep and wide. Docks and wharves for ships bearing goods from around the globe grew up along the river's banks, and the city of Portland sprang up behind them.

Portland's harbor is so good that over the years, layers of fortifications have been built along its approaches. Granite Fort Gorges and Fort Scammel were built during the Civil War, and during World War II, when Portland's Hussey Anchorage harbored as many as 60 warships and the largest convoys of the North Atlantic Fleet, huge guns and tall sighting towers were installed on Peaks and Jewell Island.

MAINE COAST GUIDE

18

Now in this electronic age, these emplacements have become obsolete, and they are slowly disappearing beneath tangles of bittersweet vines. Cruise ships and tankers make Portland their port of call, and hardy fishing boats and brightly painted ferries ply the waters.

The scale of Casco Bay is perfect for small boats. Its waters cover about 200 square miles, but the distance from Cape Elizabeth to Cape Small is less than twenty miles. The broadest sound is only a mile wide, and islands are always just moments away. Small boats can skip from island to island or wend their way up the scribbling rivers and poke into secret coves. You can brave the open ocean or squeeze through tight tickles like Whitehead Passage or under the cribstone bridge at the Gut for the sheer fun of it.

Despite its small size, Casco Bay is rich in places to explore. More than 200 publicly-owned islands and ledges lie in Casco Bay, with names like Uncle Zeke, Dog's Head, and Junk of Pork. You can find the offshore communities of Peaks, Long, Great Diamond, Chebeague, and Cliff Islands, or discover Admiral Peary's home on Eagle Island. By water, you can visit the city of Portland, Maine's largest metropolis, or discover the small, isolated outports of West Point or Sebasco, where weathered fishing shacks perch precariously on pilings. Or tour the Bay's great lighthouses—Portland Head, Ram Island, Spring Point, Bug Light, and Halfway Rock.

You can choose to stay in luxurious hotels in Portland or at the rambling Chebeague Island Inn, reminiscent of a different era. You can camp on the water at Winslow State Park in Freeport or by the beach at Hermit Island Campground, or you can rough it offshore on wooded Jewell Island. And when the sun rises, you'll awake to another marvelous day of exploring Casco Bay.

PORTLAND AND THE CITY ISLANDS

1. Fort Williams and Portland Head Light

Casco Bay begins where the high, rocky bluffs of Portland Head fall into the deep channel leading into Portland Harbor, a site as strategic as it is bold and treacherous. Maine's oldest lighthouse sits at the top of the bluffs, and the stronghold of Fort Williams spreads behind it. The fort and light command sweeping views of the open Atlantic to the south and east as well as the vital channel to Portland Harbor. The fort and its stunning grounds are now a municipal park of Cape Elizabeth (799-7652), open to the public during daylight hours, and the lighthouse, which is still a working aid to navigation, houses a small museum in the lighthouse keeper's quarters.

A little cobble beach lies tucked between the bluffs at the head of the bight called Ship Cove. It is only steps from a parking lot, offering portable boats instant access to the open ocean and the humbling, rock-hard beauty of Portland Head. The launch, however, can be difficult or even dangerous when ocean swells are running, and parking is limited to the park's daylight hours.

By sea. In calm weather, the small cobble beach at Ship Cove is open to the east and well-protected from prevailing southwesterlies. But if ocean swells are running, they tend to wrap around Portland Head and break onto the beach. The higher beach is

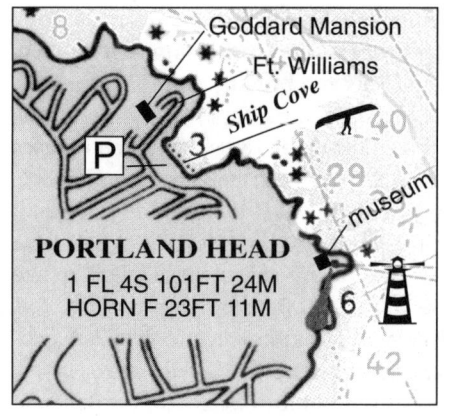

rockier and steeper than the lower portions, which are exposed as the tide drops. Launching will be easiest at mid to low tide. Try to anticipate the landing conditions at the time of your return. Do not anchor off the beach, since this is a cable area.

Like all capes, the trip around Portland Head is somewhat of a rite of passage, particularly in a small boat. The great expanse of ocean stretches to the horizon on one side, and the indomitable rocks claw the sky on the other, with white froth foaming at their feet. Be sure to avoid the rocks themselves, and be careful in the turmoil of reflected swells bouncing off the cliffs. If you explore along the coast in either direction from Portland Head, you can enjoy the million-dollar views of Cape Elizabeth's great waterfront mansions.

If you cross Portland Harbor Channel, use extreme caution (see p. 24). Ram Island and Ram Island Light lie directly opposite the launching beach. Cushing Island, with several small, tantalizing sandy beaches, lies to the north of Ram, but landing is not allowed. You can follow its coast north and then east into Whitehead Passage or jump over to Peaks Island. You can survey the granite forts on House Island from the water, but the island is private. Please do not land.

About 50 yards out and 20 yards north of the lighthouse lie the remains of the *Nancy*, one of the few ships in the area to have sunk with cannon aboard. The iron cannonballs were originally around 3 inches in diameter, but the balls found by divers have been scaled down by rust to about 1 1/2 inches, not much bigger than a golf ball. Even more disappointing, when the cannonballs were brought to the surface, they crumbled away entirely from the salt which had penetrated them.

By land. From Rt. 295 in Portland, take exit 6A to Rt. 77 to South Portland. Go left on Broadway, then right at the second light onto Cottage Road, which becomes Shore Road at Cape Elizabeth. The park will be on the left. From the south, take US Rt. 1 north to Rt. 207 and turn right. At Rt. 77 turn left and head north. At a blinking light, turn right onto Shore Road. The park will be on your right.

Park by the beach at the first parking lot on the left. There is additional parking beyond the small hill toward the lighthouse. Parking is ostensibly for daylight hours only, though if you were planning a trip overnight or longer, you might be able to arrange longer-term parking by speaking with a park caretaker, whose sheds are past the second lot, or by calling the park at 799-7652.

Ashore. Porta-potties are located at the top of the hill and by the rotary near the lighthouse.

You can wander through the military buildings of Fort Williams. There are examples from various time periods, from the poured concrete gun emplacements on the rocks above the water to the brick officers quarters along oak-lined promenades to a three-story stone shell, reminiscent of a Scottish castle, with formal granite arches, corner stones, and lintels. This is the shell of what was once the Goddard Mansion, built by Civil War colonel and timber baron John Goddard beginning in 1853. It took four years to complete.

Two years after Goddard's death in 1870, Fort Williams began as the Battery at Portland Head, a sub-post of Fort Preble at Spring Point. In 1898 it became its own fort, guarding the entrance to Casco Bay. In 1900, after passing through Goddard's heirs, the mansion was sold to the government for use as noncommissioned officer's quarters. This use, however, was eventually discontinued, and vandals and weather took their toll.

The day the United States entered World War II, after the bombing of Pearl Harbor, the old coast defense test-fired its guns. The concussion was so strong it damaged several new storage buildings nearby. The fort soon became the headquarters of the defenses of Portland Harbor, which sheltered the convoys of the North Atlantic fleet and the shipyards that built the Liberty ships. The defenses consisted of guns and sighting towers on many of the Casco Bay islands as well as anti-submarine nets strung across deep-water entrances to the harbor. The fort was eventually decommissioned in 1964.

Portland Head Light has guided mariners into Casco Bay past these notoriously treacherous rocks for over 200 years. The light was commissioned in 1787, when Maine was still a part of Massachusetts, but under direct authorization from George Washington it received federal funding for its completion in 1790. This was Maine's first lighthouse and the second in this young country (Boston Light was built first, lit in 1716).

Like most things new, there was an element of trial and error in its construction. Upon its completion, the 58-foot-high tower was discovered to still be obstructed by a nearby headland, so it had to be raised. But because the walls of the tower sloped inward, the additional height reduced the floor area at its top, and the original lantern for the lighthouse wouldn't fit. Eventually, a smaller lantern was installed and its 16 whale-oil lamps were first lit on January 10, 1791. However, there was inadequate ventilation for the smoke from the lanterns. And the keeper's quarters turned out to be damp and cold.

The Lighthouse Board visited the lighthouse in 1852 and still found problems. The reflectors were scratched and the tower was being undermined by rats. They recommended a Fresnel lens to focus and intensify the light, and in 1855 it was installed.

The Civil War reaffirmed the importance of shipping, so after it ended the tower was raised another eight feet, and new lenses were installed. Curiously, by 1883 the tower had been lowered 20 feet, only to be built 20-feet higher the following year. Finally, in 1885 they seem to have gotten it right. The top of the tower was enlarged, and a more powerful lens was installed.

Yet even so, the three-masted bark *Annie C. Maguire*, in ballast from Buenos Aires, ran up on the ledges at Portland Head on Christmas Eve, 1886. She hit them so hard that the light was said to have shaken as though hit by an earthquake. The entire 15-man crew was saved by breeches buoy, but the incident is enshrouded in mystery.

The crew claimed Captain O'Neil misjudged his distance from the rocks because he was blinded by a swirling blizzard, but actual weather records show that the night was a mild 46 degrees with only a light rain. Observers on shore could see that the ship was headed for disaster, and crew members later claimed they did, in fact, see the light.

Even more suspicious is the fact that the ship's owners had gone bankrupt and upon entering the harbor, the ship was to be attached by the Portland Sheriff for her Boston bankers. Furthermore, the ship was old, having been on the seas for 34 years. It is unclear whether the Captain knew of the impending impoundment of the ship. Even if he did, would he have scuttled the *Annie C. Maguire*, especially with his wife and two small children aboard that fateful night?

The wreck was auctioned for $177.50, and the high bidder salvaged her fittings and rigging. The rest broke apart and settled on the bottom. Divers claim that all that is left of her is a portion of her bowsprit.

The *Annie C. Maguire* was not the last ship to meet her end at Portland Head. The next year the *D.W. Hammond* was driven by fierce winds onto the rocks. In a blinding snow storm in 1915, the *William L. Elkins* met the same fate, scattering her load of pickled fish, bound for New York City, all along the shores of Cape Elizabeth. In 1932, the schooner *Lochinvar*, carrying 40,000 pounds of haddock, crashed in the exact spot as the *Annie C. Maguire*.

The light is now a searchlight type with a 1000 watt bulb projecting a 200,000-candle-power beam 27 miles out to sea from the tower that rises 101 feet above the water. The light was automated in 1989, and now a small but fascinating museum (799-2661, $2 admission charge) is located in the keeper's quarters.

Henry Wadsworth Longfellow, a Portland native, often walked to this spot for quiet contemplation, eventually befriending the keepers, and it is thought that Portland Head Light was inspiration for his poem "The Lighthouse."

2. Ram Island

Treeless Ram Island lies to the east of Portland Head and south of Cushing Island. Ram Island Ledge Light, which has a sooty appearance and a ladder-like bridge to it, stands on Ram Island Ledge, slightly further to the south.

Ram is state-owned, though it really belongs to nesting birds. You will be an uninvited guest.

By sea. Ram Island is quite exposed, but the small rocky beach on its southwest shore makes landing possible. Several other cobble pockets lie to seaward, but swells make them dangerous.

Ashore. Use care in climbing the eroding embankments up from the beach. The windswept plateau is covered by low, dense stands of sumacs, thick grasses, and ruthless nettles. Please walk carefully, and avoid the island altogether if birds are nesting.

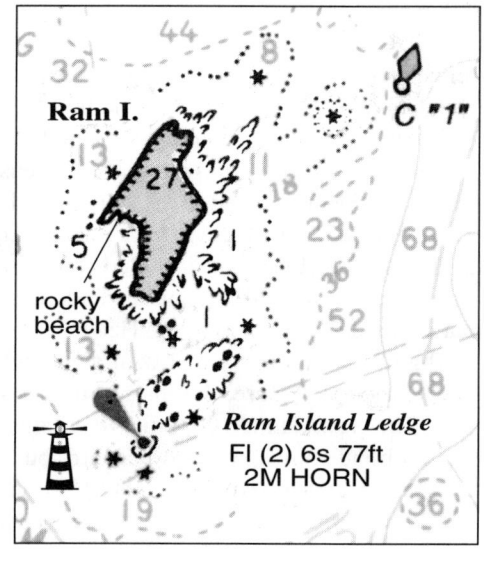

Because they are low and treeless, Ram Island and Ram Island Ledge are every bit as treacherous as Portland Head across the channel, and many ships have met their end here. On the night of February 24, 1900, the steamer *Californian* left its berth at Portland's Grand Trunk Wharf just before midnight, bound for Liverpool, England. Less than an hour later, Captain John France had unknowingly let his ship stray slightly from its course, and before he discovered his mistake, she grated onto Ram Island Ledge. Surfmen from the Cape Elizabeth Lifesaving Station rowed to the steamer, but the seas were so rough that the passengers and crew stayed on board. The next day the lifesavers returned, and her 21 passengers and all of her cargo were rescued. For six weeks, though, the steamer lay hard aground until she could be salvaged, bleak testimony to this danger so close to the shipping lane.

Two years later, money had been appropriated for a lighthouse, but construction had not yet begun. As if to underscore the need, a British three-masted schooner, the *Glenrosa*, struck the ledge that fall. The crew took to lifeboats and landed on Ram Island, but the *Glenrosa* broke up within several days. The *Cora and Lillian*, a ninety-five-foot fishing schooner, repeated the performance less than three months later, piling high up on the ledge to be destroyed by a southeast storm two days later.

The next spring stones for the lighthouse were cut and shaped at the Bodwell Granite Quarry on Vinalhaven and shipped to Portland. Work continued throughout that summer. At first, construction was restricted to the few hours each day when the ledge was above water. It continued throughout the next summer and even into the winter of 1904-05.

That January the lime schooner *Leona*, fully loaded and sailing out of Rockland, was caught in a blinding southeasterly. The Captain decided to make for the safety of Portland Harbor, but the *Leona* struck a ledge east of Ram. The boat came to rest on her side where waves broke completely over her. In addition to drowning or freezing to death, there was another danger. A lime ship was a potential bomb, and all it took to make it one was water. Water and lime combine in a very exothermic reaction, giving off enough heat to burn a ship to the waterline in an instant. The captain and crew abandoned ship immediately in the small lifeboat, but since they were wrecked on a lee shore, they had to row against the ferocious wind and waves and streaking snow. It was three in the morning, and for three hours the men pulled at the oars. As the gray dawn broke, the captain lit several distress flares at intervals in the almost vain hope that someone might see them.

While the storm raged, the workers on Ram hunkered down in their temporary shelter, occasionally checking outside to see how things were faring. Early in the morning, one of the men thought he saw the glow of a flare. Together, they made their way to the shore, where out of the snow and waves the little lifeboat appeared, carrying four exhausted forms. The workers directed them to the small landing beach on the back of the island and then up to the shelter. The *Leona* exploded before noon, and no trace of her remained.

That winter, the workers finished the light. A total of 699 four-ton granite blocks formed the tower. The light was fitted with a third-order Fresnel lens, and it was officially lit on April 10th, 1905. Its completion coincided with the increasing popularity of the Casco Bay islands as resort destinations and of boating as a recreational pursuit. The light became a popular spot for boaters and picnickers, with whole families coming out in fair weather to spread their blankets and tour the tower. Fishing parties landed here too, and a few hardy harvesters raked the ledges for sea moss to be sold as an emulsifier.

The light is now magnified by a 300-mm plastic lens and powered by an underwater cable from Portland Head. Still, danger will always lurk on Ram. As recently as 1960, the *Andarte* struck the ledge when her radar was obscured by heavy snow. She was a total loss.

3. Portland Harbor Channel

The main approach to Portland Harbor is the Portland Harbor Channel, running from Portland Head to Spring Point. This major shipping lane is deep, fairly wide, and well-marked. Still, small boats should use it or cross it with extreme caution. It is likely to be shared by tankers, freighters, cruise ships, tugs and barges, and other highly unmaneuverable vessels, as well as fishing boats, and pleasure boats of all kinds.

In the fall of 1997, lobsterman Bill Coppersmith was working the waters of the Channel between Portland Head and Ram Island when he pulled up something unusual. "When the trap broke the water," he said, "it just glowed." Inside was a completely white, albino lobster, the only one of its kind ever seen. "It almost looked like a toy," he said. "Then I looked it over and realized this is for real. It's not painted or anything."

The lobster, weighing a pound and a quarter, was a keeper. Bill kept it in the tanks of his fish stores for several months and fielded questions and requests from various aquariums and scientists before deciding to set it free again in the channel. As one of his clerks put it, "It just seemed that's where it belonged."

By sea. The short length of the Channel runs from the relatively protected waters of the inner harbor to the exposure of the ocean at Portland Head. The tide floods northward and ebbs southward, both with an average maximum of about 1.1 knots. On the ebb, when wind or ocean swells often oppose the current, the swells can grow quite large and make for rough going out past Portland Head.

Large ships, often accompanied by a flotilla of tugs and the Portland Pilot boat, can appear almost stationary even while ghosting along at an incredible speed to maintain steerage. They can be on top of you unexpectedly. Be sure you have plenty of room to cross, or stay well inshore, out of the shipping lane. In limited visibility, monitor VHF channel 16 for *securité* calls, or issue one yourself before you transit the Channel.

4. Maiden Cove and Casino Beach

Maiden Cove is the next cove to the north of Ship Cove, on the west side of the Portland Harbor Channel. The cove's sandy beach, called Casino Beach, is private, reserved for residents of the clustered houses nearby known as Cape Cottage Park.

By sea. Landing is not allowed.

Ashore. Cape Cottage Park was a resort development built in 1898 by the Portland and Cape Elizabeth Railway. Trolleys would bring guests from the big city to the broad lawns and gardens of the huge pillared Cape Cottage Casino. Luxuries included a dining room with four fireplaces, chefs and pastry cooks brought in by steamer from New York, a second-story ballroom with a balcony for the orchestra, a separate theater, and bathhouses by the beach. But by 1909, it was considered unprofitable. In 1922 it was sold to new owners who ran it for a couple of years as the Cape Cottage Inn before turning the Casino into a private residence and selling off lots for exclusive homes. The Casino stood next door, just to the north of the Goddard Mansion (see Portland Head Light entry, p. 19).

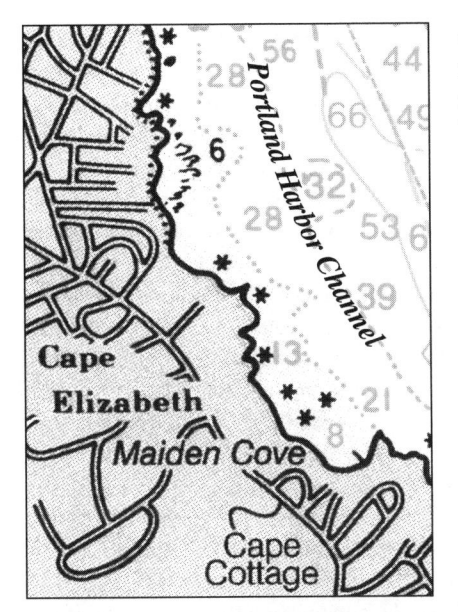

5. Danford Cove

Danford Cove is a large bight on the South Portland shore of the Portland Harbor Channel, just north of Maiden Cove. High bluffs ring its shores with small beaches at their feet.

Near the turn of the century, the electric trolley lines were extended from Portland to the Casino at Cottage Park. That made all the shore along the trolley line ripe for development. Cliff Cottage, overlooking Danford Cove, was originally a frame cottage that took in boarders. But in 1900 it was developed into the Cliff House, a massive, four-story frame building with 85 rooms and a piazza that wrapped around all four sides of the building for a total length of an eighth of a mile.

On June 13, 1914, the Cliff House was destroyed in the largest fire in Cape Elizabeth's history (At the time, South Portland had not yet separated from Cape Elizabeth).

6. Willard Beach

Willard Beach is a surprising crescent of sand ringing Simonton Cove among the tightly-packed houses of South Portland. In the summer it teems with sand-encrusted children whose screeches of delight are carried by the sea breeze. The cove itself is one of the larger mooring fields in Portland Harbor.

The north end of the beach is reserved for punts and dinghies. Portable boats can be launched here for excellent access to Peaks Island or Little or Great Diamond Island or points beyond. Parking, however, can be a challenge.

By sea. See chart next page. This beach is usually calm and in the lee of prevailing winds. Boats are only allowed on the northern portion of the beach.

By water you can explore Fort Preble, just to the north, and run out the breakwater to Spring Point Lighthouse. The Diamond Islands lie to the north, and Diamond Island Pass stretches toward Chebeague Island in the distance. Use caution crossing the Portland Harbor Channel, and watch for fast-moving yellow-and-red ferryboats plying between Portland, Peaks, and the Diamond Islands. Often tankers will be anchored in the special anchorage designated by four yellow buoys between House, Peaks, and Little Diamond Island. Before taking a closer look, be absolutely sure their anchors are down.

By land. Take Broadway in South Portland north to the intersection at Port Harbor Marine. Turn right on Pickett Street to an intersection at Fort Preble. Turn right again. The entrance to the north end of the beach is at the far end of a field on your left, next to the houses. You can drive closer, but it takes several turns in the residential neighborhood to find Beach Street which leads to the gate. Parking is difficult here, since there are no designated spots for boaters or beachgoers, and both compete for on-street parking.

Ashore. In season, restrooms, outdoor showers, a phone, and snacks are available at the beach concession at the center of the beach. If you need to stretch your legs, the ledge and scenic fishermen's shacks mark the southern terminus of the Spring Point Walkway that wends it way north and west for a mile along South Portland's waterfront, connecting Willard Beach, Fort Preble, Spring Point Light, Spring Point Marina, and Bug Light.

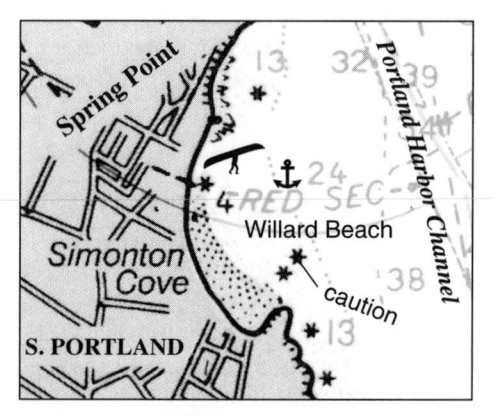

William Simonton arrived in this area in 1718 and built a warehouse and what may have been the first wharves in Portland Harbor on the point at the south end of the beach. His operation was a busy shipping point for the West India trade, exporting lumber and fish and importing sugar, molasses, and rum. Cargoes were landed on the beach and hauled by oxen to Portland.

After the great age of sail, the beach and surrounding points were dominated by fishermen's shacks and wharves, and Simonton Cove was dubbed "Gurry Cove." One of the prominent fishing families was the Willards. Captain B. J. Willard pioneered swordfishing in Maine and at one time managed the Forest City Steamboat Company. In addition, he was an author who wrote about his own life's story. One book, *Life History and Adventures*, features his dog Spot, who looks almost identical to the dog of the same name in the "Little Rascals" TV series. A photo shows the dog wearing a handkerchief-like bonnet to which is attached a small wooden perch, and balanced upon the perch is a grackle, head held high.

In 1896 an electric trolley line was installed from Monument Square in Portland to Willard Beach, and the beach took on new importance as a resort attraction. To ensure ridership, the Cape Shore Railroad Company built an elaborate two-story casino at the beach, surrounded on all sides by verandas. But the Casino, as it was called, was only open for one short season before it burned to the ground. The cause of the fire was never determined. The trolley company turned its attention to building the Cape Cottage Casino at Maiden Cove (see p. 24). The rambling Willard Haven Hotel eventually filled the need for lodging at the sandy shore, and it lasted through the Depression.

Despite the tides of change, this sandy crescent is as popular as ever. A stone at the beach's main entrance commemorates a lifeguard who manned the chair here for 35 consecutive summers, helping two generations of South Portlanders learn to swim safely and love the water.

7. Spring Point and Fort Preble

From the water, Spring Point is obvious from the brick buildings of Fort Preble. A long breakwater extends into the harbor, its end punctuated by a spark-plug lighthouse.

Most of the buildings of Fort Preble are occupied by the Southern Maine Technical College, but the site has attracted several other water-based groups. The small Portland Harbor Museum displays local maritime history in a building near the water, and in the summer, the innovative children's Fish Camp holds forth closer to the wharf. The office of Friends of Casco Bay, a group dedicated to the health and well being of the Bay, is just up the hill.

Visitors are allowed to explore the fort, walk out on the breakwater, or stroll the Spring Point Walkway, a pleasant path along the waterfront. With a short carry, it is possible to launch portable boats from the small beach just to the west of the breakwater, though parking is limited.

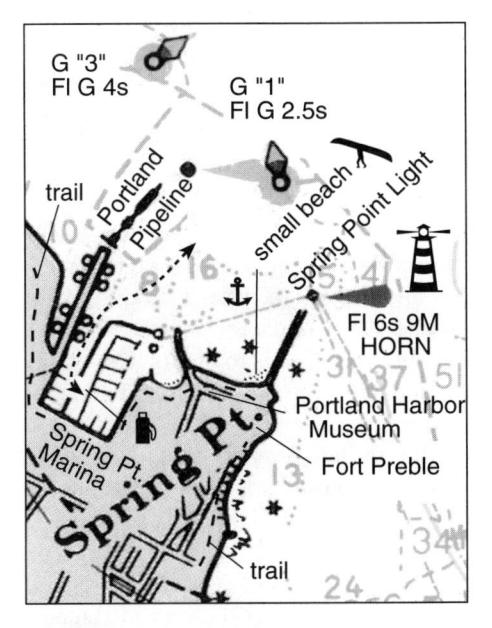

By sea. A small sand beach lies just to the west of the breakwater, an easy carry from the car. The breakwater protects it from any ocean swell, but it is partially exposed to prevailing southwesterlies. At high tide, the beach is almost non-existent, but it can still be used for launching. At low, however, it dwindles to mud flats.

Farther to the west, past a small wharf, there is another small sand beach that can work well for launching portable boats. Southern Maine Technical College's launching ramp is right beside it, but the ramp is reserved for their sailing programs. Trailered boats should be launched at the South Portland boat ramp instead (see p. 30).

The small beach faces Fort Gorges, with views beyond to Falmouth, past the Diamond Islands, or over the oil pipeline terminal to Portland's Munjoy Hill, crowned by the Portland Observatory. Beware of shipping traffic and Casco Bay Lines ferries running between the islands. Current floods to the northwest here as it wraps into the mouth of the Fore River and Portland Harbor, and it ebbs to the south and southeast. Maximum current of both ebb and flood averages about 0.9 knots.

By land. Take Broadway in South Portland north to the intersection at South Portland Marine. Turn right onto Pickett Street and take a left at the next stop sign onto Fort Road. This road leads through the campus to the waterfront.

There are several parking spots near the Portland Harbor Museum, located in a low brick building on the right. It might be possible to arrange long-term parking through the College, depending on the time of the academic year, by calling 767-9500.

Ashore. The Indians called this area Purpooduck, and in a flare-up during the

French and Indian Wars in 1703, they killed 25 settlers here. The corpses were later found in a single grave. Just over a hundred years later, during the administration of Thomas Jefferson, Fort Preble was commissioned, and it was completed by the War of 1812. The fort was enlarged and modernized during WW II but quickly decommissioned at the war's end.

Spring Point Light, at the end of the breakwater, marks Spring Point Ledge, treacherous more because of its proximity to the channel into Portland Harbor than because of its size. In a howling winter storm in March, 1876, the *Harriet S. Jackson* was attempting to run for cover and plowed up on the ledge so far that when the tide dropped in the early gray dawn, the ship listed so far that a plank was laid ashore and all the crew walked to safety. The light became active 21 years later, in 1897, and it was automated in 1934, more than fifty years before the automation of Portland Head Light. The breakwater, added in 1951, makes a fun hike or a perfect fishing spot.

The Portland Harbor Museum (799-6337, open everyday but Monday) is located in what once was an ordinance shop. It displays maritime exhibits on Portland Harbor and shipbuilding in the 19th century. The Spring Point Walkway leads in both directions along the waterfront, for pleasant strolling.

8. Spring Point Marina, Port Harbor Marine

Together, Spring Point Marina and Port Harbor Marine (marina: Ch. 09; 767-3254; dock 767-3213; service: 767-3415) is the first major yachting facility in Portland Harbor, located to the west of Spring Point and the Southern Maine Technical College Campus.

This full-service marina and boat yard has all boating amenities including repair facilities, a chandlery with charts, dockage, gas and diesel, and a restaurant.

By sea. As you approach the marina's slips, the fuel dock is to the right, with gas, diesel, water, ice, and pump-out facilities. Transient dockage is available. The marina offers easy access to the Portland islands and the rest of Casco Bay.

The yard's service dock is straight ahead and on the left. Their Travellift can launch almost any sized boat, and they can step masts, though you should arrange this ahead of time. If you prefer a ramp, use the South Portland boat ramp nearby.

By land. Take Broadway north through South Portland. It leads directly to the marina.

Ashore. Long-term parking can be arranged. The marina has showers and laundry facilities. The excellent Joe's Boathouse restaurant (741-2780) is right at the head of the wharf. The Spring Point Walkway runs through the yard, offering a pleasant walk along the waterfront out to Spring Point or to Bug Light.

Spring Point Marina is located on the site of the East Yard which was hurriedly created for building Liberty Ships to transport vital cargo to the troops in Europe during World War II. The yard exemplified the incredible American war effort, employing as many as 18,000 workers and being able to build a ship every 52.2 days during peak production in 1944. There were so many workers that the shipyard had to revive the ferry service across the Fore River between Portland and South Portland. The marina's slips now lie in the berths where the ships were built, and the fitting-out pier was converted into Portland Pipeline's tanker wharf.

9. Portland Pipeline

The long pier to the west of the Spring Point breakwater is the southern terminus of a crude-oil pipeline which runs 236 miles to refineries in Montreal, Quebec. Up to 25 tankers a month off-load oil here, where the oil is stored in tanks before being pumped northward.

By sea. Do not get anywhere near the tankers or tugs as they dock or depart, and don't be tempted to get too close to the tankers off-loading at the oil terminal near the approach to Spring Point Marina. The oil booms that encircle the tankers are moored by anchors whose lines project quite far from the boom itself.

Ashore. The pipeline was built in 1941 so tankers could avoid the Saint Lawrence River, which is only free of ice for seven months out of the year. It six-month construction was spurred by the threat of German U-boats stalking the Gulf of Saint Lawrence. Now, two pipelines make the long haul to Montreal, a 18-inch line and an 24-inch line, with pumping stations along the way. Together they can deliver 600,000 barrels of crude a day.

10. Bug Light

Tiny Bug Light, to the west of the massive oil pipeline terminal, appears even smaller amid all the industry that has grown up around it. Bug Light's real name is Breakwater Light, but the breakwater that it once marked has virtually disappeared beneath landfill, and the charts show the light tower as "Aband Lt Ho." Yet Bug Light retains her classic elegance and still earns her name by being as "cute as a bug."

Bug Light and the adjacent property is a recently acquired town park. It makes a nice rest stop with some of the best views of Portland's waterfront.

By land and by sea. Bug Light is adjacent to the South Portland boat ramp (see p. 30).

Ashore. The breakwater was first conceived after a massive 1831 northeaster pushed high-tide surges into the harbor, wreaking havoc all the way to Stroudwater and the Cumberland and Oxford Canal. Five years later the construction of a breakwater out over Stanford Ledge was approved, but funding ran out before the breakwater was completed. Mariners considered its unlit projection 1/3-mile out into the harbor as more of a menace than an improvement. Finally, in 1855, a wooden light was built at the end of the breakwater.

In 1867, after the end of the Civil War, money was appropriated to extend the breakwater 400 feet farther in to the harbor, and in 1874, the old wooden lighthouse was moved to the Lighthouse Board's First District reservation on Little Diamond Island and a new cast-iron tower was erected.

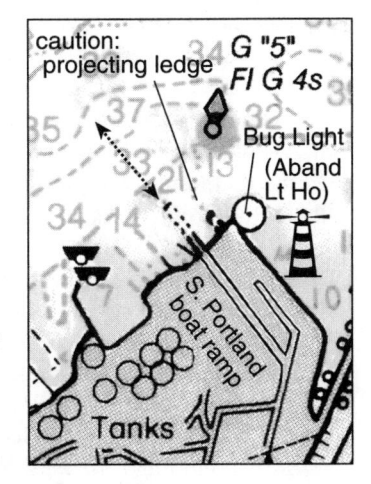

The new light was almost an exact replica of a Greek Choragic monument built in Athens in the fourth century B.C. to honor the chorus leader Lysicrates. Still, Yankee practicality prevailed, and it soon had wood-framed keeper's quarters, outbuildings, and fences attached.

The breakwater was swallowed by the war effort when the South Portland Shipbuilding Corporation filled the area north of the breakwater to form six ways for the simultaneous construction of Liberty Ships. In 1942 the U.S. Navy planned a large repair facility on the south side of the breakwater, where the South Portland boat ramp now stands and beyond. They towed in a three-section dry dock and brought in more fill, leaving Bug Light less than 100 feet from land. The Navy eventually abandoned their plans. The light, along with all lights along the coast, was blackened during the war, but with all the filling, the breakwater was no longer much of a projection into the river, and the light was never lit again.

Bug Light has recently been restored to its simple white-with-black-cap elegance, especially outstanding against its backdrop of industrial buildings and oil-tank farms.

The Spring Point Walkway leads for about a mile along South Portland's waterfront from Bug Light, around Spring Point, all the way to Willard Beach.

11. South Portland Boat Ramp

This large, well-maintained public boat ramp (Parks and Recreation, 767-7651) lies just to the west of Bug Light, directly across from Portland. It can accommodate all sizes of boats, even full-keeled sailboats launched by hydraulic trailer. It makes a perfect departure point for exploring Portland or the Fore River by water or for running out to the Portland islands and beyond.

By sea. A small fee is charged for use of the ramp. The ramp is wide enough to have an inbound side and an outbound side with floats in the middle, and it is usable at all tides. Docking time on the floats is limited. Prevailing southwesterlies blow broadside onto the floats, and strong winds from the north or northeast can make launching difficult or uncomfortable. Traffic in and out of Portland Harbor can also kick up disruptive wake.

Ledges make out a long way just to the east side of the ramp, running out parallel to it. At low tides they are visible, but at higher tides be sure to approach or depart in line with the ramp until you are well into the harbor channel. A range between the ramp and the Bath Iron Works dry dock should steer you clear. Beware of the busy traffic in the harbor.

By land. Follow Broadway north through South Portland to the stop at its end. Turn left and follow signs to the boat ramp.

Ashore. In season there is usually an attendant at the ramp who can direct you to parking.

12. Sunset Marina, Reo Marine

Sunset Marina (Ch. 09; 767-4729), farther to the west, provides transient slips, gas, diesel, and water, but they have no launching facilities. In season, Sunset runs a shuttle service back and forth across the harbor to Portland's Old Port district, so this is a convenient place to leave your boat while exploring Portland. Or you can take the shuttle the other way to eat in their Sea Dog Brewery Restaurant (799-6055), overlooking the city's skyline.

By sea. From the water, Sunset is the first marina west of Bug Light and the South Portland boat ramp. The fuel dock is located at the east end of the extensive floats.

By land. Take Broadway east from South Portland. Turn left onto Mussey Street and follow it to its end. Turn right. Go past the Centerboard Yacht Club and the Maine Shipyard. The marina will be on your left.

Ashore. Reo Marine (767-5219), located nearby, sells and services outboards and has a chandlery. The Lobstah Cafe sells fresh takeout from the Fishermen's Wharf next door.

13. Centerboard Yacht Club

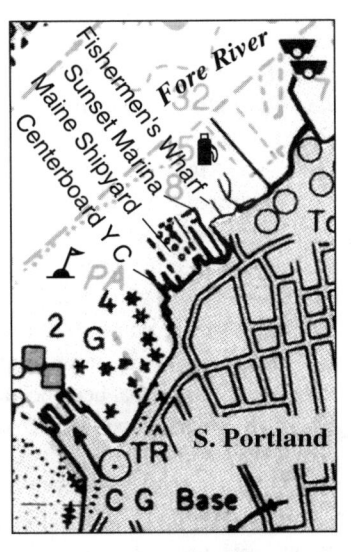

This small yacht club (799-7084) is private but friendly. It does not have the services of a marina, but the members welcome courteous visitors. Please register at the clubhouse.

A small paved ramp located next to the clubhouse is useful for shallow draft boats at most tides but low.

By sea. From the water, the small clubhouse is easily identifiable west of the old red sheds of the Maine Shipyard, with large "CYC" letters on the roof.

The club has a couple of rentable transient moorings with outstanding views of Portland. Expect to be rocked—gently and not so gently—by wakes of passing boats. Water is available at the club floats.

By land. See "Sunset Marina," above, for land directions.

Ashore. The clubhouse has pay phones and a shower.

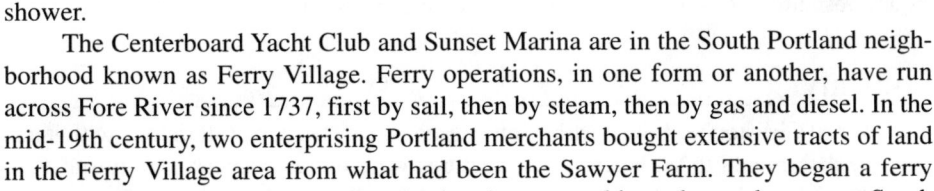

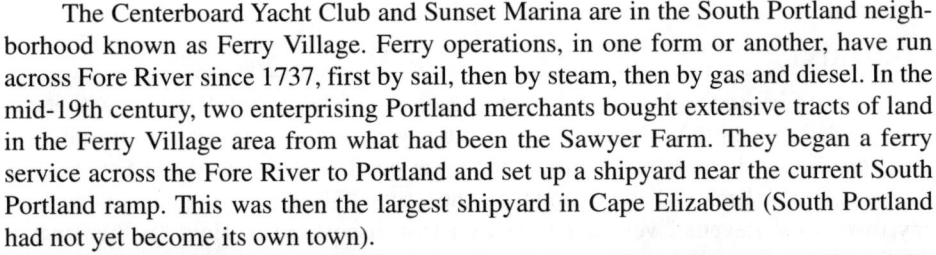

The Centerboard Yacht Club and Sunset Marina are in the South Portland neighborhood known as Ferry Village. Ferry operations, in one form or another, have run across Fore River since 1737, first by sail, then by steam, then by gas and diesel. In the mid-19th century, two enterprising Portland merchants bought extensive tracts of land in the Ferry Village area from what had been the Sawyer Farm. They began a ferry service across the Fore River to Portland and set up a shipyard near the current South Portland ramp. This was then the largest shipyard in Cape Elizabeth (South Portland had not yet become its own town).

The coming of the age of steam led to the closing of the shipyard in 1868, and the character of Ferry Village changed again. Sardine packing became a major industry for several decades, with the huge processing and canning factories built out over the water on pilings.

In 1885, the People's Ferry Company ran the *Cornelia H.*, a double-ended, sidewheel steamer, and by 1892 she was carrying an average of 60 teams of horses a day and 1400 passengers. That, fall, however, she burned at her berth. The last commercial ferry service ended in 1934, though in the summer, Sunset Marina runs a shuttle for its patrons, continuing the long tradition of Ferry Village.

14. South Port Marine

This busy marina (Ch. 09; 799-8191) lies at the foot of the bridge that spans the Fore River, linking Portland and South Portland. It is within walking distance of the supermarkets at the Mill Creek Shopping Center, or for a real expedition, you can walk across the Casco Bay Bridge to Portland.

By sea. South Port Marine launches with a travellift, and they can rig masts. The marina has no fuel, and it is located at the head of shallow mud flats. Be sure to stay in the dredged channel.

By land. South Port Marine is at the base of the new Casco Bay Bridge, on the south side. From the South Portland side of the bridge, take Broadway to Ocean Avenue. The Marina will be on the right.

Ashore. The marina has a shower and a chandlery, and they can arrange parking. Provisions of all kinds can be found at the Mill Creek Shopping Center.

South Port Marine is located in the neighborhood of Knightsville, named for master shipwright Thomas E. Knight. Knight began a shipyard here in 1850. In 1854 they launched the *Phoenix*, a 1,488-ton clipper that became part of the Red Star Lines fleet, making transatlantic runs and five trips around Cape Horn from New York to San Francisco. The Knight shipyard was active through 1877.

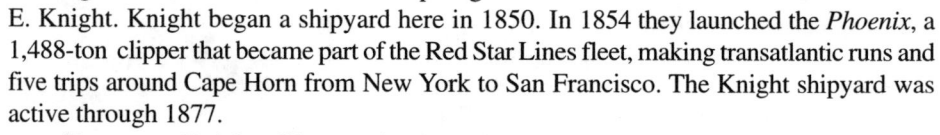

For years, Knightsville was dominated by the twin stacks of a power station located just behind the marina. Now the brick structure houses the highly-acclaimed Snow Squall restaurant. For more low-key fare, you can try Susan's Fish 'n Chips nearby.

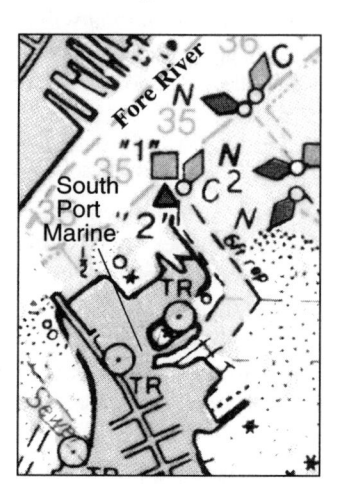

FORE RIVER

When Christopher Levett sailed into Casco Bay in 1623, he fell in love with it and became determined to settle here. Few features were more impressive to him that the river just inside the harbor. "There I found one good River wherein the Savages say there is much *Salmon* and other good fish," he wrote. "The River I made bold to call by my own name Levetts river, being the first that discovered it. How far this river is Navigable I cannot tell, I have ben but 6 miles up it, but on both sides is goodly ground." The name, unfortunately, didn't stick.

Like many rivers along the Atlantic Seaboard, the Fore River was once much deeper than it is today. One of Maine's oldest colonial villages was settled at Stroudwater, and deep-draft ships were built along its banks. The name Fore River was probably derived from the term "fore-reach," the distance a sailing vessel coasts to windward when it is brought up into the wind. As sailing ships turned into the Fore River, they would usually have come head-to-wind, fore-reaching into the prevailing southwesterlies. Today huge vessels still proceed cautiously up the river as far as the US Rt. 1, Veterans Memorial Bridge, nudged and guided by small floatillas of tugs, to off-load oil at the tank farms or swap cargo at the Merrill Marine Terminal, but beyond the bridge, the river spreads in wide, marsh-ringed mud flats.

Running up river in a small boat is like a quick trip through time, past the industrial necessities of the modern age, to the headwaters which lie quiet and peaceful between the deafening takeoffs and landings at the Portland International Jetport. A trip up the river is interesting for another reason, too. This was the site of a major 180,000-gallon oil spill in 1996, which fouled three miles of the Fore River from the dry docks of Bath Iron Works in Portland Harbor to the Stroudwater Marsh. The massive $48-million clean-up efforts appear to be paying off. The marsh, which was blackened by oil, appears to be surviving and rebounding.

Near the headwaters lies the hamlet of Stroudwater; one of Maine's earliest, and the Stroudwater Marsh (see Stroudwater, p. 34).

In 1913, to the tune of nearly a million dollars, a bridge was built across the Fore River between Portland and South Portland. Taxpayers, outraged at the cost, dubbed it the Million Dollar Bridge. It was replaced in 1996 by a new bridge with more height and wider clearance for ships below. The bridge's estimated cost of more than $165 million had the local nicknamers stumped until some official committee named it the Casco Bay Bridge.

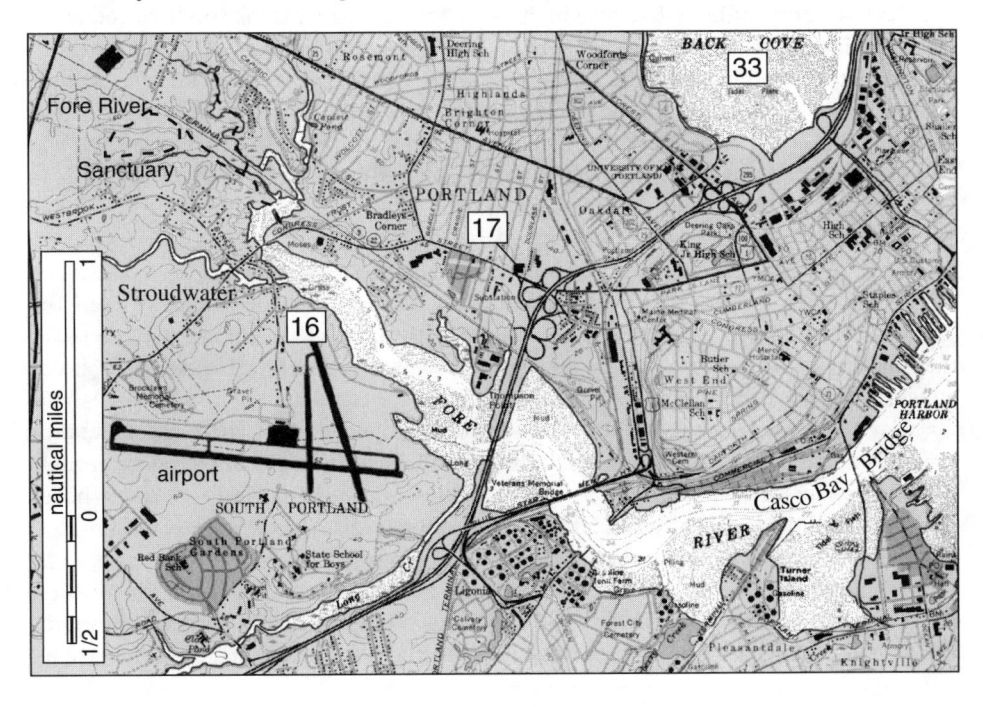

In earlier times, ferries plied back and forth across the river. Then a wooden bridge was built. In 1911 spectators crammed every inch of the Portland Bridge as it was called, climbing its trusses and clinging to its abutments to watch Harry Houdini throw himself into the Fore River, bound in chains and handcuffs—a free show as a prelude to his performance at Portland's Keith Theater. Sixty-nine years later, the Portland chapter of the Society of American Magicians held a séance on the Million Dollar Bridge in an attempt to contact the spirit of Houdini the Great. Alas, he had vanished.

By sea. Stay well clear of any shipping traffic near the bridge, preferably passing under it well away from the central channel. This is where the *Julie N.* struck the abutments of the original bridge and rolled open her oil-filled hull like a sardine can. The flood runs upriver at an average maximum of 0.6 knots beneath the bridge. Maximum ebb is about 0.5 knots downriver.

The second and third bridges, Veterans Memorial Bridge for US Rt. 1 and the highway bridge for Rt. 295, are fixed, with a vertical clearance at mean high tide of about 19 feet. Just past the bridges, you can pause for a moment and enjoy the sensation of sitting in the middle of an airport runway as planes skim overhead to land at Portland Airport. The runway lights, in fact, are built out into the water on a series of small pilings and catwalks.

Beyond this point, you are off the chart, and you will have to feel your way up river. At low, a depth of about six feet can be carried under the bridges as far as Thompson's Point, at the north end of the Rt. 295 bridge and identifiable by a collection of brick warehouses. At the southern end of the same bridge, the Fore River is joined by Long Creek from the southwest.

The upper reaches of the Fore River become very shoal. At low, they are mostly mud flats with a small tidal channel slithering through them. Exploration of the headwaters isn't recommended unless you are near the top of the tide or draw next to nothing.

Ashore. See Stroudwater, below.

15. Long Creek

The tributary of Long Creek, which meets the Fore River at the southern end of the Rt. 295 bridge, lacks much to recommend it for exploration. It trails off to the southwest past the airport and between the highway and the barbed-wire enclosure of a juvenile detention center. It is hard to imagine now that along these banks in 1678, Indians and settlers signed the peace treaty that brought an end to the First Indian War, which was also known locally by the name of the Indian Chief who called himself King Philip.

16. Stroudwater

Stroudwater is the small cluster of historic houses near the bridge where Congress Street crosses the Fore River. At high tide it is possible to land portable boats at the small park to the west of the bridge and visit historic Tate House, or you can squeeze beneath the Stroudwater bridge to explore the trails in the Stroudwater Marsh.

By sea. Feel your way up the Fore River (described above). There are no landing facilities at the park, and if the tide is falling, don't stay too long unless you've brought your hip waders. For this reason, it is not recommended as a put-in for portable boats. Boats of shallow draft and limited height can slip beneath the Congress Street bridge, which has a vertical clearance at high tide of about 3 or 4 feet.

By land. From Portland, follow Congress Street west until it drops down to the bridge that crosses the Fore River at Stroudwater. The Stroudwater Park will be on the left, just after you cross the bridge. Because of the tide, traffic, and parking limitations, this is not an ideal place to launch boats.

Ashore. Stroudwater was founded in 1727 by Colonel Thomas Westbrook who was transferred here from Portsmouth, New Hampshire as a mast agent and surveyor general for the Royal Navy, then under King George II. He set up shipyards here and a mast depot for receiving, dressing, and shipping mast trees that were felled inland and floated here. The small public park was one of the mast yards, and the houses are some of the oldest in the Portland area. Tidal mills at Stroudwater and at the dammed mouth of the Stroudwater River tributary powered sawmills.

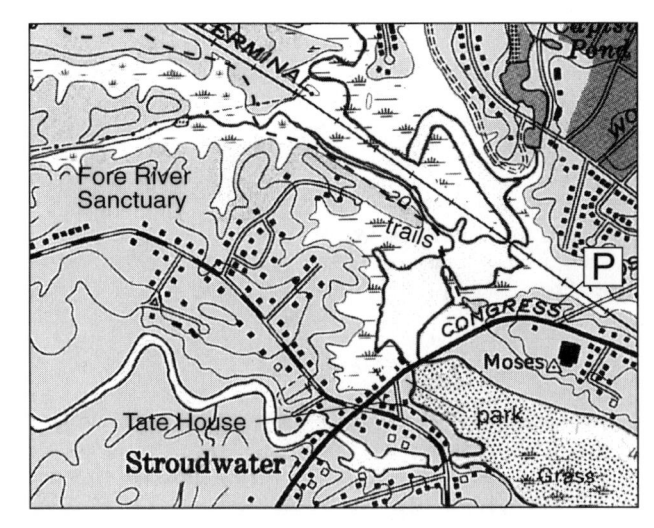

Waldo Street is named for Colonel Samuel Waldo, a friend and business partner in many ventures with Colonel Westbrook. Unfortunately, some of their ventures were highly speculative, and in 1743 the friendship dissolved when Waldo sued Westbrook for 10,500 pounds. Westbrook lost all his property, including his grand mansion, and his bankruptcy strained him so much that he died seven months later. His family and friends feared that even his body would be seized for his debts still outstanding, so they secretly buried him at night. He left a wife and a daughter.

The Tate House was built on Westbrook Street just up the hill from the mast yard in 1755 by Captain George Tate, the successor to Col. Westbrook as the British Navy's mast agent. From July through Ocotber, the house is open to the public (774-9781).

Tate's wife had a bizarre accident here in 1770. Madame Tate had discovered articles missing from their storehouse, and she presumed they were stolen. With the help of one of her sons, William, she rigged a gun to shoot whoever opened the storehouse door. But soon Madame Tate herself needed something from the storehouse. Her servant, Black Betty, refused to go, so Mrs. Tate, confident that she could open the door without disturbing the gun, went herself. The gun went off, and she was killed.

Tate's son William was arraigned in court and convicted of manslaughter, a crime punishable by death. He was spared only by a royal pardon by King George. Later it was discovered that the thieves had entered via an underground passageway.

Curiously, after his duty for the British Navy, George Tate was employed as a mast agent by the Czar of Russia. Even stranger, his son, George, Jr., eventually joined the Russian Navy and became its First Admiral and a member of the Imperial Senate for fifty years.

Westbrook built the first bridge to cross the Fore River and charged tolls for the privilege. The Stroudwater Basin lies beyond it, and the river continues under a gracefully-arched, brown footbridge. The footbridge is the beginning of a beautiful 2 1/2-mile trail system through the Stroudwater Marsh and surrounding woods known as the

On the Canal

The diary of Jerimiah P. Applegate describes in detail the slow passage through the canal, up the Presumpscot, across Sebago Lake, up the Crooked River, through the Songo Lock, through Brandy Pond, and down the length of Long Lake to Bridgton.

....Thursday, the twenty-ninth day of the month of August, in the year of our Lord, eighteen hundred and thirty nine. Weather pleasant.

I was privileged on this day because of urgent business in the town of Portland, to charter passage on a boat which plies the canal connecting the flourishing town of Stroudwater, situated at the mouth of the Fore River, with Long Pond. ...after a few minutes of aimless wandering, I made my way to the wharf, where I found my vessel waiting.

The craft which I boarded had in bold gilt letters on her blunt bow, the name "Water Witch." Her stern was square, and the masts were to all appearances too short for such a cumbersome craft. A heavy center board kept her on an even keel.

As we boarded the "Water Witch," a man collected the fare of a half penny, and another half penny was exacted at each mile marker thereafter. We set sail at 10 o'clock. The day was exceeding hot, and the poor beasts of burden on the bank were weary with the heavy load and the pitiful manner in which their drivers abused them. The scenery on either side was beautiful and verdant, and I spent much time speculating upon the game and fish to be found in these virgin wilds.

A trumpet sound brought my mind back to the boat, and I found to my amazement we had arrived at a so-called lock. Upon inquiry, I found the village to be Horse Beef (*exact location unknown*). All went ashore to seek the tavern, for all were parched by the great heat. Some of the drivers made sport among themselves and pitched quoits and wrestled. At the sound of the trumpet all returned to the craft.

Being much interested in these locks, I inquired of a man on the boat as to their construction, and I was informed that they worked by means of large beams. An iron door at the bottom allowed the water to enter. In this manner the craft was raised to the next level of the river. These locks were eighty feet long and ten feet wide with a drop of ten feet. There were, I was told, twenty seven such locks. The man in the scarlet shirt, who was seemingly the captain, called my attention to the fact that the great pines bordering the river still had what he called "the King's mark" on them, and described the mark as an arrow. And I was astonished to learn that trees so marked had been used for masts in the English and Russian navies.

As we neared Congin (*suburbs of Westbrook*), we passed a craft that was indeed strange. Seemingly it had all the colors known to man, and I was told that this was no uncommon occurrence. We hailed the "Peacock," for such proved to be her name, and which, by the way, I thought rather fitting. We encountered numerous craft of quaint description and much bantering and sport the drivers did make between them. At 3 1/2 o'clock we came to a bridge with watertight sides and bottom. This bridge crossed Pleasant River at right angles and in this way prevented the currents of the two rivers from meeting. We crossed this bridge and in the early evening we passed Gorham. As the last flushes of twilight faded, we reached Gambo (*near Newhall*) where we stopped for the night. During the evening there was much story telling, smoking, and the discussion of politics. So closes another day.

.....Friday, the thirtieth day in the month of August, in the year of our Lord eighteen hundred and thirty nine. Weather lowery.

We sailed from Gambo at 4 1/2 o'clock and two hours later arrived at the prosperous town of Great Falls (*North Gorham*). We this time went through four locks and I marveled greatly at the quickness of the lock tenders. As the weather seemed to be more pleasant, I

Fore River Sanctuary. Parking for the trail can be found at the far end of the gray and green office building up the hill on Congress Street, east of the bridge.

The trail starts by following the tow path of the old Cumberland and Oxford Canal, which was dug by hand between 1828 and 1830 to connect the Fore River with the Presumpscot, then the highway of inland commerce from Casco Bay to Sebago and Long Lake. $27,000 of the $206,000 cost of the project was raised by one of the earliest state lotteries. In its heyday, canal boats, 65 feet long and 10 feet wide with a mast and sails forward and a crew of three, would sail or be towed through the canal and in and out of 28 wooden locks to arrive at Sebago, 265 feet higher than Casco Bay. Three of these canal schooners were built in the Dyer Shipyard in the Ferry Village section of South Portland.

The canal, however, never turned a profit before the coming of the railroad put it out of business in the 1870s. It was sold at auction and bought at a bargain price by one of Portland's most notorious citizens, F.O.J. Smith (see Mile Pond, p. 72).

---

ventured out on deck. Saying farewell to the canal, with its pleasant views and peaceful villages "cradled 'mid the clustering hills," we sailed out of the Presumpscot River and across the "basin." When we reached Sebago Pond, however, the wind blew with such violence that we were forced to run for shelter at Cape Standish (*Whites Point*). But we were not alone in our plight, for we were soon joined by the "Mary Ann" and the "Jack Downing." So fierce was the gale we were forced to lie in safety. After the wind had abated somewhat, we ventured out on Sebago Pond. The waves still ran fearfully high and often the boat would almost capsize as a huge wave broke over the deck. However, by the kindness of the Lord and the skill of our helmsman, we gained the mouth of the Songo River. The moon had risen, and the only sound was an occasional night bird and the steady tramp of the men walking on the deck as they poled the boat up the river. As I stood at the railing, an old man came up, and we engaged in conversation. After some time I questioned him as to the history of the canal and found him to be very talkative on the subject.

It seems that in the year 1791, a committee of men was selected to "ascertain the practicability of a canal between Saccarrappa and Sebago Pond." Then conditions were found favorable; and, accordingly, one Woodbury Storer obtained an act of corporation under the name Cumberland Canal Company from the Court of Massachusetts.

The company united with the Falmouth Canal Company. Then came the hectic days of the War of 1812, and the financial status of the companies was disrupted. It was not until Maine became a state that a move was made to build a canal. The estimated cost, I believe, was $137,345.13. The canal was opened only nine years ago, stated the old man. I thanked the man for his kind information, and I shortly retired to my cabin, being weary from the storm.

So closes another day.

.....*Saturday, the thirty-first day of the month of August, in the year of our Lord eighteen hundred and thirty nine. Weather fair.*

I awoke this morning and found the entire ship's company bustling about. We were now on a lake and nearing shore. I inquired as to the business of the men and was told that we were at the end of our journey. At 10 1/2 o'clock, the boat nosed into the wharf at Bridgton.

So ended my first journey on the "Water Witch," and I shall try to gain passage on her for my return trip .....

From *Stroudwater Sketches*,
Deering High School, 1938

PORTLAND

Portland grew out of the water and is surrounded by it. Its downtown lies on a peninsula, bound on the west and south by the Fore River, on the north by Back Cove, and on the east by Casco Bay. This is Maine's largest city—a major shipping port, a center of law and banking, and a cultural magnet. Yet it is essentially a small and friendly village, packed with historic buildings, eclectic restaurants, an art school, major art and children's museums, a symphony orchestra, and a hometown baseball team. It is well worth visiting, whether your boat is in the water or on top of the car.

Among the wharves are several businesses of particular interest to small boaters, as well as a fuel dock, a couple of marinas, two town floats, and a launching ramp off the Eastern Promenade (see entries below).

By sea. Portland Harbor is fascinating to visit by water, but it is a busy commercial port with large, highly unmaneuverable vessels coming and going with slow but relentless momentum that cannot be reversed quickly, even if a speck of a small boat could been seen from the bridge. Avoid the major shipping channel, and give a wide berth and the right-of-way to anything bigger than you. As sailor Dodge Morgan put it, "A dinghy ride across the harbor channel is like making your way across an active airport runway on a tricycle."

For launching information, see Portland town floats (p. 41) or East End Beach (p. 47).

By land. From the Maine Turnpike, take Rt. 295 and follow signs to Portland's waterfront via Commercial Street. Or stay on Rt. 295 and exit onto Franklin Arterial and follow it to the waterfront.

Portland is also accessible through the Jetport (774-7301) or by Greyhound and Vermont Transit Lines (772-6587) or by Trailways (828-1151).

Ashore. Lodging and eating choices are wonderful and varied in Portland. The Visitor's Information Center (772-5800) can help you plan ahead.

Many fresh or organic provisions can be found within walking distance of the waterfront. The Portland Green Grocer on Commercial Street has fresh produce in a beautiful granite building. The Port Bake House next door or the Standard Baking Company farther down Commercial Street can stock you up with fresh breads or sweets. The Whip and Spoon on Commercial can take care of wine, cheese, and coffee needs. Every Wednesday in the summer, a farmers' market fills Monument Square, right in the middle of town on Congress Street. It features local produce—and local farmers. Or for local delectables like smoked salmon you can explore Portland's new Public Market on Cumberland Avenue.

A wholesome selection of beers are brewed in town, in brew pubs like the Stone Coast Brewing Company and Gritty McDuff's in the Old Port, or at Shipyard Ale, a couple of blocks up from the east end of Commercial Street.

If you are ending a small-boat trip here, you may want to visit the YWCA (874-1130) at 87 Spring Street. Or your friends may want you to. In addition to a pool and sauna, they have showers.

The Indians called Portland "Machigonne," which means either "bad clay" in reference to the clay found along the Back Cove or "knee" or "elbow" in reference to its shape. The early settlers gave it the successive names of The Elbow, The Neck, Casco, Falmouth, and Portland.

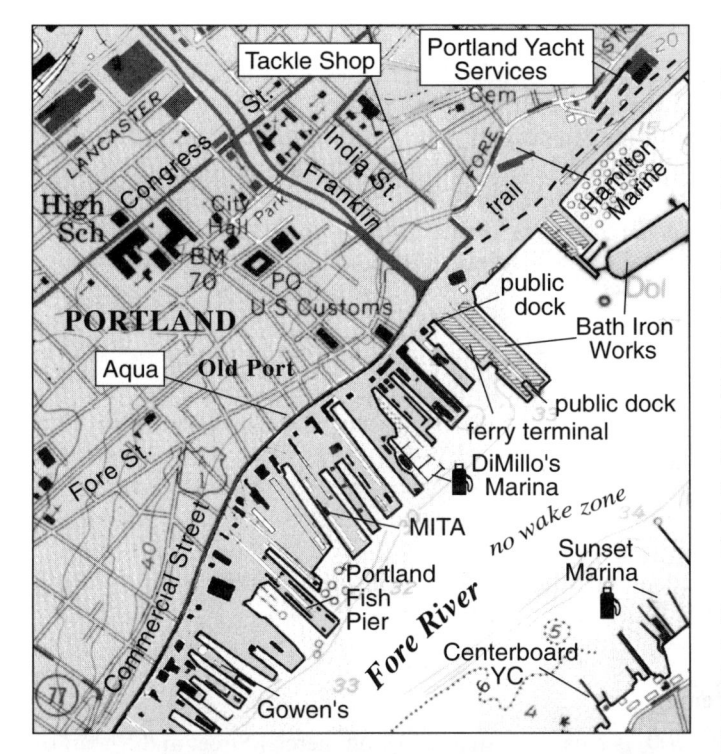

Major fires destroyed Portland twice. The first was set by the British in 1775 as retaliation by Captain Henry Mowatt for being captured and detained in the city the previous spring. The last was in 1866, set by a Fourth of July firecracker, leveling much of the downtown area. Only by blowing up buildings in advance of the flames was the fire eventually brought under control.

After the fires, non-combustible brick was, understandably, a favored building material, giving rise to the brick warehouse area along the waterfront now known as the Old Port and the workingman's Munjoy Hill neighborhood to the east. Many of the proud mansions of the West End were spared and still stand today. Portland's motto, *Resurgam*, means "I will rise again."

Portland's waterfront lies along the northern shore of the Fore River, east of the Casco Bay Bridge. The waterfront's western end is now dominated by the International Ferry Terminal, hard by the bridge. This is the home of the *Scotia Prince*, which departs on summer evenings, silently ghosting out of the harbor, lights ablaze, Titanic-style, for an overnight run to Yarmouth, Nova Scotia.

The city's wharves farther east are the heart of the working waterfront. Portland's Fish Pier harbors much of Portland's fishing fleet and Portland's fish auction, and the older wharves are still piled high with traps, nets, and gear. In many of the buildings, fish are cleaned, gutted, packed and shipped or sold on the spot. Harbor seals loll among the pilings hunting fish which are attracted to scraps.

Originally, Fore Street followed the shore, and some of the buildings on that street were equipped with steel shutters to prevent docking ships from putting their bowsprits through the windows. Some still have parts of the old Portland seawall incorporated into their foundations. In 1851 Commercial Street was built out over the tidewater to connect the railroads at either end of the city, from Union to Grand Trunk Station. The street was laid directly on top of the wharves, with a 26-foot wide railroad corridor in its center. Eventually, the shore under Commercial Street was filled in.

The east end of the waterfront is distinguished by Bath Iron Works' Portland facility, with its massive floating dry dock.

17. Johnson's Sporting Goods

Johnson's Sporting Goods (1183 Congress St., 773-5909) is Portland's oldest dive shop. With three locations in Maine, they offer complete tank servicing and air while you wait and even have an indoor pool for diving instruction. Johnson's also stocks and extensive inventory of fishing tackle.

By land. Johnson's sits on Congress Street, just west of Rt. 295 crossing. Their building, with a roof shingled in the pattern of a red-and-white dive flag, can be seen from the highway.

18. Vessel Services, Gowen's, and Becky's

Vessel Services (772-5718) operates a serious commercial chandlery at 400 Commercial Street. Here you can find a shackle that weighs more than a kayak, but their expanding line of charts, books, and rugged gear is just as useful on small boats.

Gowen Marine (773-1761), on the wharf at the same location, hauls and repairs commercial vessels, but they carry the Carolina Skiff line of small boats.

Becky's Diner, next door, opens before most humans are awake to serve strong coffee and slippery eggs to fishermen before they brave the deep.

19. Aqua Diving Academy

Aqua Diving (772-4200) is located right at 223 Commercial Street in the heart of the Old Port. They fill tanks, sell gear, and run certification courses.

20. Maine Island Trail Association

The Maine Island Trail Association was formed to promote careful stewardship of both public and private Maine islands by those who explore them in small boats. Their approach has been so successful that it has become the model for many similar water "trails" throughout the country and Canada. Anyone who plans on extensive small boat voyaging in Maine should join this organization. Their Portland office (761-8225) is located at 41A Union Wharf, and—if your boat is *really* small—you might be able to find some dock space among the fishing boats to tie up to while you join.

21. Chase Leavitt

The Chartroom (772-3751) is Portland's oldest shipping agent, located right in the Old Port where it could service ships berthed at the wharves along Commercial Street. As ship brokers and agents, they represent a vessel's interests as it approaches port, clears customs, and deals with any medical issues. Unfortunately for recreational boaters, they have stopped running their marvelous, old-world chandlery to focus on their shipping services. They continue, however, to sell an extensive inventory of charts, marine publications, and topographic maps and to service inflatables and liferafts.

By land. Chase Leavitt is one building away from Commercial St. at 10 Dana St.

22. Dimillo's Marina

Dimillo's Marina (Ch. 09, 773-7632) is right in the center of Portland's Old Port area. They have a fuel float with gas, diesel water, and electricity. A small chandlery carries boaters' basics, including snacks and limited groceries. DiMillo's Floating Restaurant is next to the floats aboard a large, blue-and-white ferry boat. They have no launching or repair facilities, but they do rent transient slips if you feel like provisioning or a night on the town.

By sea. Dimillo's fuel dock lies just to the east of the floating restaurant.

By land. Take Rt. 295 from the Maine Turnpike. Either follow signs to the waterfront or take Franklin Arterial to Commercial Street. DiMillo's is on the water side.

Ashore. Excellent restaurants are ubiquitous in Portland, most of which are within easy walking distance from the waterfront, and they run the gamut from formal to takeout. DiMillo's floating restaurant has become a Portland landmark. The ferry was once the *Newport*, which ran between Newport and Jamestown Rhode Island, and later it served as the clubhouse for the Pawtucket Yacht Club in Port Jefferson, New York.

Dimillo's has an extensive parking lot with hourly rates. See "Portland Town Floats," below, for longer-term parking suggestions.

23. Portland Town Floats

Portland has two town floats, available for public dockage. The first float lies to the west of the Casco Bay Lines ferry terminal, easily identified by their bright red-white-and-yellow ferries. Run past the ferries and the city fireboats to the float. Dock only on the west face of the float. The east is reserved for emergencies—the fireboat serves as the ambulance for the islands, docking here to transfer its cargo to a wheeled ambulance for a dash to the hospital. Maximum docking time is 30 minutes.

A newer, longer town float lies to the east of the ferry terminal slip, cut into the Maine State Pier. Again, the tie-up is limited to 30 minutes or less, and despite a small breakwater made of pilings at its outer end, it is very exposed to wake from passing boats. Access to the float by car, however, is quite good, and portable boats could be launched here.

By sea. From the water, the state pier can be identified by the large whale mural painted along the metal buildings on the pier. Blast your horn loudly for three seconds as you back out of either float.

All the cautions of Portland Harbor apply here. Of particular concern is the massive amount of boat wake here at the height of the summer, despite the huge postings of 5 mph speed limits. Be particularly wary of the *Maquoit*, Casco Bay Lines' largest passenger ferry (see p. 43).

By land. From the Maine Turnpike, take Rt. 295 to exit 7 and Franklin Arterial. The Arterial will lead directly to the State Pier. Cars can be driven down the wooden portion of the pier all the way to the float's ramp. Do not park here, but unload your boats and gear and then go park. In summer, you will probably have plenty of spectators from the crowds that fish off the end of the pier. Leave someone with your gear so it doesn't float off somewhere before it has even gotten into the boat. Also beware that the wooden portions of the pier ooze tar when it is hot, and it makes a mess if you track it into your boat.

Ashore. The Casco Bay Lines Terminal has restrooms, vending machines, newspapers, and pay phones. You can stock up on coffee, donuts, muffins, lunch, snacks, or beer at Casco Bay Variety, located just to the west on Commercial Street, or across from that, you can buy fresh-baked breads at Standard Baking Company. Public parking is available at the city garage, right at the pier, though it can be expensive for long periods. You may be able to negotiate better rates at one of the outside dirt lots near the east end of Commercial Street where it meets India Street.

A walking trail leaves from this end of Commercial around the waterfront of the Eastern Promenade, passing Portland Yacht Services (see p. 44) and ending at the East End Beach (see p. 47).

24. Casco Bay Lines

Casco Bay Lines (774-7871) steamers and ferries have served the islands of Casco Bay continuously since 1871, making it the oldest such ferry service in the country. Their brightly-painted red-yellow-and-white ferry boats are still the lifelines of the islands, plying the waters from the Portland terminal on the State Pier to Peaks Island, Little Diamond, Great Diamond, Long Island, Chebeague Island, and Cliff Island, and, in the summer, making a daily "mailboat run" as far as Bailey Island.

Proving just how inextricably intertwined Casco Bay Lines is with the daily lives of the islanders it serves, Harold Hackett, of Little Diamond Island, wrote the following:

> "Not long ago without much advance notice the company began charging fare for pets...
>
> "Island dog lovers became quite vocal, however, and one pooch was taken to the Governor protesting discrimination or something. To add to the commotion, some wag rushed about reporting that Casco Bay Lines had charged her $15 to transport a bowl of goldfish.
>
> "Every effort was made to deceive the purser into thinking the traveler petless. One heavyish woman was boarding with a suspiciously large picnic basket when midway the bottom fell out dumping three magniferous cats onto the gangplank. That received no reductions for group travel.
>
> "The elite of the secreted pets was a little pink pig with a green rhinestone collar. Invariably hidden in a briefcase, he never squealed until the boat was well underway. Finally some agreement was reached. Now four-legged pets pay, and goldfish travel free." *

If you are lucky enough to have an island base from which to explore Casco Bay or if you find yourself too tired to paddle home, Casco Bay Lines' ferry routes enable kayakers and others in portable boats to make one-way trips by shipping their boats and themselves back on the ferries. Call in advance for schedules and rates.

* Reprinted with permission, see copyright page.

By sea. Perhaps it is because the Casco Bay Lines ferries run year-round in all types of weather and conditions, or perhaps it is just because their joyous paint schemes belie the fact that these are large, steel vessels moving at considerable speed with limited maneuverability, but the captains and crews of the ferries see more than their share of small-boat stupidity, often pulling their hapless skippers out of the drink or off buoys or slamming the ferry into full reverse to avoid sinking the small sailboat that is determined to defend its right of way. Occasionally jetskiers will chase the ferries, crisscrossing their wakes to fly into the air, occasionally circling *in front* of the ferry for another run. Please, keep your distance. And hope, when you are in trouble in Casco Bay, that one of the ferries is nearby.

Beware of the tall, wide, and squat *Maquoit*, the newest of the Casco Bay Lines ferries and the largest of their passenger ferries. It moves mountains of water, even at low speeds. The wake often crests and breaks, and often it is so far behind the boat that it can hit you by surprise long after the boat has passed. The *Maquoit* generally runs "Down Bay" between Peaks and the Diamond Islands, to the inside of Long Island to Chandlers Cove on Chebeague, then to Cliff Island and back.

By land. See "Portland Town Floats" above.

Ashore. Casco Bay Lines has excellent public restrooms, located right on the water adjacent to the town floats. Parking is available right next door, though the rates can add up for longer stays. Several commercial long-term lots are located near the intersection of the east end of Commercial Street and India Street.

25. West Marine

This branch (761-7600) of the famous marine supplier is a mile from Commercial Street and Portland's waterfront, via the Franklin Arterial. They can supply you with most recreational boating needs, including charts, boating hardware, and electronics.

By land. From the Maine Turnpike, take the 295 and exit at Franklin Arterial. Turn right at the first light onto Marginal Way. West Marine is at 127 Marginal Way, on your left.

26. The Tackle Shop

The Tackle Shop (773-3474) is Portland's newest source for impassioned fishermen, particularly those of the saltwater-fly persuasion.

By land. Follow Commercial Street northeastward to its end where it makes a hard left onto India. The Tackle Shop is located two blocks up on the right at 61 India Street.

27. Hamilton Marine

Hamilton Marine (774-1772) is the Maine fisherman's equivalent of West Marine, stocking almost everything a commercial or recreational boater might need, from heavy rubber boots to engine controls and fittings to charts and sophisticated electronics. They are located at 100 Fore Street near India, within walking distance from the Old Port.

By land. Take Franklin Arterial to a left on Fore Street east. Hamilton is on the right.

28. Bath Iron Works

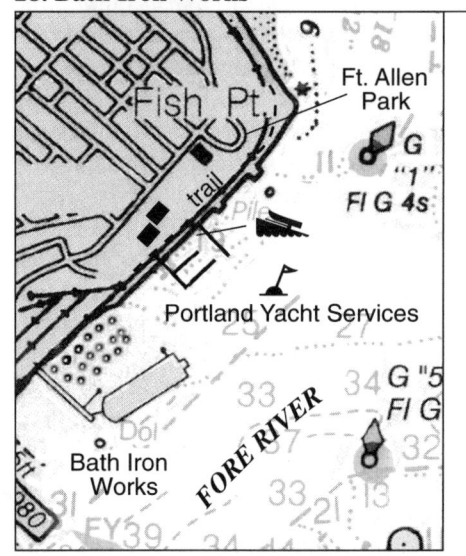

The eastern end of the waterfront is dominated by the huge, blue, floating dry dock of the Portland facility of Bath Iron Works, often cradling a large Aegis destroyer. The dry dock was used in the Pacific during World War II and then disassembled and towed, section by section, to various locations before arriving in Portland. Bath Iron Works uses it primarily to mount sonar domes on newly launched cruisers and destroyers.

By sea. Small boats can approach and observe the work here, but we don't recommend flashing your camera or camcorder. These vessels are floating monuments to our national security, and security officials at BIW might jump to the conclusion that you are making more than home movies.

29. Portland Yacht Services

Portland Yacht Services (58 Fore Street, Ch. 09; 774-1067) lies at the eastern end of Portland Harbor, just east of the Bath Iron Works dry dock. This expanding full-service yacht yard has attracted other marine-related businesses. PYS can launch most boats and perform all types of hull, engine, outboard, rigging and system repairs, and they have an extensive parts department for auxillaries and outboards.

Due to the size of their facilities and their location within walking distance of the Old Port, this is an ideal place to stage longer trips.

By sea. The Portland Yacht Services occupies a series of rambling brick and metal buildings just to the east of the large, blue, Bath Iron Works dry dock. They have a launching ramp, a small crane, and rigging capabilities. Heavy transient moorings are available and so is some limited dockage, though both are quite exposed to wind, waves, and passing wake. From here, all of the Portland islands are easily accessible.

By land. From Rt. 295, follow Franklin Arterial toward the waterfront. Go left on Fore Street. PYS is on the right, as Fore begins to climb a hill.

Ashore. PYS stores, services, or repairs boats and engines of all kinds, and they can arrange long-term parking and boat storage. Each March, they host the highly-acclaimed Maine Boatbuilders Show, which showcases the incredible talents of Maine craftsmen and the quality of their boats—many of them small, all of them beautiful.

A new walking trail leads along the waterfront past PYS either to the Old Port or to the East End Beach and Back Cove, or you can ride the Maine Narrow-Gauge Railway, departing from the Railway Museum located in one of the PYS buildings.

This site has a long history of railroads and shipping. The Saint Lawrence River, in Canada, would freeze in the winter, effectively closing Canadian ports, and in 1845, the Montreal Board of Trade decided to do something about it. They scouted both Portland's and Boston's ice-free harbors as possible locations to build a wharf and railway terminal. They finally determined which was closer by land not by commissioning study after study as we would do today, but by holding a race. The town that could deliver mail to Montreal first would get the terminal.

Mainers carefully planned a relay of fresh stage horses, and won the race for Portland. The Grand Trunk railway was built here, with a switching yard and huge grain elevators. Portland Yacht Service's buildings once housed the Portland Foundry, which built locomotives.

The grain elevators and their wharves were vast. One was 185-feet high with a capacity of 1.5 million bushels, another was 100 feet and could hold one million bushels. Canadian grain was shipped to England and Scotland. The decline of this enterprise came about when Canada subsidized a railroad to Halifax, Nova Scotia at a time when Canadian labor costs were significantly lower than American. By 1940, the wharves and elevators were rotting. When the first elevator was dismantled in 1943, 1.4 million board feet of lumber was salvaged for the war effort.

When the second elevator was dismantled in 1970, it is said that thousands of rats "ran like thoroughbreds" up Munjoy Hill. Phil O'Donnell, the harbormaster at the time, was watching from the State Pier with his dog. "A huge rat got the dog around the neck, and they both went over the side," he says. The dog was rescued by local fishermen in small boats. The forest of pilings that once supported the elevators still stand behind the dry dock.

30. Portland Observatory

The Portland Observatory is a rust-red, octagonal tower on Munjoy Hill at the eastern end of the Portland Peninsula. From the water, it is directly above the brick buildings of Portland Yacht Services. The tower is more than a landmark. It has a long maritime history as an observation post for spotting ships entering the harbor, and it is the last such structure in the country.

The Portland Observatory was built in 1807 by the enterprising Captain Moody. In the days before any kind of ship-to-shore communication, he recognized the need to signal merchants and cargo handlers of the imminent arrival of ships. Portland was a thriving port of 6,000 people, but Munjoy Hill was open field and pasture, and Congress Street was still dirt. The observatory commanded a sweeping view of Casco Bay, Portland Harbor, and its approaches, and even distant vistas as far away as Wood Island off the mouth of the Saco River and Seguin, off the Kennebec. Logbooks of ship identifications and flags were kept in the tower, and when a ship was observed through the tower's powerful Dolland telescope, it was identified, its arrival time was estimated based on weather, wind, and current, and signal flags were hoisted. Merchants and longshoremen on the waterfront wharves read the flags and prepared for the ship's arrival. Observatory logbooks show the changing trends in shipping, from sail to steam to power. Ship-to-shore telegraphy and radios eventually rendered the observatory unnecessary, and it closed in 1923.

Other observatories were located at Boston, New York, and Baltimore, but they have long since disappeared. The construction of the octagonal tower of the Portland Observatory, now owned by the city, is testimony to Captain Moody's engineering ingenuity. Eight continuous white pine supporting posts (see p. 69), each over 65' long, form a framework that is ballasted at its base by 122 tons of stone rubble. The flames of the Great Portland Fire of 1866 missed the observatory by one block, and for 188 years it has withstood storms, gales, and hurricanes.

Ironically, it almost fell prey to something called the anoibid beetle. The tower has recently been completely rebuilt to save it. Once restored, the public will again be able to climb its 102 steps to enjoy the breathtaking, million-dollar views of Portland Harbor and the islands beyond.

By sea. The Observatory is an easy walk from the Portland town floats (see p. 41), Portland Yacht Services (see p. 44), or the East End Beach (see p. 47).

By land. Take Congress Street east from Franklin Arterial. The Observatory will be on your right.

31. Fort Allen Park

Fort Allen is part of the expansive public area along Portland's Eastern Promenade, and few places present a nicer vista of the harbor. From the water the park can be recognized by the gray tower off the *U.S.S. Portland*, a heavy cruiser involved in Guadacanal and the Japanese surrender at Truk.

Fort Allen was an earthwork fort built quickly in 1814 when it was rumored that British ships were approaching Portland. From this perfect vantage point, five guns were trained on the harbor. It was named after Commander William Henry Allen, of the sloop-of-war *Argus*, who was killed in action the previous year.

Along the waterfront at the foot of the park, there is practically no trace of the grand schemes of the *Great Eastern*, a ship that from its maiden voyage became testimony to the fact that economy of scale does not apply to all things. The construction of this behemoth was begun in 1854 on the Thames in England, and when she was launched she measured 693 feet long and 120 feet wide. Her engineers covered all the bases, powering her with two paddle-wheels, a propeller, and a full set of sails on a schooner rig. But it became obvious after her first voyage across the Atlantic to New York that she was far from economical. She was too big to be moved by her sails, and she could hardly carry enough coal for her voracious engines. She finally found a job big enough for her size—laying transatlantic cable.

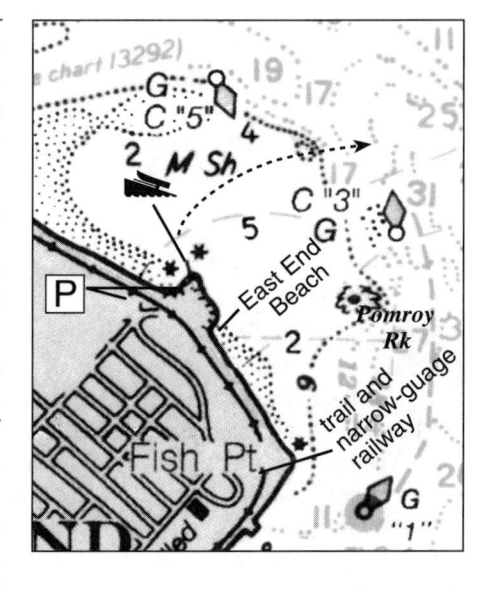

Special wharves were constructed for her at the foot of Fort Allen Park, but they were rarely used. Their one claim to fame was that they were used to receive the Prince of Wales in 1860. Eventually the wharves, and the grandiose dreams they represented, were swallowed by the sea.

By sea. Land either at Portland Yacht Services (see p.44) or East End Beach (see below) and follow the footpath to the park.

By land. Take Franklin Arterial to Fore Street. Follow Fore easterly up the hill toward the Eastern Promenade. Fort Allen Park will be on your right, just after the large yellow apartment building.

32. East End Beach

East End Beach is at the foot of Portland's spectacular Eastern Promenade. From the Promenade, high on a hill, Casco Bay stretches out in a sweeping panorama from the Spring Point Light to Cousins Island and Great Chebeague Island and beyond. Park facilities include an elaborate playground, public tennis courts, and a large, well-maintained public launching ramp.

By sea. Use the public ramp with the floating docks. The steeper commercial ramp with the pilings is reserved for landing craft from the islands for off-loading garbage trucks and other service vehicles.

By land. Take exit 7 off Rt. 295. Follow Franklin Arterial to a left on Fore Street. Take Fore up to the crest of the hill. Cutter Road, off to the right, leads down to the ramp. There is ample parking near the ramp or in the upper lots for vehicles with trailers.

Ashore. Restrooms are located in the small, white building by the little East End Beach. The new Portland Trail follows the narrow-gauge railway bed from here to the Old Port or in the opposite direction to connect with the Back Cove Trail (see below).

33. Back Cove

Portland's Back Cove is a shallow tidal cove that is almost completely landlocked to the north of the Portland Peninsula. It is generally of little interest to small-boat explorers, but at high tide, it is accessible from Casco Bay, gated by a defunct, but open, railroad trestle and spanned by Rt. 295's Tukey's Bridge.

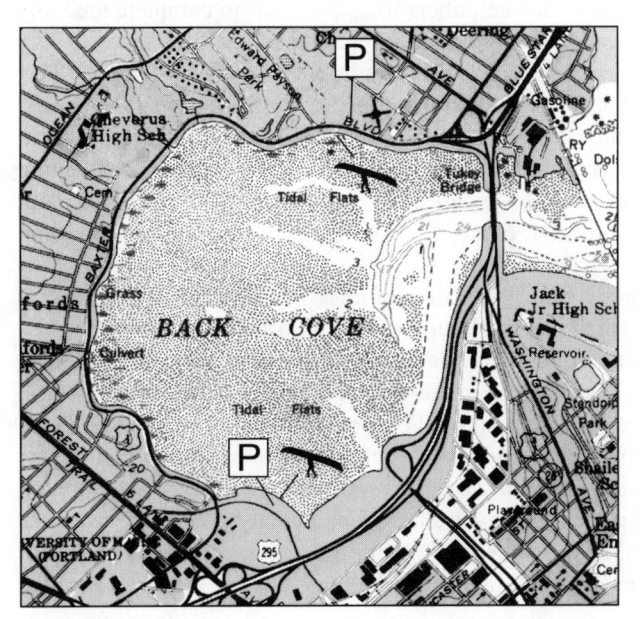

At low tide, Back Cove is mostly a mud flat. When the conditions are right, however, it is an excellent spot for windsurfing, with few obstructions to the wind, enough size for some blazing reaches but not enough to build much fetch, and water shallow enough to gain a few

47

degrees in temperature. On windy days when the tide is high, streaks of colorful sails rip across the cove.

By sea. The cove's entrance is flanked by both ends of the spectrum—the large factory of B&M Baked Beans on one side and a sewer treatment plant on the other. The open trestle spanning the entrance is known as the Grand Trunk Railway Bridge, and it was the main link between downtown Portland and the railway to Canada before the Grand Trunk Railway relocated its operations to Deering.

Tukey's Bridge carries Rt. 295 over the water, and its abutments squeeze the mouth to Back Cove. Current can run hard here, up to a couple of knots at maximum flood or ebb. This bridge is fixed, but there is plenty of vertical clearance for small boats.

If you are windsurfing from the lot on the eastern side of the Cove, you will need to carry your windsurfer across Baxter Boulevard. A small marshy area makes a good rigging and launching site. The lot on the western side of the cove is directly on the water.

The cove is almost completely rock-free and can be sailed until your centerboards—or you—start sticking in the mud. Due to potential pollution, sailing is not recommended in Back Cove after heavy rains, when the city sewer system gets overwhelmed by storm runoff, and it discharges directly into the cove.

By land. The two usual put-ins are either at the parking area opposite Shop 'n Save on the west side of the cove or off Baxter Boulevard on the east side. For the west side, take Rt. 295 to exit 6 and follow Forest Avenue. At the first light, turn right onto Baxter Boulevard. Take another right at the next light onto Preble. The parking area will be on your left. To get to the east side, get off 295 at exit 8 and follow US Rt. 1 (Baxter Boulevard) south. Park in the small dirt lot on the right.

Ashore. A pleasant walking and running trail circles Back Cove, a distance of about three miles. Governor Percival Baxter of Mackworth Island donated much of the land for this trail, and he encouraged his neighbors to do the same to complete the loop. Lunches or picnic ingredients can be bought at Shop 'n Save on the west shore.

Much to the chagrin of bean lovers, B&M does not have tours of its factory. This is the last bastion of the baked bean, a tradition that grew out of Puritan Massachusetts. The Puritans forbade labor—which included cooking—on the Sabbath. Beans were baked all day Saturday and eaten all day Sunday. The tradition became rooted in the logging camps of the Maine woods and the bean suppers of isolated small towns. Beans are still baked here in huge open pots in brick ovens, with specialized bean tasters sampling each batch.

Though it is hard to imagine now, the waters of the Back Cove once extended as far as Deering Oaks Park. Captain James Deering lived in a mansion at 85 Bedford Street, near where the University of Southern Maine now stands, and he sailed out to sea from the wharf at the foot of his fields. Huge three-masters came into the cove to take on cargo from the Portland Stoneware Co. and the Winslow Pottery factories. And as recently as the mid-thirties, John Calvin Stevens II, the grandson of Portland's famous shingle-style architect, proposed an elaborate plan for a Back Cove Recreational Park, which included dredging and diking the cove for seaplane landings, using the fill for a conventional airport, and building beaches, a lagoon, a marina, reflecting pools, arcades, a planetarium, a theatre, an amphitheater, and a huge obelisk towering above it

CASCO BAY

all. Smelling federal money, the city embraced the plans and forwarded them to the Work Progress Administration. But in the depths of the Depression, the $6-million project was rejected for being too costly.

Migrating waterfowl, mostly black ducks, use the Back Cove as a rest stop on their long journeys. In the past, the cove was declared a sanctuary for them, and city wardens had to patrol it. Observant neighbors helped too, particularly when they noticed ducks swimming in small circles. Upon investigation, they discovered that an ingenious poacher had set a trawl line by weighting it to the bottom of the cove with baited fish hooks dangling off it at intervals. Ducks that took the bait would get hooked and be confined to swimming in a radius until the poacher, under the cover of darkness, reeled in his catch.

34. Fort Gorges

Fort Gorges (pronounced *gorgeous*, which it is) is an unmistakable landmark, sitting staunchly atop Diamond Island Ledge, right in the middle of Portland Harbor. The solid granite fort is now owned by the City of Portland and kept in a marvelously rough state. It is open to the public, but it is accessible only by small boat, so it always feels like a discovery. Inside, two stories of arched gun bays form a dramatic amphitheater. A granite staircase leads to the top for views of the entire harbor and out the entrance channel past Portland Head Light. Footpaths lead through the brush to the one remaining gun, said to weigh more than 20,000 pounds.

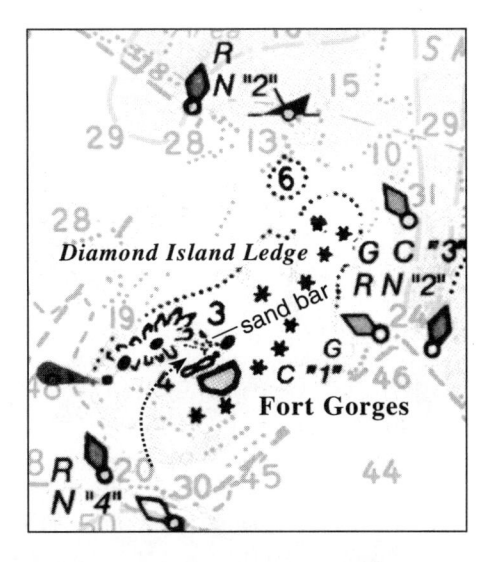

By sea. Fort Gorges is obvious from almost anywhere near Portland Harbor, sitting squarely between Little Diamond Island and the Portland Peninsula. It is only a short hop from the put-ins at Willard Beach, Spring Point, or Portland Town Floats or from the launching ramps at South Portland or the East End Beach. The fort is encircled by rocks except on the southwest. From nun "4," keep the flashing daymark on the ledge to port, and steer to the west of the fort's granite wharf. Do not attempt to approach from the north or west. Land on the small beach next to the granite wharf.

Ashore. Part of what makes Fort Gorges so much fun to explore is its unsupervised condition. There are few signs, if any, telling you what you can and cannot do or where you should and should not go or warning you of the many dangers here. Please use common sense. Watch your footing and stay away from the many edges, particularly on the third level. Granite does not make a soft landing.

The fort has no facilities at all, including restrooms. Please carry out all your trash.

Fort Gorges was commissioned in 1858 to be "constructed of large blocks with great massiveness" in the plan of a closed lunette to house 92 short range guns as part of the Eastern Seaboards Harbor Defense Plan of the Civil War. It would garrison 500 troops with four sets of officers quarters, a mess hall, a bakery, and a privy. The rest of the troops would live in the gun rooms which would be enclosed during the "severe season."

By the time it was completed in 1864, long-range guns had been developed, and the fort was essentially obsolete. Still, the fort was armed during the Civil and the Spanish American wars, but it was never garrisoned or fired upon. The gun on the top of the fort is a 10-inch, rifle-bored, Rodman gun, which was raised to the third level in 1896, but never mounted before all the guns were scrapped two years later. It could fire a 125-pound shell three miles. In the 1930s, the Coast Guard mounted a navigational light in one of the gun ports and set up a generator to power it. During World War II, rolls of steel cable for anti-submarine mines and nets were stored here, and piles of rust from the cables can still be found in the parade ground. But by 1946, the General Services Administration declared the fort surplus. It was acquired by Portland in 1960.

The Father of Maine

Fort Gorges is the only place in Maine named after Sir Ferdinando Gorges, who many claim to be the Father of Maine. Gorges, despite his Spanish-sounding name, was a naval officer under Queen Elizabeth. Eventually he was named the governor of Plymouth, England, a large navy base from which expeditions to the new world often departed and returned. When Martin Pring brought back an Indian birch-bark canoe in 1603 and when Captain George Waymouth returned two years later with five live Indians, New World exploration became Gorges' obsession.

Gorges brought Waymouth's Indians to his home and learned their language. Then he paraded them throughout the Royal Court to raise interest in, and money for, New World exploration. His efforts led to the formation of the Plymouth Company of London. The Queen granted the company the rights to colonize the New World territory known as "Northern Virginia," from 38 to 45 degrees north latitude.

The first expedition set sail in 1606 in the *Richard of Plymouth*. Thirty-two men were aboard under the leadership of Henry Chalons. But the ship was blown off course. It made landfall near Puerto Rico, where it was captured by the Spaniards.

Undaunted, Gorges sponsored another expedition with the help of the Lord Chief Justice of England, Lord John Popham. This time they sent two ships and over 120 men. The *Mary and John* and the *Gifte of God* left in the spring of 1607 and landed in Maine 65 days later to form the New World's first colony, at the mouth of the Kennebec River. They also became Maine's first shipbuilders, building the 30-ton pinnace *Virginia* on the banks of the river that fall

That winter, however, an unusually severe winter took its toll. Despite the arrival of fresh supplies the next summer, the surviving colonists couldn't face another Maine winter, and they returned to England that fall.

Not yet discouraged—and not yet broke—Gorges mounted a third expedition, then a fourth, fifth, and sixth, but they all failed. Finally in 1616, scraping the very last of his resources together, Gorges outfitted his own tenant farmer, Richard Vines with a small boat and 16 men. They landed and set up a small colony at the mouth of the Saco River, and Vines returned to England to sing his praises of Maine.

The ensuing enthusiasm was like wind in the sails of more boats, bringing more settlers to the coast and spurring the small colonies that began to dot the outer islands and mainland shores. King James eventually pronounced Gorges the Governor General over all New England, and with this honor, the aging Gorges decided he should see this New World for himself. He commissioned a new ship, but as she was launched, she flipped over and was crushed. The Father of Maine never made it to Maine. He died in England in 1646 at the age of 70.

From the top of the fort at low tide, the ribs of a wreck can be seen to the north, on Diamond Island Ledge, out near nun "2." This is the last of the *Edward J. Lawrence*, a six-masted schooner, which caught fire in 1925 while lying in Portland Harbor. The flaming ship was towed to the reef so she wouldn't obstruct the harbor when she went down. Ribs, planking, and some of the charred deck of the 410-foot *Lawrence* are still intact today, though each year less and less of her appears at low tide.

One of Casco Bay's more bizarre shipwrecks occurred on the ledge in 1883. The steamer *Brooklyn* struck what was then called Hog Island Ledge after casting off from the Grand Trunk docks (see p. 44). She was bound for England loaded with cattle, sheep, and dried peas. On impact she began taking on water, but it looked like she could be saved. Then the peas soaked up the water and expanded, forcing off several of the steamer's iron plates, and sending the *Brooklyn* to the bottom.

35. House Island

House Island sits like the rotary in a traffic circle between Peaks Island and Spring Point, at the strategic crossroads of almost every approach to Portland Harbor—the Portland Channel, Whitehead Passage, and Diamond Island Pass. It is peanut-shaped and mostly treeless. Two large, gray houses occupy its lower northern end and intriguing granite fortifications command the south. But landing, at least in your boat, is not allowed.

When Christopher Levett led an expedition from England to the New World in 1623, he had his eyes open for prime real estate. For 110 pounds, Sir Ferdinando Gorges had sold him a grant of 6000 acres at a location to be chosen by Levett himself. Of all the islands he saw in his voyage from the Isles of Shoals to Boothbay Harbor, historians believe he chose House Island. But he was not the first here. "At this place," he wrote, "there fished divers ships of Waymouth (England) this year 1623." Early European fishermen preserved their catch by cleaning and drying their fish on stages, or racks, set up in coastal locations protected both from the sea and from attack from the natives and easily accessible to the fishing boats. The harbor islands proved to be perfect sites.

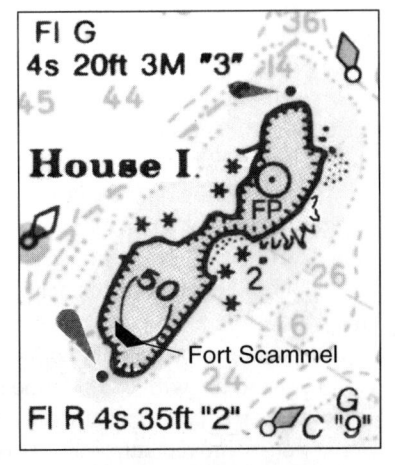

Levett was known for his excellent relations with the local Indians. Before moving onto House Island, he asked permission of Indian chief Cocawesco. The sagamores of the area were happy to have him there, in part because his presence would discourage the unneighborly Tarratines from using the shores and islands of Casco Bay for their summer headquarters.

Levett built a strong stone house against the Tarratine invasions. Eventually he returned to England, leaving ten men behind to guard his house and promising to return. He never did. Levett eventually sold his interests in Casco Bay to some English merchants. What became of the ten men is not known. Positive proof of the exact location of Levett's house is lacking. House Island seems most likely, but he may, in fact, have

51

settled on Peaks, on Cushing, or on one of the Diamond Islands.

As early as 1808, as part of the preparations for the War of 1812, a wooden blockhouse named Fort Scammel was built at the southern end of the island. During the war it was used as a prison for captured British soldiers, forty of whom are said to be laid to rest in a small graveyard nearby. In the 1850s, the wooden structures were replaced with Penobscot Bay granite, shipped aboard schooners and shaped by stonecutters into the rectangular blocks of the structures that still command the southern end of the island.

The rest of House Island was settled simultaneously by two first cousins from Monhegan Island, John Sterling and Henry Trefethen, and their brides. In 1823 they bought a long Cape Cod-style house, built around 1800, from which the island took its name. The house was divided in the center to make a duplex. Henry set up a cod drying business, with flakes of fish spread on racks, or stages, over much of the island. One season, as many as 25,000 quintals were dried there, or *2.8 million* pounds.

A family tradition holds that Henry Trefethen, charged with bringing the huge sum of $20,000 from Boston to Portland aboard his boat, had such a reputation for honesty that he did not need to post a bond of any kind. He only had to give his word that the money would arrive safely. It did, and that is how the first bank in Portland was started.

As their own fortunes rose, the Sterlings and Trefethens took increasing interest in Peaks Island, and their families became some of the founding islanders there. In 1832, long before there was a church or a school on Peaks, John Sterling built a small post-and-beam building on the island at the site of the present-day firehouse, and he gave it to the community for a place of worship and a school. After that, on fair-weather Sundays, John Sterling would set his pine ship-captain's chair in the stern of his dory, row to Peaks, put the chair over his head, and march to the small service with his bible tucked under his arm.

After the fort was abandoned by the government and after the death of Henry Trefethen and his wife in 1880, the island was taken over by hordes of rats. Six or seven years later, an eccentric character who called himself Uncle John Norwood and his three vicious dogs moved into one of the fish houses. Rosie was his favorite of the dogs, according to Jessie Trefethen, because she would "do his dishes" by licking them clean. Everyone knew him as the "Hermit of House Island."

Big changes came in 1906 when the government bought the island for a quarantine station for the immigrants flooding into the country. The Hermit's fish houses and the now dilapidated Cape Cod House were razed, and the so-called "Doctor's House," which still stands, was built on the site. The quarantine was run until around 1920, and the large cribbings for its wharf can still be seen on the shore of the island closest to Peaks.

House Island is now private again. In the 50s, there were proposals to dismantle Fort Scammel for its granite. It was spared that fate by the Dudley family, who bought the island and now hold clambakes and other functions there and give tours of the fort (799-8188).

By sea. Arriving by your own boat or landing is forbidden, and it is strictly enforced.

36. Cushing Island

Geographically, Cushing is one of the most attractive islands in Casco Bay. It sits at the mouth of the Portland Harbor Channel with bold open ocean on one side and the narrow and protected waters of Whitehead Passage and Portland Harbor on the other. It is wooded and high, and its views stretch from the Portland skyline, over House Island and Peaks, along the bold shores of South Portland and Cape Elizabeth to the sweep of Portland Head Light, and out past Ram Island and Ram Island Light to miles of unobstructed ocean.

Cushing has had many faces, from an early island farm to the site of one of Casco Bay's first resort hotels and the location of a major fort. Now Cushing is an exclusive summer enclave with large, rambling shingle-style cottages among grounds designed by the firm of Frederick Law Olmstead, famous for its design of New York's Central Park.

The island is not served by Casco Bay Lines, and visitors in their own boats are not welcome. Still, its charms can be enjoyed from offshore. A circumnavigation will take you under the bold cliffs of White Head, along the wild, undeveloped ocean side of the island, and among the tempting pocket beaches on the Portland Harbor Channel, where many of the grand cottages peek from between the trees.

By sea. See the Portland Harbor Channel (p. 24) and Whitehead Passage (p. 58).

Ashore. Visitors are only allowed on Cushing by invitation.

Because of its location Cushing has had a long history connected with the settlement of the Portland area. Some historians even speculate that this is where Christopher Levett built his house after his explorations of the area in 1623 (see House Island, p 51). When the Indian Wars broke out in 1670, mainland settlers fled to a garrison on the what was then called Andrews Island, where the duration of the war nearly forced them into starvation and prompted a desperate, and fatal, trip to Peaks Island for some stray livestock (see Whitehead Passage, p. 58).

After the Indian raids, Cushing went through a succession of owners and names, including the name Portland, which, along with Portland Head, was the first time this name was used, long before the city would adopt it. In 1735 the island was bought by Captain Joshua Bangs and became Bangs Island. Bangs leased the land to tenant farmers who produced hay for settlers on the mainland.

Eventually, in 1762, Eziekiel Cushing bought the island for $2,300 with money made from his lucrative West Indian trade. He built a grand house, complete with wine cellar, which he modestly named "Homestead in the Willows." For three years, he entertained lavishly here and then suddenly, for unknown reasons, sold the island back to Joshua Bangs. Apparently Cushing hadn't shaken his island fever, or perhaps he couldn't help but have his eye on the horizon, because he eventually bought Long Island, where he lived until his death. His Homestead on Cushing was conscripted as a hospital during the War of 1812.

The island went through a succession of other owners, but in 1858 Eziekiel's fourth cousin, Lemuel Cushing purchased the island. The Cushing family was originally from Montreal, and the Atlantic and St. Lawrence railroad line had recently been completed between Portland and Cushing's hometown. Lemuel saw an opportunity. For $10,000 he constructed a large brick hotel on the island to cater to wealthy English Canadians. He called it the Ottawa, and it would forever alter the landscape of the island.

In 1883, with business booming at the Ottawa, the Cushing family decided to develop the island as a cottage community. They hired landscape architect Frederick Law Olmstead and shingle-style architect John Calvin Stevens to come up with plans. Together they laid out lots skewed to the water and sited the marvelous cottages to take in the views.

The Ottawa burned in 1886, but business was good, and Cushing rebuilt an even grander version, this time for a cost of $75,000. A brochure at the time reads, "No spot can offer more pleasing aspects, sweeter odors, or more refreshing waters. Bathers attain supreme enjoyment, the very ecstasy of their recreation." Newspaper records state that 2,000 guests a night were not uncommon. But despite the hotel's popularity, the rebuilding incurred more debt than the short summer season could support. Cushing eventually sold it at a loss for $16,000. When this second hotel burned in 1917, it was never rebuilt.

Ironically, the cottage community that the hotel spawned was preserved by the military. Around the turn of the century, as part of the upgrade of coastal artillery defenses, the undeveloped half the island was taken by eminent domain and Fort Christopher Levett was built there. The fort, used through both world wars, eventually included brick buildings to house officers and enlisted men and large 12 and 16-inch guns. The sighting towers, which were used to aim the long-range guns, still crown the cliffs of White Head. In 1957, the fort was deemed surplus and sold to a private investor, but for more than half a century, it prevented further development on the island. Now, some of the brick officers quarters and barracks have been preserved as summer homes.

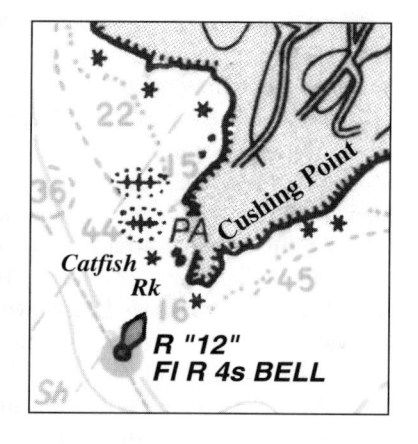

The Ottawa overlooked Cushing Island Point, the first real constriction in the Portland Harbor Channel. The point is now marked by red, lighted bell "12," but it has the sad history of having abruptly ended the sailing careers of many ships. It was particularly treacherous before the lighthouse on Ram Island Ledge. In a blinding blizzard in February, 1861, the *W.H. Jenkens,* of British registry, crashed ashore here. All hands were rescued, but the flood carried wreckage as far away as Ragged Island (see Inner Green Island, p. 102).

In December, 1870, three schooners were heading from Boston to points down east when they were engulfed in a blinding snowstorm. The *Hockman,* the *Eliza Crowell,* and the *Tiger* decided to make their way together for the safety of Portland Harbor. In the limited visibility, that meant staying very close together. But off Portland, as the *Tiger* came about, she was rammed by the *Eliza Crowell* and nearly split in half. The two ships, entangled and out of control, began to drift, while the *Hockman* tried to stand by for assistance. Just before 4 AM, all three schooners went up on Cushing Island Point.

There was only a caretaker in residence at the Ottawa House that night, and he heard and saw nothing. In trying to reconstruct what happened, crew members from each of the vessels claimed that they had seen Portland Head Light through the snow just before they went aground. Later, it was speculated that the light they saw was not from Portland Head, as they believed, but rather from the caretaker's lamps at the Ottawa House.

37. Peaks Island

Peaks Island, a mere two-and-a-half miles from downtown Portland, is Casco Bay's most populated island and part of the city of Portland. Regular ferry service to the city has gradually transformed Peaks into an island bedroom community, with lawyers, doctors, artists, carpenters, and students making the twenty minute commute daily. Yet Peaks is distinctly an island, with barefoot boys on bikes, salty dogs, rusty cars, a small market and lumber yard, a small school, and the special island blend of independence and interdependence, of isolation and of community. About 1200 year-round inhabitants call this their home, and that number almost triples in the summer.

Peaks, in many ways, is the perfect outing for small boaters from Portland and its vicinity. The trip is short, the landing is easy, and within a short stroll you can find either summer festivity or island tranquillity.

By sea. Peaks is easily accessible by small boat. A town float lies to the north of the big ferry wharf, a town beach lies to the south, and most of the beaches around the island are public.

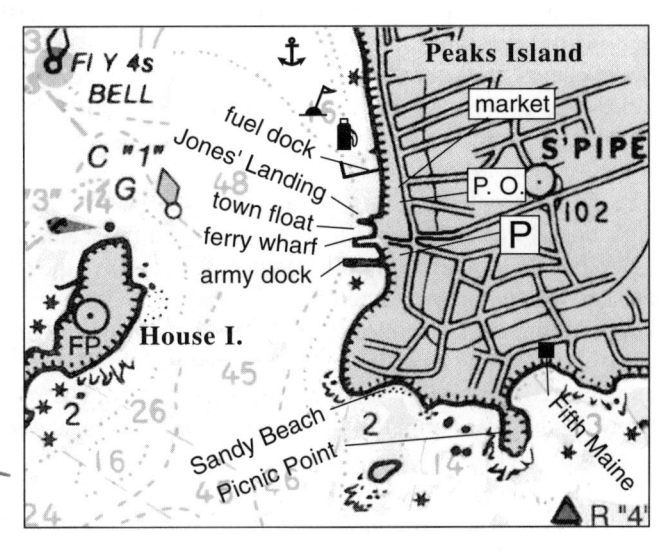

The large concrete ferry dock is easily visible on the western shore of Peaks, opposite the north end of House Island. Use caution as you approach if any ferries are arriving or departing.

The town float lies just to the north of the ferry wharf. The southern face of this dock is reserved for the emergency boats, but you can tie up along the northern face for limited periods. The next docks to the north are Jones' Landing Marina (766-5542), where the outer face of the floats is available for restaurant patrons. Longer-term dockage or mooring rentals can be arranged at the Peaks Island Marina (766-2508), also to the north and recognizable by the construction equipment ashore and Maine's largest "FUEL" sign. Gas and diesel are available at the floats.

South of the ferry wharf, a wooden wharf projects from a small beach. Beachable boats can land between the two wharves. The beach to the south of the wharf is guarded by ledges offshore, so it should be approached with extreme care. Peaks Island Kayak

(766-5004) rents brightly-colored sit-on-top kayaks from the beach by the hour, half-day, or day. You may also see flotillas of kayaks from the renowned Maine Island Kayak Company (766-2373), based on Peaks. They offer instruction and guided expeditions throughout Maine for individuals and groups of all sizes.

Ashore. Jones' Landing Restaurant serves up one of the best sunsets in Maine, overlooking the water, facing the Portland skyline. They'll also serve you dinner to go with it. Recently, The Landing has become a major small-boat destination for Sunday afternoon Reggae concerts on their deck, and the current management is booking music for several weekday evenings. Pay phones are available outside the restaurant.

A small bakery and a coffee and ice cream shop are at the top of the hill from the ferry. The market has beer, wine, food, and sandwiches. The island laundromat is right by the island's gas pumps, just up the hill from the Peaks Island Marina. Peaks Island Merchantile, an eclectic galley, craft, gift, bike, and junk shop, is across the street, and beyond it is the brick community building, with a library and public restrooms. The Peaks Island House (766-4400), right on the water near the ferry, serves breakfasts, lunches, and dinners in addition to being a bed and breakfast.

The center and the east side of the island known as the "Back Shore" is largely undeveloped, with woodsy trails, cobbly beaches, and unending views out to sea. It is not too far to walk, or you can rent bikes at Brad's Bike Shop at the Mercantile. Take Brackett or Central Avenue to cross the island, or take Island Avenue and Whitehead Street to follow the shore.

When the Indians fished and feasted here, they called the island Utowna, the Rockbound Place. Ferdinando Gorges granted the island's title to George Cleeves in 1632, but it was a difficult place to settle. Cleeve gave the island to his son-in-law, John Mitton, who was remembered as a great hunter and fowler and an even greater teller of tall tales. In one, he claimed that while he was fishing in his small boat, a merman, the son of Poseidon, grabbed the side of his boat. Thinking quickly, Mitton grabbed a hatchet and severed the beast's hands with a single blow. The merman disappeared, but his finny hands stayed gripping the gunwales, and Mitton had to pry them off before flinging them into the sea.

The island's first real settlers, John and Mary Palmer, moved onto the island in the 1670s, just at the beginning of the Indian Wars. John and Mary only stayed five years, later to be captured and never heard from again. Peaks was attacked by the Canadas in 1689, then by the Norridgewocks, and then by the Penobscots. It wasn't until 1762 that another house was built on Peaks that survived any length of time.

By the time of the Revolution, there were still only four houses on Peaks. One morning in October, a British ship anchored in what is now called Diamond Island Roads, between House, Peaks, and Little Diamond Island. The Red Coats landed on Peaks, marched along the roads with their drums and pipes, and left.

The first attempt at ferry service to Peaks and other islands in Casco Bay began in 1822 with a flat-bottomed craft with a small steam engine driving a stern paddle wheel, one of the first sailless vessels on the Bay. She was conceived and built by Captain Seward Porter on the Harraseeket River (see Porter's Landing, p. 129), but this was new technology. She was christened the *Kennebec* but quickly earned the nickname "Horned Hog" for her unique—dare we say ugly?—shape, or the "Ground Hog" for her penchant for going aground when wind or tide overpowered her weak steam engine. She was said to have been able to make forward progress in calm weather, but in head winds or seas the passengers had to tread on the paddles to keep her going. She was economically underpowered as well. In 1824, there were still only six houses on Peaks, and the ferry service proved to be a commercial failure.

Real service didn't begin until 1851 after William Jones turned his house into a boarding house and served shoreside dinners. This first summer hotel in Casco Bay started a trend, and in the next decade Peaks blossomed into one of America's first resorts. America's first summer theater was started here in 1870, and by the late 1880's, Peaks had become a 19th-century Disneyland, with twelve rambling hotels and boarding houses, six bowling alleys, an opera house, the huge Forest City Skating Rink which was later transformed into the Gem Theater, balloon ascensions, shooting galleries, an observatory, wild animal shows, and a boardwalk that ran along a length of the western shore.

Memories and stories linger on the island of a bear that escaped and got into a flour barrel and came out white, of the caged monkeys and peacocks, of the snake house, and of the man who walked on water by wearing long floating shoes. What is now called Adams Street was once called Elephant Avenue. A man at a roadside table would, for ten cents, let passersby put on headphones and listen, for the first time, to the tinny sounds of one of Maine's first phonographs. Peaks was so popular that in 1905 someone named Frank Rodway even proposed building an aerial tramway from Portland's East End to Peaks, supported by trestles on Hog Island Ledge and Little Hog Island (now called Diamond Island Ledge, the location of Fort Gorges, and Little Diamond Island).

Peaks attracted visitors from all walks of life, from the common man to the famous and wealthy. Eleanor Roosevelt came to Peaks many times as a young girl.

During World War II, Peaks was discovered again. Half the island was taken by eminent domain for the installation of a huge gun battery to protect Portland Harbor. Battery Steele, the cavernous concrete gun emplacement on the Back Shore, can still be explored. It held two 16-inch guns with the capacity to lob a shell the size of a Volkswagen 26 miles, covering the coast from Kennebunk in the south all the way to Popham Beach in the north. They were fired only once, as a test. The concussion was so powerful that it blew out many of the windows on Peaks, including some of the stained glass at the Brackett Memorial Church nearly a mile away. The guns were eventually dismantled and sold for scrap, but their huge concrete bunker still remains. Photos of the guns and the installation are on exhibit at the Fifth Maine Regiment Memorial Hall (see p. 59). If you plan to explore, use caution. The tunnels are dark, and the holes are deep.

The most famous wreck on Peaks is undoubtedly the *Helen Eliza*, which ran aground on the Back Shore in 1869. Only one member of the crew survived, and he had already been the sole survivor of another wreck in a hurricane in the West Indies. Not being one to tempt fate, he decided to give up the sea and become a New Hampshire farmer. But that, perhaps, was his undoing. He slipped off a log and drowned in a stream.

The *Helen Eliza* is rumored to have inspired Henry Wadsworth Longfellow's poem "The Wreck of the Hesperus." Instead, she was life imitating art—the *Helen Eliza* went aground thirty years after Longfellow penned his prophetic poem.

57

38. Whitehead Passage

Whitehead Passage is a marvelous tight cut between the high cliffs of Cushing Island and Peaks Island. Ocean swells roll in at one end, and the tranquil waters behind House Island lie at the other. When heading offshore, the ocean is all the more expansive for having just come through the squeeze of Whitehead Passage, and when returning, the protection of the passage is all the more comforting for its narrowness.

Whitehead Passage gets its name from the light-colored cliffs on its eastern end, the highest point in Casco Bay. Not only does the headland appear light when viewed from the ocean, but when it is viewed from Peaks, a profile of a head, known as "The Old Man of Cushing," can be discerned among the ledges and outcrops.

By sea. A current of nearly a knot runs in and out of the passage at maximum flood and ebb. At the western end, red bell "8" should be left close aboard to the north (red-right-returning) and so should the red nun and daybeacon at Trotts Rock at the eastern end. Do not cut too close to green daybeacon "3," opposite Trotts Rock, because the ledge it sits on projects beyond the mark.

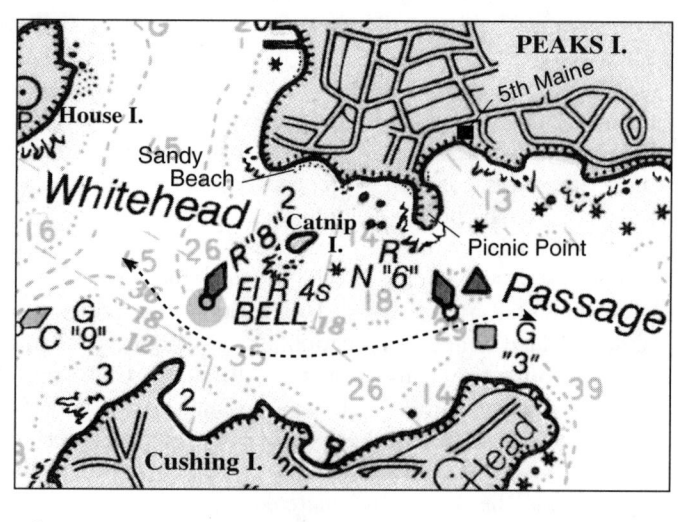

The combination of current and rocky projections make the shores of Whitehead Passage good striper territory.

Ashore. Landing is not allowed on Cushing. Sandy Beach or Picnic Point on Peaks, though, are pleasant sunny spots for lunch or rest (see following entries).

When the Indian Wars broke out in the 1670s, settlers holed up in the garrison on Cushing Island, then called Andrews Island, with little food or ammunition. The few settlers on Peaks had already fled or been massacred, and they had left behind some sheep. Tempted by their hunger and convinced that the Indians were no longer on Peaks, seven men from Andrews, led by George Felt, Jr. of Peaks, rowed across narrow Whitehead Passage and landed on Peaks. The Indians ashore waited until they had landed before brutally ambushing them. John Sterling, also from Peaks, witnessed the massacre from his dory in Whitehead Passage, agonizingly helpless to do anything. No one survived.

39. Sandy Beach

Sandy Beach is located at the western end of Whitehead Passage on the southern shore of Peaks Island. The small crescent beach gets even smaller at high tides, but in addition to being sandy, it shoals gradually, the water is protected, and it is sunny. If the beach is crowded, small boats can retreat to the little treeless island just offshore, unnamed on the chart but known locally as Catnip Island.

By sea. Unless you have exceptionally shallow draft, don't approach the beach from the west. Instead, follow Whitehead Passage eastward, keeping flashing bell "8" to port until you are close to nun "6." Then head northwest toward the beach. Stay close to the point to avoid the rock shown on the chart east of Catnip. Beach your boat on the beach or on Catnip, or anchor among the moored boats.

Ashore. If you discover you need food or drink, the market is within easy walking distance. The name Catnip Island must be a misnomer. The green stuff growing on the island is not catnip; it's poison ivy. Perhaps the name evolved from Cat *Nap* Island, which it is perfect for.

40. Picnic Point

Just north of Trotts, a beautiful peninsula projects southward from Peaks Island into Whitehead Passage. Officially, it is called Long Point. Islanders call it Picnic Point, and with good reason. A small patch of grass, low trees, and shore rocks is connected to the shore by a graceful tombolo of stones rounded by the ocean swells.

By sea. You can beach or anchor on either side of the isthmus. The cove to the east, Hadlock Cove is somewhat exposed to the ocean swells. The west side is more protected, but beware of the ledges that extend to the southwest from the peninsula as you approach. In either spot, be sure your anchor is well set.

Ashore. Picnic Point is owned by the City of Portland, and it is used primarily by Peaks Islanders. Please treat this small patch of earth on rock carefully. From Picnic Point it is an easy stroll to the Fifth Maine Regiment Memorial Hall (see below). Follow the dirt road to the pavement and turn right.

41. Fifth Maine Regiment Memorial Hall

The large yellow shingle building on the cove to the east of Picnic Point is the Fifth Maine Regiment building, a memorial to Maine's Fifth Regiment in the Civil War. It is often open to the public. Portland was strongly pro-abolition, and 25,000 Portlanders, about one fifth of its population at the time, joined the fight. Inside is a moving collection of memorabilia illuminated by sparkling sun shining off the sea and passing through beautiful stained-glass windows etched with the names of the astounding number of young men who gave their lives in the war.

Upstairs are evolving exhibitions of Peaks Island in its heyday as a tourist destination and, in more threatening times, as the site of Casco Bay's largest defenses, including the two huge 16-inch guns at Battery Steele (see Peaks Island, p. 55 for more detail).

42. Little Diamond Island

Little Diamond Island is a just over a mile from Portland, and you could almost jump there from Fort Gorges. Yet the tranquillity on this carless island is almost palpable. Grassy paths lead between clusters of turn-of-the-century summer cottages, and water sparkles from behind the shady trees at every turn. The island is served by Casco Bay Lines, with limited year-round service for the few hardy souls who winter over.

By sea. Head for the ferry wharf at the southeast end of the island made obvious by the Casino, the brown building next to it. Beware of the ledges making out from the south shore of Little Diamond, marked by nun "6."

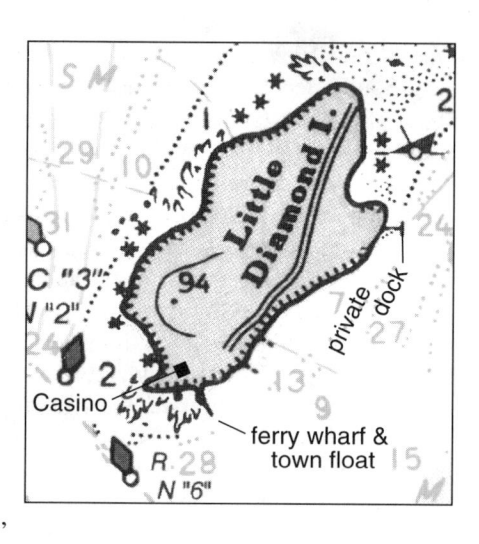

A public float is attached to the ferry wharf for limited docking. A small beach to the north of the wharf can also be used.

Low tide reveals the bones of several old hulks in Lamson Cove, between Little and Great Diamond Island. A barge, a schooner, and an old Casco Bay Lines steamer, the original *Maquoit*, were towed here from Portland Harbor for disposal.

Ashore. The pleasant footpaths invariably lead to the north end of the island, where at low tides, a path crosses the sand bar to Great Diamond Island. This was once the site of a salt works. Few places have trash pickup on a lunar calendar, but here the garbage truck needs to dash across the bar, quickly make its rounds, and be back before the bar is covered again. If you plan to cross, be sure the tide will still be low when you plan to return.

Little Diamond was bought in 1743 by the Deerings, a prominent family of Portland. By the middle of the 1800s, they were leasing small plots of land to select Portlanders who wanted to get away from the bustle of urban life by setting up summer tents and cooking over open fires. Soon, the tents were pitched on permanent wooden platforms, and by the late 1800s, the "tenting families," as they were known, were replacing their tents with balloon-frame cottages trimmed with gingerbread.

Between 1876 and 1939, four acres of the island were used as a part-time U.S. Lighthouse service station. When the iron Breakwater "Bug" Light replaced the old wooden lighthouse, the six-sided structure was moved here. The wharf and buildings of the station are still on the east shoulder of the island, but they are private.

43. Diamond Island Pass

Diamond Island Pass runs northeastward between Peaks Island to the east and Little and Great Diamond Island to the west. This is a well-protected thoroughfare, leading from the Portland Harbor area to Hussey Sound and beyond, but in the summer, it can be busy, with a constant parade of pleasure, ferry, and fishing boats. Moderate currents of up to 0.3 knots flood to the northeast, but they ebb to the southwest weakly.

The launching ramp at City Point on Peaks is useful at higher tides, and it is available for public use. So is most of the beach along the western shore of the island. The water, however, is shoal for a long way out, so it is a difficult place to land at lower tides. Beware of the rocks off City Point.

Ashore. The beautiful white-with-green-roof clubhouse of the Trefethen-Evergreen Improvement Association, with its fleet of small boats, is a landmark on the Peaks Island side. TEIA was formed in 1912 to provide a social structure for the visitors who spent the summers at the grand hotels or nearby cottages and to, as the name suggests, improve life on Peaks. Their first accomplishment was no small task. They managed to lobby the state government to pipe water to the Casco Bay islands from Sebago Lake. The underwater piping was laid in 1920, and the club bore a large portion of its expense. The pipes were just replaced in the spring of 1998. TEIA is still a summer club with a casual elegance and a schedule of summer dances, tennis tournaments, day camps, and sailing lessons.

The club's tennis courts are on the site of one of Peaks' grand old inns, the Valley View Hotel, built by William S. Trefethen. Trefethen also brought the first load of coal to the island only to discover that none of the fireplaces had coal grates, so he couldn't burn it. He used it instead to bed the first crib of his boat wharf, Trefethen's Landing. Because of the gradual pitch of the beach, it had to extend so far out that it claimed the fame of being the longest wharf in Maine. A few of its many pilings can still be seen just to the south of the club. The steamers from town used to stop at the wharf, and an island store stood at the head of the street.

The west shore of Great Diamond Island is bold and drops off into fairly deep water. For years, a rope swing has hung from an overhanging branch of a tree, and in the hot days of summer when the tide is high, passing boaters will sometimes stop for a plunge. Use caution.

44. Great Diamond Island

Great Diamond, like Little Diamond, is a turn-of-the-century summer community almost untouched by time. Paths and unpaved roads meander among beautiful shingle-style and Victorian cottages, and large tracts of woods have been left undeveloped. Remarkably, this island is part of the city of Portland. The tranquillity of Great Diamond, however, has been disturbed over the years by its dubious honor of perfect geographical positioning, so the summer community has had to share their treasure with Fort McKinley, on the north end (see Diamond Cove, p. 62).

By sea. Approach via Diamond Island Pass. The ferry wharf at the island's southern end has a public float for docking for limited periods, or you can beach your boat just to the right of it. Or you can dock at Diamond Cove.

Ashore. The walking roads on the island are public and pleasant strolling. If the tide is right, you can even cross the sand bar to Little Diamond Island (see above). Or you can follow the roads north to old Fort McKinley.

Great Diamond was originally named "Hoggiscand" or "Hog Island" for the pigs that were naturally penned there by the water. But in 1882, a Mr. Smith of Portland formed the Diamond Island Association by carefully selecting members who wished to have seaside summer residences "free from objectionable contacts."

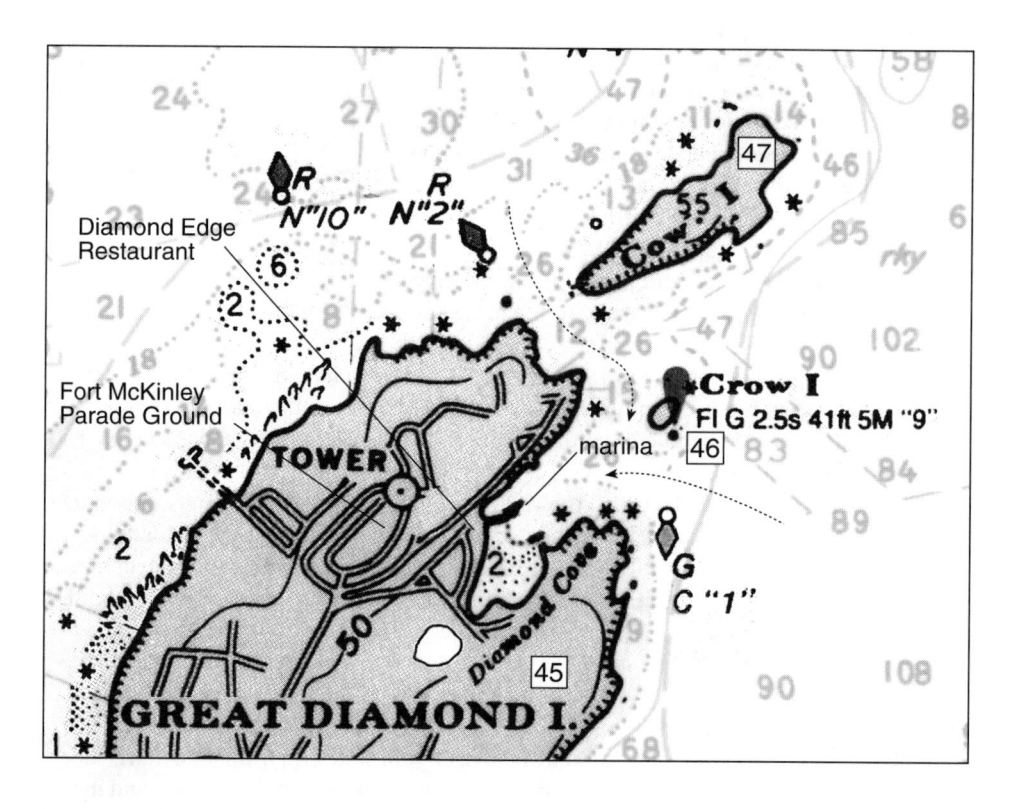

Also objectionable to the group was the island's name. The effort to change it was led—so the story goes—by a rather large woman who took personal offense to the name, particularly when mail arrived addressed to Mrs. So-and-So, Great Hog. The name Great Diamond was chosen, presumably, after the large quartz crystals found there.

45. Diamond Cove

The northern half of Great Diamond Island was once Fort McKinley, serving as an army base from the 1890s until it was abandoned after WW II. It's front door was pristine Diamond Cove at the northeast end of the island. For nearly four decades, the fort remained an empty ghost town and a destination for almost two generations of island boys exploring Casco Bay. The cove, a mere two miles from Portland, became known as Cocktail Cove for its reputation as a place to whoop it up.

All this, however, changed dramatically when a developer bought the fort and began restoring its stately buildings as luxury townhouses. Now a swimming pool graces the Parade Grounds, a restaurant, bar, gallery and small general store occupy the storehouses by the wharf, a new ferry pier and boat slips have been built, and Casco Bay Lines' "down-bay boat" now stops there.

The public is welcome ashore to dine at the restaurant or bar or to shop at the store.

By sea. Approaching from the west, pass through the marvelously tight tickle between Great Diamond and Cow Island. Favor Crow Island as you leave it to port, and turn southward into Diamond Cove as it opens up. From the east, approach from Hussy Sound with Crow Island to starboard and can "1" to port. Beware of the fast approach or departure of the ferries in this small cove.

The marina at Diamond Cove (Ch. 09; 766-5804) provides temporary dockage for restaurant patrons as well as overnight slips with water or electricity.

The moorings in the cove are private and not associated with the marina. Boaters seem to pick them up temporarily, but do not leave your boat unattended on them. At least one of the moorings on the eastern side of the cove is precariously close to the rock shown on the chart. Don't be tempted to anchor in the inner cove, past the slips, since it almost becomes a mud flat at low.

Ashore. The dockhouse at the marina sells basic boat supplies, and marina patrons can use the shower and laundry facilities ashore.

The Diamond's Edge Restaurant (766-5850) is located in a renovated quartermaster storehouse and open for lunch and dinner with reservations, and there is an art gallery nearby. Often on weekend evenings, live bands play outside at the head of the cove.

For the sake of privacy, the general public is asked not to wander among the buildings of the fort by themselves. Tours of the Parade Ground, however, are offered during the summer. The main road leads south to the island's cottage community.

46. Crow Island

Crow Island is the little nubbit that blocks Diamond Cove from Hussey Sound. It is also known as Smuttynose.

On paper, the island is actually part of the Town of Long Island, and it is owned by the state. But it really belongs to the gulls, shags, and eiders that nest there. Even if there was a reason to land, the rocky shores would make it difficult, and what little interior there is is impenetrable.

47. Cow Island

Cow Island lies to the north of Great Diamond, separated by a marvelously narrow gut between the islands and ledges. Guessing from its name, it was probably once used as pasturage for the resident milker. Later, it was taken to become part of Fort McKinley, and several concrete structures still stand on its shores. Now, the island is privately owned.

What is remarkable about Cow is its history of permissive trespass, and for this we heartily thank the owners. For generations, Cow has been the place where young boys ventured in their skiffs for an overnight adventure, or where the not-so-young headed for some misadventure. Among locals, tales of whooping it up on Cow are legendary. Everyone who has ever visited Cow owes the owners a debt of gratitude, for providing a place, all these years, where those who live on Casco Bay can exuberantly enjoy its all-too-short summers among friends, the stars in the sky, the gentle breeze, and the breathing of Hussey Sound on the shores.

We must, of course, interject a reminder. Past use by others in no way constitutes permission to use a private island. And any willingness of owners to allow visitors will be directly affected by your behavior.

By sea. Land either just north of the eastern shoulder of the island or at the small beaches on the island's southern or western shores. Beware of the several rocks shown on the chart lying just off the island.

Ashore. Most of the island is overgrown, with the exception of the eastern shoulder, where people camp. Beware of poison ivy.

48. Pumpkin Knob

Pumpkin Knob, also once known as Punkin Island, is the little bump of an island at the north end of Peaks Island, ringed with bold shores and surrounded by the surging deep waters of Hussey Sound. It is currently a private summer residence, and landing is not allowed.

By sea. The pass between Pumpkin and Peaks is delightful with pine-capped rocky shores close by on either side and established summer homes perched on the cliffs of Peaks. The minimum depth at low is about 13 feet.

Ashore. During the heyday of Peaks Island's popularity as a summer resort, little Pumpkin Knob actually supported a large hotel serviced by the Casco Bay steamers.

There is an unconfirmed reference that during the war years, the U.S. Government decided that Pumpkin Knob was an obstruction to navigation in Hussey Sound and they proposed blowing it up with TNT. Treacherous Soldier Ledge, just east of the Knob in the middle of Hussey Sound would be a much more likely candidate for the demolition experts (see Hussey Sound, below). Luckily, if the plans ever existed, *they* vanished instead of the island.

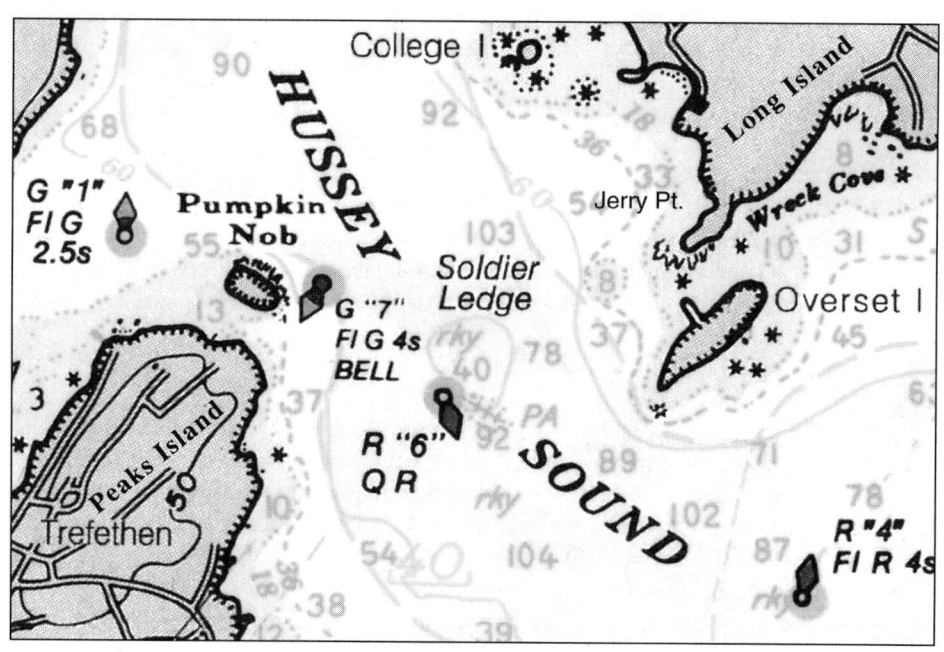

49. Hussey Sound

Hussey Sound is the deep but narrow channel between Peaks and Long Island that leads into the Hussey Anchorage. Soldier Ledge lurks almost dead center in the middle of the channel. In July 1972, the Norwegian tanker *Tamano* struck a buoy and went aground on Soldier Ledge, spilling 100,000 gallons of heavy petroleum.

This was not the first time. During World War II, Soldier Ledge ripped open the battleship *Iowa,* spilling about 50,000 gallons of oil. Newspapers didn't report the spill because during the war it was forbidden to mention the location of any battleships.

By sea. Hussey Sound is directly in line with the ocean swells. Both flood and ebb currents in the sound run at an average maximum of 1.1 to 1.2 knots. When the ebb current opposes the swells, large waves can form. Small boats should use caution, particularly when the waves are abeam. Commercial traffic is quite rare through the Hussey, but on the occasions when tankers or freighters do make the passage, they dwarf the nearby islands, and they are usually unescorted by tugs and moving fast. Don't get in their way.

Ashore. The sandy beach on the Long Island side of Hussey Sound, Fowler's Beach, is owned by the Long Island Civic Association.

A cove on the Peaks Island side of Hussey Sound became known as Aquarium Cove. The turn-of-the-century amusements on Peaks Island attracted many entrepreneurs. One, a Mr. Bennett, decided he would build an aquarium in the small cove to the north of the new house near the north end of the island. He built a concrete floor and walls to form a pool with a walk around it and a ticket office. Pumps piped water in from Hussey Sound, the pool was stocked with a seal, an eel, and some small fish, and tickets were printed in town. But before he could sell the first ticket, the eel ate the fish, and the seal ate the eel, and then the seal died. The only good to come of it was that the children discovered the sun-warmed waters of the pool, and kindhearted Mr. Bennett always allowed them to swim free of charge.

50. Overset Island

Overset Island, on the seaward end of Hussey Sound, was once offered to the City of Portland for 500 dollars. The city council refused it by a vote of 5 to 3, so it is now private. Even if it weren't, it is so steep-to and surrounded by ocean swells that landing would be difficult. It is now part of the town of Long Island.

By sea. Do not attempt to pass between Long Island and Overset, which are connected by ledge at low.

51. Long Island

Long Island is one of Maine's newest towns, having seceded from Portland in 1993. It lies directly across Hussey Sound from Peaks Island, an easy small-boat jaunt from Falmouth Foreside or Portland Harbor. The island presents one long flank to the ocean and the other to Portland's Hussey Anchorage. But its location has been a mixed blessing. During World War II, it was a fueling depot for the North Atlantic Fleet, and clean-up of the fuel storage tanks is ongoing. In the 1970s it was the proposed site for an oil terminal, which, fortunately, never came to pass. And it is just far enough away from

Portland to be a difficult commute. Yet the same geography has endowed it with several beautiful sandy beaches and its pleasant, back-in-time feeling.

By sea. There are practically no obstructions to the inner, northwestern side of the island, where there are four distinct wharves. If you are a patron, you can land at the floats of the Spar Restaurant, furthest to the west, or pick up one of their moorings. The Spar is the small building with the big deck overlooking the old ferry wharf, known as Ponce Landing. The restaurant (766-3310) serves seafood to go with the sunsets.

A public float hangs off the Ponce Landing wharf with a two-hour docking limit. The local lobstermen, however, have staked their claim to this wharf, and they discourage others from using it. Most of the lobstermen are also the town selectmen, so if they ask you to leave, it's a good idea to take heed.

The next wharf belongs to Casco Bay Lobster, and the float is their buying station. This isn't a good place to land, but in a pinch they may be able to sell you some fuel or lobsters.

The new Mariner Wharf where the ferry lands lies farthest to the northeast, past an old army breakwater. The float off its south side is public, but docking is limited to 30 minutes.

If you need repairs of any kind, land at Johnson's Boat Yard (766-3319) in Old Cove. Old Cove is the nitch on the northwest side of the island in the community shown on the chart as Mariner. The outside of their floats are free of obstructions, but a ledge lurks just off their end, in the mouth of Old Cove.

If the swell isn't running too hard, it is possible to land beachable boats on Fowler's Beach on the Long Island side of Hussey Sound or at Sandy Beach (see p. 67) on the ocean side.

Ashore. Town offices, portapotties, a pay phone, and even the Historical Society are at the head of Mariner Wharf. Clark's Store, just south of The Spar, can set you up with groceries or snacks if the Spar hasn't taken care of you already.

Big Sandy Beach can be reached on land by following—what else?—Beach Avenue, and Fowler's can be reached by following the road to the south. Neither beach has any facilities or lifeguards. The Oceanside Conservation Trust holds conservation easements for Fowler's, and it is owned by the Long Island Civic Association. Big Sandy Beach is owned by the state.

Evidence on the island suggests that for centuries, Indians lived and feasted here, and there are legends that they left intricate carvings in the part of the island known as the Dark Forest. One of the carvings was of an English ship observed by the Abenakis, but the carving, it is said, was lost in the Hurricane of 1938.

When Captain John Smith explored this region in 1614, he was so impressed that he returned in 1640 to buy this island, naming it Smith's Island. But despite his skill as an explorer and New World publicist, he had poor luck at naming islands, and the name didn't stick. He had the same problem at the Isles of Shoals.

The same fate befell Colonel Eziekiel Cushing, who lived on Cape Elizabeth and also had a fine summer residence on Cushing Island. In a moment of apparent impetuosity in about 1765, Cushing swapped a valuable tract of downtown Portland property for barren Long Island. He sent his brother Ignatius and his family to Long to develop it, and they farmed the Portland end of the island. By 1830, Long Island's census reported a population of 146, making it the most heavily populated island in Casco Bay.

During the steamboat era, Long Islanders built hotels and touted the virtues of their medicinal springs, but even then, the feeling of Long was more rural, more removed. Instead of trumped up amusements, Long Island specialized in clambakes. At one clambake, sponsored by the City of Portland for its Centennial celebration in 1886, they cooked 500 bushels of clams over a fire that consumed 16 cords of wood. A different great fire, in 1914, destroyed the hotels and many of the cottages.

52. Big Sandy Beach

Big Sandy Beach is on the ocean side of Long, tucked behind Vaill Island. The state acquired this beautiful beach in 1972 and has left it marvelously undeveloped, without fees, lifeguards, or facilities of any kind. In settled weather, it is possible to anchor between the beach and Vaill or actually beach your boat here.

By sea. Sandy Beach is flanked by two of the best-named coves in Casco Bay: Wreck Cove and Shark Cove. Run in toward Wreck Cove, between Overset and Vaill Island, then turn to the north, between the beach and Vaill.

A sand bar runs from the northeast end of the beach out to Vaill. At low it is shallow enough to wade across. If your boat has a draft of more than a couple of feet, be sure you are not over the bar when you anchor. If you plan to beach your boat, beware of the ocean swells that roll in here. They can make landing or launching a kayak or dinghy difficult, and sometimes they even poop unsuspecting sport boats. The swells tend to increase in fair-weather afternoons with building southwest winds, so leaving can be more difficult than arriving.

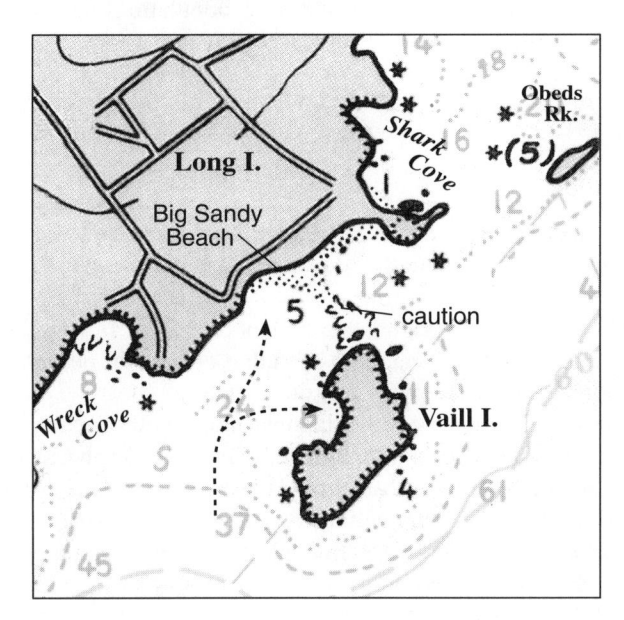

Ashore. Sandy Beach is long enough for strolling, and its sand is fine enough to sing when you drag your feet. The public beach ends at the peninsula to the north. The sandy crescent that fronts on Shark Cove is private.

There may be a dumpster or trash can by the road at the southern end of the beach. Otherwise, please take all your trash with you.

Clark's Market is within easy walking distance by following Beach Road to the north.

53. Vaill Island

Vaill Island is a small apostrophe-shaped island, directly off Long Island's Sandy Beach. Its rocky flank curls back from the ocean, and it cuddles a miniature harbor in its lee, ringed by a cobble beach.

The harbor makes a pleasant daystop, offering a sense of offshore remoteness and isolation, yet only a stone's throw away from its bigger neighbor.

By sea. See the approach and chart for Sandy Beach on the previous page and enter the middle of the cove.

Ashore. Visitors will want to confine themselves to the harbor's beach. Vaill is also known as Marsh Island, for the swampy areas among its ledges. The rest of the island is entwined with poison ivy, and the few areas where you might find room to step will probably be occupied by nesting gulls. There is no room to camp.

Recently, Vaill has earned the dubious distinction of being ground zero for the resurgence of the plague of the browntail moths.

Browntail moths were inadvertently imported to this country from Europe at the same time as the gypsy moths, in 1897. They feed on the leaves of hardwood trees and shrubs, often causing complete defoliation. If the fine hairs on the browntail moth come in contact with human skin, they can induce severe rashes and itching, similar to poison ivy and often more persistent. By 1915, the browntail moth had spread to most of the area east of the Connecticut River and into Nova Scotia, but for unknown reasons, its population began declining. By the 1970s, the last remaining populations of the pests were found in a few isolated areas of Cape Cod and on one or two islands in Casco Bay. The largest population was on Vaill.

Then several years ago, again for unknown reasons, the moth populations began a dramatic resurgence, spreading to most of the islands of Casco Bay and now to the mainland.

54. Harbor de Grace

Harbor de Grace is a wonderful cleft in Long Island's eastern shore, tucked behind a rocky headland. Unfortunately, the chart leaves out the "de" in its French name, which loosely translated means "Blessed Harbor."

In fair weather this is a fun harbor to poke into, but don't count on Harbor Grace if you are looking for a protected anchorage in foul weather. Its mouth is open to the ocean swells and southerly winds, and lobsterboats occupy its few deep spots.

By sea. Harbor Grace is easily identified by the octagonal house with a white mast-style flagpole perched on the rocky peninsula north of the harbor mouth, known as "The Nubble." From seaward, clear Obeds Rock and run straight in.

The chart shows a rock dead center in the entrance. The rock is actually an extension of the ledges from the south and shows clearly at midtide or less. Favor the Nubble to clear it. The entrance has about 12 feet of depth at low, and the area just inside has about eight. The rest of the harbor shoals rapidly.

THE WESTERN SHORE

PRESUMPSCOT RIVER

The Presumpscot River was once Casco Bay's most important river. The Indians used it as their main trail between Sebago Lake and Casco Bay, and the early settlers used it to float masts and lumber. Shipyards, brickyards, tanneries, and mills sprouted on its banks, and fish and ice were taken from its waters. But with the crescendo of industrialization, the Presumpscot gained the dubious distinction of becoming the most polluted river running into the bay. The water is cleaner now. Fish return for spawning, blue heron tiptoe through the marshes, and migrating birds alight on its still waters. Yet the Presumpscot, remarkably, remains a forgotten river.

At high tides, small boaters can explore the beautiful 2.8-mile tidal inlet from the Martin Point Bridge to the Lower Falls Dam in Falmouth, wending upriver through a broad saltwater estuary into a freshwater river cradled between steep, wooded banks and tinged with an earthy aroma. This is an ideal jaunt for anglers or bird watchers or for those who—within sight and sound of the city of Portland—want to feel strangely close to the Indians who paddled here long ago.

The Presumpscot, in many ways, was the lifeblood of the Abenaki tribes in the area. They settled at Lower Falls where the abundant fish congregated to jump upriver, and they planted corn along its banks. By canoe, they could travel upriver to the numerous connecting trails that converged at Sebago, or they could head downriver to the rich clamming and fishing grounds on the Casco Bay islands.

When Christopher Levett explored the area in 1623, he wrote, *"In the same Bay I found another River, up which I went about three miles, and found a great fall of water much bigger than the fall at London bridge, at low water; further a boate cannot goe, but above the fall the River runnes smooth againe.*

"Just at this fall of water the Sagamore or King of that place hath a house, where I was one day when there were two Sagamors more, their wives and children, in all about 50. and we were but 7. They bid me welcome and gave me such victualls as they had, and I gave them Tobacco and Aqua vitae."

This was a taste of things to come. Several years later, that same Sagamore, Skitterygusset, sold all his land on the east side of the river to Francis Neale Small to the tune of one gallon of spirits a year. The deal is the oldest recorded deed in Falmouth.

After European settlers arrived, the river became the main trade route from inland to trading posts at Richmond Island and later on Casco Neck or what is now known as the Portland Peninsula. Early colonists described the Presumpscot as "a foot deep in fish," and they were quick to take advantage of it. They hunted the abundant fowl and corralled smelts in numerous weirs, and they discovered banks of marine clay, which was ideal for brick making. Soon, they were cutting pines for masts and floating them downriver, and they were harnessing the river's falls for saw mills, grist mills, and cotton mills. Among the logs that made the trip down river were the eight 65-foot long white pines cut on Pikes Hill in Windham to form the vertical members of the Portland Observatory (see Portland Observatory, p. 45).

The lower estuary is called Presumcok Cove on the Atlantic Neptune chart of

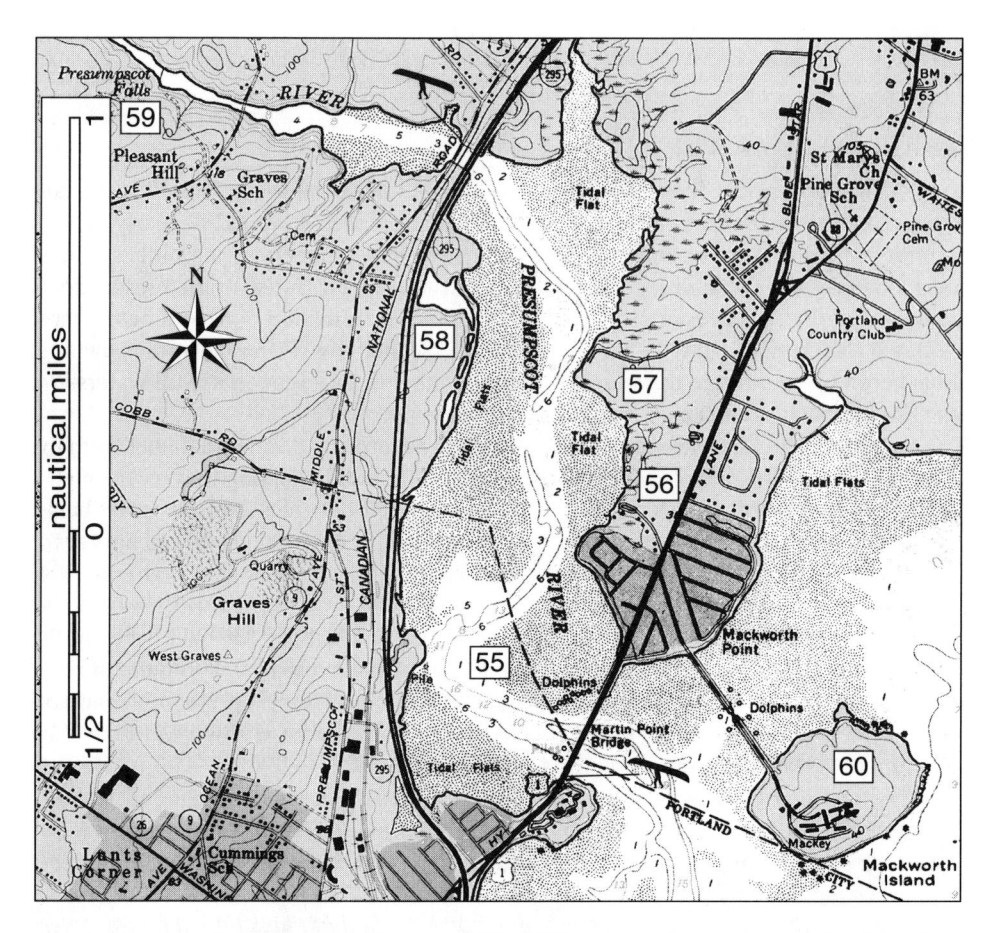

Casco Bay (see DesBarres sidebar, p. 139). With its ready access to inland lumber, cotton for sails from the river's mills, and the easy access to the ocean, the estuary was ideal for shipbuilding. The first ship was launched on the Presumpscot in 1734, and in the heyday of shipbuilding, as many as sixteen shipyards flanked the shores. One of the Presumpscot-built vessels was the first American-built ship to carry grain to Europe.

By the 1940s, this short, 25-mile river had as many as seventeen dams and mills at almost every conceivable location, including sawmills, power stations, and paper mills. By the 1960s, the river could barely be seen beneath the surface froth of what was described as "root beer foam." Its fumes turned the paint on nearby houses black, and helicopters were used to dust the river with lime to neutralize its stench. The river was so foul that when two determined college students paddled its entire length in 1969, they threw up afterwards. Fortunately since the Clean Water Act of 1972, the Presumpscot has rebounded remarkably, and fish and fowl have returned.

The upper Presumpscot is home to land-locked salmon and—before the dams—to the Presumpscot jumper, a variety of salmon found nowhere else. Anadromous fish return to the lower Presumpscot from the sea to spawn, and after decades of dams and pollution, this migratory pattern is reestablishing itself. Blue-back herring and rainbow smelt are returning. Elvers, baby eels also known as glass eels, journey from as far away as the Sargasso Sea to mature inland. Predatory mackerel arrive in the early spring, followed by menhaden, stripped bass, and voracious bluefish. Hopefully someday the endangered Atlantic salmon, silversides, will return too.

By sea. Follow the approaches described in the sections below.

55. Presumpscot River Basin

The Presumpscot River Basin lies between what is now the East End Beach and Mackworth Island. This is a broad, shoal area, much of which become mud flats at low tide. Near the top of the tide, however, small boats can follow an unmarked, shifting channel that curves through it to Martin Point Bridge, and portable boats can be launched near the bridge itself. This is a prime fishing area, both for bluefish and, more recently, for stripped bass, which congregate when the ebb flushes smaller fish out of the river estuary.

Martin Point Bridge was completed in 1828, but it was begun an astounding 21 years earlier. Its progress was first interrupted by the depression caused by the 1807 Embargo Act prohibiting foreign commerce and then by the War of 1812. This first bridge was destroyed by ice. A new bridge was completed by 1868. This time the construction took seven years, due to the Civil War. When the 1868 bridge needed to be replaced, the construction took even longer, interrupted this time by World War II.

By sea. At high tide, most of the Basin is navigable, with no obstacles other than the shallow depths. At lower tides, however, you may need to feel for the unmarked channel.

Portable boats can be launched at high tide off the old abutment from the 1868 bridge on southeast side of the Martin Point end of the bridge. The put-in, however, is high, and parking is limited to a short stretch of pavement leading to it.

The fixed bridge has a vertical clearance of about 12 feet at high tide. Once under the bridge, beware of the line of wooden dolphins to the north, designed to break up winter ice.

By land. From Rt. 295N, take exit 9 and follow Rt. 1 north from Portland toward Falmouth. The turnoff to the put-in is just before the bridge, on the right.

Ashore. When the stripers or blues are running, fishing is excellent off the Martin Point Bridge, particularly at the bottom of the ebb.

With the Presumpscot as Casco Bay's main link with inland Indians, the Basin was of vital strategic importance, both to the settlers and the Indians, and much blood was shed to control it. Casco Bay Fort, built on the Neck, was ground zero when the Indians attacked Portland during a five-day siege in 1690. For many years after that the Portland Peninsula was known as "Deserted Casco." Ten years later, another fort, Fort New Casco, was built on the shore of the Basin near where the causeway to Mackworth Island leaves the mainland.

56. Jim Whitney's Boathouse

A red boathouse perches on the eastern bank of the Presumpscot estuary in the first bight past the Martin Point Bridge. This used to be Jim Whitney's boathouse and his father's before him. Jim was a boatbuilder and pilot by trade, but his real passion was duck hunting. He came by it naturally. His father, J.A. Whitney, was a commercial duck hunter for the Boston markets, and he even set up a skeet shooting clubhouse to keep his aim sharp when he wasn't in the blinds along the banks of the river.

Jim carved elegant, oversized decoys and built ingenious duck boats in the boathouse. Hand tools lined the walls and benches, and shavings blanketed the floor. Jim stored his powder and packed his shot in the small steel shed next door, which originally stored gunpowder during World War II. Jim's love of birding was passed to his son, who tragically drowned while hunting during a hurricane.

Among birders, Jim became a legend. At the time, his family never fully realized the value of Jim's craft, and when he died they sold most of his work in a yard sale. Needless to say, many hunters and collectors were sorry they missed that one.

Jim's boathouse was sold and eventually converted into a private residence. His decoys, mostly oversized geese, can occasionally be found in antique shops along with their oversized price tags.

57. Gilsland Farm

Gilsland Farm occupies the high bluff on the east bank of the Presumpscot estuary. It is the headquarters of Maine Audubon (781-2330), which maintains pleasant walking paths around the property and runs nature courses, a library, and a small store in its acclaimed contemporary building. At high tides, it is possible to land near one of the trails and explore this beautiful preserve, where you might catch glimpses of heron, egrets, occasional kingfishers, or even eagles.

By sea. On the chart, the farm occupies the V-shaped point which projects into the river from the east. The point is mostly a high bluff surrounded by marsh. When the tide is out, it reveals extensive mud flats. At high tide, though, canoes or kayaks can approach the lowest point of the bluff at the indent on the north side, where there is a wooden observation blind. The trail system leads from the blind.

This should be considered a pleasant high-tide stop, not a launching site. Do not stay too long, or you will be visiting the creatures in the mud.

By land. Take Rt. 295 to Rt. 1 north toward Falmouth. Signs will be on the left about a mile after Rt. 1 crosses the Martin Point Bridge.

Ashore. Trails lead throughout the property and to Audubon's award-winning visitor's center, where there is a small store, restrooms, and drinking water. For most of this century the farm was owned by David Moulton, who raised prize Jersey cattle here. Moulton's other passion was peonies. He planted seven acres with 400 varieties he collected from around the world. Some still bloom in the spring and early summer throughout the meadows. The farm was given to Maine Audubon by his descendants in 1974.

58. Mile Pond

On the west bank of the Presumpscot, just as it bends to the west and passes beneath Route 295, grasses and cattails ring a small pond, called Mile Pond. The chart shows several other long and narrow ponds just south of it. Together, these pools are all that's left of a bizarre scheme in 1861 to turn the Presumpscot into a major *freshwater* sea port.

Perhaps inspired by the Cumberland and Oxford Canal at the head of the Fore River (see Stroudwater, p. 34), F. O. J. Smith conceived the idea of building a canal across Staples Point—at the south end of the bridges—to divert the entire Presumpscot into Mile Pond. From there, more canals would carry it down the west bank of the river and across the southwest corner of the river estuary, where a large dam would keep it from spilling back into the original river bed. Finally, a last stretch of canal would carry the river through Martin Point, where a 900-foot long dam would enclose a 100-acre freshwater dockage area. The dam would raise the height of the river in the canal system twenty-two feet and submerge Lower Falls. Seagoing ships would then be able to pass through the dam via a lock and steam upriver as far a Cumberland Mills, where Smith envisioned a thriving industrial complex.

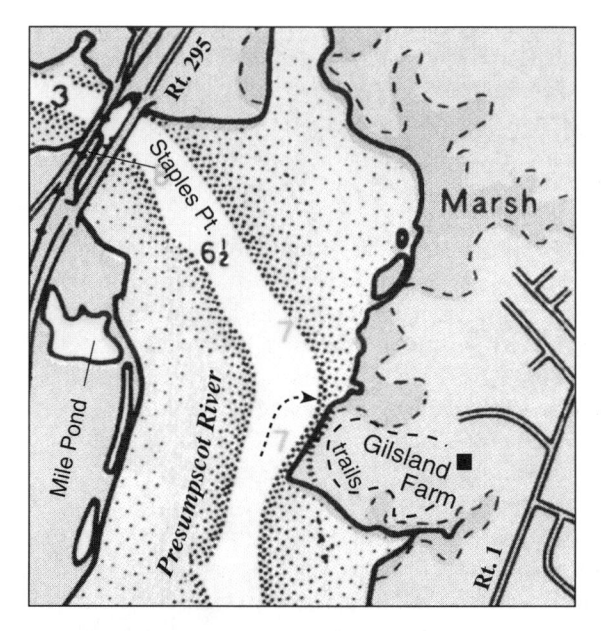

"If Portland cannot go to the distant waterfall (Lower Falls)," Smith wrote, "...then substitute it for the opposite idea, of bringing the waterfall to the city on the seaboard, and what was before a worthless waste becomes of priceless value to the world."

Smith was not a crackpot. He was, however, a scoundrel. As historian Herbert Adams wrote, "He was born a scoundrel, lived a scoundrel, and thrived as a scoundrel. Scurrility made him rich, famous, and, of course, a congressman." Smith was the precocious son of a tavern keeper. He was admitted to the Maine Bar at the age of nineteen, became a State congressman and then a U.S. congressman. But his dealings were far from above board. He started a wildcat bank in Westbrook, which he had to back up with federal money that was illegally borrowed from a Massachusetts bank. Then the Secretary of State hired him to surreptitiously sway popular opinion in Maine about resolving the border dispute between Canada and Maine. Maine paid him from a "secret fund," but he might have been receiving other secret money—bribes by the British government. With Smith's "help," the border dispute was resolved, but Maine gave away more than half of the disputed territory.

Smith was an equally unscrupulous wheeler-dealer in his financial life, peddling his political clout to Samuel Morse for a quarter share of Morse's telegraph and then having the audacity to sue and harass Morse for the remainder of the inventor's life.

Smith shrewdly invested in western Maine land and timber and set himself up in a huge mansion just outside of Portland surrounded by 70 acres of manicured lawns, gardens, and forests. The house had a two-story front door, a dome, and the finest private library in the state. Smith called it "Forest Home." His neighbors called it "Smith Castle." He owned more than six newspapers, built the International Hotel on Congress

Street, and the Union Street Theater. He even founded the Portland Gas Works, but he quickly abandoned it and its investors. It may have been the Cumberland and Oxford Canal that turned his attention to the waterways near Portland. When the $200,000 canal went bankrupt, he bought it at auction for twenty cents on the dollar.

For the Presumpscot project, Smith formed the Presumpscot Land and Water Power Company and propped up John J. Speed as President. They purchased land and dug the stretch of canal between Mile Pond and Martin Point 130-feet wide and ten-feet deep. But after five years, Smith was broke and could find no more backers. He is remembered as "Maine's Greatest Failure." The frogs in the ponds, however, croak their thanks.

59. Presumpscot Falls and Smelt Hill Dam

The stretch of the Presumpscot from the salt-water estuary to the fresh water at Presumpscot Falls, also known as Lower Falls, makes a beautiful transition from marsh to inland woods. Heron or egrets wade in the lower marshes, and kingfishers swoop from the wooded banks. It passes from the low bridges at Staples Point to the high, graceful span of the Presumpscot Falls Bridge, to the Lower Falls hydro station.

This was the settlement of the Aucocisoco Indian tribe led by Chief Skitterygusset, and the place where Christopher Levett met so amicably with this Sagamore (see Presumpscot River, p. 69). At the time, the beavers had dammed the river just above the falls so completely that the Indians used the dam as a footbridge to cross. When the settlers arrived they built mills on the south bank here. The first, a sawmill, was built in 1646. In 1732, as one of their many business ventures, Samuel Waldo and Thomas Westbrook (see Stroudwater, p. 34) built the first man-made dam over the falls to power a grist mill and a paper mill. On the opposite side, a single and double saw mill were built, and finally, at the height of the shipbuilding on the river in 1850, a triple sawmill was added along with a fulling mill and a combing mill that produced wool cloth.

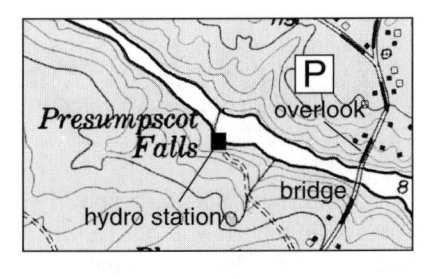

The dams, however, blocked the river's salmon from reaching their spawning beds and the Indians' fishing grounds, adding to escalating tensions between the Indians and the settlers. Retaliation was swift and bloody. The Abenakis attacked Thomas Wakely and his family who lived on the west bank just above the falls, massacring the parents and six of their children and kidnapping another, Elizabeth, aged 11 (see p. 76).

The first ship was built on the river in 1734, and the 600-ton mast ship started a shipbuilding boom. By the middle of the 1800s, the banks between the Lower Falls and the Presumpscot Falls Bridge were lined with shipyards: the Knight Shipyard, right at the dam which launched the largest Presumpscot-built ship, the Hamilton Shipyard, the Waite's Landing Brickyard and Shipyard, the Batchelder and Skillins Shipyard, and the Smelledge Shipyard. A large mast yard was even squeezed between the shipyards for loading the mast ships. Between the shipyards and the sawmills and the log drives, there were fears that the sawdust and bark and deadheads might clog the river.

The first bridge was built across the river in 1751. The Smelt Hill Bridge was a wooden covered bridge financed through a Massachusetts grant that allowed local residents to raise the necessary 1200 pounds sterling by lottery. The cement Presumpscot Falls Bridge replaced it in 1913, and at the time it was an engineering marvel, the longest single-span cement bridge in New England, with a span of 160 feet. The bridge, along with the Martin Point Bridge, effectively put an end to river shipbuilding.

And finally, another first for Lower Falls. When the Smelt Hill Dam was built in 1890, it became the sight of Maine's first hydroelectric plant. The plant supplied power to S.D. Warren's paper mill in Westbrook and thousands of homes. The dam, however, slows the flow of the lower section of the Presumpscot River and traps its sediments. The stretch of the river between the dam and the S.D. Warren paper mill in Westbrook is still the most polluted. In 1996 heavy rains created floodwaters so high that they destroyed the hydro facility, and S.D. Warren began negotiating with Central Maine Power to purchase the dam and demolish it. Removing the dam would enable the river to more easily purge itself of pollutants and help restore populations of migrating fish to the reaches of the river above the falls. It would also help S.D. Warren meet federal water quality standards. The deal, however, is in a state of flux. S.D. Warren was bought by the Sappi Company, and Central Maine Power is reorganizing to brace for deregulation.

By sea. From the Presumpscot estuary, pass under the triple bridges of Rt. 295, the Grand Trunk Railroad, and Middle Road's Staples Point Bridge, the latter having the lowest vertical clearance at high of only four or five feet. Beware of tidal currents running hard under the bridges. From here the channel favors the right, northern side of the river and passes beneath the high, graceful span of the Presumpscot Falls Bridge.

Portable boats can be launched off the embankment at the north end of the Staples Point Bridge, where Rt. 9 crosses the river.

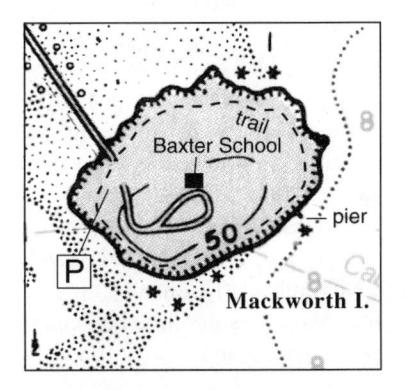

By land. To reach the put-in, take exit 8 off Rt. 295 (exit 9 if you are heading south) onto Washington Avenue. Head north on Washington and take a right onto Ocean Avenue (Rt. 9). Ocean Avenue becomes Middle Road. Follow it until it crosses the river. Park on the shoulder on the east side of the road at the north end of the bridge.

60. Mackworth Island

Mackworth Island is located just off Mackworth Point, at the mouth of the Presumpscot River. This beautiful, state-owned island is the site of a school for the deaf, and its shores and woodsy perimeter are open to the public for basking, hiking, or quiet contemplation. Mackworth is connected to the mainland by a long causeway.

By sea. Curiously, even though you may arrive by car or on foot, you are technically not allowed to land by boat. Most of Mackworth is surrounded by very shallow water at high tide and extensive mud flats at low, and all but its southwest shore is rocky. The island's southeast flank, though, is very approachable, and small beaches lie on either side of a granite pier. The rule against arriving by boat seems in this case to detract from Mackworth's rich history and very islandness. If you do approach, use caution to avoid the rock shown just off the pier on the chart. It is is actually a collapsed cribbing for the old wharf that once extended from the pier, and it is revealed at low.

The shallow waters at the mouth of the Presumpscot between Martin Point and Mackworth are prime areas for bluefish and stripped bass.

By land. From Rt. 295N, take exit 9 to US Rt. 1N. Cross over the bridge from Martin Point to Falmouth, and take the third right and follow the causeway to Mackworth. The parking lot on the island can hold about 20 cars.

Ashore. Mackworth is managed by the Bureau of Parks and Lands (287-3061). A gentle 1.25-mile walking trail leads around the perimeter of the island, along the island's bluffs, through the beautiful and varied stands of woods planted by Baxter, and past the small burial plot where each of his 19 exuberant Irish setters is remembered by a bronze plaque.

Before European settlement, when the Presumpscot River was the main highway between Casco Bay and Sebago Lake, Mackworth's location had strategic importance. By some accounts, the island was the home of Cocawesco, the Indian sagamore of Casco. By others, it was the site for the summer village of the Wabinaki led by sachem Skitterygusset. They called the point Menikoe.

Arthur Mackworth arrived in the area in 1630, straight from England, with some of his influential friends, one of whom was Richard Vines, Sir Ferdinando Gorges' agent. Mackworth set up housekeeping on the point, and four years later, Vines gave him a grant which also included the island. Mackworth promptly had a house built there and moved into it, raised a family, and spent his years in public service as Gorges' deputy of Casco Bay, raising crops and livestock, trading with the Indians, and steadfastly practicing a strong religious life. He died in 1657, before relations had soured between the settlers and the Indians. He was buried on the island and is remembered for his outstanding calmness, civility, and honor in this rugged new world.

But Indian resentment of settlers mounted until it was sparked by a senseless incident on the Saco River. Several English sailors saw an Indian woman and her child paddling a canoe on the river. Legend among the English at the time was that Indian children were born innately knowing how to swim, and seeing the woman and the child, the sailors decided to test the theory by capsizing the canoe. The child drowned.

The Indian happened to be sachem Squando's wife. Indians retaliated at Mackworth and along the Presumpscot, violently massacring the Wakely family and capturing and enslaving their 11-year-old girl. From August through November 1675, nearly 50 settlers were killed near the mouth of the Presumpscot. Historians consider this the beginning of the Indian or King Philip's War, a bloody struggle which would last for the next 35 years.

James Rennie brought a lighter historical note to Mackworth when he bought the island in 1808 and built a large two-story home there. Rennie, a Scot, was an experienced ventriloquist and a notorious practical jokester. Legend has it that he played one too many a trick on the local lobstermen until they put an end to it by throwing him into the bay. But Rennie's real claim to fame was his uncanny ability to tame the wildest of horses with hypnotic voicings, an art, he said, that was passed down from father to eldest son. He became known as "The Whisperer."

"The Whisperer" only stayed on Mackworth a short time. Apparently, somewhere in his past Rennie had woven his hypnotic charms into his business life. He fled to Jamaica without a trace, and creditors quickly claimed his house and island and auctioned them off.

The island changed hands and names several times in the ensuing years. During the Civil War, it was used for a training camp, Camp Berry, whose massive granite wharf still projects from the east side of the island. The island passed through the ownership of Lemuel Cushing, of Cushing Island, before being sold, in 1888, to the Honorable James P. Baxter of Portland.

Baxter built a 22-room cottage, and Mackworth became an expansive summer estate during the golden Victorian and Edwardian periods. A windmill pumped fresh water from the island springs. A wooden bridge was built in 1914 to link the island to the mainland. And in 1916 the original cottage was moved to make room for an even grander one. When the family's horses were brought to the island each summer, their hooves were bound in leather to keep them from splitting the planks of the bridge.

Baxter's son, Percival, became the governor of Maine from 1921 to 1925, and he took over the island around the same time. Camp Berry had largely deforested Mackworth by the end of the Civil War, and Baxter planted one hundred thousand pine and spruce trees and used his influence to have the island declared a bird sanctuary by an act of the legislature.

Baxter gave the island to the State of Maine in 1946, and seven years later he financed a new causeway and the School for the Deaf. He is also remembered for encouraging landowners to donate the land for the trail around Portland's Back Cove (see Back Cove, p. 47) and for his gift to the state of Mount Katahdin and Baxter State Park.

FALMOUTH FORESIDE

From the water, Falmouth Foreside can be recognized by a forest of masts swaying in the wind (and swells) between the mainland and Clapboard Island. Geographically, this is an exposed and unlikely place for the center of Portland's boating activity. Instead, it has grown up around the venerable Portland Yacht Club, long-established Handy Boat, and the Falmouth Town Landing, each listed below.

By sea. Falmouth Foreside is reached by heading around either the north or south end of Clapboard Island. The anchorage and its approaches contain several ledges, but they are well marked—Lower Clapboard Island Ledge, Jones Ledge, Prince Point Ledge, York Ledge, and Sturdivant Island Ledge.

Ashore. See individual listings below.

With the growth of Portland, Falmouth Foreside metamorphosed from an Indian settlement to a rural farming area to an elegant summer community to one of Portland's most affluent suburbs, with manicured lawns leading from grand houses to the water's edge.

An Abenaki tribe had a permanent settlement near the Foreside's abundant aquifer, and when George Waymouth explored Casco Bay, they let him fill his casks here.

During the cottage era, the spring was known as Underwood Spring. It was unaffected by drought or freshet, and it seemed to have no perceptible source.

One resident was known as the Lantern Lady because she always lit a lantern

MAINE COAST GUIDE

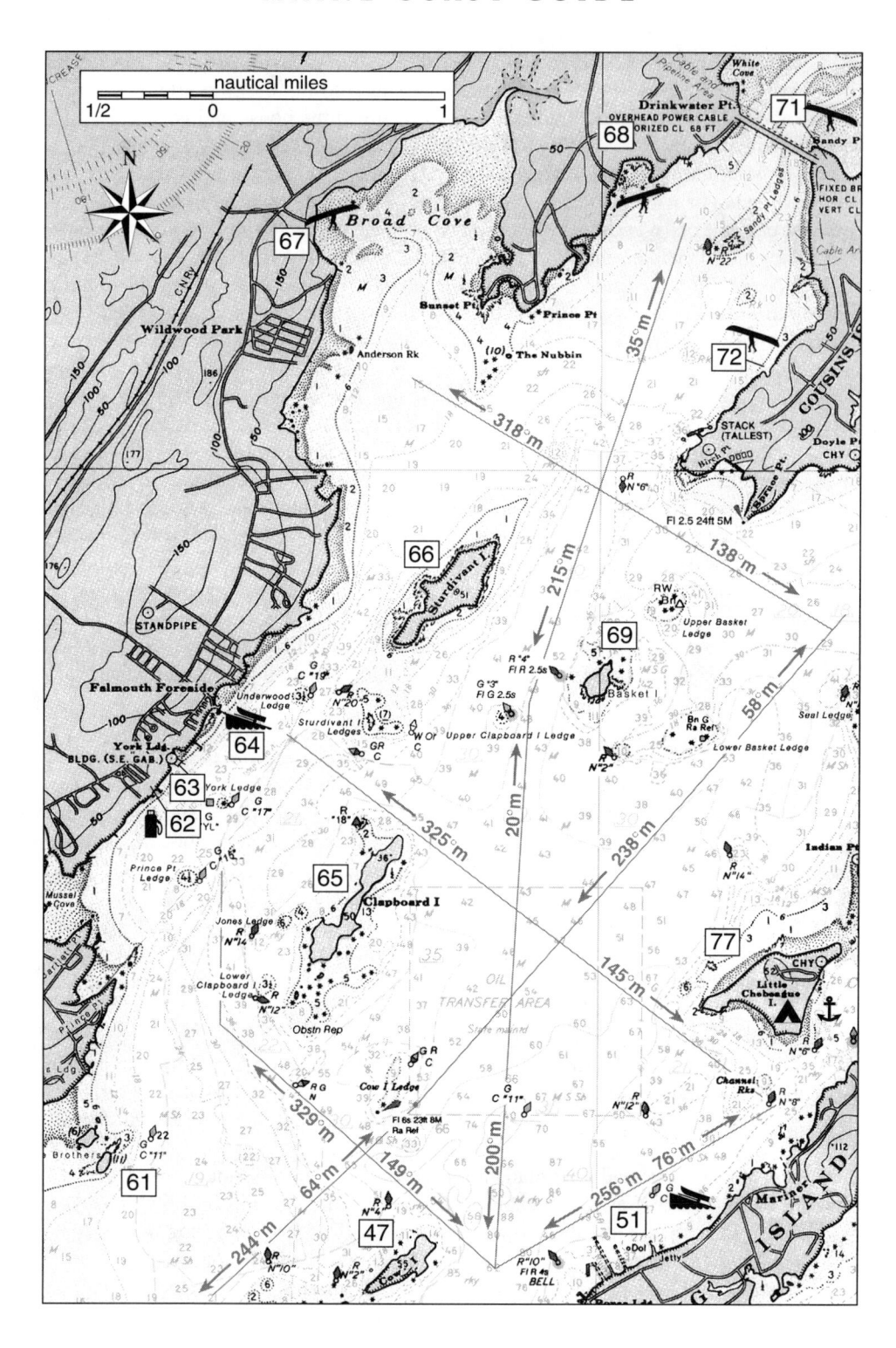

when her sea-captain husband put to sea and kept it burning until he returned. When he didn't return from one voyage, the Lantern Lady kept the lamp burning, and upon her death, the lantern duty was passed to her daughter. The oil lamp eventually gave way to an electric one, but for nearly half a century the lamp was kept burning. Lantern Lane is still on the maps.

61. The Brothers

The Brothers, or the Two Brothers, as they are called on earlier charts, are a pair of islands off Falmouth Foreside, just north of Mackworth Island. Both are private. A small white cottage is nestled near a small beach on the north end of the inner island. The outer island is uninhabited and crowned by tall oaks.

By sea. The Brothers define the eastern extremity of a large mud flat extending northeast from Mackworth Island and the southern entrance to Falmouth Foreside. The water to the west of the islands and between them is shoal. Beware of the large ledges that extend to the north and to the southwest of the outer island. Its rocky shores make landing difficult except in the smallest boats.

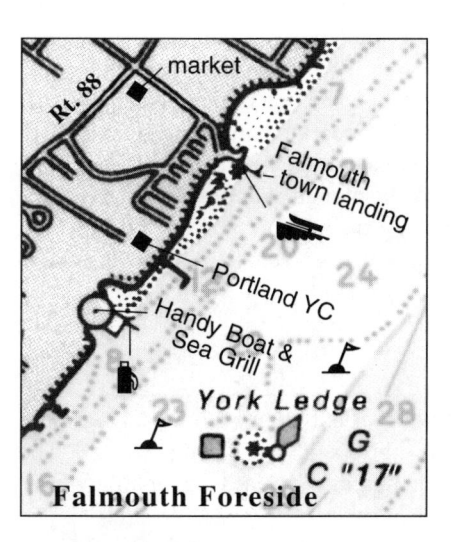

62. Handy Boat

Handy Boat (781-5110) grew in tandem with the Portland Yacht Club as one of greater Portland's earliest boat yards and marinas. This full-service facility has a fuel float with gas, diesel, water, and ice, and full launching, hauling, rigging and repair services.

By sea. Handy Boat is the southernmost operation along the Foreside. The fuel float is north of the hauling slip. They have transient dockage or mooring rentals if you would like to stay. They do not have a boat ramp, but they can launch boats of any size with their Travellift.

By land. From Rt. 295N, take exit 9 onto Rt. 1N. Cross the Martin Point Bridge and take Rt. 88N to the right. Look for signs to Handy Boat on the right.

Ashore. A pay phone, a marine store, and the Falmouth Sea Grill (781-5658) are located in the Handy building. Long-term parking and boat storage can be arranged.

63. Portland Yacht Club

Despite its apparent misnomer or misplacement, the Portland Yacht Club (781-9820) is located in Falmouth Foreside, just north of Handy Boat. This venerable club is one of the oldest in the country, and having survived the Depression and two world wars, it ranks as one of the oldest yacht clubs in continuous operation. It is the largest yacht club in Maine, and it annually sponsors the Monhegan Island race, among others. The club is still busy doing what it has always done—promoting boating among friends and passing boat-handling skills and traditions to the next generation.

While obviously a club, its service and facilities are open to visiting yachtsmen who are members of clubs with reciprocal privileges.

By sea. The long, high wharf of the Portland Yacht Club stretches into the water just north of Handy Boat and is recognizable by the dockmaster's house on its end. Launch service is available. The dockmaster can be reached on channel 09 or 68. The club also has a paved launching ramp near the clubhouse with adequate water at most tides.

By land. From Rt. 295N, take exit 9 onto Rt. 1N. Cross the Martin Point Bridge and take Rt. 88N to the right. Look for a small sign for the Portland Yacht Club on the right.

Ashore. PYC welcomes guests from registered yacht clubs. Please sign the guest book. Pay phones, ice, water, showers, and laundry are all available at the clubhouse. The dining room serves lunch and dinner. Unlike many yacht clubs, this one does not have a swimming pool or tennis courts. In fact, the idea of building those facilities was strongly outvoted in 1984 by a the majority which chose to keep boating at the core of the club's focus.

The Portland Yacht Club was founded by several avid yachtsmen in a downtown office as the nation was struggling to recover from the Civil War and as Portland was rebuilding itself after the Great Fire of 1866. The year was 1869. Early meetings were held in members' offices until a clubroom was rented in 1873 on Custom House Wharf. Membership and interest in the club and the luxury of boating barely survived the Depression and the First World War, but in 1946, when a cottage became available on the water in Falmouth Foreside, the few members took the plunge, purchased it for $15,000, and moved. The cottage, incidentally, sat on the site of a former power station which provided electricity for the trolleys that ran along the Foreside's Rt. 88 between 1899 and 1933 (see the Castle, p. 127).

64. Falmouth Town Landing

The Town of Falmouth has a large wharf with a float and paved launching ramp north of the Portland Yacht Club, opposite the northern end of Clapboard Island. The ramp can be used at all tides, but it is busy. At the height of the season, you may have wait, and parking will be scarce or non-existent.

By sea. The most direct approach to the landing is around the north end of Clapboard Island. The town float has 3 feet of depth at low and a docking limit of 15 minutes. You may be able to find the harbormaster (781-7317) here or in his skiff nearby, or you can reach him on channel 09.

By land. From Rt. 295N, take exit 9 onto Rt. 1N. Cross the Martin Point Bridge and take Rt. 88N to the right. After several miles, the Town Landing Market will be on the right. Turn right at the market. The landing is at the end of the road.

Ashore. Groceries, sandwiches, snacks, a pay phone, and a sense of history can be found a short stroll up the hill at the Town Landing Market. In the late 1800s, this market began as a tea room, then a restaurant, then an ice cream parlor. In the 1940s it became the market that it still is today.

65. Clapboard Island

As a harbor, the only protection Falmouth Foreside gets is from long, narrow Clapboard Island. While temptingly close, Clapboard is private, and exploring is not allowed.

Ashore. Clapboard holds two grand summer estates, a far cry from its modest value as timberland in the early days of settlement. Men from Richard Trelawney's fishing station on Richmond Island off Cape Elizabeth would make small-boat forays to the Casco Bay Islands to cut timber and saw it into lumber. On this island, they sawed—you guessed it—clapboards. On Stave Island (see p. 112), they cut barrel staves.

Clapboard was put on the map, literally, in 1651, when Massachusetts formally claimed "all the Maine land south of latitude N043° 43' 12" with the eastern point on Upper Clapboard Island in Casco Bay." This demarcation was relatively short-lived, because in 1677, Massachusetts purchased from the heirs of Sir Ferdinando Gorges the rest of his claim, extending all the way to the Sagadahoc (Kennebec) River.

On a hunting trip in 1897, Clapboard caught the eye of Henry Houston, a magnate of the Pennsylvania Railroad. In a single summer, he had his army of craftsmen build a huge 12-bedroom, 10,000-square-foot summer "cottage." They paneled it with Oregon pine and pinned it to the island with 13 massive granite fireplaces. Its granite wharf is on the island's southwest shore.

The ledges off the island's northeast end were the final demise of the salt schooner *Adalaide*, which had taken a terrible beating in a storm on her way to Portland Harbor. She managed to unload her cargo, but she was surveyed, found unsafe, sold at auction, and towed to Long Island where her fittings were to be salvaged. But while she was being stripped, another storm ripped her from her docks and drove her onto the ledges off the northeast point of Clapboard. The impact ripped her heating stove free, and the stove, which had been going for the salvage job, spilled hot coals and set her on fire. The tide eventually lifted her free and she sank about 1000 yards off Handy Boat. She now lies in 15 to 50 feet of murky water and is described by divers as a "crushed matchbox."

66. Sturdivant Island

Sturdivant Island lies just northeast of the Falmouth Town Landing, though it is part of the town of Cumberland. Sturdivant looks today the way it and many other Maine islands must have looked a couple of hundred years ago when they were first settled as subsistence farms. Its terrain rolls, with fields cleared to the south and a trim wood lot of hardwoods standing proudly on the crest to the north. A farmhouse and barn hunker down in the lee of a hill on the backside of the island. The only modern structures are the few cottages that dot the windward shore.

By sea. Flood and ebb currents run between Sturdivant and the mainland at an average maximum of 0.3 knots.

Ashore. The island is private, and landing is not allowed.

The Sturdivants were one of the early families to settle in Cumberland. Ephram Sturdivant was a sea captain who put to sea at age 12, and he was the first in Maine to import merino sheep from Portugal. Later he became a state legislator and senator.

67. Broad Cove

Broad Cove is just that—broad. It is also shallow. The mouth of the cove is more than a mile wide, open to all southerly quadrants with only a minimum of protection from Sturdivant Island. Inside the cove, the water never gets deeper than 15 feet at low, and most of it shoals into extensive mud flats.

The cove's shores are shared by Cumberland Foreside, on the west, and Yarmouth, on the east, and neither shore has good access to the water. At the high end of the tide, however, portable boats can be launched from the end of Town Landing Road in Cumberland.

By sea. The put-in is in the wide basin due west of the word "Broad" on the chart. The name Town Landing Road overstates it a bit, at least in modern times. You will need to carry your boats around the guard rail at the end of the street and down the bank to a muddy shore. This entire area becomes mud flats at low, so if you plan to return, read the tide tables and wear a watch.

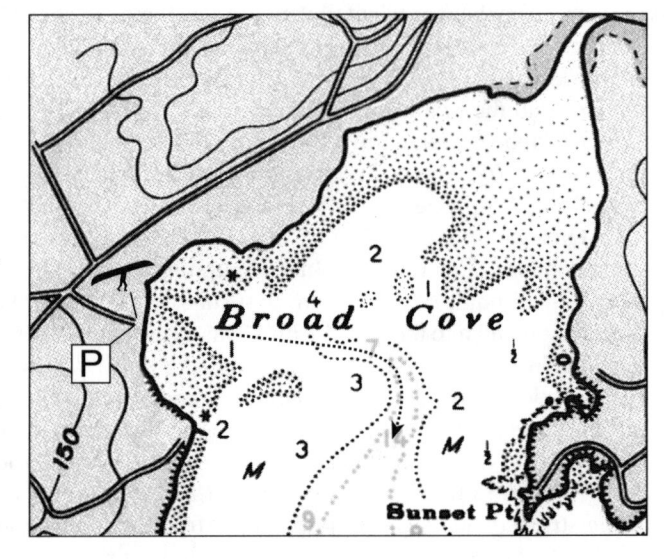

There is little to explore in Broad Cove itself other than a small estuary at the foot of the fields from beautiful Broad Cove Farms. From the put-in, though, easy excursions can be made to Basket Island or Great or Little Chebeague, all of which are visible.

Broad Cove has silted in over the years, but despite its shallowness, this was the center of Cumberland's shipbuilding. Shipyards here produced the 406-ton brig *N.M. Haven* in 1863, the 609-ton *Woodside* three years later, and the *Grapeshot*, a clipper that made one of the quickest roundings of Cape Horn on record.

On a fall night in 1780, the schooner *Rhoda* was anchored in Broad Cove, and all the crew had gone ashore except the anchor watch of two cabin boys, John Barr and Perez Drinkwater. (For more on the Drinkwaters, see Sandy Point, p. 86). Doubtless, captain and crew were making merry on shore leave, but in the morning they were sobered by the sight of the anchorage. The *Rhoda* was gone.

The captain and crew rounded up townspeople and weapons and an old sloop for the search. Soon they found the two boys off Chebeague Island's Deer Point in one of *Rhoda's* small boats. The boys claimed that in the night, a boat from an English cruiser had slipped the anchor of the *Rhoda* and put out for Monhegan.

The sloop sailed on in pursuit. Off Monhegan the crew spied their boat and pretended to be in distress. The ruse fooled the English, and the crew of the sloop boarded the *Rhoda* and reclaimed her. The next morning the sloop encountered another English cruiser off Seguin, and they managed to capture it and tow it to Portland where they exchanged it for "the more needed substantials of life."

By land. From Rt. 295N, take exit 10 onto Rt. 1N. In about four miles, Tuttle Road will cross Rt. 1. Pass under it and turn right, and turn left onto it. Where Tuttle Road meets Rt. 88, cross 88 onto Town Landing Road and follow it to the water.

Ashore. Parking is limited to the end of the road or along its shoulders.

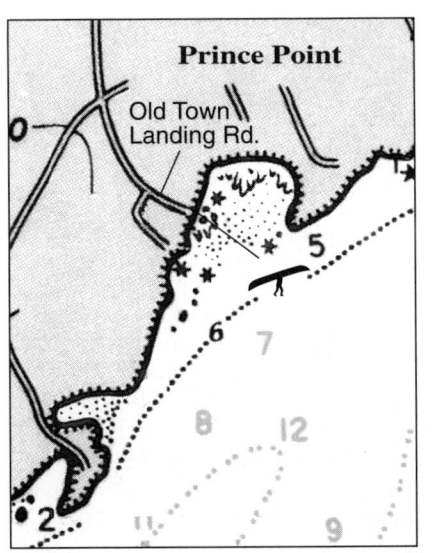

68. Prince Point

Prince Point separates Broad Cove from the unnamed body of water between Yarmouth and Cousins Island. A small and difficult launch site lies in the small cove between Prince Point and Drinkwater Point, at the end of a very steep, narrow, and rutted road. This is basically a local access point, used by nearby residents and clammers and is included here only for completeness or in case of emergency.

Portable boats can be launched here, and even light trailerables could be run down to the small beach if you had four-wheel drive and a lot of courage. Parking, however, is virtually non-existent along the narrow road.

By sea. This small cove nearly dries out at low. The put-in is marked on the chart by a ledge at the northern branch of the forked road. Beware of the rock a considerable distance off the point on the east side of the cove.

By land. From Rt. 88 in Yarmouth, follow Prince Point Road. It eventually seems to tee with another paved road, though the stretch to the right is actually the continuation of Prince Point Rd. Directly across the tee is the dirt Old Town Landing Road which leads, precipitously, to the shore.

69. Basket Island

Basket is a small island in the northern part of the Hussey Anchorage, sitting like a bullseye almost equidistant from Clapboard Island, Sturdivant Island, Cousins Island, and Great and Little Chebeague. The island is owned by the Nature Conservancy and managed by the Cumberland Mainland and Islands Trust and members of the Portland Yacht Club.

Basket is a beautiful wooded island, diminished only by the looming proximity of the power plant on Cousins Island. It makes a pleasant small-boat outing, not far from the mainland and within relatively protected water.

By sea. See chart next page. Beware of the large ledges projecting from the east side of the island. Upper and Lower Basket Ledges, each marked with a daymark, lie a good distance off the island and are good fishing grounds. The best approach is from the west, just north of flashing nun "4." Another option is to skirt the northern point of the island, pass between the island's northeast shore and the rocks shown just offshore, and land at the small beach by the ledge that projects from the island to the east. Sometimes there is even a small mooring here.

Ashore. Day visiting is allowed but no camping or fires. Beware of poison ivy in the interior. If you circumnavigate the island's rocky shores, you'll find several attractive pocket beaches where you can pretend you're a seal.

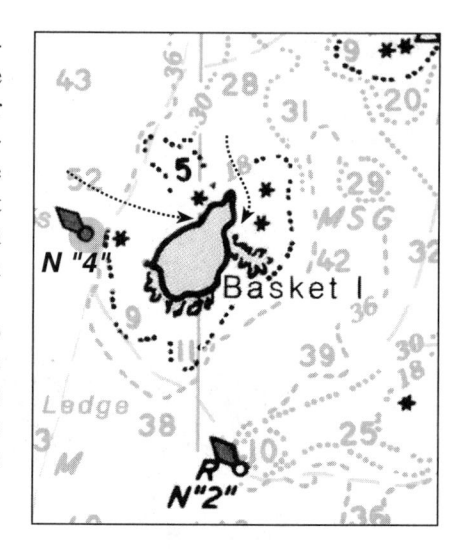

70. Cousins Island town float

Cousins Island can be identified from almost anywhere in Casco Bay, day or night, by the tall, blinking stack of the Wyman Power Station on its southern end. Ironically, since the power plant was built, the island has been distinguished not by its islandness, but by the fact that it is connected to the mainland by a long bridge. The bridge, however, gives boaters with portable boats the opportunity to drive farther out into the bay before launching at one of the island's several sites (see additional entries below).

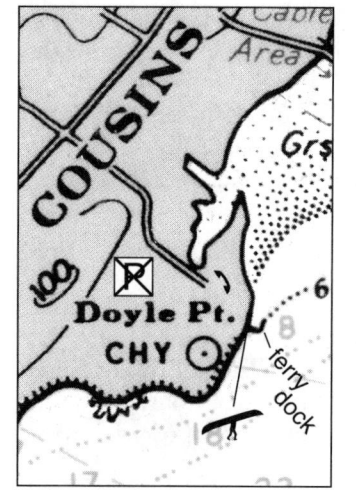

The main access to the water is the town wharf and float, at Doyle Point on the east shore. The wharf is also Chebeague Islanders' point of access to the mainland. Portable boats can be launched at the small beaches at the head of the wharf, but the wharf and the small road leading to it are busy when the Chebeague Island ferry lands here, and there is no parking at all.

By sea. The eastern side of Cousins is connected to Littlejohn Island by a causeway with shoal water on both sides of it. The town wharf is due south of the causeway, on Doyle Point.

If you land on the town float, be sure to leave its front face free for the ferry from Great Chebeague. Small beaches on either side of the wharf work for launching portable boats when there is no ferry traffic.

By land. From Rt. 95N, take exit 16 in Yarmouth and head north on Rt. 1. At the first light, take a right and follow it until it tees with Main Street in the center of town. Take Main, which is Rt. 88, to the right. Follow it out of town, under the highway bridge, past the harbor, and up a hill. Then follow signs to the left for Cousins Island.

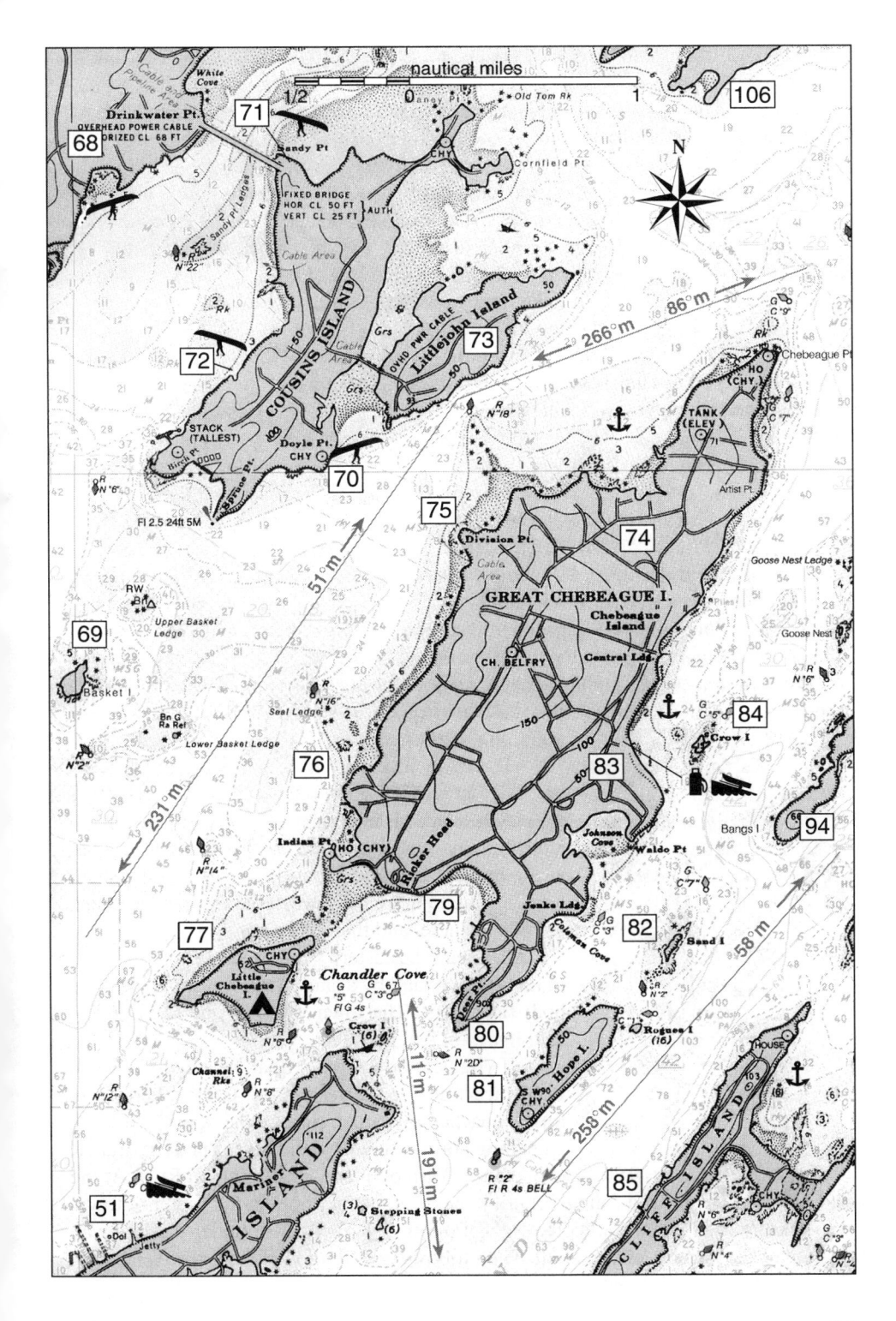

CASCO BAY

Once on the island, follow the main road to Wharf Road, the last possible left before the power station. The wharf is at its end.

Ashore. Cousins Islanders, like most islanders, are acutely aware of their island's limited resources. Parking is a particular rarity on Cousins, a situation aggravated by the fact that Cousins, which is part of the town of Yarmouth, is the point of mainland access for Chebeague Island, part of the town of Cumberland. There is absolutely no parking near the Doyle Point landing. In the past, Chebeague Islanders leased a lot on the point to the north with parking there for nonresidents at $8/day, but this is changing as the towns try to work out the parking problem. A small launching ramp projects from the Doyle Point lot, but it's reserved for the Chebeague Island Transportation Company. A pay phone is near the wharf.

The Indians lyrically called Cousins Susquesong (Littlejohn was called Pemasong), but their meaning has been lost. The less poetically inclined colonists called it Hog.

John Cousins was a man from the Royal River area with an impeccable reputation. In 1645, he bought the island directly from Sir Ferdinando Gorges via Gorges' agent Richard Vines. But at the time there was still some dispute over the original grants to the New World, so Cousins was careful enough to get another deed from Gorges' rival, the Rigbys, through their agent George Cleeves. Historians are unsure, though, why John Cousins wanted the island. Like many islands in the Bay, Cousins laid claim to a medicinal spring, one which would promote health, vitality, and longevity. But only two years after his purchase, Cousins sold half of the island to another settler, and when the Indian Wars of the mid-1670s scattered the Casco Bay settlers, Cousins, by then quite old despite the water, went to York.

Cousins may have built his homestead between Blaney's Point and Cornfield Point at the north end of the island. Evidence turned up at Cornfield Point suggests that it was cultivated long before white settlers arrived. Other parts had been wooded forever. In 1728, James Parker reported that Cousins had stands of massive trees, many of which were *six to eight feet* in diameter!

Eventually, a small farming and shipbuilding community established itself. The island once had a blacksmith shop and two small shipyards, one at Sandy Point, near Cornfield, and one near Birch Point, which is now dominated by the power plant.

71. Sandy Point

The west side of Cousins Island has two put-ins for portable boats, one at Sandy Point, hard by the bridge, and another on Madelon Point, to the south. Of the two, Sandy Point is easier. It has a longer carry, but more parking.

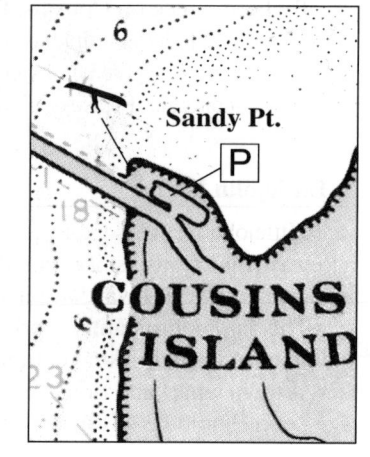

By sea. All of the water on the west side of Cousins is shoal. The channels beneath the bridge barely hold twelve feet at low, and north of the bridge the depth dwindles to six or less in a snaking channel, which may or may not be marked by sticks driven into the mud. Near the top of the tide, however, the whole area is wide and clear. Sandy Point Ledges, south of the bridge, are well marked by nun "22," and they show themselves at lower tides.

Sandy Point lies to the north of the bridge on the Cousins Island side, and despite the extensive mud flats near it, it is actually sandy. Launching boats here requires carrying them down a high embankment, but the wide path is well maintained as part of the Sandy Point Park, and its slope is gradual.

By land. See directions to Cousins Island, above. The parking lot for the Sandy Point Park is on the left just after you cross the bridge.

Ashore. Sandy Point Park is blessed with plenty of parking, though if you plan to leave your vehicle here for an extended period, you should probably inform the Yarmouth police (846-3333). A plaque here reminds you, lest you should forget, that the Cousins Island Bridge is actually called the Ellis C. Snodgrass Memorial Bridge.

In keeping with Cousins Island's legendary aquifer or perhaps by coincidence, one of the most renowned Cousins Island families was called Drinkwater. Their name still graces the charts where the bridge touches down on the mainland at Drinkwater Point. John Drinkwater, in addition to having two daughters, had either nine or 14 sons, depending on who is telling the story, and each son in turn became a master mariner and captain of his own square-rigger. Being Mainers of independent spirit, they found government regulations irksome, and they decided to strike back. One day they each sailed into Boston Harbor (some versions claim it was New York), and each vessel, registered from Cousins Island, Maine and commanded by a Captain Drinkwater, applied for customs clearance. Needless to say, it was a rough day for the fledgling bureaucracy.

72. Madelon Point

Madelon Point is not really much of a point at all, and it is unnamed on the chart. A small beach is jammed with fishermen's skiffs, gunwale-to-gunwale, and traps are loaded and off-loaded from the ledges. Portable boats could be launched here, but there is little room for strangers and less for their cars.

By sea. Madelon can be recognized by the boats moored off its small beach, south of the broad bight on Cousins' west side and just south of the 3-foot sounding.

By land. Once on Cousins, follow the main road. Madelon Point Road is the last possible right. Madelon Point has space for a few vehicles, but you won't make any friends if you block the drives of the nearby cottages or the access to the ledges where lobstermen load and off-load their gear. Please don't leave your car here for anything more than a short daytrip.

73. Littlejohn Island

Littlejohn Island is Cousins Island's smaller Siamese twin, connected at the hip by a causeway. Like Cousins, it is possible to drive to Littlejohn, but its small size, rugged terrain, and narrow causeway have helped it keep its feeling of a true, unconnected island.

This is predominantly a private island, with little to offer the boater other than a quick tour of a small island community and a glimpse of Great Chebeague through the trees. A town wharf and float hangs off the eastern side of the island, but parking is very scarce and should be left to the islanders.

By sea. Littlejohn is best seen from the water. You will be forced close along its eastern shore by red nun "18" that marks the string of rocks that run out from Chebeague's Division Point. Just south of the nun, there is a town dock, which can be used for limited docking if you want to explore by foot, but leave room for the joyous kids who often are taking the plunge here. Maximum flood currents can run up to nearly 0.5 knots to the northeast. Ebbs are only 0.1 knots to the southwest.

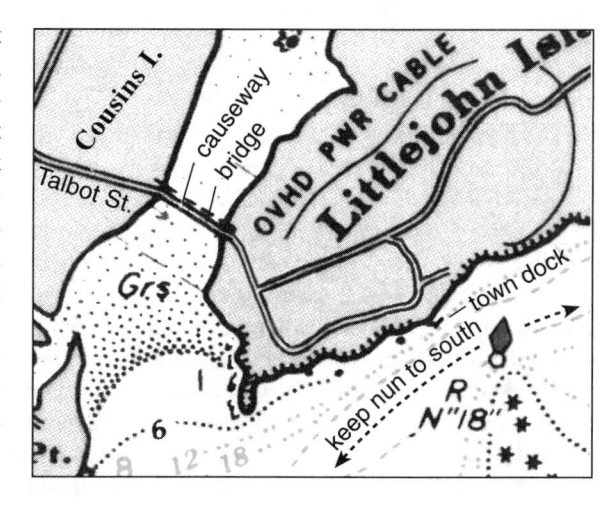

The causeway between Littlejohn and Cousins could be a possible small-boat put-in at higher tides, though boats would need to be carried across sections of marsh. There is a small turnout where you might be able to park on the Cousins Island side. The other end of the causeway actually has a wooden bridge section, so at high tides it is possible to circumnavigate either Littlejohn or Cousins. Beware, however, of strong tidal currents beneath the bridge. They can reach several knots and, surprisingly, they flood to the south and ebb to the north. The bridge's minimum vertical clearance is four or five feet.

By land. Follow the directions for Cousins Island, above, and then turn left on Talbot Street just after the small Cousin's Island Chapel and the Community House. There are only a handful of parking spots near Littlejohn's float, so this does not make a good put-in for portable boats.

Ashore. The road makes a tight loop around the southern end of the island, up steep hills and around tight turns, with no room anywhere to turn around. Please do not take this as a Sunday drive if you are pulling a trailer.

John Cousin got Littlejohn as part of the package when he bought Cousins in 1645. There is speculation that this smaller island was called Little John's Island to distinguish it from his larger one, but the name doesn't appear on a deed until 1732. Supporting the theory is the name of a spring, which is supposed to have been on the south end of the island, known as Little John's Drinking Place.

Littlejohn's small size and rocky nature attracted few early settlers, but eventually, near the turn of the century, a large portion of the island was sold to the Atlantic Improvement Company of Massachusetts, which laid out tight lots and built cottages and a small summer hotel.

CASCO BAY

CHEBEAGUE AND VICINITY

74. Great Chebeague Island ⚓ ⛳ 🛏 🍽 🚗

Great Chebeague is Casco Bay's largest island that is not connected to the mainland by a bridge. It stretches four miles from Chebeague Point at the northern end to southerly Deer Point, and it averages more than a mile across. With only about 350 year-round and 1,700 summer residents, the island feels all the more spacious.

Chebeague's sheer size lent itself to farming, with small communities clustered near the many steamer landings and wharves used for shipbuilding and fishing. Open fields and large woods still lend the island a rural feeling, and town businesses like the school, post offices, churches, and market are still not consolidated in one location, but instead are scattered over the whole island. Overlaid on this rural setting is Chebeague's rich "cottage industry," literally catering to a summer community, that has the grand Chebeague Island Inn and the Chebeague Island Golf Course as its centerpieces.

Chebeague is an easy destination for small boats and a pleasant place to explore by foot or bike, play an offshore game of golf, or have dinner at the Inn. Landing is easy at the stone wharf or at one of the several other locations listed below.

By sea. The ferry landing at the Stone Wharf is in the large bight opposite Littlejohn Island. The harbor is wide open to the north, but surprisingly protected from the summer southwesterlies. When approaching from the southwest, be sure to find and keep to starboard red nun "18" near the boats moored off Littlejohn to avoid the string of rocks that projects from Division Point.

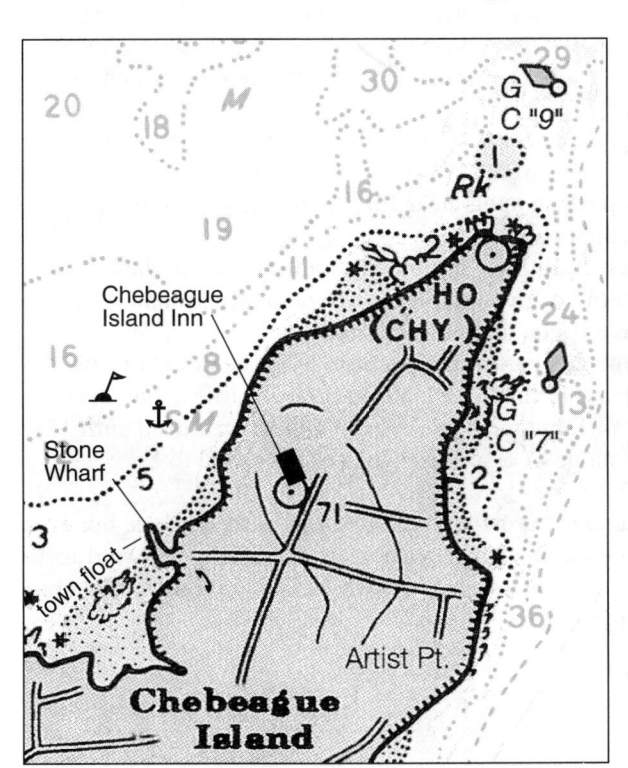

Docking time at the town float is limited. If you plan to explore for a while, drop your passengers off before anchoring or picking up one of the moorings maintained by the Inn. Or beach on the small beach to the north of the wharf.

You can also land at any of Chebeague's public beaches or at its boat yard. See individual entries below.

If you don't want to take your own boat, public transportation is available from Portland via Casco Bay Lines (774-7871) or from Cousins Island via Chebeague Island Transportation (846-3700).

89

A Little Hamilton in all of Us

In the 18th century, Chebeague Island was settled by Scots. Among them was Ambrose Hamilton, a real father of Maine. Hamilton purchased land from one of the island's two earliest settlers, Captain Waldo (see Division Point, p. 91) and sired anywhere from 12 to 26 children, depending on who is doing the counting, and as many as 194 grandchildren!

In the mid 1850s, the Hamilton clan began the lucrative industry of stone slooping. Beginning on a small scale, they built sloops to carry ballast stones to the many shipyards in Casco Bay. Gradually they built more and bigger boats to carry Maine granite for building, eventually evolving a design for stone sloops that averaged 60 feet in length with a 20-foot beam. They had a flat bottom so they could get close inshore or even be beached, and they were rigged with a large, single sail. Stone slooping reached its heyday in the years following the Civil War, when as many as thirty Hamilton boats carried Maine granite cut for building nearly every stone fort, breakwater and lighthouse from Eastport to Delaware as well as for the public buildings, bridges, and monuments of many of our great cities.

But these were the glory jobs. The bread and butter of the business, more often than not, was transporting what was called "grout," the rough stones which filled the cores of breakwaters and wharf cribbing. Most of Casco Bay's bedrock is gneiss, being made up of the same minerals as granite—mica, quartz, and feldspar—though formed under less pressure. The result is a stratified, softer, more slate-like rock. The Hamiltons mined the gneiss along the shores of many of the Casco Bay islands with drills, wedges, and dynamite.

An unconfirmed report ties one of the Hamilton stone sloops to the wreck of the passenger steamer *Portland*, one of the worst maritime disasters of its time. On November 26, 1898, the steamer left Boston loaded with Thanksgiving passengers headed for her home port of Portland. But that night or early the next morning, the *Portland* disappeared in a howling gale. Wreckage and bodies washed up on the beaches of Cape Cod Bay between Peaked Hill Bars and Highland Light, but none of it provided clues as to what happened. One hundred and seventy six lives were lost.

Almost fifty years later, in 1945, a scallop dragger from Rockland pulled up the bell of the *Portland*. Divers eventually thought they discovered the wreck, and the story surfaced that deeply embedded in the side of the *Portland* was the bow of the *Addie Snow*, one of the Hamilton stone sloops. The ships apparently collided in the blizzard and sank like, well, stones.

The stone business, however, was subject to the boom-and-bust cycles of the building trade. The resourceful Hamiltons branched into the West Indian trade, shipping dried fish and salted clams south and to Portugal. And those who stayed at home capitalized on the emerging discovery of Casco Bay Islands as resort destinations by going into the boarding business and eventually building a hotel.

The close-knit Hamilton clan settled the east end of the island. Their business enterprises became so diverse that money made by the Hamiltons usually was spent among the Hamiltons, and the area where they lived became known as Stingy Hill.

Many Hamiltons and their descendants are still on Chebeague. The saying among islanders is that "there's a little bit of Hamilton in all of us."

Ashore. There is a pay phone at the wharf, but no other public facilities.

The venerable Chebeague Island Inn (846-5155) sits atop the hill overlooking the wharf. This is a classic Maine summer inn. A huge porch wraps around the exterior, where guests can watch passing boats or golfers on the nine-hole course. Inside, a great room is warmed by a huge fieldstone fireplace, and shelves are filled with well-thumbed books. The Inn has both a restaurant (reservations recommended) and a pub, and on most Saturday nights there is music and dancing.

Chebeague has two other bed and breakfasts, the Chebeague Orchard Inn (846-9488), run by veteran sea kayakers who offer a 15% discount if you arrive by sea kayak yourself, and the Sunset House Bed and Breakfast Inn (846-6568), overlooking the second hole of the golf course.

The Great Chebeague Golf Club (846-9478) is open to the public and includes a challenging water hole. The tee is near the Stone Wharf, and the green is across a small indent in the harbor on what is locally called Noddle Head. If you miss the shot, you can retrieve your ball at low tide. Another unique feature of the course is the small family graveyard within its boundaries. There are no surviving relatives, so the graves are tended by club members.

The level roads make strolling, running, or bicycling easy. Bicycles can be rented near the Inn at Great Island Bike Rentals (846-6568), or you can take the Veterans' Taxi (846-4876). Doughty's Market and the post office are a mile from the Inn, to the right.

Chebeague has three public beaches: Chandlers Cove, at the south end of the island, Sunset Landing on the west, and just north of Division Point (see individual entries below).

The Abenakis settled on Chebeague and called it T'Cabie or Chebidisco, the Land of Many Springs. One of the largest was said to be near Central Landing, on the east side. Even as late as 1870, a small band of the Penobscot tribe summered on the island.

Early European settlement involved speculative ownership, including the original grant to Sir Ferdinando Gorges, and a piece owned by Colonel Thomas Westbrook (see Stroudwater, pg. 34), who was interested in the mast timbers growing there.

Chebeague Islanders made recent history in their battle to save the Pilot Crackers. Nabisco decided to discontinue making Pilot Crackers, a New England staple for accompanying chowder for over 200 years. Chebeague Islanders mounted a campaign to save the crackers from extinction and managed to convince Nabisco executives that Crown Pilot Crackers were a symbol of tradition and good taste. Swayed by the public outcry (and, no doubt, by the PR potential), Nabisco reinstated the crackers with a parade of boats to Chebeague and a generous contribution to the Chebeague Island Historical Society.

75. Division Point

Division Point is on the west side of Great Chebeague Island, opposite Littlejohn Island. Another less obvious point, unnamed on the charts, lies just to the north of Division, and a long line of rocks projects outward from it a long way over toward Littlejohn Island. A public beach is in the bight just north of this point.

By sea. Be sure you are on the north side of the rocks before you approach the beach. If you are approaching from the southwest, be sure to keep the nun "18" near Littlejohn to starboard. The area off the beach is a cable area, so you take your chances if you anchor out.

Ashore. Division Point was the point at which Chebeague was divided between its two earliest settlers, Captain Waldo and Colonel Waite. A line ran from Division Point south to Waldo Point, with Waldo on the northeastern half of the island and Waite on the southwest. Waite, however, was suspected after the Revolutionary War of aiding the English, and he was forced to abandon his 1400 acres on Chebeague. For years afterwards, his horses ran wild on the island until they died during a severe winter.

76. Sunset Landing

Sunset is also on the west side of Chebeague, just north of "The Hook"—called Indian Point on the charts—near Little Chebeague. Sunset used to be one of many steamer landings on Chebeague, when small communities clustered around each landing.

Sunset is now one of Chebeagues public "beaches," though the beach is little more than a tiny sand bar between shoreside ledges. It makes a pleasant rest stop or site for a sunset picnic, with unobstructed views to the west past Basket Island and the power plant on Cousins to Cumberland Foreside and Yarmouth. Most boaters, however, pass it up for the more expansive Little Chebeague, just to the south.

By sea. The chart shows a shoulder of land just north of Indian Point with several diverging roads. Sunset Beach lies at the end of the road that leads farthest to the west, just north of the small wharf, also shown. From the water, no beach is obvious, but its location can be identified by the concrete footing of the old ferry wharf that still perches on the rock. The sand bar beach is behind this ledge. Approach carefully from the northwest.

The waiting house that once perched on the wharf was swept away one winter gale. It washed ashore on Little Chebeague where it was moved and rebuilt into a cottage.

77. Little Chebeague Island

At low tides, Little Chebeague is connected to Great Chebeague at "The Hook" by a wide and rich sand bar. Sandy beaches run down the length of its eastern side and across its southern end, encircling its wooded interior. The island is owned and managed by the Maine Bureau of Parks and Lands and open to the public, though it is not served by any ferries. You are welcome to land and carefully explore or beach yourself on the sand.

By sea. The easiest approach is from Chandler Cove (see p. 94), on the east side of the island, where you can land on Front Beach or anchor off. The chart indicates that this is a cable area, so place your hook carefully. Beware of pilings from the old Navy wharf and the ledge near the 26-foot sounding on the chart. At high tide, a slight ocean swell will work its way in through Chandlers Cove.

The beach on the opposite, northwestern side of the island, the Back Beach, shoals very gradually. The shallows make landing difficult, and boats need to be anchored way out. But the broad expanse of sand warms the incoming tides for pleasant swimming.

Ashore. Low-impact camping is allowed, though the island has a reputation for ticks in early spring and summer and for a few dense groves of poison ivy. Do not camp in the fragile dune grass behind the beach. The island's interior has become quite overgrown, and it is difficult to explore. The remains of a few of the old summer cottages are still standing.

Little Chebeague's Back Beach and sand bar have been rich clam flats for centuries, and the native people who feasted here left behind deep middens of shells along the eastern shore. *The overgrown shell heaps are an important archeological site; under no circumstances should they be disturbed.*

In the latter half of the 18th century, the island was cleared by white settlers for pasture, and it supported a farm for over a hundred years along with various fishing activities including a fish-rendering plant along the shore. But with the end of the Civil War and the advent of the steamboat, the entrepreneurial spirit reached Little Chebeague. In 1865, the current farmer built a steamboat wharf, a hotel, and a "bowling saloon." Eleven years later, it attracted 2,000 Maine Civil War Veterans who camped in the pasture for their eleventh reunion.

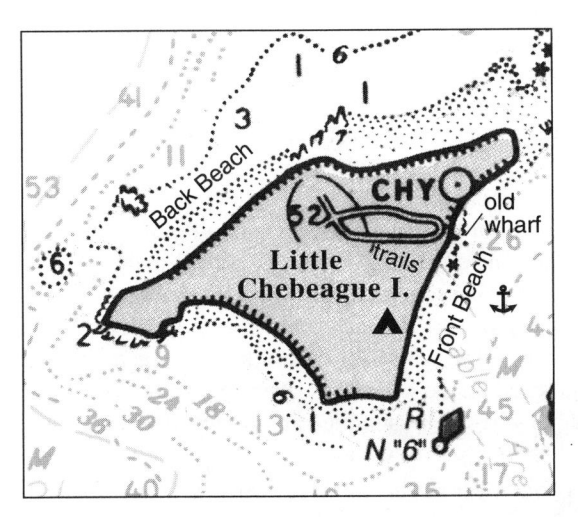

In the 1880s the hotel was enlarged and then sold to an investor from Chicago who expanded it into the exclusive 70-room Waldo. The Waldo boasted a dining room which could seat 150 and the modern luxuries of gas lights, running water, and even toilets. Clamshells were mined from the old Indian midden to pave the elm-lined "clamshell walk" from the steamboat landing to the hotel. Guests were served fresh vegetables and dairy products from the island farm, and a small cottage community grew up around the hotel and its social life.

One of the festivities was the Fourth of July celebration in 1893. It was to be the last. Somehow a firecracker landed on the Waldo's upstairs roof or inside the hotel's grand tower, which housed a water tank. Sparks touched off the dry wood, and a dense fog obscured the fire from neighboring islanders who might have been able to help. All the guests got out safely, but the hotel burned to the ground. Without the hotel, interest in the cottage community waned, and the cottages were either sold or abandoned.

In 1912, Harry Atwood chose Little Chebeague as the perfect place to demonstrate his "hydro-aeroplane," an early version of a seaplane. He trailered his invention from Lake Winnipesaukee to Portland, where he reassembled it on Custom House Wharf. Then he flew to Little Chebeague for five days of flights, the first flying in Portland's history. Unfortunately, the weather didn't cooperate, and of the five days, he was only able to fly for two. On one of those days, though, he flew out to Halfway Rock and back, a distance of about 15 miles, which he covered in 15 minutes, setting a new record for ocean flying.

Peaceful times ended in 1942 when the U.S. Navy took over the island for a firefighting school and a recreational center for its sailors. They built a new wharf, and the entrance to the Hussey Anchorage through Chandlers Cove was secured by scuttling several vessels between Long and tiny Crow Island and stringing submarine nets the rest of the way across. Fires were set and extinguished in the rusty metal structure that was built to resemble a compartment of a ship. It still stands on Front Beach.

Lobster bakes and baseball games were held on the island for the sailors. A wooden boxing ring was built, and a skeet-shooting range was set up near the Prichett Cottage, whose fallen chimney is still marked on the chart as "CHY."

In 1950, when the federal government no longer needed the island, it offered it to the State of Maine for a dollar. Frugal Mainers thought the price a bit steep and refused the offer. The island was sold at auction for $6,250 to John Absmeier, a New Yorker who also bought Jewell Island at the same time for a bargain price. In 1965 he announced a partnership with a contractor from Long Island, New York to develop the islands. They planned an airstrip, a hotel, and a cottage colony, but fortunately, nothing ever came of their grand plans. When Absmeier died twenty years later, his estate sold Little Chebeague to the State of Maine, which now forked out $155,000 for it.

You may happen to meet Richard Innes. Innes married a granddaughter of the island's farmer/caretaker and has devoted much of his retirement to researching Little Chebeague's history and keeping some of the trails clear of the choking bittersweet.

78. Crow Island

Casco Bay has several Crow islands. The smallest lies just north of Long Island, crowned only by a few bushes. Low tide reveals the remains of two wrecks between the two islands. These were the *Maude M. Morey* and the *Zebedee E. Cliff*, both four-masted schooners, built in 1917 and 1920 respectively. The government purchased the ships in 1942 to use as a breakwater as part of the war effort. They were later burned, so just the lower portions of the hulls remain.

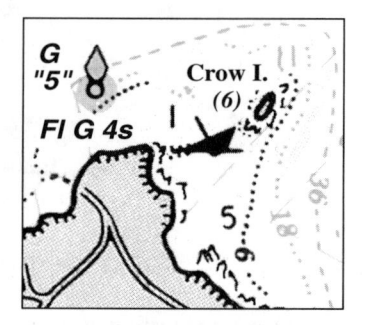

79. Chandler Cove

This large cove at the south end of Chebeague Island is where the Casco Bay Lines ferry docks from Portland. Chebeague Islanders still call the ferry "the steamer." The wharf is on the east shore of the cove, and it includes a public float.

By sea. The water at the float is deep at all tides, but docking is limited to 30 minutes.

Ashore. There is a pay phone at the wharf. The crescent beach at the head of the cove is one of Chebeague Island's three public beaches.

80. Deer Point

Deer Point projects southward from Great Chebeague toward the northeast tip of Long. The channel between Long and Chebeague snakes through Chandler Cove and around Deer Point.

By sea. The snaking channel is complicated by a strong tidal current, which floods westward and ebbs eastward and can set you out of the channel. An 11-foot spot off Deer Point is marked by nun "2D." Small boats can avoid the worst of it by keeping inside Chandler Cove. A chop usually makes up at the eastern end of the channel, between Deer Point and Long Island, when the ebb opposes the southwesterlies.

Ashore. On July 6, 1929 the fog was so thick that the Casco Bay steamer *Pilgrim* lost the channel and went hard aground on the rocks at Deer Point. It was high tide, and when it dropped, the huge three-story steamer was left high and dry. She was pulled off by a Coast Guard cutter eleven hours later and towed to Portland for repairs.

81. Hope Island and Rogues Island

Hope Island is high and round. A large white house stands on its southern end in stark contrast to the backdrop of dark spruce. It makes a good visual landmark for boaters to the south, but Hope and its little sidekick Rogues Island are private, and landing is not allowed.

By sea. The house's chimney is marked on the chart, and the southern end of the island is marked by flashing red bell "2." A tight channel cuts between the north end of Hope and Sand Island, marked by can "1" and nun "2."

Ashore. Please do not land. In 1914, a business tycoon from Philadelphia approached Great Chebeague aboard his private yacht. The yacht rolled in on the swells between Long Island to port and an intriguing high, wooded mound-shaped island to starboard. The island was Hope, and he bought it. The man was Senator George Elkins.

Elkins built a 24-room "cottage" high on the southern end of the island, and soon formed the Hope Island Club with the families of four other Philadelphia businessmen. Each spring, the servants would sweep away the cobwebs, and the families would move in. Jackets and ties were required for dinner, cocktails were served on the porch, and promptly at seven, everyone would file in for dinner at the 22-foot-long dining table. During the days, the families would tackle repair projects or tree work or picnic on their island getaway, nearby Rogues Island.

But sadly, few have either the money or the time to afford such a lifestyle today. In 1992, the descendants of the original Hope Island Club put the island on the market for $1.8 million, and everyone in Casco Bay who was familiar with the bold landmark of the prominent, white Hope Island cottage feared that Hope would fall to the pressures of development.

When the island was sold the following year, rumors circulated that the purchaser was actor Mel Gibson, who had recently discovered the Maine coast while filming *The Man Without a Face* on Deer Isle. The rumors turned out to be false. Instead it was bought by a private individual from New York state. The island now sports a massive new boathouse, new caretakers' quarters, endless stone walls, and a small chapel.

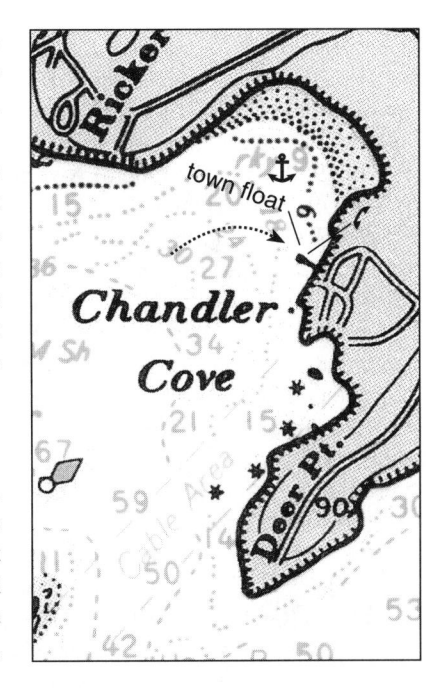

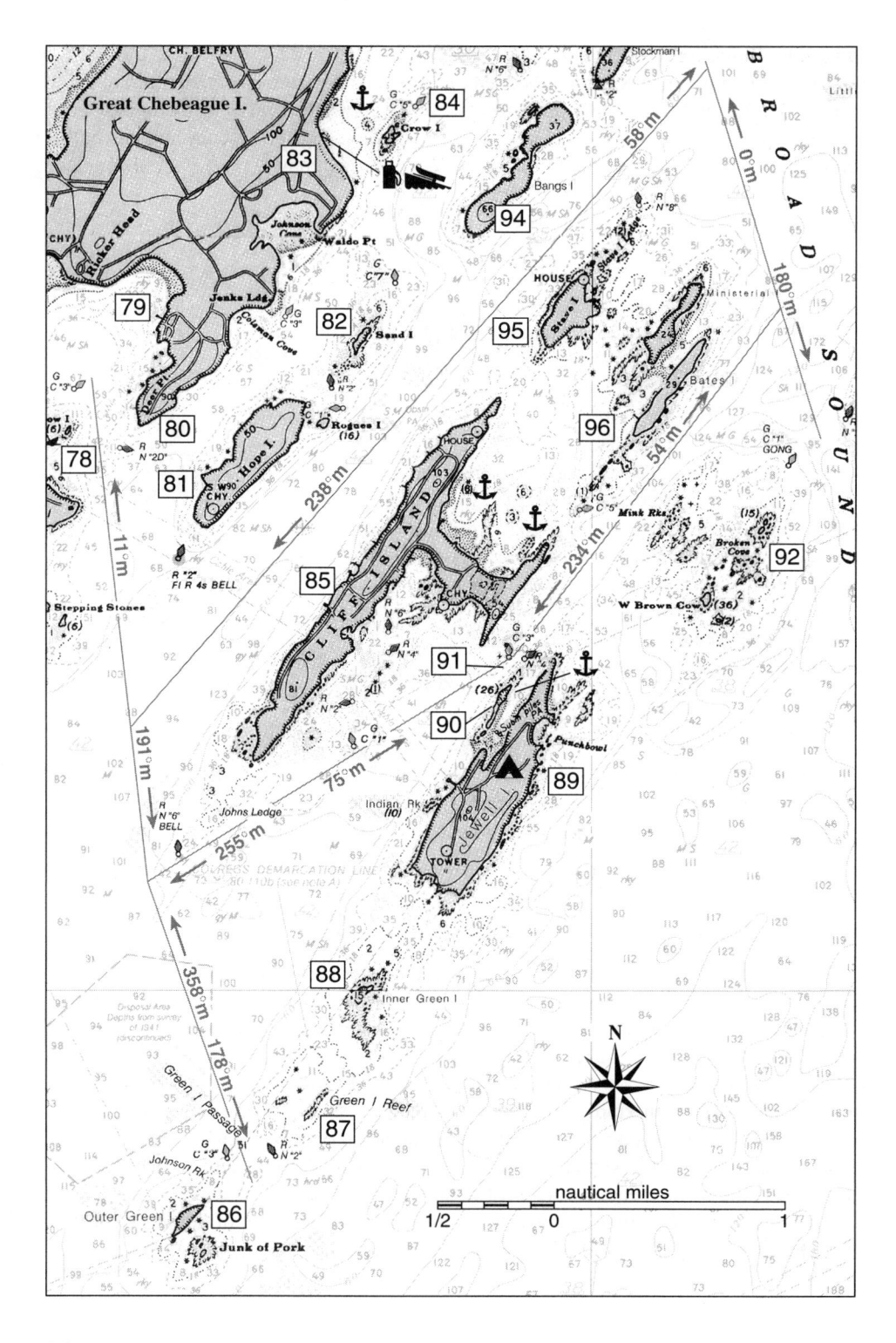

MAINE COAST GUIDE

Previous caretakers of the island claim that its interior holds some of the oldest cellar holes in Casco Bay, remnants of earlier settlers now long forgotten, and that the "cottage" was home to several ghosts who made their presence known by footsteps, thumpings, and other strange going ons, preferably when the generator had quit. The "cottage" was recently replaced by something more contemporary, much to the dismay of preservation-minded locals and the now homeless ghosts.

82. Sand Island

Sand Island is well named. This low mound lies just north of Hope Island, ringed by sand. It is private but well shared. On warm days, boaters often stop here to sprawl in the sun.

By sea. Don't let the island's sandy west shore fool you. It is still made of rock, and extensive ledges stretch off its north and south ends. The pair of moorings of the west side of the island belong to the owners, though many boaters seem to use them if they are unoccupied. Be prepared, however, to move your boat if you are asked to. If you anchor, be aware that the island is quite exposed and that the southwest winds will build in the afternoon.

Ashore. In season, sea birds may nest in the scrub at the center of the island. If so, leave the island to them.

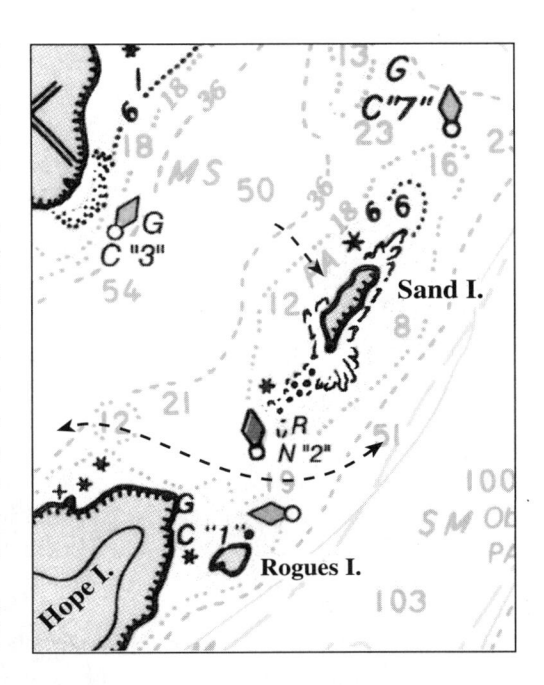

83. Chebeague Island Boat Yard

At first glance, an island seems like an unlikely place for a boat yard, away from dealers in bottom paint and rope and rigging and pieces of mahogany and teak. But then, few things are as important to islanders as boats. So it is at the Chebeague Island Boat Yard (846-4146).

This is a quiet but industrious place, where boats are hauled by marine railway and skidded to the field on cradles by tractor and where spring winds carry the hum of sanders and float boyhood dreams of the summer ahead on the water.

By sea. See chart next page. Chebeague Island Boat Yard sits in an obvious field on the east side of Chebeague, due west of small Crow Island. Gas and water is available at their floats, though at low the floats only have several feet of depth. If you are stuck for diesel fuel, delivery can be arranged by truck. The boat yard also rents moorings by the night.

Ashore. The boat yard has limited marine supplies. Doughty's Island Market (846-9997) is a short walk up the road to the right.

The beach to the north of the boat yard is Central Landing, where the steamers once stopped, and beyond that is the location of Fenderson's clam factory which cooked, shucked, and canned the island's bounty between the 1890s and 1920s. The clams were known all along the Atlantic seaboard as Chebeague Island Littleneck Clams, giving rise to a sense of island identity captured in the poem "Long Island for poverty, Peaks for pride. If it hadn't been for clams, Chebeague Islanders would have died." Workers went on strike in the 1920s, but they underestimated the stubbornness of the owner who, rather than give in to the striker's demands, closed the factory.

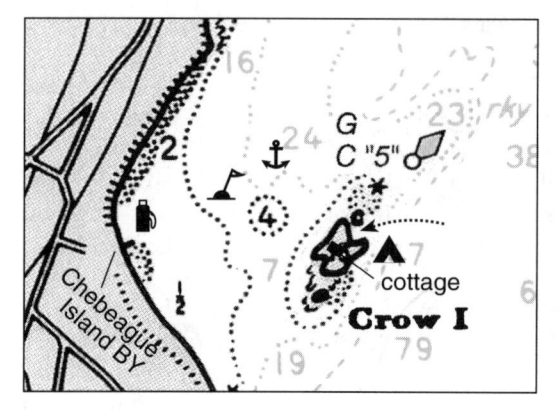

84. Crow Island

This tiny island lies just to the east of Great Chebeague, opposite the Chebeague Island Boat Yard. Yet despite its size, there is an almost perfect sense of completeness here. A small cabin nestles among a few staunch pines, the sun warms the ledgy shore, and oaks shade a grassy glade by a beach of white shell sand, all surrounded by the blue-black water.

Now the island is owned by the Maine Bureau of Parks and Lands and meticulously cared for by Chebeague Islanders and the Maine Island Trail Association. The cabin is swept clean and free of graffiti, and the pens haven't been borrowed from the logbook.

By sea. Bring boats in on the beach at the northeast end of the island in the lee of prevailing southwesterlies, or anchor to the west of the island.

Ashore. The cabin was once a summer cottage owned by a Chebeague Islander, and it originally was perched on the rocks closer to shore before it was moved to its present location. For many years, Crow has been a traditional picnic and excursion island for Chebeague Islanders. Please respect their privacy.

Camping is allowed, but low-impact techniques, including carrying off human waste, are a must for this island. Camp stoves rather than fires are recommended, and small groups and limited stays are encouraged. If another party is already on this small island, consider an alternate site.

THE OUTER ISLANDS OF WESTERN CASCO BAY

85. Cliff Island

Cliff Island is Casco Bay's outermost populated island. Year-round islanders work either on the island or they fish, or they commute for 45 minutes aboard the Casco Bay Lines ferry to jobs in Portland. The few island children go to school in one of Maine's last one-room schoolhouses.

This is a small, tight-knit community. Surprisingly, Cliff is still a part of Portland, though it feels a million miles from it. Visitors may walk the few public roads on this long, narrow island and get a feeling for living together and apart.

By sea. Cliff is in the shape of a distorted H that forms a well-defined crotch between the legs north of the crossbar, giving rise to one of its original names—Crotch.

Visitors have three possible places to land. The ferry dock and public float hangs off the island's west shore, but docking periods are limited. A small commercial wharf with fuel and a small store is in Fisherman's Cove, on the east side of the island, just south of the crossbar of the H, though you may have to pick up a mooring here. Or you can anchor or beach your boat north of the crossbar. Notice, though, that this area is divided down its middle by a long ledge. High tide covers the ledge and often allows ocean swells to work into the anchorage. At low, the water is shoal for a fair distance from the beach.

Ashore. You can't get too lost on Cliff. If you keep on walking, the road is bound to return to where you began. The main road that loops around the island is—surprise!—Island Avenue, and a couple of short cross streets shortcut across it.

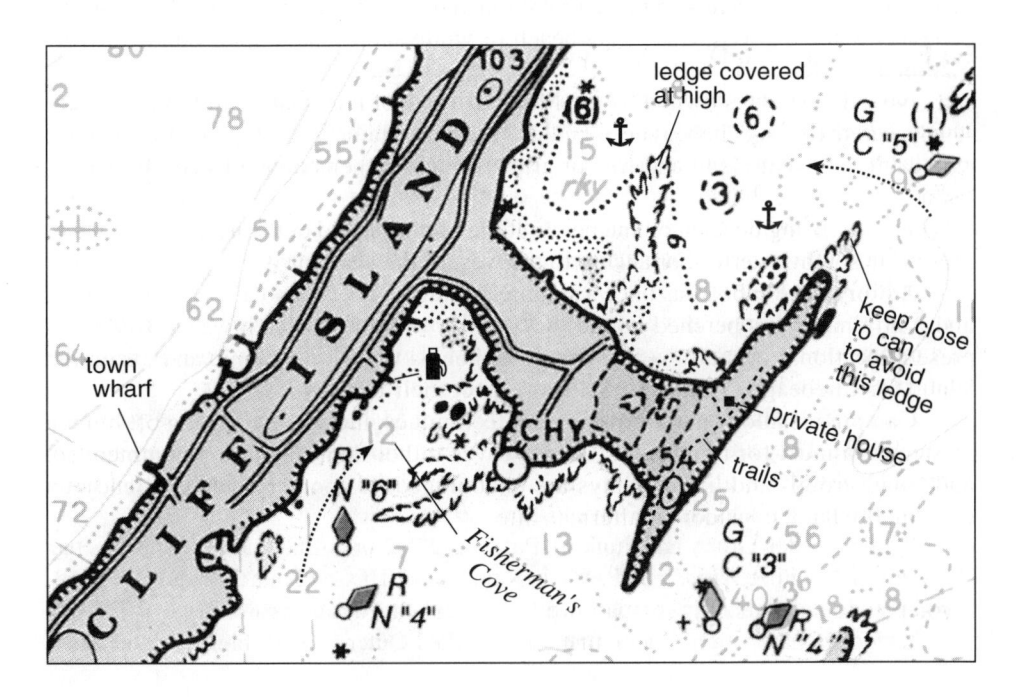

MAINE COAST GUIDE

The island's ball field is on the crossbar of the H. Also perched there, high on a cliffy bluff on the southern side, is the Pitkin's cottage that was used for the filming of *The Whales of August*, starring Bette Davis and Lillian Gish. Filming, however, ran behind schedule, no doubt due in large part to the logistics of shooting on an island, and in the true Hollywood fashion the bushes in this stunning location had to be sprayed with green vegetable dye to make them look "right."

Thanks to a generous gift, the cliffs on the eastern leg of the H are protected by the Oceanside Conservation Trust (772-8806) and are open to the public. A narrow trail leaves from the east end of the beach on the north side of the crossbar.

Crotch Island was largely settled by Seventh Day Adventists, who ran both the school and the church. They fished or farmed and the Sabbath was observed on Saturday. In the winter, the islanders turned to boat building, and over the years they developed a design for a fishing boat that became a classic, the Crotch Island Pinky, characterized by its high ends and a stern that tapered almost to a point.

Cliff's population crested in the early 1900s, with as many as 50 Portland High School students hailing from Cliff. But limited boat schedules severely curtailed higher education, and many families moved off-island when their children reached high school.

The same dilemmas exist today. In the face of budget cutbacks and declining enrollment, islanders have had to fight hard to keep their school open. A record low number of school children recently prompted a campaign to attract more year-round islanders to Cliff, preferably ones who will help keep the community alive with school children and jobs which they can manage from the island. The effort worked almost too well; for a while the island was overrun with the crews from national television and magazines and by visits from curious families looking for a simpler life.

86. Junk of Pork and Outer Green Island

Junk of Pork and Outer Green Island are the southern terminus of a series of ledges and islands extending northeast toward Jewell Island. Junk of Pork is a tall rock formation that was once part of Outer Green. It has an unbalanced appearance, as if the next storm will topple it into the sea. From the deck of a rolling ship making landfall after a long passage, it might fit the hallucination of a junk of pork sticking out of the sea. Perhaps that was its price long ago. Or perhaps somebody named it that because they just couldn't stand one more Hog Island.

Larger Outer Green is a bluffy, flat-topped island that sometimes appears to float on a mirage on the horizon like a mesa out West. This is a different frontier, an outer rampart of Casco Bay, with stiff breezes, crashing surf, and reeling gulls.

Both of these islands are owned by the State of Maine, but neither is easy to visit by small boat. They are exposed to wind and swells with no good places to go ashore. Their sides are sheer, and their tops belong to the birds. The few mariners that have visited these treacherous islands haven't done so by choice.

By sea. Outer Green and Junk of Pork lie 2 1/2 or 3 miles across unprotected bluewater from either Whitehead Passage, Ram Island, Hussey Sound, or Jewell Island. If you plan to make this trip, prepare well and pick your weather carefully.

A wooden navigation beacon that once marked Outer Green's highest point has long since disappeared, but the island would be hard to miss. High bluffs form its bold coast. Scattered rocks pepper the surrounding deep water, as shown on the chart, often attracting bluefish and stripers. Green Island Passage, to the north, is well marked (see Green Island Reef, below).

Ashore. Landing on Outer Green is not recommended. These high bluffs have long been breeding grounds for seabirds. Junk of Pork is the only place along the Maine coast where storm petrels (commonly known as Mother Cary's Chickens) come ashore to nest. Please do not land during nesting season, if at all.

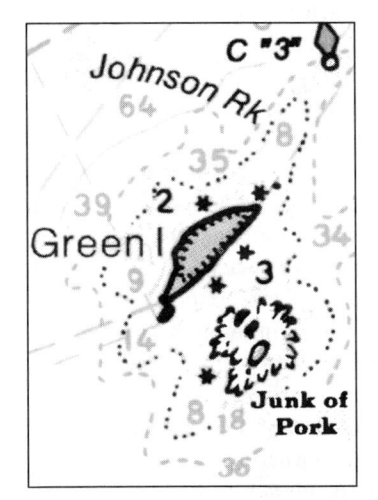

Outer Green played a role in the history of Jewell Island. When the settlers, holed-up in a garrison there, ventured to Outer Green to harvest corn they planted, Jewell was attacked by Indians (see Jewell Island, p. 103). Modern historians, however, doubt that corn would have been planted on Outer Green. More likely, the settlers would have planted on Jewell itself, or returned to their own fields, or planted closer to Jewell, on Inner Green, perhaps.

In a winter storm on January 12, 1891, the three-masted schooner *Ada Baker* blew out her sails and was wrecked on the reefs on the east side of Outer Green. Her foremast toppled onto Junk of Pork and her crew of six managed to scramble to safety.

The U.S. Revenue Cutter *Woodbury* had been waiting out the gale in Rockland Harbor, but when the storm eased up, she steamed out on her rounds of aiding mariners in distress. In the early afternoon, she sighted a signal from Junk of Pork and discovered the crewmen. The breakers were still about 30-feet high, pummeling the rocks, and the *Woodbury* could not approach. She stood offshore, hoping that the sea would abate enough to drift a line to the rock to pull the men to safety. But night fell. The *Woodbury* steamed to Portland and commandeered dories from a fishing vessel and recruited reinforcements from the Cape Elizabeth Lifesaving Station. They returned at dawn. The wind had backed to the west, and all six men were rescued.

One of the last visitors to this island—though from the tales, he has visited many others—was a hermit who lived here alone for years except for several dogs. One winter a severe winter storm hit the coast, and in its wake, fishermen went to the island to check on the welfare of the hermit. All they found were some torn clothes and the skeleton of a dog, providing a feast for speculation about whether the man ate the dogs, or the dogs ate the man.

87. Green Island Reef

Green Island Reef is the spine of the ledge between Outer and Inner Green Island. In total, it presents almost a mile of merciless rock broadside to the prevailing winds. However, the most-remembered tragedy here was not swept onto it from the sea but fell from the sky.

Soon after World War II, Cliff Island lobstermen began to find pieces of aircraft wreckage in gear they set off the reef, and in 1960, a large fragment was recovered and brought ashore. A Frenchman visiting Cliff at the time felt sure he knew what they had found.

Shortly before Charles Lindbergh flew the Atlantic, two Frenchmen had attempted the same feat, but in the reverse direction. The fliers, Nungesser and Colie, and their plane, *L'Oiseau Blanc* or "White Bird," had disappeared without a trace, though some believe that it was last heard from as it passed over Seguin. Now, here was wreckage of what might be their plane, proof positive that the French had conquered the Atlantic before Lindbergh.

The speculation, despite its hopeful press coverage in the *Paris Match*, was just that—speculation. At the request of historian and flying enthusiast Edward Rowe Snow, the fragment was analyzed and found to be from the World War II era.

Years later, the mystery of the wreckage was thought to be solved. When the United States finally committed itself to an involvement in the war, nineteen squadrons of Royal Navy pilots came to the Brunswick Naval Air Station between 1943 and 1945 to train in Corsair fighters. In the middle of a snowstorm, one of the pilots radioed the Portland Airport that his plane was out of control and that he was bailing out. A Coast Guardsman stationed at Halfway Rock heard a stuttering engine, and then nothing. The plane was thought to have gone down a mile and a half southeast of Jewell. At the time, neither it nor the pilot was found, but the recovered fragment suggests that the crash might have occured farther to the west. No trace has ever been found of *L'Oiseau Blanc*.

By sea. This is no place to be in any size boat in foul weather or when a sea is up. Green Island Passage is a narrow but deep cut through the reef. It is well marked, but strong tidal currents through the passage can set boats to either side, toward the breaking foam.

The same currents make the rocks and ledges of Green Island Reef, along with the shores of Outer Green Island, excellent fishing grounds for stripers and bluefish.

88. Inner (Little) Green Island

Inner Green, or Little Green as it is sometimes called, is smaller and much lower than Outer Green and a much easier rampart to visit. There is, however, very little reason to do so. Like its bigger brother, Inner Green is state-owned, treeless, and home to nesting birds. But because it is low and just a stone's throw from Jewell Island, it feels less exposed.

By sea. The west side of Inner Green faces away from the ocean swells, and the northwest shore slopes to a rocky beach. Beware of the submerged rocks shown on the chart to the north.

Ashore. You will probably want to restrict your visit to the rocky fringe around the perimeter of the island. The center is low scrub, rocky, and birdy.

After a severe storm in February, 1861, the waters off Inner Green were littered with puzzling wreckage. The *Eastern Argus* reported "a lot of knees, dunnage plank and deck planks together with a beam with four boat lashings on it, two of which had been cut by an ax; a lot of hard bread, now much soaked, and part of the top of a medicine chest with the word 'Broadicia' marked on it, together with sundry ships articles apparently belonging to a vessel of about 300 tons." A piece of a chart was also found, with courses marked on it from the Straits of Gibraltar. Inquiries, however, revealed that the 346-ton British bark *Broadicia* had cleared from New Orleans on December 2 the previous year, bound for Glasgow, where she was laid up.

During the same storm, another boat, the British bark *W.H. Jenkens*, had been wrecked on Cushing Island Point (see p. 53). All hands were saved, but the ship broke up. Upon questioning the captain and crew, it was discovered that the *W.H. Jenkens* had been outfitted with secondhand equipment from the retired *Broadicia*, and that, much to everyone's relief, a second ship had not gone down.

Another mystery washed up in 1919 when a large, 120-foot stern section of a ship came ashore along with tell-tale wreckage and cargo, including barrels of molasses and pork. More wreckage was found on Little Bull Ledge, just east of Ragged Island (see p. 201). A hatch was discovered with numbers and letters on it which led to the identification of the wreck as the *Lohocla*. The next day its forward section was found off Saco Bay by fishermen from Biddeford. The bodies of her captain and crew were never found.

Sailors are a superstitious lot and quickly attributed *Lohocla's* bad luck to her cavalier name, "alcohol" spelled backwards. The ship was only one year old.

The hulk remained on Inner Green for more than a decade until a Cliff Island fisherman burned it during the Depression to salvage her iron fittings and fastenings as scrap.

89. Jewell Island

Jewell is a large, magnificent island in the outer row of islands in the center of Casco Bay, as mysterious as it is beautiful. The Maine Bureau of Parks and Lands manages it as an undeveloped state park, but it can only be reached by private boat. It has a small harbor and several beaches of sand and gravel interspersed with cliffy shores. The interior is wooded, with numerous clearings for campsites and trails that lead to tunnels and towers, spooky remnants of a major World War II gun battery.

The island's allure, however, has worked its charms on plenty of boaters, in vessels of all sizes. On a busy summer weekend, the little harbor will be packed with yachts and runabouts hanging on precariously short scope. Kayaks and dinghies will be pulled up on the beaches, and the campsites will be staked out early. Jewell, more than any other island in Casco Bay, runs the risk of being over-used.

By sea. See chart, p. 105. Jewell lies due east of Cliff Island. Its small harbor is formed on its west side near the north end, between Jewell and Little Jewell Island, also known as Harbor Island. Deep water extends in as far as two pilings in the southern end of the harbor, a short way past the small cottage on Little Jewell. One of the pilings gets just barely submerged at the very top of the tide, so if you only see the top of one, proceed cautiously. Beyond the pilings, the water shoals rapidly. At low, a sandy bar stretches from Jewell to Little Jewell.

The harbor is exposed from the north and, to a lesser degree, the southwest. Gusty afternoon southwesterlies can blow through the cove, but the bar at its southern end breaks practically all of the sea, depending on the tide.

If you anchor in the harbor, be sure your anchor is well set. The holding ground is good mud, but you will probably have to hang on a short scope to limit your swing and leave room for other boats. Because everyone else is also on short scope, good blows from the southwest often wreak havoc here.

Deep-draft cruising sailboats need to anchor along the centerline of the cove from the pilings northward. Smaller boats can work their way farther in. Some even tie off to the pilings, but you should use caution in doing this—one powerboat caught a bolt on its small bowsprit on the top of the piling as the tide dropped. Its owner—I won't name names!—was camping on the island, and in the morning he woke to the stunning sight of his 24-foot boat standing vertically on its transom.

Jewell has several beaches where beachable boats can land. The most dramatic and difficult is Surprise Beach (see sidebar, p. 106), at the north end of the island, just north of the Punchbowl on the chart. Approach west of the long offshore ledge, which is often frothing with swells. The same swells may be rolling onto the beach, making landing—and leaving—difficult.

The sea has worn the southern end of the island into several cobbly beaches between the spines of ledge. Swells can make landing dangerous except in calm conditions.

The remains from an old wharf project from the west side of the island, and a sandy beach lies just to its south. The fill for the wharf is now a grassy area which makes a wonderfully open but exposed campsite.

Finally, some of the easiest beaches to land on are at the head of the harbor or against the ledge on the harbor's east side.

Ashore. From the harbor, a trail leads directly across the island to the lagoon-like Punchbowl, on the east. At low tides, a ring of ledges encircles a broad crescent beach and a pool of water, which gets warmed by the sun. The lone sentinel on Halfway Rock winks offshore. Curiously, red pine roots that periodically get exposed in the beach are thought to be 5,000 years old, though red pine has always been considered a non-native species.

Other trails lead south to the elaborate ruins of a World War II gun emplacement. A large gun was erected on its southern end, and aiming towers, bunkers, mess halls, generator buildings, and roads were built inland.

You can carefully climb to the top of a concrete observation tower and gasp at the view of Casco Bay in its entirety. On clear days you can make out Mount Washington in New Hampshire. The round pads poured in the floors mounted observation telescopes which took fixes on enemy ships or periscopes and, together with eleven other such towers, helped aim the long range guns that guarded Portland Harbor from Two Lights, Peaks Island, and Jewell. Thankfully, no shots were ever fired. In 1942, a German submarine surfaced and was spotted off Jewell Island, and it was pursued and attacked by destroyers. Its exact fate, though, is unknown.

Farther along the path, past collapsing tar-papered barracks, you will find an enormous concrete circle with a hole in the middle for Jewell's twin gun emplacement. The six-inch guns could fire a 100-pound shell as far as 15 miles. Dripping concrete tunnels lead underground into the bunker with massive, rusting doors, open floor pits, and tunnels branching to unknown destinations, all in a blackness thicker than ink. If spelunking runs in your blood, bring a flashlight, but please be careful. This is not a convenient place to have an accident.

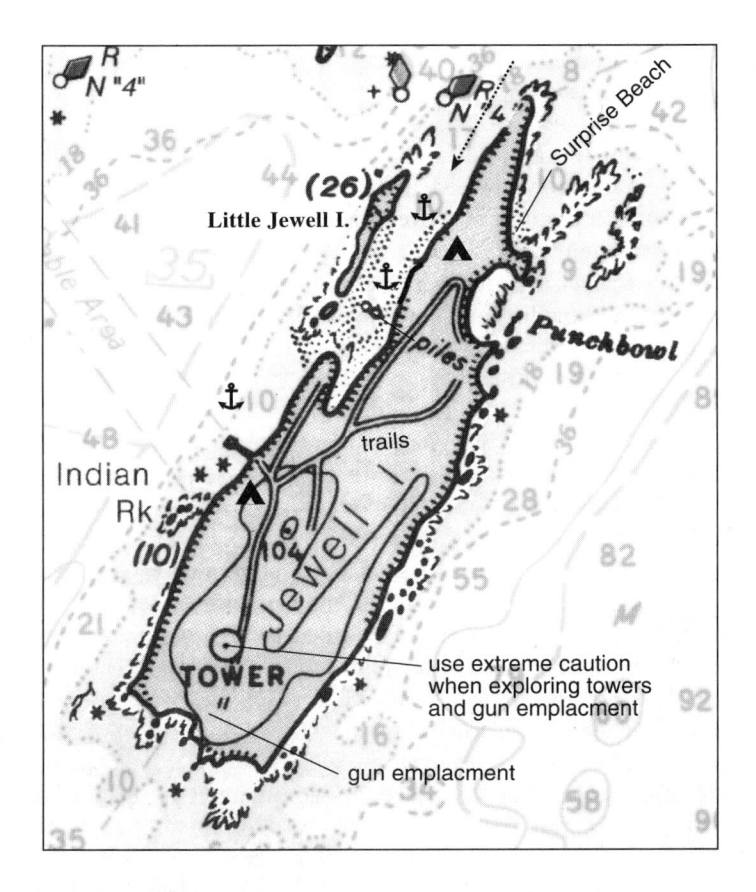

Camping is allowed on Jewell. No reservations or permits (other than fire permits) are required and no fees are taken. Yet these privileges will only continue as long as campers are considerate and careful. Please use only existing clearings for campsites, and use the several nearby outhouses (bring your own TP) and keep them clean. Also please respect your neighbors by keeping your voices down.

In recent years, the Maine Island Trail Association has assumed much of the on-site management of Jewell. Volunteers have built the outhouses and placed fire rings near the campsites to stem the proliferation of fire sites and keep the fire danger in check. If you plan to have a fire, please use the rings. Please do not cut firewood on the island. Gather it instead, or, better yet, bring it with you, along with your fire permit. Be sure, of course, that your fire is thoroughly doused before you leave.

And don't be surprised if you meet some of Jewell's many ghosts.

Strange tales of horror and mystery begin with the early settlers. George Jewell, of Saco, used the island as a fishing station, where he dried and salted his catch. After years of squatting on the island, he eventually purchased it from the Indians in 1637. But he lived on the island only a few years before slipping into Boston Harbor in a drunken stupor and drowning.

In 1676, during the worst of the Indian Wars, settlers from Harpswell and nearby islands fled to a garrison they built on Jewell, but even this offshore outpost couldn't protect them. A raiding party of Indians landed at the beach north of the Punchbowl, and a bloody battle ensued with the exiled settlers. One of the victims was James Lane, from the Cousins River (see Lanes Island, p. 121). Another, Richard Potts of Potts Harbor (p. 155), had to watch his wife and children being carried away.

Surprise Beach

During the 1676 attack of Jewell, maurading Indians landed most likely at the beach north of the Punchbowl, thereafter known as Surprise Beach. The chilling fate of the exiled settlers is described a year later:

When the fore said exploits were done by the Indians in and about Casco Bay several of the English removed to Jewell's Island where they hoped to be more secure from the Indians, but their barbarous enemy finding so little resistance made against them on the mainland, a considerable party of them came with their canoes to destroy that island about 3 weeks after the afore mentioned mischiefs. There was a fortified house upon the said island where the English that either kept upon the island or repaired thither, hoped to have secured themselves, but at that time when the Indians assaulted the place many of the English were absent, few left in the garrison, but women and children, some were gone to other places to fetch Indian corn others were in a boat employed about fish. amongst whom was one Richard Potts with two more.

The wife of said Potts was washing by the waterside where she was surprised with her children and carried away in sight of her husband who was not a little distressed with that sad spectacle, but was not able to afford any relief either to wife or child, although one of the children spying his father in his boat ran into the water calling for help. But an Indian ran after him to catch him up. The poor man in a great agony, being within half a shot, was about to have fired upon the Indian but then fearing he might wound his child, which the villain had laid hold of, he forbore, rather suffering him to be carried away alive, then be exposed to so manifest danger of his life or limbs, by shooting at the Indian.

It is said that some of the Indians were killed by them in the garrison: They speak of a lad it is said that at one shot killed two or three of them. Some guns were found afterwards under the fort, which were supposed to have belonged to some of the Indians that were killed. Some that were abroad when the fort was assaulted desperately broke in through the Indians, whereby at the last many of the people were preserved, some flying away from Jewell's Island in a canoe toward Richmond Island. They met with a ketch to which they made known the distress the people were in. Who there upon went to the place, and took in all the people they found there, and carried them off to a place of more safety. Yet were there several persons said to be killed and carried away at that time. Viz 3 men who were known to be killed, two women and two children that are supposed to be yet alive though in the enemies power.

From Hubbard, 1677, reprinted in
History of Jewell Island Maine,
by Peter Benoit, 1996

Title to the island was eventually acquired by a Colonel John Tyng. Tyng, in his later life, became convinced that he would return to earth exactly one hundred years after his death, and he built an elaborate, baize-lined coffin for the voyage. Until then, he put it to good use storing dried beans. He specified in his will that the lands he leased out in Dunstable, Massachusetts would revert to the leasee, Tyng himself, in 500 years. And Jewell was to pass through a specific line of succession, presumably so Tyng could assume ownership upon his return. His heirs, however, remained unconvinced. When Tyng died in 1797, he left Jewell to his great grand niece and her father. Amelia Dolliver was blind, but after ten years she could see that Tyng was not, in all likelihood, going to return, and they sold the island.

Jewell eventually fell under the long tenure of Captain Jonathan Chase. Chase has been described by more fanciful historians as an unscrupulous sea captain and smuggler. In fact, he was probably just a fantastic story-teller who fancied a nip now and then. He claimed to have been captured by pirates in the West Indies, and there may be some truth to this. Less believable is his story that the pirates, being staunch Masons, freed Captain Chase when he, being an ardent Mason himself, gave them secret Masonic signs. Chase retired to Jewell, where he built a house at the head of the harbor and a farm.

After an October hurricane in 1846, Captain Chase made the gruesome discovery of the corpses of five sailors and a ship's boy, washed ashore on the east side of the island from the wreck of their mackerel schooner, the *Active* of Castine. Chase, whose own son had been lost at sea nine years earlier, had the sad task of retrieving and burying the bodies. He placed them in a wooded glen near the head of his southwest field and marked the graves with rock slabs. Peter Benoit's marvelous *History of Jewell Island* contains a blurry photgraph of the crude gravestones jutting at odd angles from the forest floor. The field ran from the southwest shore of the island toward its center, but most of it has been reclaimed by spruce. The gravesites have disappeared.

Chase hired a Cliff Islander, Sam Pettengill, to help him with the farm and to be a caretaker in his absence. With inspiration from the island's name and the mysterious graves, Chase and Pettengill are likely responsible for the many tales of pirate loot buried on the island.

One of the tales, probably inspired by the *Active*, involves a pirate ship getting wrecked on the ledges of nearby West Brown Cow (see p. 110). The pirates managed to get the treasure into their dories and row it to Jewell, where they sank it in caverns near the Punchbowl and covered it with huge rock slabs.

Another tale recounts the arrival on Jewell of a stranger from St. John, New Brunswick, who claimed he had a map that pinpointed the burial place of Captain Kidd's treasure. He said the map was given to him by Kidd's personal servant, whom he had befriended, at the pirate's deathbed.

But the man from Saint John had not brought along a compass, so, after much haggling, he engaged the services of a local skipper who had a good compass but a reputation for honesty that deviated from the straight and narrow—none other than Captain Chase himself. They were seen setting out together with the map and compass and picks and shovels.

The skipper was seen again several days later before he departed for a trading voyage. However, the man from St. John was never seen again. Before long the islanders could no longer stand their curiosity, and they decided to do a little digging themselves. They combed the island and discovered a freshly dug hole with an imprint at its bottom of something that looked like a chest. The man from Saint John, they assumed, had found the treasure and quietly stolen away.

Many years later, so the story goes, long after Chase had passed on, a hunter on Jewell made a gruesome discovery. Wedged in a crevice between some rocks, he found a weathered human skeleton. Even though all its features and clothes had rotted away, the skeleton was identified by a silver ring and some brass buttons as the man from Saint John.

Chase's reputation was sealed many years later, after his heirs sold the island in 1882 to the McKeen family, descendants of the first President of Bowdoin College. When they were renovating and expanding Chase's farmhouse, they discovered an alcove that contained some empty liquor bottles. Chase had been on the island when the Quaker Joshua Dow was elected as the Mayor of Portland on the platform of temperance. Soon after his election, Dow managed to pass a prohibition bill in Maine, one of the hardest drinking states in the Union. The McKeens had a good sense of humor and intrigue, and from the time of the discovery of the bottles they called the house "The Smugglery," and Jewell Island's harbor became known as Smuggler's Cove. The fact that one of the McKeen girls inadvertently found a human skull on a beam in the basement when she was playing hide and seek only put icing on the cake.

This branch of the McKeens were wealthy New Yorkers who lived in Brooklyn and retired to Jewell as rusticators and, some would say, eccentrics. The family was known to raise some of their farm fowl in their Brooklyn apartment in the winter and then ship them with their baggage on the train to Maine. They kept two stubborn mules on the island, Jack and Jill, which were wryly called "jack horses" by the island caretaker. And it was said that once when a calf fell down the island well, it wasn't missed until the water went bad.

The McKeen family lost their summer home to fire in 1911. They had another built on the same site, but many years later, the house and most of their land was taken by eminent domain for the coastal defense battery during World War II. It suffered from neglect and vandalism, and after the war, it, too, went up in smoke.

When the government deemed the island surplus, if offered it to the State for $1, which Maine legislators, being careful with their taxpayer's money, thought was too steep. The same New Yorker who bought Little Chebeague also bought Jewell at auction. His estate sold it to the State of Maine twenty years later for $200,000. It only takes one trip to Jewell to know that even at that price, it was a bargain.

90. Little Jewell Island

Little Jewell Island forms the western flank of Jewell Island harbor. At low, a sand bar connects the two at the harbor's southern end.

Jewell Island is an undeveloped state park, and its harbor and shores are busy with pleasure boats of all kinds. Little Jewell, however, is private, with a small brown cottage at its center.

Stanley Cushing was known as Hikey to his fellow Cliff Island lobstermen. In the early 1950s, he had moved off Cliff to Portland, but he still fished the Cliff Island waters. He built the small cabin on what was then called Harbor Island so that in the summer months, his wife and children could join him out on the bay.

The pleasure, however, was short lived. On September 29, 1958 some Cliff Islanders noticed Hikey's boat running in erratic circles before it beached itself on the sand beach in the northeast crotch of Cliff Island. Hikey, who had been fishing alone, was caught in the potwarp that trailed astern, and attempts to revive him were unsuccessful.

By sea. See Jewell Island above.

Ashore. Hikey's small cabin is still maintained by Hikey's descendants. If residents are here, please respect their privacy and do not land on the adjacent beaches.

91. Cliff/Jewell Island Passage

An unnamed, deep-water channel runs between Cliff and Jewell Island, marked at its tightest spot by can "3" and nun "4," just before the mouth to Jewell Island Harbor.

In late August, 1863, in the middle of the Civil War, the revenue cutter *R. M. Dobbin* overtook a small fishing sloop in this passage and took aboard the sloop's two sailors. The two men were Thurston and Alexander, Confederate escapees from Fort Warren on an island in Boston Harbor. They were part of a group of six led by Charles W. Read, a bold lieutenant in the Confederate navy with a mission to interrupt Yankee shipping.

Earlier that summer, Read had captured the fishing schooner *Archer*, and, after transferring his crew and munitions aboard her, slipped into Portland Harbor where in such a local craft he anchored off Long Wharf undetected. Under the cover of darkness, he and his crew silently highjacked the revenue cutter *Caleb Cushing*, a topsail schooner, and stood out to sea. The next morning, just as Read's slight breeze was dying, several steamers were commandeered for pursuit. Read was wallowing in the calm without even enough breeze to come about. When he saw the approaching steamers, he knew he was caught. But at least he could permanently take the *Caleb Cushing* out of service. He ordered his crew to set fire to her, and then he surrendered. He and his crew were taken to Fort Warren.

Before long, they hatched a plot to escape. Under the cover of darkness, some of the men would swim to a nearby island, find a boat, and return for the others. Read, however, was not a strong swimmer, so the two strongest men were elected. On a moonless night, they set off, but they were never heard from again. In the second attempt, the next two, Thurston and Alexander, managed to survive the cold water and the long swim, but it took them so long to find a small boat and launch it that Read and the last of the group were caught. Thurston and Alexander put to sea, bound for Saint John, New Brunswick. Their trip, however, ended in the passage between Cliff and Jewell Island.

92. West Brown Cow and Broken Cove

A treacherous maze of rocks lies at the southeastern end of Broad Sound, equidistant between Jewell and Eagle Island. It is aptly named Broken Cove. One small island lies at the southern end of this group, named West Brown Cow for its dark brown bluffs, and the Mink Rocks lie to the west.

This dangerous area is noted primarily as a place to avoid. The rocks are marked only at the northern end of the group at the entrance to Broad Sound by green gong "1." All other sides must be given a wide berth.

During settled weather, however, lower tides reveal a small sand bar between the islets of Broken Cove, which makes a good rest stop for paddlers. West Brown Cow is too high for convenient landing.

By sea. Caution should be used to avoid this area when passing inside of it, between Mink Rocks and Bates Island, or south of it, between West Brown Cow and Jewell Island, particularly when visibility is limited. The safest way to approach the Broken Cove sand bar is from the north, but it is possible to cross over the seven-foot spot shown on the charts and enter from the southwest.

Ashore. West Brown Cow and Broken Cove are owned by the State of Maine, reserved, primarily, for the birds.

Like almost every rock along the Maine Coast, this one has had its tragedies. In December of 1952, Buster Estes, a local lobsterman, his son, and nephew were lost when duck hunting on one of the Broken Cove Ledges. Their lobsterboat was found with a chafed anchor line off Cape Elizabeth, and their skiff was wrecked on Jewell's back shore. It is speculated that while the hunters were ashore with their skiff, the lobsterboat parted its anchor rode and went adrift. When the hunters went after it in their skiff, they may have capsized.

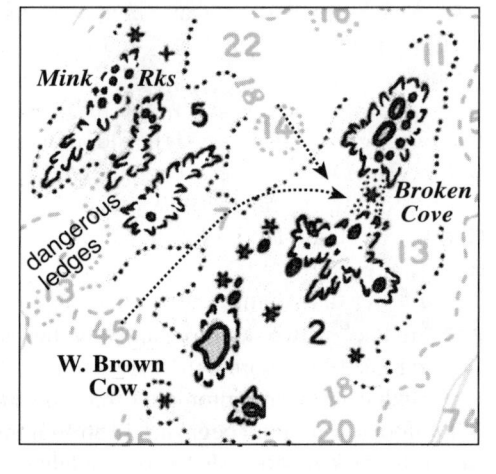

One of the Jewell Island tales describes a treasure-laden pirate ship from Bermuda foundering on Brown Cow Ledge. Captain and crew managed to escape with their treasure in a longboat, which they rowed the short distance to the Punchbowl on Jewell. They dug a hole in the pebbly beach and lowered their chest into it. Then they capped the hole with a huge, flat rock so heavy that the combined strength of all the men could just barely move it. That way they would all need to return together to retrieve the loot! Old Captain Chase, master story-teller of Jewell, claimed that some of the crew eventually did return to carry off the treasure and even stopped by to visit at his house. And when they had left, Chase supposedly found the treasure chest's empty rectangular hole in the Punchbowl.

CASCO BAY

93. Halfway Rock

Lonely Halfway Rock lies almost exactly halfway between Cape Elizabeth and Small Point, on the seaward horizon off Jewell, among a bevy of treacherous ledges. In southeasterly storms they form a lee shore, hidden except for the breaking seas, which shoot foam and spray high enough to be visible from Peaks or Bailey Island as an icy-white scrawl on the horizon.

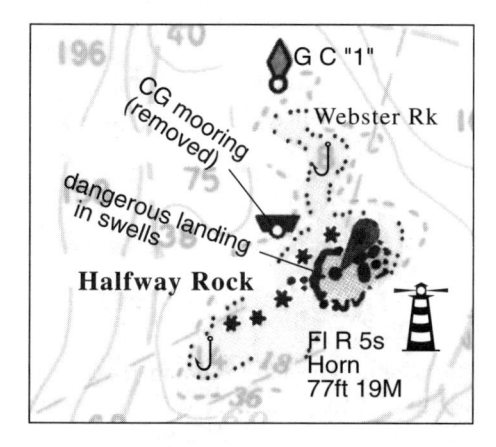

Small boaters are drawn out to Halfway Rock for the promising fishing around the ledges, but the island itself has no landing facilities, and few, if any, attempt the difficult landing in the ceaseless surge. This would be a remote and exposed place to have an accident.

By sea. Do not approach Halfway Rock unless the weather is settled. Even then, the ocean surge and the lack of any wharf or beach makes landing extremely difficult. The Coast Guard mooring shown on the chart hasn't been there in recent years.

Ashore. Among the unfortunate vessels that discovered Halfway Rock the hard way are the brig *Samuel*, wrecked in 1835 with the loss of two, and, presumably, the *W.H. Jenkens* before she drifted ashore on Cushing Island in February, 1861 (see Inner Green Island, p. 102).

Both catastrophes prompted recommendations for a light on the rock, but work on the 66-foot tower didn't begin until 1869. Granite was quarried on Chebeague and shipped out to the rock in stone sloops (see sidebar, p. 90). But that fall, before much progress could be made on the light, the Rock took a beating in the Hurricane of '69. The schooner *Lydia* hit the rock lightly, but managed to put in at Bailey Island despite losing her mainsail, her rudder, her lifeboats, and her anchors. The following year, construction ground to a halt for lack of funds. Completion money was eventually appropriated, and Halfway Rock Light was lit for the first time in August, 1871.

The keepers and their supplies were landed by small boat in calm weather between the swells and surges. A wooden boat ramp and an igloo-shaped boathouse were eventually built, but they were soon washed away. In 1888, a new two-story boathouse was built, affixed to the tower. In 1960, the boathouse was replaced again, and a helicopter pad was built on the rock, but two years later, twenty-foot waves engulfed the Rock, and most of the outbuildings and half the helipad were washed away. In February of 1972, a severe gale washed away the fuel tank for the generator and portions of the boat ramp, and the crew had to be airlifted to safety. The light was automated in 1976, but the fuel tank was washed away again in what has become known as "The Perfect Storm" in 1991. This storm also washed away the tanks and put out the lights at the Isles of Shoals and Boon Island, leaving the entire outer coast from Cape Ann to Seguin in the dark and prompting the conversion of the generators to solar systems. Now the only keepers of the rock are the seals who bask on its foam-washed ledges.

111

94. Bangs and Stockman Islands

Bangs Island lies east of Great Chebeague and east of little Crow Island, on the west side of Broad Sound. Stockman lies across a narrow gut to the north. These fairly large islands are state owned, acquired in 1974 and managed by the Department of Inland Fisheries and Wildlife as wildlife habitat. Both islands lack either a good anchorage or a good landing beach, and the vegetation ashore is thick. The only trails on 55-acre Bangs are made by deer, and they are considerably more agile at ducking under tree boughs and through thickets than their two-footed counterparts.

By sea. Beware of the ledge projecting from the west side of Stockman. Goose Nest Ledge, between Stockman and Great Chebeague, wears many different shades of bottom paint. The ledge is not marked when approaching from the north, and it lurks in water that seems wide and clear. Keep track of where you are in this area.

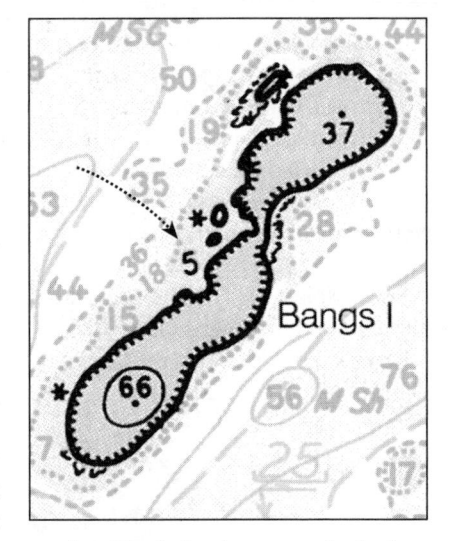

Bangs has a narrow waist. The most protected spot to come ashore is south of the waist on the west side. If you anchor off here, be sure your anchor is well set. The bottom may be rocky, so a tripline is recommended. Stockman is bold on all sides with several small cobble pockets, depending on the tide.

Ashore. The deer population on Bangs warrants care to avoid deer ticks which can carry Lyme disease. Wear long pants tucked into socks and spray your ankles with insect repellent.

95. Stave Island

Stave Island, along with Ministerial and Bates, are fragmented geographic extensions of Cliff Island. Together they compose a little mini-archipelago north of Cliff, which encircles a relatively protected basin of water. With only one or two cottages and few trees, this is the way Casco Bay must have appeared a hundred years ago.

All of these islands are privately owned, and landing is not allowed, but their convoluted shores and the soft lay of the land make them fun to poke around by water.

By sea. The area between Stave and Ministerial is a minefield of ledges.

Ashore. Stave was once owned by Abner Harris, the founder of one of Portland's old ship chandleries, the Harris Company. He built the house on the hill, fenced in a lobster pound, erected a small fish shack, and bought and sold lobsters for the Portland market. Abner sold the island in the mid 1940s to Charles Olsen, a Cape Elizabeth fisherman, but since then the ownership has become fragmented. Now Stave is divided into seven different parcels.

96. Bates and Ministerial

Bates and Ministerial are long narrow islands connected to each other by a sand bar at low. Together they are almost a diminutive reflection of Cliff Island to the south.

Both islands are private. The crotch to the north of the bar makes an adequate anchorage in settled summer weather, though it can be rolly.

By sea. Notice that almost half of Ministerial lies under water as long ledges stretching to the south. And the west side of the island is a rock garden. Approaches directly to the bar, however, are clean.

The slot north of the bar makes a pleasant daystop on anchor, and if it is calm, it is even possible to spend the night here. If swells are running in Broad Sound, though, they tend to funnel in and make it rolly, particularly at high. Protection from the south is good until the tide covers the bar. At the top of the tide, boats with very shallow draft can slip over the bar.

Ashore. Legend has it that the first squatter on Bates is the island's namesake, Jane Bates. The surprise for that era, of course, is that she was a woman. She lived there all her life, wearing rugged men's clothes, fishing and clamming for a living. Her death was either equally peaceful or extraordinarily puzzling. Her body was found washed up on Richmond Island, south of Cape Elizabeth. She had apparently drowned and been carried by the ebb. But for some unknown reason, she was elegantly dressed in a bright kimono, clothes nobody had ever seen her in before. One can't help but guess that she might have dressed for her own death. At a time when island hermits often were found frozen to death in their cabins or half-eaten by rats, what more dignified way would there be to go?

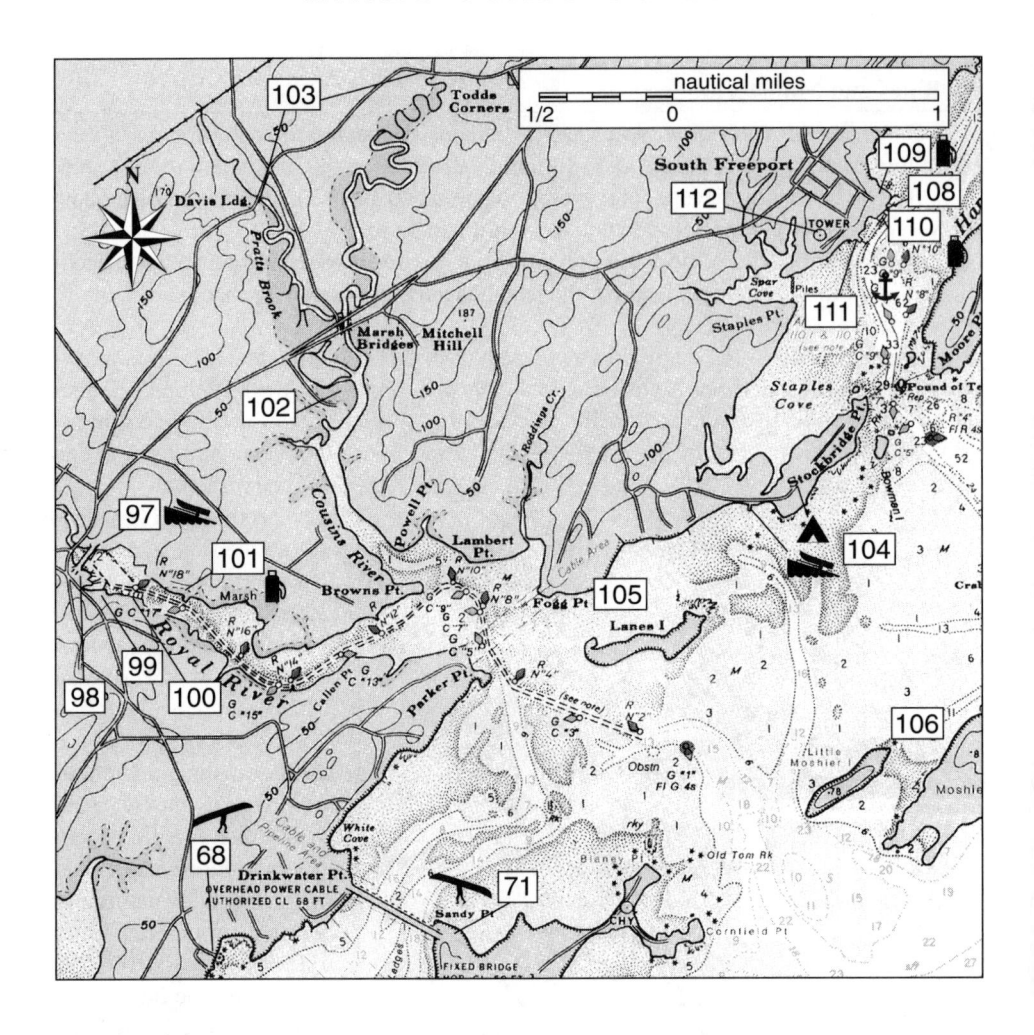

Ministerial was once owned by the notorious—if not nefarious—Captain Chase of Jewell Island (see page 103), but he kept it only for a few years before selling it to Joseph Sturdivant of Cumberland (see Sturdivant Island, page 81). For the past 36 years, Bates has been the retreat of John Rich, whose forty-year career had him chasing around the globe for late-breaking news as a national news corespondent.

CASCO BAY

WESTERN RIVERS AND ISLANDS

ROYAL RIVER

The portion of the Royal River that is navigable from the sea is a short and winding scrawl that etches its way from a basin just below the lower falls to the shallows between Cousins Island and Lanes Island. Together, the several Yarmouth boat yards and the town landing cater to nearly every boating need in the nearly perfectly protected boat basin.

By sea. See detail chart next page. The boat basin is somewhat removed from Casco Bay, but the run out the river, or up it, between high banks and marshy shores and past some of Yarmouth's fine homes, can be pleasant in its own right. The channel out of the river has been recently dredged, and it's well marked.

By land. Follow directions for individual listings below.

Ashore. The Royal River runs from its source at Sabbathday Lake some 30 miles to Casco Bay, draining 142 square miles. In the early days of the colony, Broad Arrow pines were floated down the river to the British Navy's waiting ships in the harbor, but the river was named for William Royall, who settled here in 1636. The U.S. Geodetic Survey lost the second "l" in a typographical error in the 1930s.

Yarmouth sprang up where the river flowed over four natural falls. A sawmill was built at Gooch's Falls, a grist mill at Baker's Falls, a textile mill at Cotton Mill Falls, and a tannery and foundry at Pumgustock Falls, where the fresh water finally meets salt. Pumgustock was the Indian word for "Falls Goes Out Place."

The banks of the river were rich in clay, and a brickyard was set up on Mill Road. Small flat-bottomed boats would float bricks to the harbor. In the winter, the ice would freeze to depths of 10 or 15 feet, thick enough to support ships built far inland and skidded over the ice to the sea. Near the Yarmouth Falls, one ship got away from the oxen that were pulling it, accelerated past the team, and slammed into the bridge at the foot of the hill.

Later industries along the banks included a paper mill at Baker's Falls and a chicken processing plant at the Upper Falls. As late as the 1960s, the Royal River was awash in chicken parts, which during the spring freshet would hang from the branches of trees and bushes along the riverbank. Like many Maine rivers, though, the Royal River is far less polluted now.

97. Yarmouth and the Yarmouth Town Landing

Yarmouth Town Landing is on the east bank of the Royal River hard by the bridge for I-95. This is a well-maintained facility, with a concrete ramp, separate floats for recreational and commercial users, and plenty of parking. It is used by recreational boaters, commercial fishermen, and clammers. The Yarmouth harbormaster (846-2418), who's office is on-site, charges non-residents $10 per day for ramp use.

By sea. See chart next page. The town ramp is on the north side of the Royal River boat basin, hard by the bridge. The river was dredged over the winter of 1996 and 1997, so there is deep water at the ramp and floats at all tides.

By land. Take I-95 to exit 17. Head south on Rt. 1. Take the first left on Rt. 88S, then take your first left again on Bayview Street. Cross over I-95 and take the first right on Old Shipyard Road, which leads to the landing.

Ashore. Portable toilets and trash facilities are located ashore. A pay phone is on the wall of the harbormaster's building. The ramp fee includes parking for the day, but overnight parking must be arranged with the harbormaster.

Each year, on the third weekend in July, Yarmouth celebrates the bounty of the sea with its Clam Festival, complete with parades, music, dancing, shucking contests, and, of course, feasting.

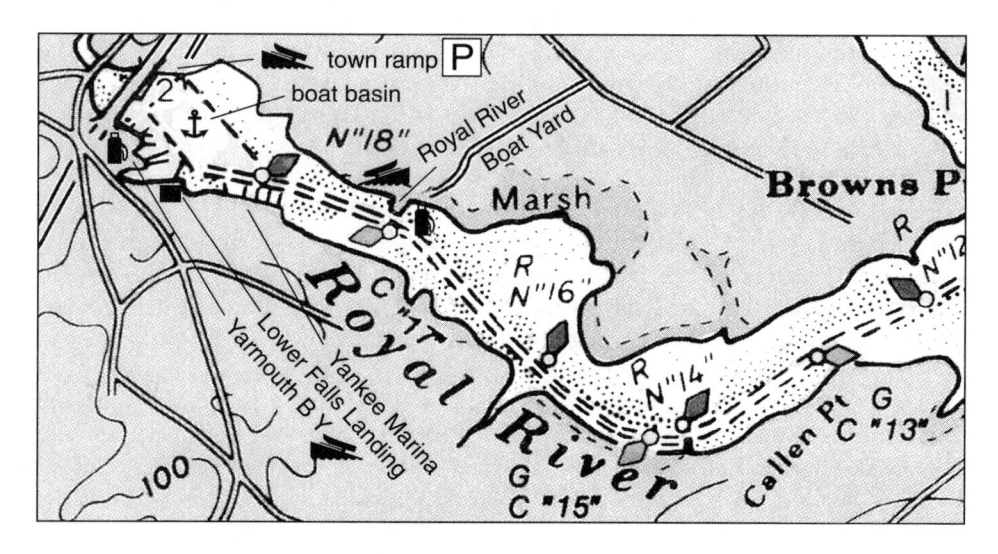

98. Yarmouth Boat Yard

Yarmouth Boat Yard (846-9050, Ch. 09) specializes in outboard-powered boats. They have a dirt launching ramp that is usable on the top half of the tide and gas, water, and pump-out facilities on their floats.

By sea. YBY is at the head of the Royal River boat basin on the south side. Transient dockage and moorings are usually available.

By land. Follow the directions for the town landing, above, but continue on Rt. 88S until you pass under the I-95 bridge. YBY will be on the left.

Ashore. YBY repairs outboards, and they have an Evinrude parts department and a marine store. They also can arrange long-term parking or storage.

99. Lower Falls Landing

Lower Falls Landing is the large gray shingled building on the south side of the Royal River boat basin. As recently as 1980, this building was a sardine cannery, buying and packing herring for the world market. In its heyday, it produced an average of a million cans of sardines a week. The cannery closed with the decline in the herring fisheries, but it found new life when it was renovated into office and retail space, most of which now house business related to boats or boating.

By sea. The docks directly off Lower Falls Landing belong to one of its businesses, East Coast Yacht Sales, and there is no regular dockage here for transients or for patrons of the Landing's restaurant, The Cannery. Temporary dockage can be arranged either at Yarmouth Boat Yard, just to the north, or at Yankee Marina just to the south, or possibly through East Coast Yacht Sales in the unlikely event that their docks are empty.

By Land. Follow the directions to the town landing, but continue south on Rt. 88. Pass under the I-95 bridge. Lower Falls Landing will be on your left.

Ashore. In addition to the restroom in the lobby, the old cannery now houses a well-equipped marine chandlery (Landing Boat Supply, 846-3777), a sail loft (Maine Sailing Partners, 846-6400), a waterfront restaurant (The Cannery, 846-1226), and a specialty foods shop which can put a five-star picnic together for you (Royal River Provisioners, 846-1332). Or you can tempt yourself by browsing the showroom of East Coast Yacht Sales.

100. Yankee Marina

Yankee Marina (846-4326, Ch. 09) is a full-service marina and boat yard just east of Lower Falls Landing. They dock, haul, repair, and store boats of all sizes. Their concrete ramp has deep water at most tides, and in the summer when the yard empties out, there is plenty of parking. The Casco Bay Rowing Center (846-3277), organized to promote the sport of rowing, has a launching dock here for members.

By sea. Coming upriver, Yankee Marine is the first complex on the south bank, with its unmistakable large sheds and docks. They have water and pump-out facilities on their docks, but no fuel. Transient slips are available by reservation.

By land. Follow the directions for Lower Falls Landing, above.

Ashore. Yankee Marina can perform almost any kind of repair, and ice and showers are available. You can explore Lower Falls Landing or the Cannery Restaurant next door while you wait.

101. Royal River Boat Yard

Royal River Boat Yard (846-9577) is a low-key, family-run boat yard on the north bank of the Royal River. They cater to very loyal commercial and recreational boaters alike, launching, hauling, storing, and repairing boats of all kinds. They have a paved boat ramp, with adequate water depth at all tides, and they can find you long-term parking somewhere in the yard.

By sea. This is the first and only yard on the right as you approach the boat basin. Gas, diesel, ice, and water are available on the fuel dock.

By land. Follow the directions for the town landing, but stay on Bayview Street until you see the boat yard's sign on the right.

COUSINS RIVER 🍴 ⤴

The tidal Cousins River merges with the Royal River near its mouth. Its deeper lower section is considerably shorter than the Royal, but its upper estuary makes a nice paddling adventure. It can be accessed either by sea or from Walter Greene's boat yard on its banks, and portable boats can explore its creeks from put-ins near its headwaters.

By sea. For boats with deeper draft, navigation on the lower portion is limited to higher tides. Walter Greene's yard is on the left bank.

The upper reaches of the Cousins are lovely scribbles through salt marsh, but, unfortunately, they are interrupted by busy US Rt. 1 and I-95. The Rt. 1 bridge's 3-foot vertical clearance at high tide limits upriver travel to the smallest boats, or the northern section of the river can be explored from the put-ins at Davis Landing or Todds Corners.

By land. See entries below.

Ashore. A pair of bald eagles nests near the lower section of the river and you may be fortunate enough to see them perched along the shore or riding thermals nearby.

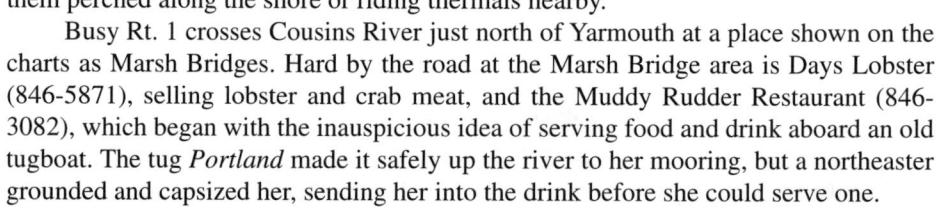

Busy Rt. 1 crosses Cousins River just north of Yarmouth at a place shown on the charts as Marsh Bridges. Hard by the road at the Marsh Bridge area is Days Lobster (846-5871), selling lobster and crab meat, and the Muddy Rudder Restaurant (846-3082), which began with the inauspicious idea of serving food and drink aboard an old tugboat. The tug *Portland* made it safely up the river to her mooring, but a northeaster grounded and capsized her, sending her into the drink before she could serve one.

A short distance south of Marsh Bridges, next to I-95's exit 17, is a major tourist information center, with clean restrooms and fresh water. Delorme's Map Store (846-7100), across the street, features the world's largest globe and sells a complete selection of Maine topographic maps and NOAA charts as well as DeLorme's famous Maine Gazetteer.

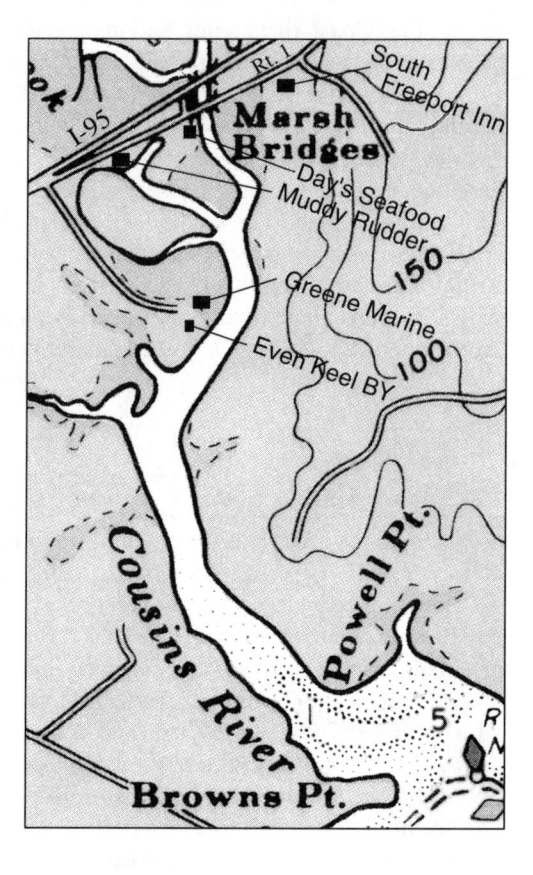

102. Greene Marine and Even Keel Boat Yard

Even Keel Boat Yard and Greene Marine are tucked together on an upland point in the midst of Cousins River saltmarsh. Even Keel (846-4878) is the small yard of the sons of Carroll Lowell, fourth-generation boatbuilders. They can design and build you a boat or store or repair one you already have.

Greene Marine (846-3184) is the surprising yard of Walter Greene, designer and builder of world-class racing multihulls. Pulled up in his yard are thoroughbreds like *American Eagle*, a pencil-thin, feather-weight trimaran which finally beat the old clippership speed record from New York to San Francisco, as well as other go-fast boats and works-in-progress. Greene continues a tradition of shipbuilding on the Cousins and Royal rivers that has included more than 300 sailing vessels since the 1800s.

Ashore. Walter Greene first amazed the ocean-racing world in 1978 when he sailed his modest, self-designed, self-built trimaran to a first in her class in the prestigious Round Britain Race. He then chartered the same boat to another skipper who won the grueling single-handed Route de Rhum race from St. Malo, France to Guadaloupe.

Greene doesn't limit himeslf to any one construction technique. His high-tech repetoire includes cold-molding or vacuum-formed wood and epoxy techniques as well as glass, carbon-fibre and cored laminates. And he doesn't limit his projects. He built a copy of the space shuttle for Maine's Children's Museum in Portland, and he recently completed an 18-foot sailing Docksider for a Maine shoe company.

Greene Marine also stores and repairs boats that can make it up the shallow river to his yard. So if you have a challenging repair, or need a new boat for a world challenge, you've come to the right place.

By sea. Greene Marine and Even Keel should be approached near high tide. The yard is on the west bank of the Cousins River. Both yards can haul boats of most sizes as long as their draft is not too deep.

By land. To get to the boat yards, take I-95's exit 17 and follow Rt. 1 north. After a Ford dealership on the right, look for a small dirt road and follow it to its end.

103. Pratts Brook and Todds Corners

Just upstream of the Marsh Bridges, Cousins River divides. The main branch tends to the north to Todds Corners. The smaller branch, Pratts Brook, winds to the west to Davis Landing. The NOAA chart still shows a road crossing this branch from the Marsh Bridge area, but this crossing is long gone.

Within about two hours either side of high tide, it is possible to launch canoes or kayaks into the small creeks at either Davis Landing or Todds Corners. Of the two, the Todds Corners put-in is the easiest.

By sea. See chart, next page. The bridges of Rt. 1 and I-95 limit access to the upper portions of the Cousins River from seaward. The smallest boats may be able to work through the culverts to explore the marshes farther upriver, but otherwise they will need to be launched from the put-ins.

By land. Both put-ins are reached from Old County Road. From exit 17, take Rt. 1 south and then take your first right, then right again onto Old County Road. The first

MAINE COAST GUIDE

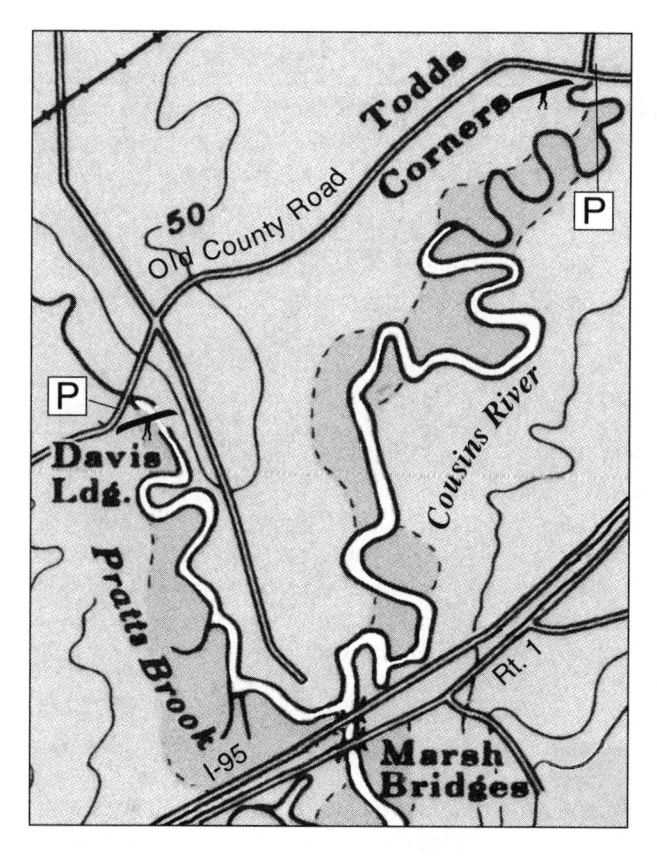

creek you cross is the Pratts Brook put-in.

The put-in for the upper portion of Cousins River proper is just before the intersection of Webster Road. Shoulders at both put-ins are wide enough for parking, but be careful of fast traffic.

104. Winslow Memorial Park, South Freeport

Winslow Memorial Park (865-4198) is a town-run park and campground with tent and RV sites on the South Freeport shores of Casco Bay. Because the campground does not accept reservations, there is a good chance you can get a site, even at the height of the summer season. Short walking trails lead along the shores and by a sandy swimming beach.

Within two hours either side of high tide, there is enough water to launch trailerable boats from the park's paved ramp. You do not have to be a camper to use the ramp, but in either case, a small fee is charged. Portable boats can be launched from the small beach next to the ramp.

By sea. Winslow Park occupies most of Stockbridge Point, inside Big and Little Moshier Island and just northeast of Lanes Island. All of the water between these islands is very shoal, even on the high end of the tide, and low reveals extensive mud flats. If you plan to launch here, your timing with the tide is crucial, both when you leave and when you return. Kayaks generally have enough water except within two hours of low tide. Trailered boats will need more. Launching may be further complicated by the ramp's broad exposure to winds from the southwest which generally pick up in the afternoon.

The ramp is just west of the narrowest point of the neck. The chart shows a narrow channel leading from the ramp area out through the shoals, but park attendants recommend that you try to find the deep water closer to Lanes Island. From the ramp, head first toward the ledges that make out from the north end of Lanes. Near the ledges, turn south and run out to the deeper channel that heads toward Royal River.

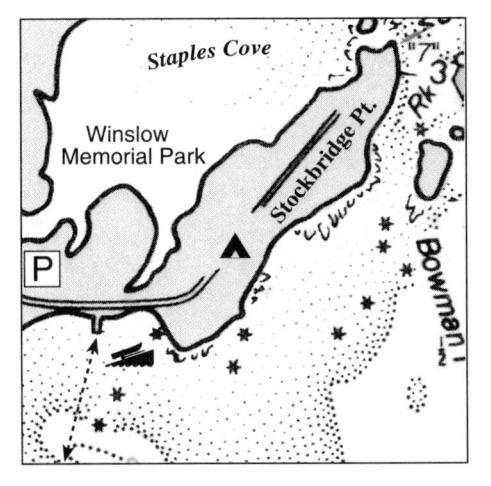

If you are camping here and need to return when the tide is down, you could tie your boat to the town-owned dock at the end of Stockbridge Point, just north of Bowman Island, and walk back to the campground. Follow the approaches for the Harraseeket River (see page 124).

By land. Take exit 17 off I-95 and head north on US Rt. 1. Go right on South Freeport Road. In .8 miles, turn right on Staples Point Road and follow it to its end.

Ashore. The park has a large lot for cars with trailers, though an additional fee is charged for parking. The campground has toilets, showers, trash receptacles, grills and picnic tables, and a small playground. Block ice is available at the gatehouse.

105. Lanes Island and Fogg Point

Wooded Lanes Island sits just offshore at the mouth of the Royal River and just off Fogg Point on the South Freeport shore. Lanes is a tempting exploration for small boaters heading out from either the Royal or Cousins River or from Winslow Park, but the island is private.

By sea. Lanes is surrounded by shallow water, most of which becomes a mud flat at low. A cluster of ledges projects from its north end. In 1753, little Roddings Creek, to the west of Fogg Point, powered a tidal sawmill.

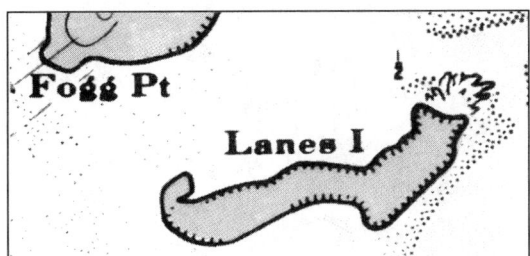

Ashore. Lanes Island's position in the rich clam flats and at the convergence of several canoeable rivers made it an ideal location for Indians. They used Lanes as a burial ground and, supposedly, for councils of war.

Its history is closely tied to the nearest mainland, Fogg Point. This was the location of the first cabin of William Royall before he later moved to the banks of the Royal River. In 1658, James Lane settled here from Malden, Massachusetts. His deed included Lanes Island, Moshier Island, Rodding's Island (which might have been Little Moshier), land at Little River, east of Wolfe Neck, and Sandy Point on Cousins Island. During the first Indian wars, James Lane fled to Jewell Island, but he was killed in the surprise Indian attack on Jewell in 1676 (see Jewell Island, p. 103).

MAINE COAST GUIDE

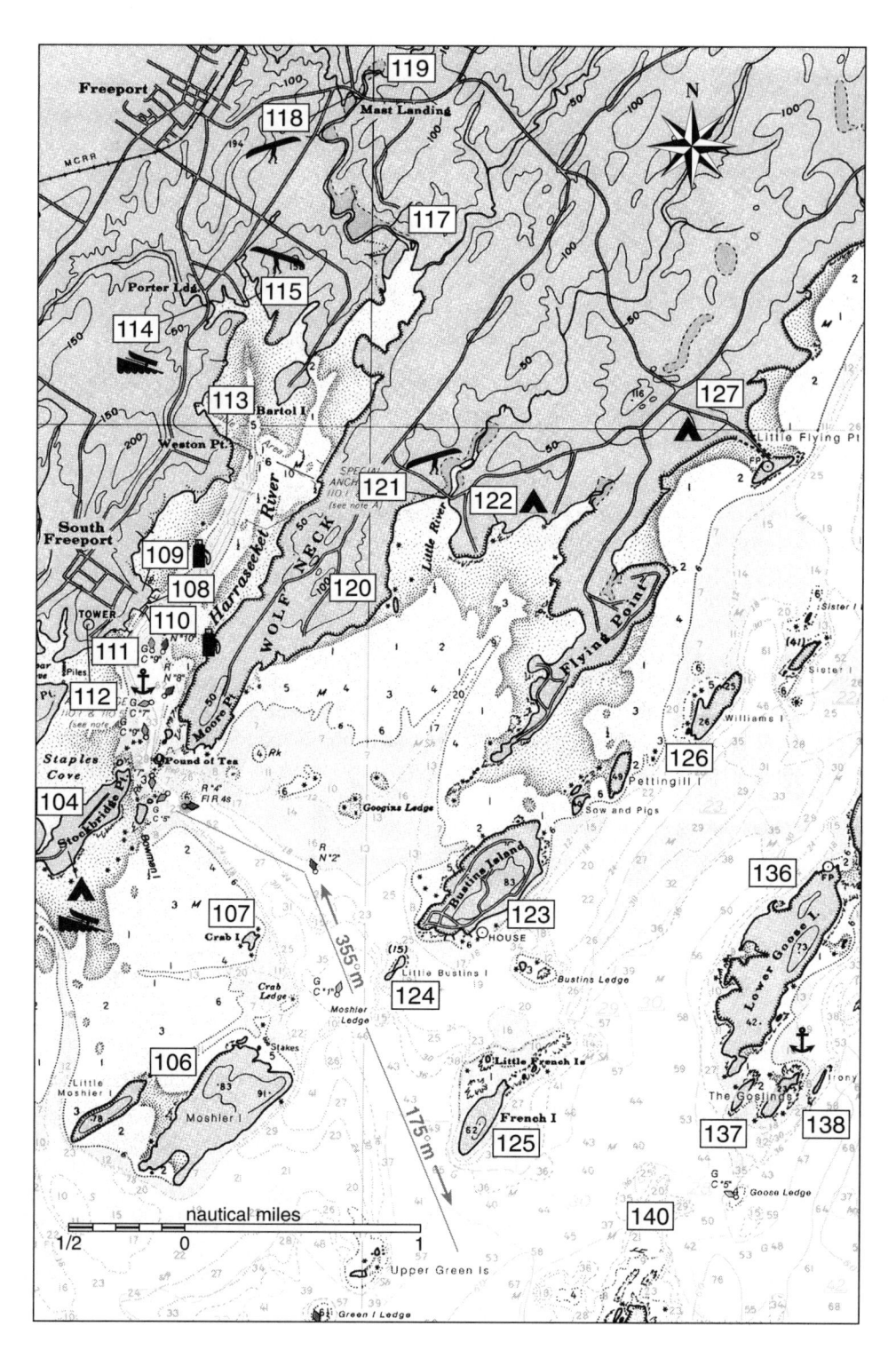

After the first wars, Lane's sons, Samuel and Henry, resettled on Fogg Point. They lived in uneasy truce with the Indians typical of settlers of the times. On a late afternoon in July, 1688, an Indian and his squaw appeared at the Lane homestead and asked if they could spend the night there. This was a somewhat delicate situation for the landowners, whose father had been killed by Indians just twelve years before. But night was falling, and the Indians seemed friendly, so the Lanes agreed.

In the morning, however, the Indians called from shore out to Lanes Island, where more Indians had spent the night. Five of the Indians canoed to Fogg Point and joined the original two, building a fire close to the Lane house. Concerned that his house might burn and outraged at the Indians' cavalier attitude toward the fire, Samuel Lane told the Indians to move their fire. To be sure they got the message, he carried their coals to the water's edge himself. This angered the Indians. One of them tried to attack Lane, but he was rebuffed, so he resorted to threatening the Lanes' hogs with his hatchet. The Lanes saved their bacon by overpowering him and driving the Indians from their land.

The town constable was alerted. The belligerent Indian was apprehended, brought before a judge, and fined. His defense sounds remarkably familiar: he claimed he wasn't responsible because he was drunk on rum he had bought from John Royall, William's son, who in turn claimed the rum was stolen.

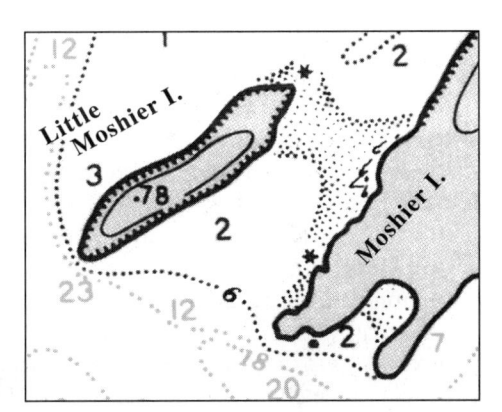

106. Moshier and Little Moshier Island

Moshier and Little Moshier Island dominate the horizon from Winslow Park. They are high and wooded—and enchanting. But like Lanes Island, they are private.

By sea. Moshier's west side is completely shoal, and at low a mud flat reaches over to the north end of Little Moshier. The beautiful grove on Moshier is on the southwestern point, approachable from the shallow pocket between the two islands or from the smaller cleft at the southern end of Moshier.

Beware of the one lone rock off the island's otherwise bold east side.

Ashore. There are cottages on the north end of the island and on its east flank. The owner of orthern cottage, a contractor from the Boston area, built his house by shuttling materials out to the island by helicopter, including huge vats of wet cement for the foundation.

Like Lanes, Little Moshier was an Indian burying ground. The islands take their names from Hugh Moshier, a member of the English court whose imagination was captured by the exciting discoveries being made across the Atlantic. In 1640, he gave up his established life for one of voyaging and adventure, and he settled here. The larger island, whether from strength of character or self-promotion, became known for a time as Great Moshier.

107. Crab Island

Crab Island is a little bump north of Moshier Island in a sea of shoal water, not much bigger than the little camp in its center. A few bushes and trees clamber for footholds on the rest. This island was once owned by the estate of Admiral Robert E. Peary (see Eagle Island, p. 161), and it is still private.

HARRASEEKET RIVER

The Harraseeket River is short, sweet, and strong. Its upper reaches form in the woodlands of Mast Landing and scrawl through marsh-lined banks to the wide and shallow expanses inside Wolf Neck (often alternately spelled "Wolfe Neck"). The river's mouth narrows again, studded by tiny Pumpkin Knob and Pound of Tea Island.

This well-protected water creates an almost perfect harbor. It is taken advantage of by two marinas, a yacht club, and the town floats in South Freeport, as well as the flotilla of boats on moorings. Despite the number of boats in the lower section, the intriguing headwaters are seldom explored.

By sea. The broad shape of the lower portion of the Harraseeket holds a lot of tidal water, which every tide sucks and pushes through the harbor and its mouth. Currents can reach 3 or 4 knots in the harbor and may even reach 4 or 5 on a spring tide. Careful maneuvering is required both upon entering the harbor and once inside.

From the sea, the narrow entrance to the Harraseeket River bends to the right, with crosscurrents swirling around Pound of Tea, the island in its mouth. The well-marked channel passes to the south and then west of the island. Deep-draft boats, however, may be swept out of the channel by the current. Shallower boats, including most of the harbor's lobster fleet, blast through the slot between Pound of Tea and Pumpkin Knob, but strangers should probably leave this corner-cutting to those in the know. Definitely do not pass inside of the little island to the north of Pound of Tea, known locally as Pumpkin Knob, since it is connected to Wolfe Neck by ledge.

Once inside, a marked channel runs toward the marinas and the town dock. Again, maneuver carefully, taking the current into account.

The upper reaches of the river can be explored near the top of the tide. Trailered boats can be launched at the town ramp at Dunning's Boat Yard, and portable boats can be launched at the Flying Point Road turnout (see the following entries).

By land. Most of the Harraseeket can be reached either from the village of South Freeport, from the ramp at Dunning's Boat Yard, or, with portable boats at the top of the tide, from the turnout off Flying Point Road.

Ashore. On the west bank of the lower Harraseeket, the town dock and harbormaster's office is flanked by Brewer's Marine to the north and Strouts Point Wharf Company to the south. Farther to the south is the shingled clubhouse of the Harraseeket Yacht Club. The stone tower of Casco Castle, shown on the chart, rises above the yacht club. An elegant convenience store serving sandwiches and cappuccino is another block up in the little town center (see entries below).

L.L. Bean needs no introduction. They are nearby in Freeport, and they run a shuttle service from South Freeport to their store. Inquire at Brewers (see Freeport, p. 116).

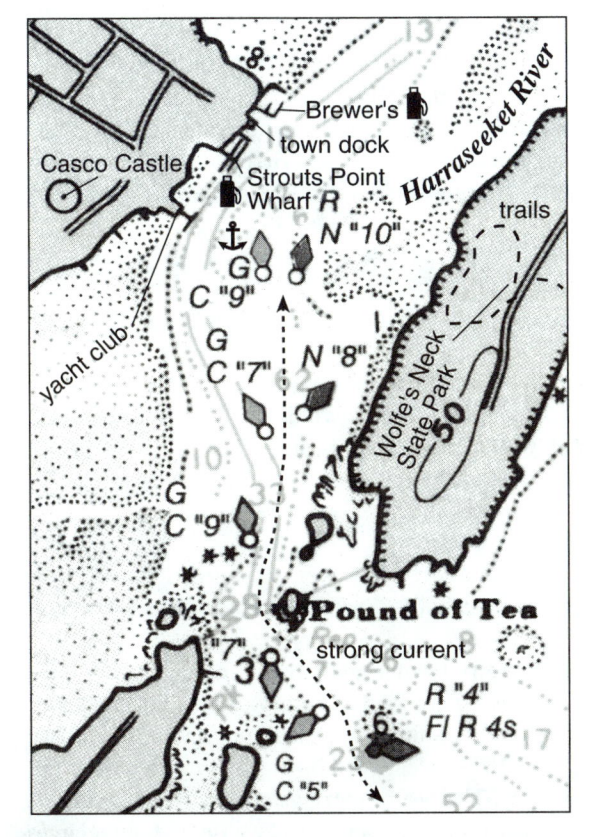

In the early days, abundant forests grew nearby, and early colonists quickly discovered the soft, straight, and limber pines and firs and began exporting them as masts. Soon the British Admiralty sent a Surveyor of Pines and Timber who blazed "the King's broad arrow" with an ax in the bark of the best mast trees, reserving them exclusively for the Royal Navy.

With the abundance of lumber, a succession of shipyards soon flanked the banks of the lower portion of the river—the Porter Yard, which built the infamous *Dash*, the Soule Brothers Shipyard, the Strouts Point Wharf Company, and Talbot and Bliss Brothers. This teeming location was called Strouts Point Village, though the name was changed in the 1880s to South Freeport. Photographs from that time show rocky fields rolling to the river banks, treeless except for the shipyards where trees gained a second life in the colossal ships growing on the ways. Strouts Point Marine, Brewer's South Freeport Marine, and the town docks are where the shipyards once stood (see following entries).

108. South Freeport Town Dock

The South Freeport Town Dock is at the center of all the Harraseeket waterfront activity, directly at the end of Main Street and flanked on either side by the commercial marinas. The floats are very busy with local fishermen and lobstermen landing their catch, the small ferry to Bustins Island loading and off-loading passengers, and pleasure boats coming and going.

Docking on the town float is allowed for limited periods—just about enough time to order a lobster roll at Harraseeket Lunch next door. You may be able to launch portable boats here, but parking is scarce unless you pay to park at either of the boat yards.

By sea. Use the red building of Harraseeket Lunch as a landmark. The town docks are just to the north, with a small, elevated building, the harbormaster's office (865-4546), above them.

By land. The village of South Freeport can be reached from the south at exit 17 from I-95. Take Rt. 1N to South Freeport Road, on the right. Follow South Freeport Road to the village. Turn right at the four-way stop onto Main Street and follow it to the water.

Ashore. Harraseeket Lunch is a classic Maine takeout right at the water's edge. Their fare includes succulent crab rolls, clams, and lobsters. If you prefer, you can buy live lobsters next door at Harraseeket Lobster. A pay phone is on the side of the building.

Main Street leads up from the water past the Atlantic Seal Bed and Breakfast (865-6112), owned by Captain Tom Ring who also runs tours out to Eagle Island (see p. 161).

109. Brewer's South Freeport Marine

Brewer's (865-3181) is a full-service yard, just north of the town floats. They can launch your boat, park your car, and fix either or both. They can fill your tanks with gas, diesel, or water, and they can pump out your holding tank.

By sea. South Freeport Marine is just north of the town docks, with several work floats moored just offshore. Gas, diesel, water, and electricity are on the outermost dock, but beware of the strong currents that can run by its outer face. Brewer's rents dock space or moorings to transients, and they run a launch service, which can be reached on channel 09.

By land. As you reach the water on Main Street, Brewer's is on the left.

Ashore. Long or short-term parking is available. Showers, laundry machines, and ice are available ashore.

Brewer's has made a remarkable recovery from a catastrophic, multi-million-dollar fire in the early spring of 1999 to continue more than a century of boat building and repair on this site. This was the Soule Brothers Shipyard, which built and managed 30 large merchant vessels between 1839 and 1879, eventually buying out the neighboring shipyard, the Strouts Point Wharf Company. The last of their weathered sheds survived the fire and still stands by the water between Brewer's and the town dock, with a large weathervane on top.

110. Strouts Point Wharf Company

Strouts Point (865-3899) is a marina and boat yard just south of the town docks and Harraseeket Lunch. Ted Wengren, the owner of the marina, is an architect, and he lives above the yard. He was tired of looking down on an eyesore, so he built a series of beautiful, classic boat sheds of his own design. Strouts hauls, stores, and repairs boats of all kinds. They sell fuel and have a small marine store.

By sea. Strouts is located south of the red buildings of Harraseeket Lunch. Gas, diesel, water, and ice are available at their fuel dock. The dockmaster can be reached on channel 09.

By land. Look for the signs and the dirt driveway to Strouts Wharf before you get to Harraseeket Lunch.

Ashore. A small marine store is located at the head of the floats, and showers are available. Parking, however, is limited.

Strouts Point Wharf Company occupies the site of a second Porter Shipyard. The original Porter yard was at Porters Landing, farther upriver (see p. 129).

111. Harraseeket Yacht Club

This local yacht club has an active junior sailing program and an extensive cruising fleet. They may have a guest mooring for larger boats or be able to direct you to one, but they have few, if any, amenities for transient boaters other than a pay phone.

By sea. The yacht club is the southernmost facility on the west side of the river.

By land. Follow the directions above, but take your last possible right off Main Street. The yacht club is on the left, down by the water.

112. The Castle

From the water, the Castle is one of South Freeport's most distinctive features. Its crenelated stone tower rises above the small village like a misplaced Scottish stronghold. In fact, it is all that is left of the grand dreams of Amos Gerald.

By sea. The stone tower of the Castle is clearly visible on shore above the South Freeport Yacht Club clubhouse. The chart shows the tower near Spar Cove.

By land. The Castle is private property, but glimpses of it can be seen from the road. From Main Street, head south on Harraseeket Road. The Castle will be on the right.

Ashore. Amos Gerald was a consummate turn-of-the-century promoter. He got nicknamed the "Electric Railway King" for building an electric trolley between Yarmouth and Brunswick in 1902. To increase ridership, he built Casco Castle, a large inn that overlooked the Harraseeket and would have given Disney a run for his money. The inn and its grounds sported the medieval stone tower, manicured gardens, a real moat with a suspension bridge, a small zoo, a saltwater swimming pool, and a baseball diamond on the hotel grounds. Bathing pavilions and a boathouse were constructed by the shore of Spar Cove where a wooden dam with a sluiceway trapped tidal water in the shallow cove where the sun would warm it.

But this dreamland was just that. The great resort had everything but timing. It was built just as the automobile blossomed. Just twelve years after it was built, the Castle had burned and the "King" had died. Trolley ridership waned until the line had to be abandoned in 1927. Now, the only monument to an idea whose time had come—and gone—is a procession of the old dam pilings across the mouth of Spar Cove, which are still shown on the chart, and the hollow tower of a castle in the sky.

The Castle is now private property, with a new house built nearby. Wonderful photos of the Castle and early South Freeport can be seen at the small post office next to the village variety store, a short walk up Main Street from the town landing.

113. Weston Point and Sandy Beach

Weston Point lies on the west bank of the lower Harraseeket, north of the village of South Freeport. It is now an area of private homes, but it is still known as Cushing-Briggs for the shipyard that occupied the site from 1855 to 1880.

A very small beach is located on the north side of the point. It is public, though it is used primarily by Cushing-Briggs residents. Lightweight portable boats can be launched here, but it is a difficult put-in. The beach lies at the foot of a long flight of stairs down a steep embankment, and water depths are only adequate on the top half of the tide.

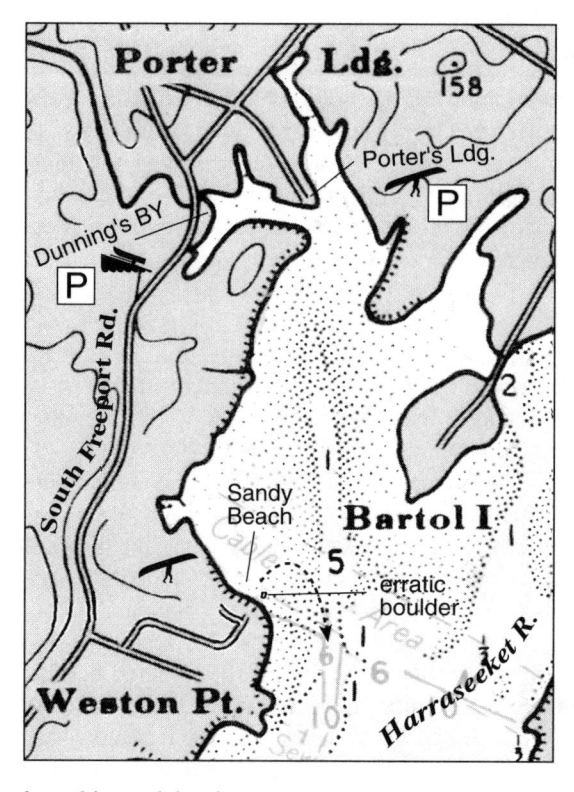

By sea. Sandy Beach lies just to the west of a large light-colored erratic boulder along the shore. Note that the area immediately off the beach is a cable area.

By land. From the South Freeport Road, turn east on Cushing-Briggs Road and then left onto Sandy Beach Road. After a hard right turn, then a hard left, the main part of the road dead ends at a large red-and-white arrow sign at a small turnout. Park in front of the sign. The steps to the beach are just to its left.

Ashore. In 1878, the Cushing-Briggs yard launched Freeport's largest ship, the *John A. Briggs*, of a staggering 2,110 tons burden. All the town schools and businesses were shut down for the day and her launching celebrations were attended by the Governor of Maine and James A. Garfield, who three years later become this country's second assassinated president.

The *John A. Briggs* outlived the age of sail. She met an ignominious end as a coal barge, lost in December, 1909 with her entire crew of seven off Seaside Park, New Jersey.

114. Dunning's Boat Yard

The town of Freeport recently purchased this small boat yard in the upper estuary of the Harraseeket and built a launching ramp for clammers and recreational boaters.

By sea. This new concrete ramp lies at the end of the more southerly creek shown on the chart at Porter Landing, next to a gambrel-roofed boathouse. For about three hours either side of high, the water will be deep enough for an outboard. After that, once the water gets to the base of the eel grass in the marsh, there will only be two feet of water or less. Lest the extensive mud isn't obvious, a sign at the ramp reads "Warning—no water at low tide." Time your launch and return carefully. The ramp is limited to daylight use only.

By land. From South Freeport, follow the South Freeport Road northward. The ramp will be on the right. From Freeport, take South Street out of town. The ramp will be on the left just after the intersection at the small village of Porter's Landing.

Ashore. Parking is very limited and not allowed overnight. Do not block the boathouse, which is currently the home of Falls Point Marine (865-2145), specialists in marine challenges of all kinds. Picnic tables are by the water's edge.

115. Porter's Landing

In addition to the ramp at Dunning's, the Town of Freeport also maintains a small float at the tip of land between the two creeks at Porter's Landing. At the top half of the tide, this is an easy put-in for portable boats, and the float makes a good staging area.

By sea. This area flats out at low. Follow the directions for Dunning's, above, within a few hours of high tide. The light gray float is obvious.

By land. From Porter's Landing, take the Mast Landing Road north, then take the first right to the end. Parking is limited, though not likely to be crowded, since there is no longer a launching ramp here.

Ashore. The village of Porters Landing was settled by Seward Porter in 1782 and sprang up around the Porter's saltworks. Later the successful Porter Shipyard was located here. Before the railroads. the landing served as a vital port for Freeport and towns as far inland as Lewiston. Freight was shipped aboard packets from here to Portland and Boston, and granite was hauled here by oxen from local quarries to be loaded aboard stone sloops (see Great Chebeague Island, p. 89).

At the outbreak of the War of 1812, the Porter yard built the *Dash*, probably Freeport's most famous vessel. Before large standing navies were fully established, privately owned vessels were licensed by the government to interrupt British shipping during the war. The *Dash* was one of the most successful of these privateers. Crewed by Freeport and Harpswell men, she made fifteen captures in seven cruises! But in the spring of 1815, the *Dash* and all aboard her disappeared without a trace. For years, its ghostly form was said to be seen reaching for home through the fog. The eerie sight was immortalized in John Greenleaf Whittier's poem *The Dead Ship of Harpswell*.

Seward Porter was blessed with eleven sons, and the *Dash* was a family enterprise. She was commissioned and owned by Seward and Samuel Porter, who were then in business in Portland, though they were on shaky financial footings. The early successes of the *Dash* saved them from bankruptcy, but when she was lost, three of the Porters, John, Jeremiah, and Ebenezer, went down with her. The original working model of the *Dash* is now on display at the B.H. Bartol Library in Freeport.

There is an interesting footnote about Captain Seward Porter, both humbling and praiseworthy. By the early 1800s, the steam engine had begun to become common, and its possibilities didn't fail to attract the attention of this mariner. In 1822, he installed a steam engine with paddlewheels in a flat-bottomed boat and began the first steamer service in Casco Bay (see Peaks Island, p. 55) and the Kennebec River. Steam power, however, was new technology. She was christened the *Kennebec*, but she quickly earned the nicknames "Horned Hog" and "Ground Hog" both for her ugliness and for her tendency to be overpowered by headwinds and cross currents, which often carried her aground. Some say that there were many times the passengers had to tread on the paddles to keep the boat heading to their destinations. This innovative operation was a harbinger of the future, but needless to say, it was a commercial failure.

116. Freeport

No discussion of Freeport is complete without mentioning the store that put the town on the map, L.L. Bean (865-4761). What began as a small company making rugged hunting boots has grown into an international retailing giant, renowned for its guarantee of quality and satisfaction. Bean's line of canoes, kayaks, and camping gear is of particular interest to coastal boaters, as are the several other high-quality outfitters in town. Unfortunately, Bean does not rent gear.

By sea. As they say in Maine, "You can't get there from here." At least not by water. So, unfazed, L.L. Bean runs a shuttle service from the South Freeport waterfront to their store in downtown Freeport. Inquire at Brewer's South Freeport Marine (see p. 126).

By land. From the south, take exit 18 off I-95 and follow Rt. 1N into town. From the north, take exit 19 and turn left.

Ashore. Outlet stores of every shape and variety seem to jockey for positions near the Maine institution of L.L. Bean. Outdoor enthusiasts should check out North Face and Patagonia. Rings Marine (865-6143), nearby, rents canoes and small boats. The Harraseeket Inn (865-9377) and several motels and Bed and Breakfasts are in town. Casco Bay Yacht Exchange (865-4016), south of town on Rt. 1, carries a huge inventory of small boats. They are mostly used, but anyone of them could be new to you.

117. Pettengill Farm

Heading upriver, the upper reach of the Harraseeket River tends to the northeast, makes a sharp turn to the west, and then slaloms to the northeast through graceful turns of salt marsh. High on the north bank, after the river's first turn, the wooded shores open up into fields of grass and old stone walls. A weathered salt-box farmhouse hunkers behind an ancient oak, bounded by tough old apple trees. It presides over a view that has hardly changed since the early 19th century when it was built.

This is the Rodick Pettengill Farm, which remained in the Pettengill family virtually unchanged, without running water or electricity, for almost a century and a half. Mildred Pettengill, or Millie as she was known locally, was the last occupant. She lived here, unmarried, with her brother Frank, working the farm through thick and thin. Millie was known as a stoic Yankee. It was not uncommon on blustery winter days to see Millie, in her sixties, walking to Brunswick, eight miles away.

Millie lived here until 1970. She eventually gave the farm to the Freeport Historical Society, which restored the exterior of the farmhouse and now uses the property for special functions. If none are under way, you are welcome to stroll the grounds and feel, firsthand, what it must have been like for the early settlers to eke an existence out of this wild place called Maine.

By sea. Exploration of the upper Harraseeket must be done near the top of the tide. The farmhouse is not easy to see from the water. It sits in a field on the north bank where the river bends to the left, from a northwest to southwest, near a small brook shown on the chart. Half of the road shown on the chart leading from the word "Mast Landing" southward is the driveway to the farm.

Land where the river comes closest to the steep bank, at an obvious outcrop of rocks, which are the remnants of an old granite pier. Follow the path up through the field.

If you travel farther upriver, you may see the remains of salt hay staddles in the marsh beyond the landing place. Many early farms harvested salt hay as feed and bedding before upland hayfields were fully established or to supplement the upland hay. The hay was cut with scythes and stacked on groups of cedar posts driven into the marsh, called staddles, to keep the flood tides from reaching the haystack. The hay was brought ashore as needed, often in the winter when the marsh froze hard enough to support horse or oxen, who would wear wooden bog shoes strapped to their hoofs to keep them from sinking into the peat. If the haystack was frozen, chunks would have to be cut off with a hay saw.

Eelgrass, which grows lower on the marsh than salt hay, is not easily digested by farm animals. Its sealed hollow structure, however, gives it a natural resistance to water, and early settlers harvested it to be used as thatch for roofs.

By land. Follow Bow Street out of Freeport. It becomes Flying Point Road and crosses the upper Harraseeket, known as the Mill Stream. Take the next right, Pettengill Road. The drive to the farm is chained, so you will have to park along the road and walk the beautiful drive. The land on either side of the road is private until it opens out into the fields of the farm.

Ashore. This stunning farm is undoubtedly a challenge for a small historical society to fund and maintain. Inquiries or donations can be sent or hand-delivered to the Freeport Historical Society, Harrington House, 45 Main Street, P.O. Box 358, Freeport, ME 04032 or call at 865-3170.

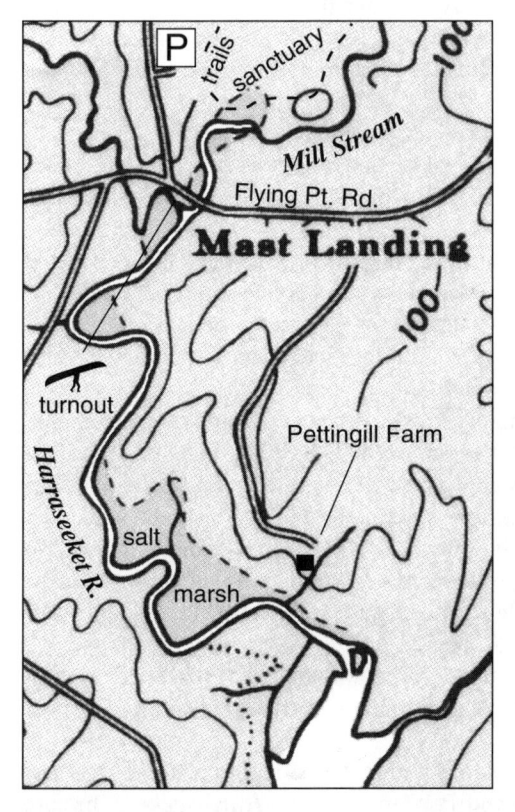

118. Flying Point Road Turnout

Where Flying Point Road crosses the upper Harraseeket River, a small dirt road leads down to the river on land owned by the Freeport Conservation Trust. At high tide it becomes a convenient portable boat put-in for exploring the upper Harraseeket estuary.

By sea. The put-in is just before the twin culverts that pass beneath Flying Point Road. At higher tides, canoers or kayakers can pass through the culverts to wend their way a short distance upriver to the Mast Landing Sanctuary (see p. 132), or they can follow the river seaward.

By land. From Freeport, take Bow Street out of town. It becomes Flying Point Road. Follow it until just before it crosses the river. You'll see the turnout and put-in on the right.

Ashore. The turnout and the shoulder have enough room for several cars to park.

119. Mast Landing Sanctuary

The Mast Landing Sanctuary is a beautiful and historic nature preserve along Mill Stream at the headwaters of the Harraseeket River, above the Flying Point Road bridge. Reaching it by small boat is possible though not particularly practical, since coming in at the top of the tide does not allow much time to explore before the tide drops. Still, Mast Landing should not be missed.

By sea. Follow the Harraseeket upriver and through the twin culverts beneath Flying Point Road. At high tide, canoes and kayaks can navigate as far as the Mill Dam.

By land. From Freeport, take Flying Point Road to a left on Upper Mast Landing Road. The sanctuary is on the right.

Ashore. The sanctuary has self-guided nature trails that run through the woods and follow the river. Maps are located at the trailhead near the parking lot.

From 1634 to the Revolutionary War, inland pines were cut for masts in Freeport, Durham, and Pownal, hauled by oxen to Mast Landing, loaded into specifically-built mast ships, and shipped to England (see sidebar).

When the sanctuary was created, timbers from an ancient corduroy road were discovered, preserved in the salt marsh. This was part of the King's Highway, built in 1762 as a route for British soldiers to maintain contact with coastal outposts during the skirmishes of the French and Indian Wars. Old stone slabs at the Mill Dam are the remainder of a tidal dam across the upper Harraseeket, known as Mill Stream. Though it is hard to believe today, by the mid-1800s, this trickle powered a sawmill, a shingle mill, two gristmills, a fulling mill, and a woodworking shop. The miller's house still stands, now occupied by caretakers.

The milled lumber was brought to Portland by the little steamer *Tyro*. *Tyro's* smokestack was hinged so it could be lowered to pass beneath the bridge and continue further upriver to the mill.

Mast Landing was also a steamer landing with a wharf and two stores. The last steamer running between Mast Landing and Portland was the *Harraseeket*. The fare was 50 cents.

The sanctuary is owned and operated by Maine Audubon, which runs various programs here throughout the year. For more information, they can be reached at 781-2330 or at 118 US Rt. 1, Falmouth, ME 04105.

Masts and the Broad Arrow

When English explorer Captain George Waymouth brought the *Archangel* into Pentecost Harbor, near the St. George River in 1605, he found "notable high timber trees, masts for ships of four hundred tons." As much as gold or cod, masts were the New World's bounty.

In Europe, the lightweight and supple softwoods such as firs and pines suitable for masts were in short supply. England's forests were cut for firewood in the Middle Ages, and by the 17th century, the closest supply for mast timbers was in the Baltic. There she competed with the French, Spanish, and Dutch for the great Baltic firs, prized by the British Admiralty for their resilience and durability. But the Baltic was 1,000 miles away and not under England's control, and the route could be blocked easily at the straits of Denmark. New sources were needed.

As early as 1609, the Jamestown Colony was sending home the first shipment of masts from its virgin forests. By the mid-1600s, the colonists in America had established a flourishing trade in masts, lumber, and other naval stores to Europe and the Caribbean. They were not pleased when the British Admiralty awoke to the fact that its supply of mast trees in North America was in danger. In 1685, a Surveyor of Pines and Timber was appointed to survey the Maine woods "within 10 miles of any navigable waterway" and mark all suitable trees with "the king's broad arrow," the symbol designating Royal Navy property. The broad arrow was to be blazed with an ax on "all trees of the diameter of twenty-four inches and upwards at twelve inches from the ground." Woe to anyone who damaged or stole the king's property. The fine was £100!

The Broad Arrow Policy was observed with all the enthusiasm that greeted Prohibition more than two centuries later, and the same native ingenuity was applied to circumvent it. Mast trees were partially burned in mysterious fires or splintered in unusual gales. Some of the great pines were surreptitiously fed into the sawmills, but never, under any circumstances, would the floorboards of any colonial home exceed 23 inches in width.

Mast trees were usually cut in the fall, when they were full of resin. The trees were carefully felled on prepared beds, limbed, and squared. During the winter, the rough timbers, or baulks, were dragged by brute strength onto sleds and hauled out of the woods by teams of oxen. Since one great tree could weigh as much as 18 tons, this was a difficult and dangerous process, requiring great skill and the efforts of as many as 100 oxen.

Where mast roads met, communities sprang up, and often the shape of the town square was determined by the clearance needed to turn the long timbers. The Bliss-Holbrook Tavern in Freeport, now the stores opposite L.L. Bean, was sited at an angle so the masts could make the turn.

Every mast road led to the nearest navigable waters, often a tidal marsh. "Mast Landing" still appears on charts for many locations along the Maine coast. In Casco Bay the main landings were at Stroudwater on the Fore River and at the headwaters of the Harraseeket. Here the baulks were delivered to a mast agent, slipped into the water, and towed to a mast depot.

At the mast depot, the baulks were graded and hewn to the specified 16 sides. Typical dimensions required an inch of diameter at the butt for every yard of height. Then the masts were loaded aboard special mast ships through large stern ports for transportation to England for final shaping and fitting. Some of these mast ships were of 400 to 600 tons burden and could carry 30 to 50 of the enormous baulks below decks.

The Broad Arrow Policy could never be effectively enforced in the wilds of the New World, but the supply of great pines was sufficient to provide a crucial resource for the Royal Navy for 125 years, until the monopoly was finally ended by the American Revolution.

120. Wolfe's Neck State Park

Wolfe's Neck State Park (865-4465) is a 200-acre park with wide walking trails and picnic spots along Casco Bay and woodsy trails along the Harraseeket River. There is a modest admission fee.

"Wolf Neck" on the chart is not named for the animal. As early as 1666, the area was settled by Thomas and Anne Shepherd. Their daughter Rachel married Henry Wolfe, but his name was sometimes spelled "Wolf."

The park straddles the road near the word "Neck" on the chart. It is approachable by water from either the Casco Bay or Harraseeket side, but only at the top of the tide.

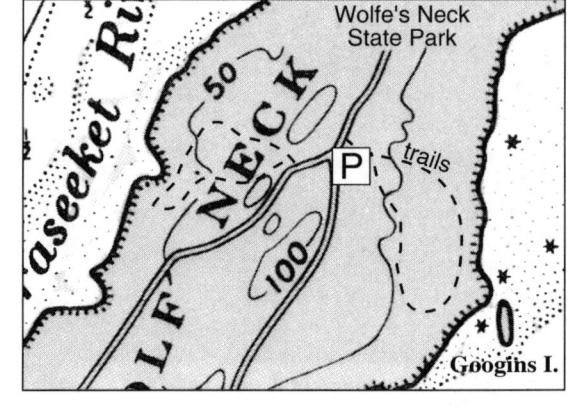

By sea. There are no launching facilities here, even for portable boats. From the Harraseeket near the top of the tide, head for either of the two small indents shown on the chart near the word "Harraseeket." Hike up the bank through the woods until you come upon the trails. From Casco Bay, follow the deep water between Bustins and Moshier Island until you pass the mark at Googins Ledge. Then work your way through the shallows to the shore just south of the small island shown on the chart, just off the broadest portion of the neck. Do not disturb the ospreys which nest every year on Googins Island.

By land. From Freeport, follow Flying Point Road. Take a right on Wolf Neck Road and pass through the farm fields until you see signs for the park on the left.

Ashore. Henry Wolfe is said to have planted an orchard, but he found that the Indians also liked apples. To get rid of the Indians, he had to cut down all his apple trees except one that had apples so sour nobody would touch them.

An old saltbox house sits close to the road before the entrance to the park. It once was the home of Captain Greenfield Pote. Pote was a staunch 18th-century sea captain who was usually voyaging at sea. In the brief periods when he was ashore, he lived in Falmouth (now Portland) in a typical saltbox of the period. Legend has it that in 1760, he had just finished one of his brief shore leaves and was waiting favorable winds to depart Portland Harbor. But day after day brought bad weather or contrary winds. Finally, when his weather window opened, he put out to sea.

When Captain Pote returned weeks or months later after his successful voyage, he discovered that a complaint had been filed against him—the day he had finally left had been the Sabbath! Pote was so infuriated that he vowed he would no longer live in such a town, nor pay taxes there. And in 1765, true to his word, he picked up his house, loaded it onto a flat-bottomed scow, and moved it to some farmland he had purchased on Wolfe Neck. Curiously, the house sits with its back to the road. Either the road moved after the house, or it is another strong testament to the Captain's independence. Captain Pote rests in the nearby graveyard.

121. Little River

A small stream runs to a bight to the east of Wolfe Neck, snaking through farm fields and slipping gently beneath a small wooden bridge, where it empties into the glistening bay. Little River is indeed little. It is also know by a more Puritan name, Recompence River.

The vistas where the dirt road crosses Little River are stunning. You can bask on the shoreside rocks, or, at high tides, you can carry portable boats down a makeshift ramp and splash them in the river for a quick exploration. If you need a place to stay, Recompence Shore Campsites is nearby.

By sea. The put-in is on the northwest side of the bridge, down the ramp made of sloping logs with cleats nailed to them. The tide will need to be fairly high for enough water to paddle upriver or to float over the shoals on the bay side of the bridge.

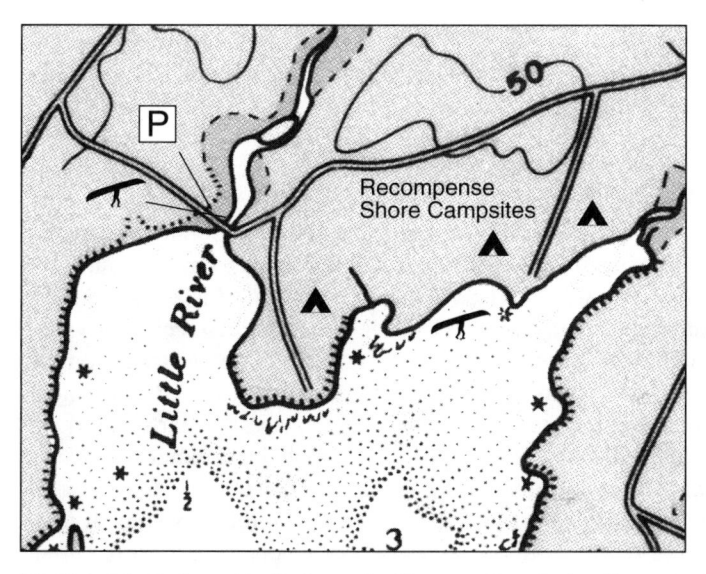

The bridge has a vertical clearance of about three feet at high, and outside the bridge, the water opens into a wide, shallow bay, fully exposed to the southwest. On the ebb, the deceptively gentle current in Little River can set up large standing waves where it meets the opposing wind. At low, this is all mud flat.

By land. Follow the directions to Wolfe's Neck State Park, but take Burnett Road, the first possible left off Wolf Neck Road. Parking is just before the bridge, on the left.

Ashore. Wolfe's Neck Farm surrounds Little River, and the farm's cattle may be grazing nearby. The farm raises organic beef, and it is run by the Wolfe Neck Foundation. The office is east of the river, farther along Burnett Road, on the left.

122. Recompence Shore Campsites

Recompence Shore Campsites (865-9307) is a marvelous array of tent sites tucked in the woods, on the edges of expansive hayfields, or on the shores of the Casco Bay. Proceeds from the campground help support Wolfe's Neck Farm, which is intertwined with the campground. Reservations are recommended.

Like most of the Freeport shore, the coast here is very shallow, confining swimming on the tidal beach and boating activities to near the top of the tides.

By sea. On the chart, the campground is located on the series of small points halfway between Wolfe Neck and Flying Point. Near high tide, portable boats can be launched down one of a couple of sets of stairs to the small tidal beaches at the campground, or they can be run over to Little River (see above).

By land. Take Bow Street out of Freeport. Bow becomes Flying Point Road. At a Y, stay to the right on Lower Flying Point Road and take the first right on Burnett Road. The campground office will be on the right.

Alternatively, take a right off Flying Point Road onto Wolf Neck Road and then take your first left onto Burnett Road. Follow Burnett over Little River. The campground will be on your right. The office will be on your left.

Ashore. There is an organic vegetable garden next to the campsites in the West Bay area with an honor-system farmstand. The campground has showers, restrooms, laundry facilities, limited groceries, a pay phone, and ice.

Wolfe's Neck Farm (865-4469) encourages visitors. Their office and farm store sit across the road from the campground. They sell cuts of their organically raised beef—everything from Porterhouse steaks to kabobs. Their organic pork includes hams, smoked pork chops, and breakfast links or patties. Now that's camping!

123. Bustins Island

Bustins is a wooded 80-acre island on the north side of Broad Sound, half a mile wide by a mile long. Geographically, Bustins lies just a few miles from the mainland, but temporally, it is an island lost in time. This is one of a handful of islands along the main coast where the summer community has changed very little since turn-of-the-century rusticators first built their simple cottages here. There is no electricity on the island, and no phone lines. Water is pumped by hand, and meals are served by the light of kerosene or gas lanterns. Technology has arrived in other guises—solar systems are the rage and more and more cellular phones are packed in with the summer gear.

This is a private place—a tight-knit summer community with grandparents and great grandparents who have come to Bustins every summer of their lives, with marriages between one summer family and another, with childhood memories of ratting around on the island barefoot. This island's enchantment has bound families together for almost a hundred years—a constant in a sea of change.

The most pervasive quality of Bustins Island is its peace and tranquillity, and the island's residents cherish it. Uninvited visitors are not encouraged. There is no store on the island, and no inn or restaurant.

By sea. Bustins is easily identified by one of Casco Bay's most distinctive homes, The Nubble, an octagonal tower built in 1909 on a ledge just off Bustins itself.

Bustins Ledge is a large but low rock southeast of the island, unmarked by any buoys. In good visibility it is obvious, but in fog, be sure you are well away from it. A large underwater ledge lurks to the east of the visible portion of the rock.

The Bustins Island dock is tricky. A ledge extends south from The Nubble to just opposite the dock, so the dock must be approached from the south, inside the ledge. But another rock lurks southwest of the dock and has to be avoided. Often it is marked with a red stick.

Ashore. There are no vehicles on Bustins, just footpaths.

John Bustian is the first recorded owner of a Bustian Island in 1660. Over the next one hundred years, ownership passed through many hands before it was purchased in 1797 for $300 by James Bibber. Bibber and his wife cleared the land with oxen, built a house, and farmed the island. Their daughter and son-in-law carried on the tradition, and for years the island was called Bibber's Island on the charts. After fifty-six years, the farm was sold out of the family, and it was gradually divided. In 1885 a school with eleven pupils was established in one farmhouse.

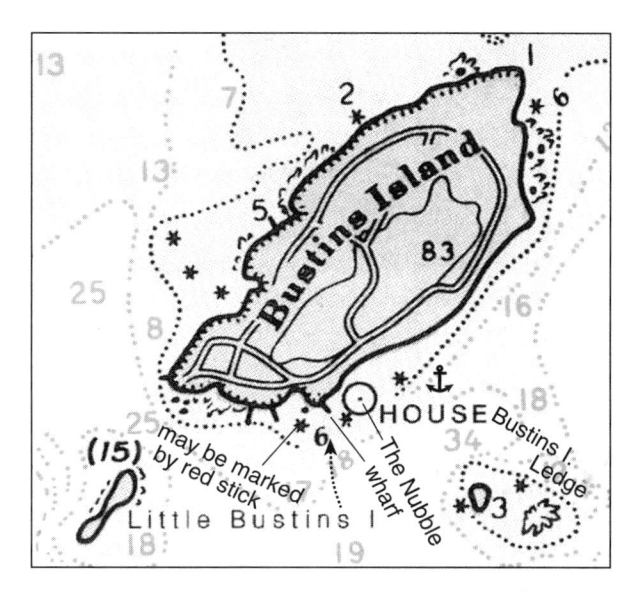

The rusticators discovered Bustins in the late 1800s, and from then until about 1910 the island sang with the ringing of hammers as the summer cottages went up. After the steamer *Phantom* began regular service to the island in 1888, a general store was established, followed by the Ship's Inn, with a small restaurant. The community attracted actors and artists. Helen Keller visited briefly, and Cole Porter attended Nautical Camp Wychmere for boys, which was begun on the island in 1903 and ran for several years. Captain Donald MacMillan was a summer resident when he wasn't exploring the Arctic. And even somebody named L.L. Bean had a cottage here.

One early resident, Charles Guppy, came up with the ingenious idea of rigging a large kite to his dory to spare him the work of rowing to South Freeport and back for his supplies. He and a friend launched his big red kite from South Freeport for its maiden voyage, but they hadn't gone far before a sudden gale descended upon them and grabbed the kite, lifting the bow of the dory and skimming it over the waves. When the dory hit the beach on Bustins, it was dragged clear over the beach and up a full boatlength into a field. After such a promising beginning, Guppy decided to stick to the oars.

In 1913, the residents of Bustins banded together and petitioned the state to become a Village Corporation, with jurisdiction over all municipal matters except taxation. The new Corporation promptly banned all but the most necessary motor vehicles. Three years later, the residents built a community center that became the focal point of the summer activities and housed the small island library. Each cottage was named, and each section of the island got an unofficial name—or reputation: Rum Row, the Bible Belt, the Gold Coast, the West Side, and Shanty Town.

Following World War II, with the new-found popularity of auto travel, few people had the time or the desire to spend a whole summer on the island. With lack of ridership, the Casco Bay Lines steamer dropped Bustins from its route. The Ship's Inn closed, and, after hanging on until the early 1970s, the island store folded.

Archie Ross, from nearby Chebeague, stepped in to fill the gap. He began a shuttle service to and from the Freeport town landing in the *Victory*. Several years later, the Victory hit some pilings while Archie was helping a sailboat in distress. Residents of Bustins and neighboring islands rallied in support, raising enough money to built a new boat, which Archie named the *Marie L* after his mother. And for fifty years, up through the summer of 1996, three times a day, seven days a week, from mid-May to mid-September, Archie and the *Marie L* made the run out to Bustins and back. Now, the service is on the *Maranbo II*.

124. Little Bustins Island

Little Bustins Island lies due south of Bustins. This small, private island sports a cottage owned by descendants of the Soule brothers, who ran one of the major shipyards in South Freeport (see Brewer's Marine, p. 126). Please do not land.

By sea. The passage between Bustins and Little Bustins is wide and deep with no obstructions other than the ledgy shore of Bustins.

125. French Island

French Island lies due south of Bustins Island, punctuated by Little French Island to the north. These wooded islands are private, with a cottage hidden among the trees.

By sea. These dark islands make a good landmark at the north end of Broad Sound and at the southwestern end of the unnamed sound to the west of Upper and Lower Goose Island. But they present several dangers.

A long, unmarked arm of ledge reaches from French Island to the northeast. When passing to the east of French Island, keep well away from the area of the ledge. When passing to the west, you will first need to estimate your position and steer between the French Island ledge and Bustins Ledge, due north of French and also unmarked. The visible portion of Bustins Ledge is a low, treeless rock, which is sometimes difficult to see. Often it is occupied by seals. The rest of the ledge is underwater, to the east.

Do not attempt to pass between French and Little French Island—they're not quite as separate underwater as they appear above.

Ashore. Please do not land.

French Island is the southernmost island in the town of Freeport. In the years following the Civil War, in an effort to protect dwindling stocks of mackerel and herring, the town paid a bounty of a dollar for each seal killed. Other towns bordering Casco Bay had similar bounties. As proof of kills, the seal's noses were presented to the town treasurer for payment.

One day, two Indians appeared before the Freeport treasurer with 205 seals' noses, which the Indians, with some hesitation, claimed they had killed out on French Island. The treasurer became suspicious. He had the noses examined, and it was discovered that they were, in fact, carefully crafted out of seal hide. The Indians, it seemed, had discovered a lucrative cottage industry—the manufacture of seal noses to trick unsuspecting town officials. But Freeport's treasurer had sniffed it out.

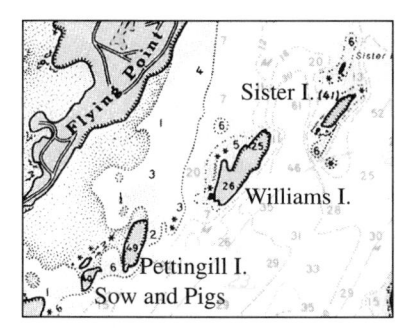

126. The Silver Islands

A string of small private islands lies between Bustins Island and Merepoint. Early charts call them the Silver Islands (see below), perhaps for the silver birches that may have grown there. Today they are known as Sow and Pigs, Pettingill, Williams, and Sister Island. Together they form a string of stepping stones that can offer small boats a series of lees to escape the prevailing southwesterlies while working to the southwest or northeast.

By sea. The water between the Silver Islands and Flying Point is shoal. At low, Sow and Pigs and Pettingill Island are actually connected to Flying Point by mud flats. Small rocks lie to the north, just off each island.

Ashore. Most of these private islands have cottages on them and landing is not allowed. Sow and Pigs was once known by the equally charming name of Kittywink.

Joseph F.W. DesBarres, Atlantic Neptune

In the age of exploration, maps and charts of the coast were as much an interpretive art as a science. Not only did they depict the geography of the coast, but they also reflected impressions and wishful thinking. A dangerous cape would loom larger on the chart than, perhaps a bigger, but more benign island. Imaginary towns like Norumbega would be placed where the cartographer hoped they would be. And fanciful sea creatures would surface and spout offshore.

For the mariner, these early charts were useful tools, but imperfect. In the middle of the 16th century, the Hydrographer in Ordinary to Charles II referred to "the common scandal of their badness." To correct the problem, surveyor Joseph F.W DesBarres began surveying the east coast of Canada and the United States in 1764. The result, published ten years later, was the *Atlantic Neptune*, a series of beautiful charts with remarkable detail and accuracy with the astounding coverage from the Saint Lawrence to the Mississippi. They became the standard charts for almost a century.

DesBarres' methods were meticulous. He would establish a baseline 350 fathoms long along the shore of a harbor, and then from each end of the baseline, he took bearings of objects on the opposite shore. With these two fixes, he could calculate the distances, the other sides of the triangles, by trigonometry. In the same manner, he took fixes from shore on distant headlands, points, and islands. "Next I went along the shore and reexamined the accuracy of every intersected object, delineated the true shape of every headland, island, point, bay, rock above water, etc. and every winding and irregularity of the coast; and, with boats sent around the shoals, rocks and breakers, determined from observations on shore, their positions and extent, as perfectly as I could."

The Atlantic Neptune chart of Casco Bay is fascinating, showing some early place names and spellings. In addition to the Silver Islands, Maquoit Bay is spelled Magout, Quahog Bay is spelled Cohauk, and Ragged Island is the more logical Rugged Island.

MAINE COAST GUIDE

THE CENTRAL BAYS

MAQUOIT BAY

Maquoit Bay is hugged against the Freeport and Brunswick shores by Merepoint Neck. The Bay is wide and long and open to the southwest, with extensive shoaling towards its head.

With the exception of Little Flying Point at its mouth, the little tuck of Bunganuc, and the small estuary at its head near Wharton Point, Maquoit is almost featureless. There are no real harbors, and the only access to it is from the Wharton Point ramp, which is limited by the tides (see below for individual entries). For these reasons, Maquoit is the most overlooked of all the large bodies of water on Casco Bay.

Ashore. In the late 1600s, the west shore of Maquoit Bay was the site of an incongruous settlement attempt by a group of families from Eleuthera, a large cay in the Bahamas. In 1685, these families were driven from their homes by the Spanish, and they fled to Boston. When the proprietors of what was then North Yarmouth heard of their plight, they presented a petition to the town proposing that some of them be resettled here. As a result, 200 acres were granted to the Eleutherans between the eastern boundary of North Yarmouth and Bunganuc Brook. Nine families moved here, cleared several acres and planted about sixteen acres with corn. But pioneer life in the northern latitudes was tough for those used to living in the tropics, and they eventually moved away.

127. Flying Point Campground

Flying Point Campground (865-4569) is actually on Little Flying Point on the west shore of Maquoit Bay, where Little Fox Island is connected to the mainland by a causeway. This campground caters primarily to a semipermanent RV community, though it does have a handful of tent sites clustered near the water. Reservations are accepted, though a three-night minimum stay is required on holiday weekends.

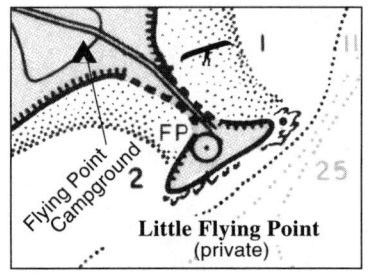

By sea. Little Fox Island is unnamed on the chart, but the flagpole of the house there is shown as "FP." The island is connected by to Little Flying Point by a causeway, and portable boats can be launched at the small beaches on either side of it. The water is too shoal, however, to be navigated on the lower half of the tide.

By land. Take Bow Street out of Freeport and follow it as it becomes Flying Point Road and then Lower Flying Point Road. It eventually leads to an extreme Y, where you will see signs for the campground. Go right. The campground drive will be on your left. There is no parking at the put-in, so you will need to shuttle your vehicle back to your campsite.

Ashore. The campground has showers, toilets, and laundry. Little Fox Island—called Tobacco Island in early records—and the causeway that leads to it are private.

In 1756, Thomas Means and his family lived in a little cabin by the shore, just above

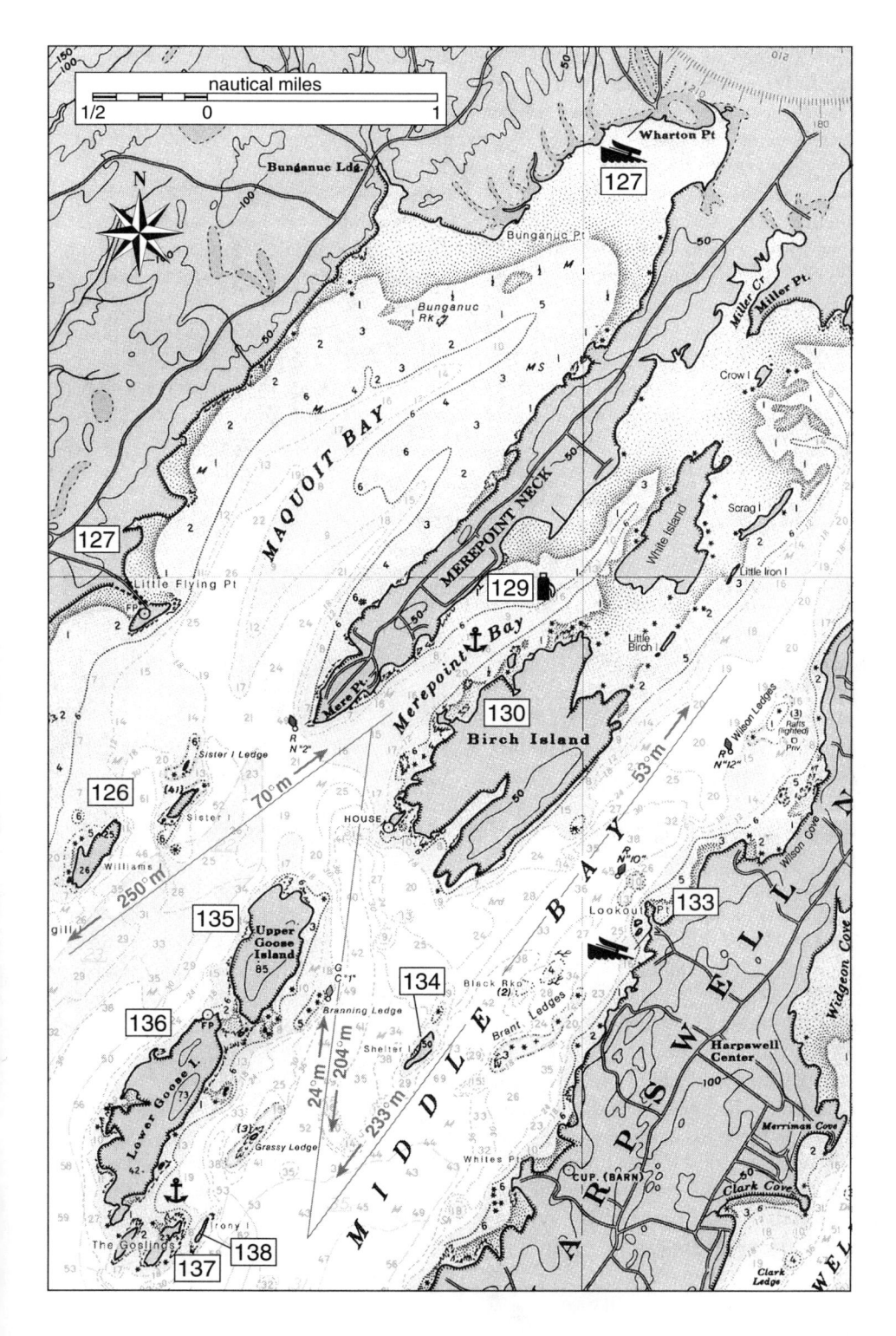

CASCO BAY

Little Flying Point. That May, Indians were raiding the coast, and outlying settlers were advised to seek the protection of the nearest garrison house. For the Means family, the closest garrison house was only about a half-mile away on Flying Point, but for some reason, perhaps because it was so close that they could get there quickly, they delayed.

The Indians attacked the cabin at dawn. Thomas Means was killed. His pregnant wife was holding their youngest child, Robert, aged eighteen months, in her arms when a bullet passed through him and into her breast, killing the child and wounding her. Her sister, Molly Finney, had been living at the Means cabin, and the Indians grabbed her, along with the Means' oldest child, Alice. A hired hand, Martin, was in the upstairs loft. He finally found his gun and fired. The shot wounded one of the Indians and scared them into a retreat. Alice managed to wriggle away from her captor, but Molly Finney, aged 16, was dragged into the woods.

The Indians eventually marched Molly Finney to Quebec and sold her to a Frenchman as a housemaid. She was discovered, though, by Captain William McLellan, of Falmouth (now Portland), and he managed to help her escape on his vessel. Tradition gives the Means Massacre a happily-ever-after ending. Molly Finney and her gallant savior were married upon their return.

128. Wharton Point

Wharton Point is at the broad and shallow head of Maquoit Bay, which at low tide becomes one of Casco Bay's most extensive mud flats. Surprisingly, there is a small gravel launching ramp at Wharton Point, with parking in a nearby turnout. This is the only public access to Maquoit Bay, but because of the tidal limitations, the ramp does not see a lot of use.

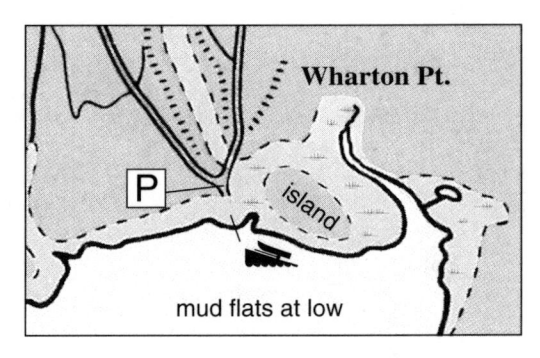

By sea. Depending on your draft, this ramp is usable from one to two hours on either side of high tide. Keep an eye on the wind, too. The ramp faces the prevailing southwesterlies with the long fetch of Maquoit Bay and beyond. When the afternoon wind is up, waves can pile into the shallows at the head of the bay and become quite steep.

As a put-in for portable boats, the ramp or the flat beach next to it can be used anytime except an hour or so on either side of dead low. Following the small creek and estuary tucked to the north of Wharton Point is a pleasant, if brief, adventure.

By land. Take the Brunswick exit from I-95 and merge onto busy US Rt. 1 heading east. Soon after the merge, take a right onto Church Road. From Church, take a right onto Woodside Road and follow it to the water.

Or from downtown Brunswick, follow Maine Street south out of town. Maine becomes Maquoit, and it ends at the point. This is the route of the old Twelve Rod Road.

Ashore. You can park in a turnout in a field above the ramp. The wooded island in the marsh to the east of the ramp is state-owned and managed by the Department of Inland Fisheries and Wildlife.

In 1691, during the latter part of the Indian Wars, the English heard rumors that Indians were planting the abandoned cornfields on Jewell Island. They mounted an expedition to attack them, but when they reached Jewell, they found it deserted. They sailed on to the head of Maquoit Bay and landed to investigate the Brunswick area. Again, they found no Indians.

As they began to return to their ships, however, they were suddenly attacked by both the Indians and the French. Forty men were caught on the shore, and a major battle ensued. The ships were hard aground at the shallow head of the bay, so they couldn't flee. The fighting continued through the night and into the next morning until the tide refloated the ships and the English managed to get away.

Twenty-seven men were either killed or wounded, and after the skirmish, the survivors placed an urgent request for shoes and socks which they apparently had left behind (or were they sucked off by the mud?) as they pushed and pulled their longboats way out to deep water.

Resettlement began near the turn of the century. Wharton Point is named after Thomas Wharton who owned it in 1717, the year that Brunswick's first real road, Twelve Rod Road, was laid out from the "southerly bastion of Fort George (on the Androscoggin) in a straight line to Maquoit." At this time the land that rolls gently down to the east bank of the creek in the headwater estuary was the farm of Matthew Thornton (1714-1803), who would later become one of the signers of the Declaration of Independence.

MIDDLE BAY

Middle Bay is more of a sound than a bay, a broad stretch of water to the west of Harpswell Neck. Like Maquoit Bay, its head shoals extensively, with broad low-tide flats in Middle Bay Cove, where the Indians used to portage their canoes across Harpswell Neck.

By sea. Trailered or portable boats can be launched or hauled near the top of the tide from the ramp on Simpson's Point at the head of the bay or from the Harpswell ramp at Lookout Point (see entries below).

Ashore. Harpswell Neck is one of the predominant features of Casco Bay. It is the longest neck in the bay and the widest, stretching from Brunswick southwestward more than eight miles and culminating in the twin arms of Basin Point and Potts Point that embrace Potts Harbor. Gentle hills of fields and woods roll to the water's edge, and summer homes cluster along its numerous pockets and points.

The Indians called this place Merriconeag, or "Quick Carrying Place" for the narrow portage between Middle Bay Cove and Harpswell Cove. Six years after Captain Smith explored the coast in 1624, he returned in the *Plough* to spend a year in Casco Bay with some settlers. The place he stayed may have been the southern end of Merriconeag.

In 1659 Colonel Shapleigh of Kittery purchased the Neck and neighboring Sebascodegan Island. Some of the first settlers hailed from Harpswell in England, and gradually the neck became known as Harpswell.

To the Indians, it was already known as something else. This was the place where one of the "Yangees", as they called the English, had cheated them. A settler had promised to pay for furs with whiskey, but instead had given them water from his well. Ironically, his name was Thomas Purchase, one of Brunswick's original settlers. Thomas

Purchase was more successful in his dealings with the Indians elsewhere. As early as 1624-1628 he was one of the first to trade with the powerful Canibas and Anasabunticooks near the falls of the Androscoggin River, in Brunswick, acquiring salmon and sturgeon which he cured and exported.

Peace was as ephemeral as trust, and Indian raids were frequent. Thomas Purchase's cabin was one of the first to be burnt to the ground (see New Meadows Lake, p. 205). In 1714, only two settlers remained on the Neck, but the population had rebounded by the time the French cunningly exploited the Indian's distrust for the English and spurred them into the French and Indian War. During attacks, the settlers fled to local garrisons or to blockhouses on Shelter or Jewell Island.

129. Merepoint

Merepoint Neck is a long and narrow peninsula between the upper portions of Maquoit Bay and Middle Bay. Merepoint Bay lies between the Neck and Birch Island to the east.

The best access to the bay is from Paul's Marina (729-3067, Ch. 09). Paul's is a small, low-key, and mostly local affair. They launch boats with a crane and have floats with fuel, water, and pump-out facilities. A small general store is ashore.

By sea. Most of the middle portion of Merepoint Bay is a mooring field, and Paul's is at the center of it, on the bay's west shore. If you have a deep draft, stay among the moored boats at low tide, because the bay shoals rapidly towards the Marina. At low tide, the outer floats at the marina only have a few feet of water. In late summer, the Bay's shallowness is complicated by an abundance of sea grass. Rafts of floating grass can clog saltwater intakes on outboards.

By land. From downtown Brunswick, follow Maine Street south out of town. Go left on Merepoint Road and look for signs to Paul's Marina on the left.

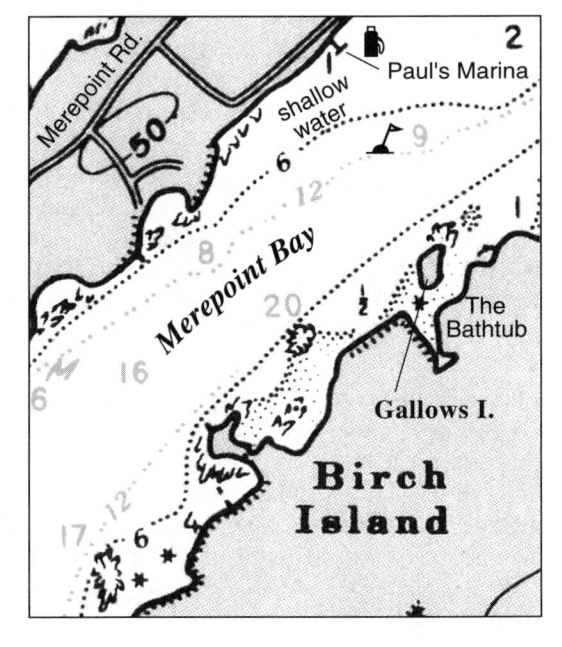

Ashore. Paul's can provide long or short-term parking as well as boat storage and limited repairs. Portapotties and a pay phone are available. The marina operates a small, friendly general store at the head of the dock with basic marine supplies, ice, and delicious ice cream.

For a dangerous side trip, ask directions to the boatshop of Richard Pulsifer (725-5457), who builds exquisite Casco Bay Hamptons (see sidebar, p. 232). Expect to *need* one.

Merepoint may be named after an early settler on the point, a Mr. Marr. This may have been the John Mare who is referred to as having lived there. Or the name may have been a corruption of the French word *mer*, meaning sea, though there is no evidence that the French ever occupied the point.

The southern end is now a private association with a small yacht club near the mouth of Merepoint Bay. The next landing to the north is Birch Island's mainland base.

130. Birch Island

Birch Island, on the east side of Merepoint Bay, is one of Casco Bay's several summer community islands. Simple island cottages are connected by wooded paths and island tranquillity is tempered by a relaxed social scene. Uninvited visitors are not encouraged.

By sea. Birch Island lies directly to the east of Paul's Marina. The community landing is on the island's west shore, in Merepoint Bay. The Little Island off the northwest flank of Birch is Gallows Island. The bight behind it, where the incoming tide is warmed by the sun-baked mud flats is known as The Bathtub. A large cleft in the southern end of the island would make a nice anchorage if it wasn't open to the southwest.

Ashore. The island was originally named for the silver birches that covered it. It changed hands several times, primarily as a woodlot, and for many years it was not settled. During the Indian Wars, an advance sentry was posted on Birch to warn settlers on Harpswell Neck of approaching Indians. He would signal from the hill on the west side of the island, and the settlers from Harpswell would flee to the blockhouse built on Shelter Island, nearby in Middle Bay.

Walter Merriman was Birch's first settler. Merriman was a ship carpenter indentured to a Cape Elizabeth ship owner for his passage from Ireland. He settled on Harpswell Neck with his wife, and they had several children. Merriman eventually bought some of Birch Island, and his son built a family homestead there. The year was probably shortly after 1776.

Other settlers soon followed, and a farming community evolved, with barns and houses and a school. Just after the Revolution, Birch Island was suspected of being a way-station for British goods being smuggled into the fledgling United States. By 1849, there were 48 students in the island school.

Through much of the 19th century, the west side of the island was dominated by "The Farm." In 1875, it was owned by John Miller. According to the Bath papers, Miller was said to be "a very passionate man, frequently beating his wife in a brutal manner." On Thursday, July 29, one of Miller's sons tried to stop one of the beatings. But Miller shot his son in the head with a shotgun and killed him. Miller was convicted and sentenced to life imprisonment. He deeded the farm to his wife for the remainder of her life under the condition that she never remarry. Her heirs eventually sold the farm to James Coffin and his second wife. Their son, Robert Peter Tristram Coffin, would eventually win the Pulitzer Prize for his poetry.

The Coffins sold the farm in 1883 to Fred Johnson, who in addition to running the island farm became the island's biggest promoter. He developed his land into cottage lots and helped to establish steamer service from Portland in the 1920s.

However, after nearly 50 years of settlement, the social structure unraveled. Birch was too small to absorb its expanding population, and young people felt that it held little opportunity. When they moved off, their families often followed, rather than live apart.

Adding to this restlessness, gold was discovered in California, and many Birch Islanders gave in to its lure. Many buildings were abandoned and left to fall into their cellar holes.

Birch was later rediscovered as a summer community, and the land is now private. The Harpswell Heritage Trust, however, holds conservation easements on about 42 acres to protect the island from overdevelopment.

131. Simpson's Point

Simpson's Point is not labeled on the charts. It is the point at the end of the road to the left of the word "Pennellville" on the chart, at the head of Middle Bay. The State of Maine maintains an excellent concrete ramp here, though its use is limited by water at low tide and parking space, both of which are in short supply.

By sea. The ramp is deceptively steep, which might make you think that the bottom keeps getting deeper and deeper. It doesn't. The ramp reaches past most of what flats out, but at low, there is only a foot or so of water for a long way out. Three hours either side of high, though, will allow plenty of water for outboards.

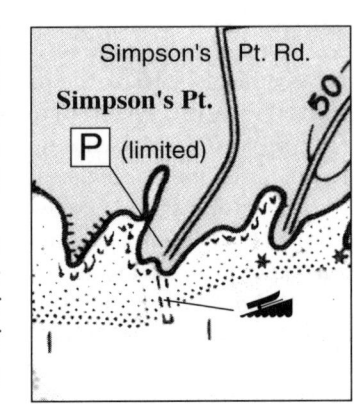

Use caution if the southwest wind fills in. The ramp heads into it, with only a little protection from White and Scrag Island, so swells can build.

By Land. From Brunswick, follow Maine Street south out of town. Turn left on Merepoint Road and left again on Middle Bay Road, heading east. Simpson's Point Road will be on the right, with the ramp at its end.

Ashore. Be particularly cautious with two-wheel drive vehicles on the steep ramp and go easy on the clutch. Geographical fate didn't bless Simpson's Point with much parking space, so be sure to obey the parking signs and park in as tight a space as possible.

For a long time, Simpson's Point and neighboring Pennellville were shipyards and the center of much of Brunswick's shipping activity. When the wharf here was replaced in 1837, it was referred to as New Wharf. Fifty years later, George Wheeler wrote "...it is still called New Wharf, though now old and dilapidated."

132. Middle Bay Cove

Middle Bay Cove lies just to the west of the narrowest portion of Harpswell Neck. At low tide, it is a mud flat, but at high, it becomes a surprisingly wide and multifingered cove that is pleasant to explore.

Little has changed since the days when this was one of the most important links in the Indian canoe routes through Casco Bay. Hugging the western shore, they would follow the southernmost creek through the marsh and then portage across the isthmus to the creek that leads into Skolfield and Harpswell Cove. This carry completely eliminated any open-ocean paddling in the brunt of the southwesterlies. From there, they could paddle around Prince Point and follow Long Reach to the Gurnet and up the New Meadows River.

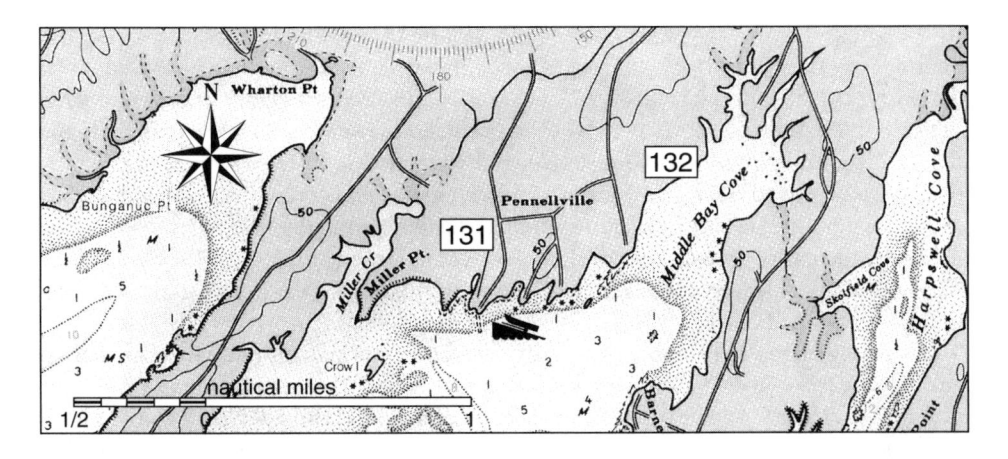

They named this place Merriconeag, which meant "Quick Carrying Place." The name was used loosely and was often applied to the whole peninsula, which settlers later renamed Harpswell Neck.

By sea. You could still make this portage, but you would have to scale the fences and traipse across the private fields of the old Skolfield farm and also cross the sometimes very busy road leading out Harpswell Neck.

The wooded shores of the cove itself and its marshy headwaters make a pleasant exploration for those who don't link their personal contentment to any particular destination.

By land. Because of the open farm fields, the carry is perfectly visible from the low dip in the Harpswell Road, through the fields and past the lily pond of this stunning farm. From downtown Brunswick, take the Bath Road briefly before taking a right on Rt. 123, the Harpswell Road. The carry is just before a sign marking the Harpswell town line.

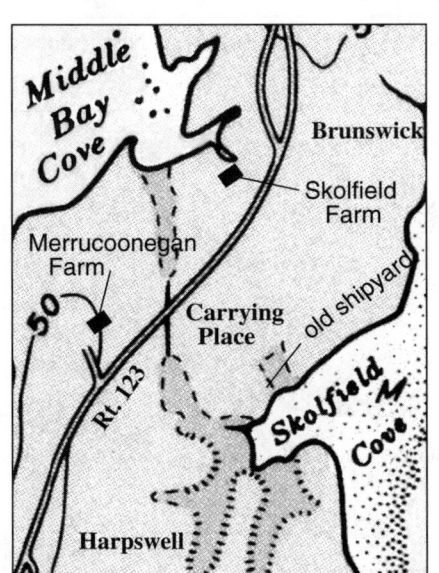

Ashore. The Brunswick-Topsham Land Trust owns the southernmost of the fingers at the head of the cove. The land to the south of that, where the chart shows the marshy connection across the neck, is the Skolfield farm.

In the 1740s, Thomas Skolfield bought 200 acres and settled jst across the Harpswell line, working the farm and raising eleven children. At the turn of the century, the Skolfields turned to shipbuilding, beginning a long family tradition tied to the sea. In the next century, the descendants of Thomas Skolfield launched more than 60 vessels. Skolfields not only built the ships, they also owned and captained them, sometimes with wives and children aboard. Forty members of the family became mariners. Six died at sea from disasters or sickness. Only one ever lost his ship.

Thomas Skolfield's grandson, George Skolfield, moved his operations from the Androscoggin River in 1802 and started the shipyard at the farm down on the banks of Harpswell Cove. As his reputation for fine work and fine vessels grew, George became known as "Master George." The town of Harpswell also took notice of him. In 1836 the town tried to tax him for a half-finished vessel on his ways, a very uncommon practice. Towns usually taxed a ship only after she was launched and could begin earning returns for her owner. But Harpswell underestimated Master George. Instead of paying the tax, he moved the entire operation a few hundred feet across the town line into Brunswick. Pleased with the unexpected revenue, Brunswick was more than happy to float the tax until the ship was floating.

The keel for a new ship was usually laid in the spring, and the vessel would be launched in November before the small bays and coves froze. A typical shipyard employed 60 to 100 men and by man and ox power alone produced huge ships weighing as much as 1800 tons at a rate of about one a year. A ship of that size would cost roughly $75,000, but it would usually pay for itself in its first year at sea. Most of the Harpswell fleet went into the West India trade or the coal and oil trade, and a ship would make about three round trips to the Caribbean and another three along the coast each year.

The original Skolfield house, called Merrucoonegan Farm, is on the hill on the Harpswell side; Master George's newer house is across the dale in Brunswick.

The site of the old shipyard is difficult to see from the road or water. Some of the old ways remain, and grassy mounds cover what were once piles of wood chips. The shipyard consisted of a boarding house for workers, a cookhouse, a blacksmith shop and steam-box, and an ox barn. For a launching, they would hire local boys for $1 a day to dig a channel in the mud from the ways into deeper water. Harpswell Cove has since filled in dramatically (see Inside Passage, p. 186).

133. Lookout Point

Lookout Point is a distinctive nub on the west side of Harpswell Neck, about halfway down its length. A small beach flanks a launching ramp, and two cute, but private, little islets lie just offshore.

By sea. The breadth of Middle Bay is greatly reduced in its mid-section by the lethal Brant Ledges, east of Shelter Island, and by Black Rock, which the cormorants seem insistent on painting white. With care these obstacles can be passed on either side, but passing to the west is easiest. Once well clear of Black Rock, Lookout Point can be identified by the red sheds of Allen's Lobster Wharf and the two little islets just south of the point. Approach the ramp north of the islets.

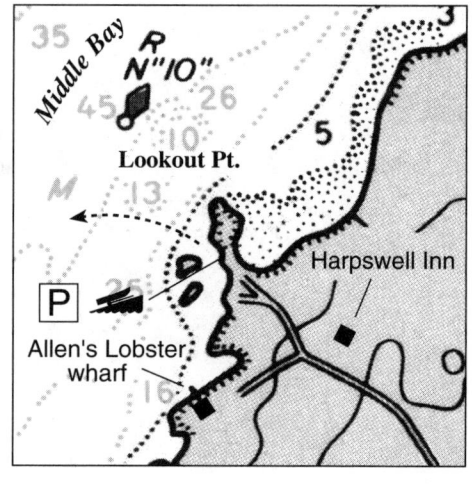

The paved ramp has deep water at all tides, and there is some space for roadside parking. If your boat has a mast, beware of the powerlines near the ramp.

By land. Take the Harpswell Road (Rt. 123) out of Brunswick (see Middle Bay Cove, p. 146) and take a right on Lookout Point Road, where you will see signs for the Harpswell Inn.

Ashore. Not only is Lookout Point blessed with a good ramp and two small beaches, but there is some roadside parking, and the Harpswell Inn (833-5509, 800-843-5509) is right next door. They may be able to arrange long-term parking for you, and they can certainly tuck you in for the night. The Inn's beautiful building began in 1761 as a cookhouse for the workers of the local shipyard, owned by Joseph Curtis and Albion Estes.

134. Shelter Island

Shelter Island lies in the Middle of Middle Bay, halfway between Harpswell Neck and Upper Goose Island. This is a private island, with a camp that blends so well with its surroundings that it is practically invisible.

Shelter points its rust-stained rocks straight into the southwesterlies like a ship riding at anchor. It has no harbor or cove or even much of a lee to speak of. Instead, Shelter Island got its name from the stout, wooden blockhouse that the settlers of Harpswell Neck built here during the Indian Wars. The island is high for its width, with broad expanses of water in all directions. They posted a sentinel on Birch Island who would signal them if he saw Indians advancing in canoes, and the settlers would flee to the blockhouse.

Now, the island's high trees are the perfect shelter for ospreys, which nest in three of them. A conservation easement given to the Harpswell Heritage Trust protects all of the island's seven acres.

135. Upper Goose Island

Upper Goose Island is a 94-acre wooded island to the north of the Goslings on the western side of Middle Bay, due south of the entrance to Merepoint Bay. The Nature Conservancy owns most of the island, which for a while was the largest great blue heron rookery in New England, with more than 250 nests in the island's hemlock, beech, and yellow birch trees. Some trees held as many as ten nests. But for unknown reasons, the colony left in 1992, possibly because of the presence of a predatory owl or osprey. One hundred and fifty pairs relocated on Little Whaleboat Island (see p. 152).

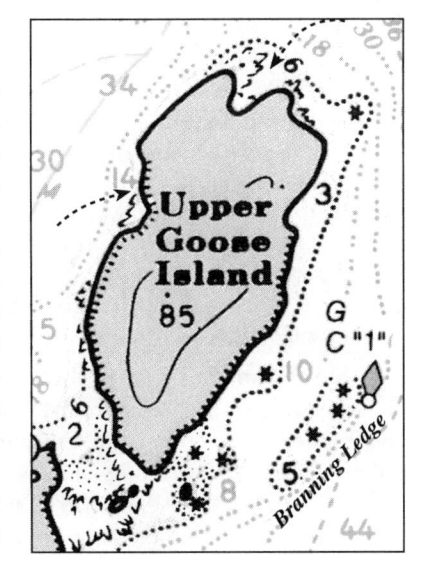

Ashore. Some heron may still nest here, or they may return. The Nature Conservancy urges you to refrain from visiting the interior of the island during the herons' nesting period—between early April and mid-August—when they are particularly prone to human disturbance.

To explore the shoreline's rocky ledges, gravel beaches, and salt marshes, land at the large gravel beach on the western shore or in the north cove. Ospreys, eiders, and other sea ducks are common sights, as are harbor seals on the southeast ledges.

A small cove at the northeasterly end of Upper Goose Island is said to be the location of the Fountain of Youth. This great freshwater torrent was exposed only for very short periods at low tide, bursting out of the tidal mud and shooting as high as a foot. Its water was said to have life-giving properties, and those who drank it were supposed to live to a ripe old age. Many settlers claimed they owed their long lives to its magical properties. We, alas, haven't been able to find it.

136. Lower Goose Island

Lower Goose is a large, wooded island connected to Upper Goose by submerged ledge. Most of the island is owned by several families who have summer cottages here. In recent years the anchorage formed by Upper Goose and the Goslings to the south (see below) has become an increasingly popular cruising destination, particularly on weekends, transforming this tranquil and secluded spot into a beehive of activity. Please respect the privacy of the island residents by keeping your presence to a minimum.

By sea. At high tide it is possible for kayaks and other boats with minimal draft to sneak between Lower and Upper Goose Islands.

Ashore. Please do not land.

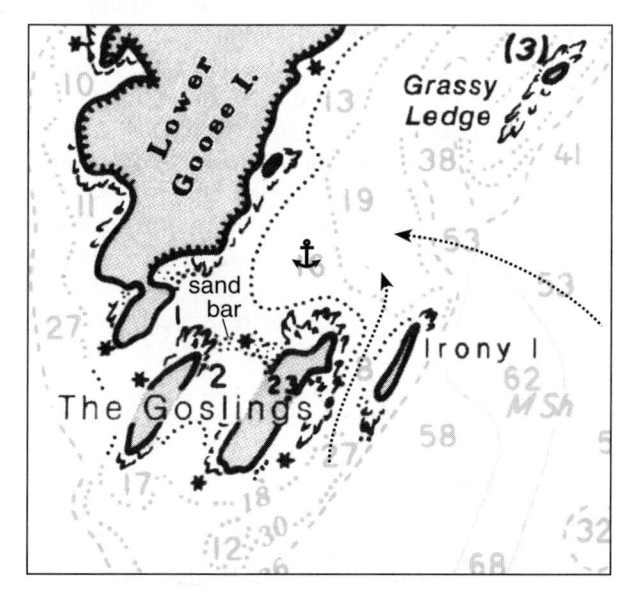

137. The Goslings

Several small islands lie to the south of Lower Goose Island, forming a relatively protected anchorage. They are the Goslings to the geese. All are wooded and beautiful and fragile, and all are private. Currently the owners do allow careful landing and exploration, though this permissiveness is contingent upon careful use.

These islands are blessed with the dubious distinction of both beauty and location. They form a lee from prevailing southwesterlies, and the anchorage to the north has become a very popular cruising destination. Since the Goslings are an easy small-boat pilgrimage from Yarmouth, Freeport, or Harpswell, there are many boats and moorings vying for swinging room and many boaters looking for something explore. Please respect these islands and their owners' request that fires are not allowed and leave nothing behind.

By sea. The two easternmost islands both have small beaches and are connected to each other by a shell bar at lower tides, with a ledge between them. The third island is connected to Lower Goose by a similar bar. At higher tides, a shallow channel runs between the middle island and the one closest to Lower Goose. Small boats can approach by running between the two westernmost Goslings, but deeper-draft boats should come in from the east, north of Irony Island, halfway between Irony Island and Grassy Ledge. Grassy Ledge, to the northeast of the anchorage, is unmarked except for the colony of harbor seals that often are basking and barking there.

138. Irony Island

There is nothing ironic about Irony Island. It is exactly what it is called, irony. This little piece of ledge east of the Goslings has so much iron in it that it has rusted, and if you get too close, it would probably throw your compass off. The same vein runs farther up Middle Bay, through Shelter Island and, not surprisingly, Little Iron Island.

By sea. Irony Island marks the southern edge of the entrance to the Goslings anchorage. For the daring, a narrow channel with eight feet of water runs to the west of the Irony. Boats with deeper drafts or skippers with more caution usually go around Irony to the outside.

Ashore. There is little reason to ago ashore on this privately-owned island. On the east side, a small brass plaque is cemented to the rocks that reads, "Captain Ted Langzettel, lost off this island Sept. 2, 1962, born July 7, 1912, Captain of Portland Pilot Boat and his own cutter *Corineus*."

139. Harpswell Fuel Depot

The chart indicates a large, lit wharf south of on the west side of Harpswell Neck. It lies at the foot of a broad, cleared field that might look rural if it weren't for a few scattered, institutional-looking buildings.

This was the site of a fuel depot for the Brunswick Naval Air Station. Tankers off-loaded jet fuel at the wharf. The fuel was stored in shoreside tanks and then piped ten miles to the base as needed. The Navy operated the depot from 1954 until 1980, when it was turned over to private contractors. But by 1992, the depot was considered too costly, the tanks were removed, and the view improved dramatically. Fuel is now trucked to the air station from a storage facility in Searsport.

Once the inevitable ground contamination has been cleaned up, the property will revert to the town on Harpswell. An oceanographic institution from Florida has approached the town with a proposal to develop the site into a marine laboratory.

140. The Jackknife

Lobstermen have named the stretch of water to the west of the Harpswell Neck between the Goslings and the Whaleboat islands the Jackknife. Perhaps it got that name from the way it has to skew around Goose Ledge and the ledges north of Little Whaleboat, but its name has a new meaning now. The Jacknife is rich in lobsters, and therefore it is equally abundant in lobstermen and lobster traps, having one of the highest concentrations of traps in Casco Bay. By convention, strings of traps are usually set parallel to the shore. But here, the direction of the shores is quite subjective, and traps get set on top of each other. When one string is pulled, it often brings up incredible tangles of warp, traps, and buoys. And when that happens, you can bet that every hand is holding a jackknife.

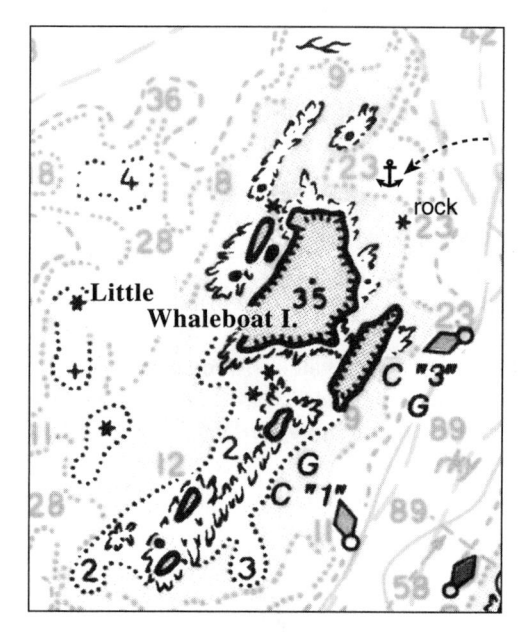

141. Little Whaleboat Island ⚓

This is a privately owned island. Landing is not allowed, but it holds other attractions for those exploring by water. The island forms a good lee from prevailing southwesterlies for resting or anchoring, and the cluster of ledges and an island to the west form a micro-archipelago with several osprey nests and an occasional blue heron that moved here from Upper Goose (see p. 149).

By sea. Approach from the northeast, using care to avoid the lone rock off the island's northeast flank and the long line of ledge that extends off the north point. The lone rock is completely covered at high tide and barely shows at low, lying about halfway between green can "3" and the ledge showing to the north.

Little Whaleboat Island lies due west of a smaller island, unnamed on the chart. This littler Little Whaleboat Island is joined at the hip to Little Whaleboat by a ledge at low. At high tide, small boats can pick their way between the ledges and rocks to the southwest of the island and pass between Little Whaleboat and Littler Little, or they can approach from the north, favoring the east side of the channel between them to avoid the submerged ledges on the west.

The cut between Little Whaleboat and the miniature island to the west should only be attempted in shallow-draft boats, and then only near the top of the tide. Please keep your distance from the nesting birds and do not land.

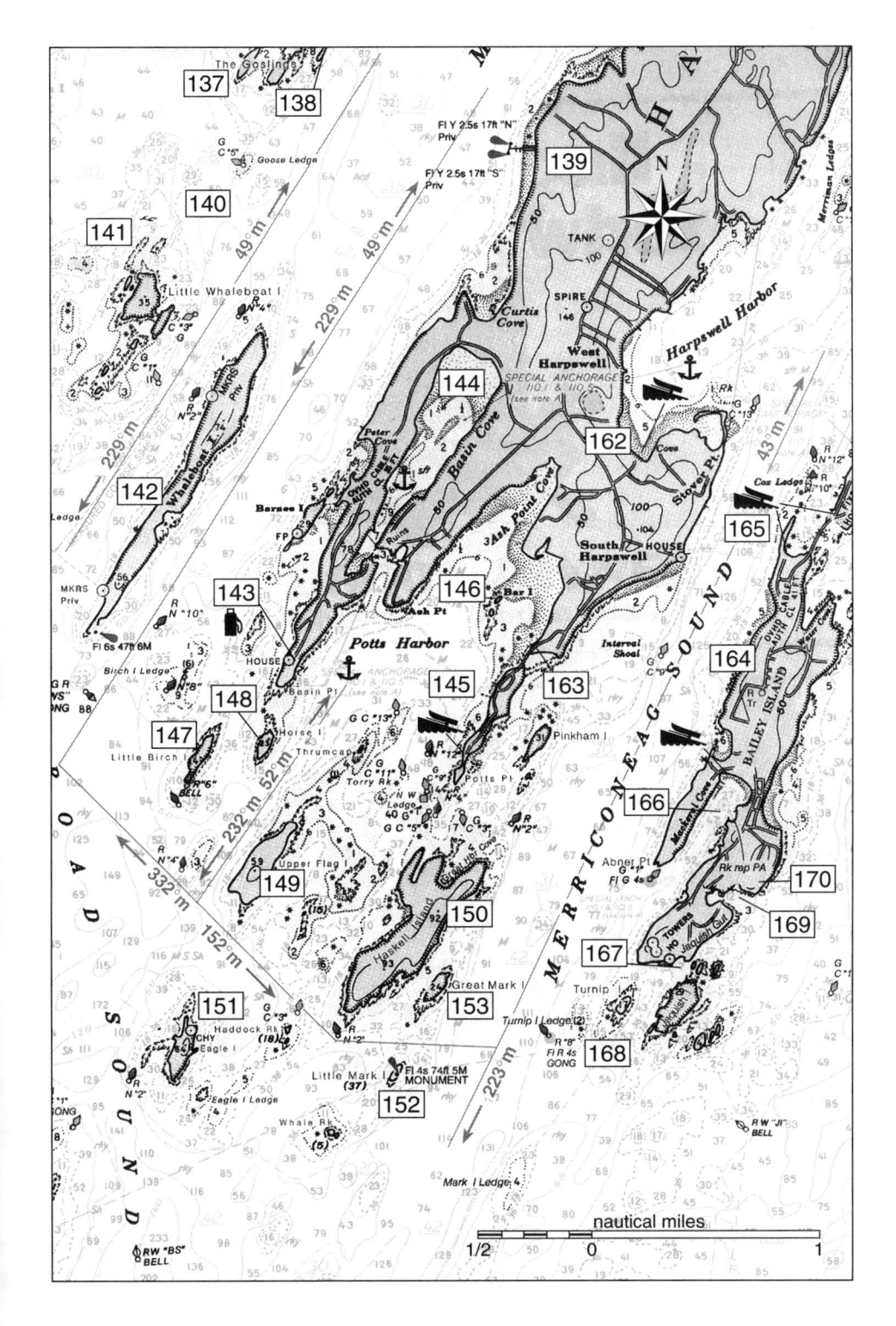

CASCO BAY

153

142. Whaleboat Island

Whaleboat Island is a long and narrow spine of ledge, stretching between Broad Sound and Middle Bay. Its north and south ends are wooded, and they are connected by a lower, rocky waist.

This is a private island, but the Bureau of Parks and Lands holds a conservation easement on it. Small boats sometimes land either along the middle section, on either side, or on the northwest shoulder.

By sea. Whaleboat's shores are bold rock, with only a few cobbly clefts in its shoreline. A narrow band of submerged ledge fringes it here and there.

Near the top of the tide, the easiest place to land is on the west side of the island's midsection, in a small cobble pocket that faces north. On the chart, the stem of the "b" in "Whaleboat" points to it. If you have enough water to clear the submerged ledges just off the pocket, approach it heading south, staying far enough out to avoid the ledges projecting from the shore on your left. High tide also fills the small cove southeast of the waist. Beware, however, of submerged rocks.

A clearing on the wooded northwest shoulder lies just north of the northern mile marker shown on the chart. Again, you will need to be aware of the few submerged ledges, depending on the tide.

Because of its shape and orientation, Whaleboat affords practically no lee to the afternoon southwesterlies, and the relatively deep water makes anchoring a precarious proposition. If you do anchor, be sure your anchor is well set, or you may be visiting Whaleboat for longer than you planned.

Ashore. The thick underbrush on Whaleboat generally confines exploration to the northwest clearing or the treeless midsection. Fires are not allowed ashore.

Like so many of the Casco Bay islands, Whaleboat provided offshore protection from local Indian tribes. The first deed describing Whaleboat was written in 1774 when Jacob Mitchell passed a quarter of the island to his son David "in consideration of love and good will and also 40 shillings lawfull money." The first real settlers seem to have been the Jacob Blake family, who bought Whaleboat in 1788 and farmed it until 1861. Paul Merryman of Harpswell began to put together the many stray pieces of ownership, and by 1889, for the grand sum of $1,085, he owned the island in its entirety. In 1954, it was purchased by the painter Stephen Etnier, who escaped here for peace and solitude. And now Whaleboat is for sale again. Unfortunately, the value of Maine islands has skyrocketed, and they are often developed to justify their price tags. Is it Whaleboat's turn?

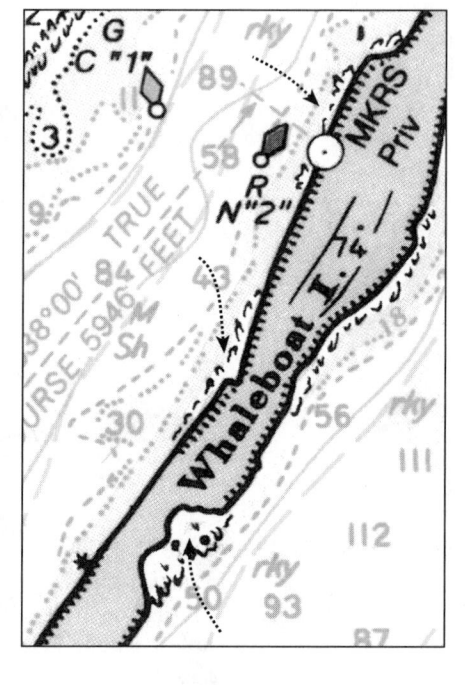

CASCO BAY

POTTS HARBOR AND BROAD SOUND

POTTS HARBOR

Potts Harbor is a broad expanse of water lying between the open arms of Basin Point and Potts Point at the end of Harpswell Neck. Boaters in small craft can explore several sandy islands here, work up into the almost land-locked Basin Cove, or twist eastward through the harbor's back door to Merriconeag Sound and Bailey Island. Potts also makes an ideal departure point for exploring Broad Sound or Eagle Island.

Potts Harbor has enough room to hold a small armada, and in fact it does when the Harpswell Lobsterboat races are held here each year. But as an anchorage, it is quite broad and exposed, with only minimal protection from the islands and ledges to the west and south—Little Birch Island, Horse Island, Upper Flag Island, and Haskell Island. Most boats are docked or moored off Dolphin Marine on Basin Point. When it blows, absolute shelter can be found in Basin Cove, which hides in the northwest corner of the harbor.

Potts Harbor is named after the Potts family of Harpswell who became famous when Jewell Island was attacked by Indians (see Jewell Island, p. 103).

By sea. The main entrance to Potts is from the southwest, west of Upper Flag Island, between Horse and Thrumcap Island. It is wide and free of obstructions. There is also a backdoor, from the east, which follows a convoluted but well-marked channel between Potts Point and Haskell Island. A third entrance is possible by carefully wending through the unmarked ledges west of Haskell, but this is best left for those in the know, particularly where this channel joins the marked one near Torry Rock and Northwest Ledge.

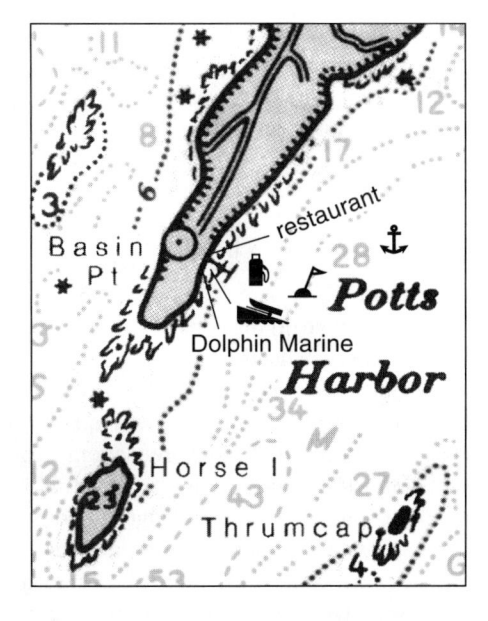

Boats can be launched at Dolphin Marine or docked at the town dock on Potts Point (see entries below).

143. Dolphin Marine

Dophin Marine (833-6000) is a marvelously low-key boat yard in a staggeringly beautiful location on the Potts Harbor side of Basin Point, at the western tip of Harpswell Neck. Boats are stored in a grassy field that rolls to the water's edge, with a backdrop of sparkling water and islands strewn like stepping stones to the horizon. This is an ideal place to stage a small-boat expedition. Geographically, all of central Casco Bay is easily reached from Basin Point, and Dolphin Marine provides almost anything you could need.

Or, if you are already on the water and the day blows up cold and gray, Dolphin's cozy restaurant can serve up steaming cups of coffee or bowls of chowder to put the warmth back in your bones.

By sea. See Potts Harbor, above. Dolphin Marine is on the harbor's west shore.

Dolphin has a paved launching ramp with water at all but the lowest tides. A small ramp fee is charged if you launch your own boat, and Dolphin can launch bigger boats with their hydraulic trailer. Transient moorings are available.

Dolphin pumps gas, diesel, and water on their floats. The water, however, is drawn from the restaurant's well, so major tank-filling is discouraged. Depth at low is six feet.

By land. Follow Rt. 123, the Harpswell Road, south from Brunswick through West Harpswell. Following signs, take a right to Basin Point.

Ashore. Dolphin provides short or long-term parking or boat storage in their field, and they can handle boat and engine repairs of all kinds. The restaurant has restrooms, a pay phone, and ice. And in season, the field has delicious blueberries.

144. Basin Cove

Basin Cove is an almost completely landlocked cove off the north corner of Potts Harbor. This is what the cruising guides call a true hurricane hole, completely protected from wind and surge from every quarter, though visiting yachtsmen rarely attempt to take deep-draft boats though the mouth of the cove without local knowledge. Not only is it narrow and shallow, it takes an S-bend, and at every turn of the tide it becomes a sluiceway with currents reaching 4 or 5 knots. This is as close as Casco Bay comes to having a reversing falls, where tidal water cascades into the cove on the flood and out of the cove on the ebb. In small craft, however, the challenge at the cove's mouth can be pure excitement.

By sea. The entrance to Basin Cove is between Ash Point and the longer arm of Basin Point at the north corner of Potts Harbor. Where the entrance bends to the west, all the water volume of this mile-long cove is squeezed at the turn of the tide between two fingers of ledge like a watermelon seed. At maximum flood or ebb, it can run as strong as 4 or 5 knots.

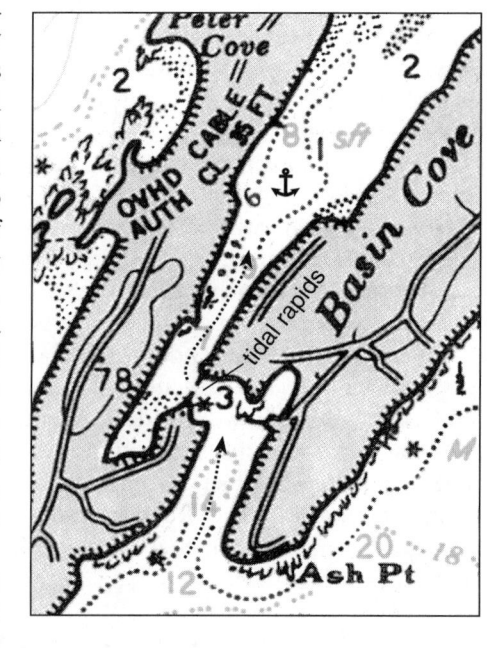

Though the chart still shows the tidal dam and marks the ruins of the Old Mill, the mill has disappeared completely, and all that is left of the dam is some rubble on the ledges. The deepest channel through them lies about a third of the way across the mouth from the southern shore.

If the current is running against you, shallow draft boats can work against it by finding the along-shore eddies, but taking it bow-on can't be avoided at the actual race. Occasionally, paddlers come here just to play in the current.

Once inside, there are few obstructions other than the shoal water in most of the northern half of the cove.

By land. There is no public access to Basin Cove, though it is an easy jaunt from Dolphin Marine (see p. 155).

Ashore. All of the cove's shoreline is private, including the extensive wooded section on the west bank near the mouth.

Basin Cove's water energy was harnessed by the earliest settlers. The last of the mills was built by a Portland grain company in 1867. They built a stone dam across the mouth of the cove with one-way floodgates. The pressure of the flood would swing the gates open and let water into what they called the Mill-Pond Basin, but when the tide turned, the pressure of the ebb would shut the gates. Head pressure would built to eight to ten feet at every high tide. Water was forced into a sluiceway and turned the waterwheel and grindstones of the mill, which perched on pilings by the banks.

Typically, raw corn was brought to Portland by schooner from New York or Baltimore and then lightered by smaller vessels for grinding at the Old Tide Mill at Ash Point, as it was known. "It furnishes a tide power of great value, from its accessibility by sea, the depth of water admitting the passage of vessels of several hundred tons, quite to the dam."

When the mill was abandoned, it stood empty for a long time. Its windows were boarded, and, of course, it was haunted. It became known as the House on Stilts. And while its eeriness challenged the courage of local boys to pass near, Clara Burnham, a summer resident of Bailey Island, romanticized it in another way. In a book she wrote in 1906 called *Open Shutters,* the heroine's moods were shared by the mill. When the heroine was happy, the Old Mill would be also, and it would mysteriously open its own shutters. The Old Mill finally succumbed to a winter storm in 1934.

145. Potts Point

The east side of Potts Harbor is defined by Potts Point, though much of the point is almost an island, connected to the rest of Harpswell by a short causeway. A long wooden town wharf projects off the west side of Potts Point into Potts Harbor. This might be a convenient stopping spot for stretching the legs or for dropping off the crew for a trip to Estes Lobster House, while you anchor out. Portable boats or very light trailerable boats might be able to be launched at a small ramp slightly south of the wharf, but parking will be a problem at both locations.

By sea. See chart next page. The wharf is the most major of the wharves on this side of the harbor. Please do not block the face of its float, which is in constant use. If you need to stay for any period of time, you may be able to rig up a stern anchor and tie off to the wharf parallel to the numerous skiffs on outhauls there.

At the very end of the Harpswell Road, a small ramp leads into soft sand, but calling is a ramp may be an overstatement. For any but the lightest trailered boats, hauling or launching will be difficult, particularly at anytime other than high tide. The small beach, however, is fine for launching or beaching portable boats, assuming you are able find somewhere to leave your car. The *"Don't Even THINK of Parking Here"* sign nearby suggests that you won't.

By land. The wharf is almost at the very end of the Harpswell Road (Rt. 123) out of Brunswick. The ramp is at the end of the public portion of the road.

Ashore. A short walk to the north and over the causeway will bring you to Estes Lobster House, a large, high-volume restaurant overlooking both Potts Harbor and Merriconeag Sound (see Estes Lobster House, p. 170).

146. Bar Island

Small, grassy Bar Island lies between Ash Point and Potts Point, tucked in the shoal northeast corner of Potts Harbor. It is owned by the Maine Bureau of Parks and Lands, and careful day use, managed by the Maine Island Trail Association, is permitted. It makes a nice rest stop to stretch your legs or have a picnic.

By sea. Like most of the islands in Casco Bay, the bedrock that forms Bar is oriented in a southwest to northeast direction, with submerged ledge extending well to the south of the island and shoaling mudflats to the north. The deepest approach is from due west.

Ashore. Camping and fires are not permitted.

147. Little Birch Island

Little Birch is the westernmost of the cluster of islands at the mouth of Potts Harbor. This low nine-acre hummock is crowned by scrub, and a sandy beach spills off its north end. The State of Maine acquired Little Birch in 1979, and it is managed by the Department of Inland Fisheries and Wildlife. The beaches make a nice rest stop for weary paddlers and a pleasant place for a picnic.

By sea. Little Birch can be distinguished by red bell "6" at it southern end. Land on the sandy spit at the island's north end.

Ashore. No camping or fires are allowed. Please avoid the island during the nesting season.

148. Horse Island

Horse Island is similar to neighboring Little Birch, though slightly smaller. Like Little Birch, Horse is ringed by nice sandy shores. This island, however, is private.

By sea. The ledges that make out a long way to the north from Horse Island and to the south from Basin Point meet at a pronounced rock, shown on the chart. Passing between the two is recommended only for the brave of heart or the shallow of draft.

Ashore. Please do not land.

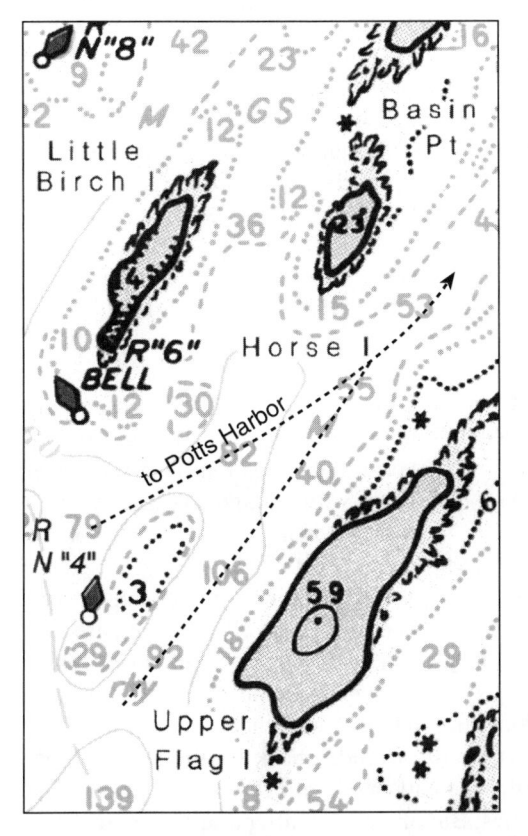

149. Upper Flag Island

Upper Flag looks like a tear running down the chart, and from the water, its profile is similar. Its southern end is rounded, high, and treeless, while the trailing north end tapers and gets low and sandy. At the narrower north end, the island's contours create a basin that traps fresh water and supports the tall cattails that wave in the wind and give the island its name. Upper Flag is private.

By sea. Use extreme caution in the rock garden between Flag and Haskell Island or avoid it altogether.

Ashore. Though this island is privately owned, some unsightly evidence at the north end suggests that it is sometimes used as a place to whoop it up. These visitors, however, are not the first. The infamous Captain Mowatt of the British Navy is said to have anchored his sloop *Canceaux* here in October, 1775 to ready his crew before sailing to Portland and burning it to the ground (see Portland, p. 38). And when Admiral Peary returned from his North Pole expedition in 1909, he let his sled dogs have the run of the 60-acre island (see Eagle Island, p. 161). Until fairly recently, there was a small camp on the island's east side.

150. Haskell Island

Haskell is the largest of the islands defining Potts Harbor. It is high, with craggy bluffs and deep forests. Its eastern and southern shores stand tough against the ceaseless ocean swells, while Potts Harbor is formed in its lee.

With the exception of the southern end, most of Haskell has been owned by the same families since the turn of the century. Landing is not allowed, but Great Harbor

Cove, at its north end makes a pleasant anchorage.

By sea. Great Harbor Cove is well protected from the southwest. From Potts Harbor, follow the twisting channel to the east and enter the cove from between can "3" and nun "2." From Merriconeag Sound, keep nun "2" to starboard and then run south into the cove.

Ashore. Early on, Haskell was a major fishing center, as illustrated by one of its first names. Haskell and Upper Flag and perhaps some of the smaller adjacent islands were known as the New Damariscove Islands. The original Damariscove Island, off Booth Bay, was one of the most important fishing outposts along the New England coast, bustling with activity many years before the Pilgrims landed at Plymouth. Haskell's operation was probably set up in much the same way, with fields cleared for pasture, and racks, or stages, set up for the delicate task of drying fish to preserve them.

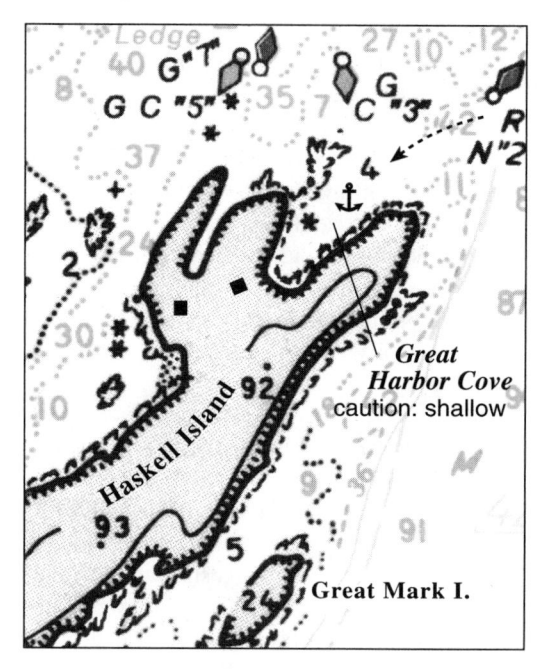

Eventually, the island acquired the name of a captain of a coasting vessel, and with the growth of the city that would become Portland, Haskell became the location for a large beef farm, with enough livestock to support its own slaughterhouse for the city market.

The animals most people associate with Haskell, however, are rats. It is said that in the late 1870s Haskell became overrun with rats. The only person with a strong enough constitution to live with them on the island was an old lobsterman named Humphrey, who built a crude shack by the shore. Other local lobstermen made a habit of keeping a weather eye out for the old hermit and occasionally bringing him bait and supplies. But one winter, after a severe storm, they noticed that no smoke came from the old man's chimney. When they rowed ashore to investigate and opened the door of the shack, squealing rats scurried in all directions, away from the meal they were having of the old lobsterman in his bunk.

So Haskell belonged to the rats until two enterprising brothers from North Harpswell, the Mills boys, came up with a plan. They caught as many of the meanest tomcats they could find and ferried them to the island to let them have at the rats. In time, the toms had the rat population in check, and the Mills brothers built themselves a fish house and moved in. They fed the toms old bait scraps as a reward for a job well done.

Eventually, rats were no longer seen on the island. The toms, on the other hand, multiplied and grew more and more wild. They were so fierce and territorial that they wouldn't let anyone other than the Mills brothers on the island. One day, the owner of the island tried to show it to a prospective buyer, but when he landed, the toms drove him off. The owner returned several nights later and spread poison on the island. The Mills boys awoke to such a shocking feline body count that they fled the island, never to return. Or so the story goes.

The truth, or another version, is much tamer and more circular. In their later years, one of the brothers, Oliver Douglas, did actually winter over on Haskell, alone in a small cabin, and *he* became known as the Hermit of Haskell. One winter, he was found dead by a caretaker of the summer places on Haskell who had come over from Harpswell, and the rats had, in fact, discovered his body. But the rampant populations of wild rats and cats multiplied in people's imaginations, not on Haskell.

BROAD SOUND

Broad Sound runs in a north-south direction diagonally across the grain of the islands and ridges in Casco Bay. It leads from the Royal and Harraseeket rivers out past Potts Harbor and Eagle Island.

By sea. Much of the tide that affects inner Casco Bay floods to the north or ebbs to the south through Broad Sound, with average maximum floods of nearly a knot and average maximum ebbs of 1.3 knots. Small-craft boaters need to watch for set, particularly in limited visibility.

151. Eagle Island

High Eagle Island stands like a sentinel at the entrance to Broad Sound, in almost the exact geographic middle of Casco Bay. The island is high with spectacular views of Casco Bay in every direction.

This was the home of Admiral Robert Peary, the controversial discoverer of the North Pole. Eagle Island and Peary's house are now a state park open to the public. A beautiful trail circles the perimeter, and the ship-house is full of the Admiral's furnishings and artifacts from the far north.

Eagle must either be reached by private boat or aboard one of the several charter boats that make the trip from Portland or South Freeport. Either way, the island always feels like a discovery in its own right.

By sea. The dock at Eagle Island is near the northwest tip, and a small beach lies to the north of that. In the approach, nun "2" marks the end of a long ledge from the west side of the island. Some moorings are available, but you may have to anchor in 16 to 30 feet of water. Be sure your anchor is well set. The anchorage is exposed, and the current in Broad Sound runs swiftly.

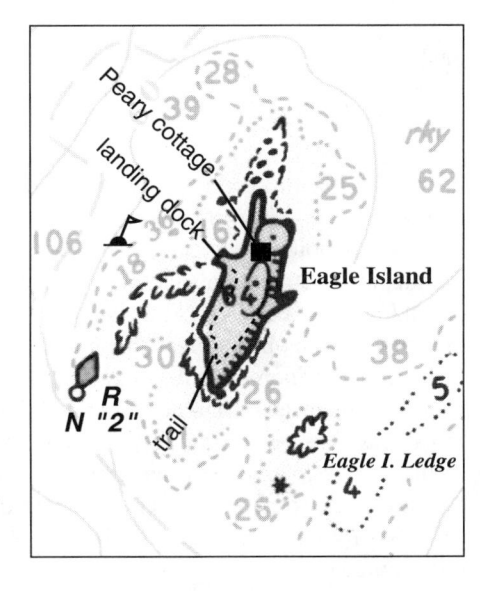

By land. Tours to Eagle Island depart from downtown Portland and from South Freeport. For more arctic history, visit the Peary-MacMillan Arctic Museum located on the first floor of Hubbard Hall on the campus of Bowdoin College in Brunswick (725-3416). Exhibits include a kayak brought back from North Greenland by MacMillan, as well as photos of Inuits hunting from their kayaks.

Ashore. A resident caretaker collects a modest fee for exploring the Peary cottage and trails around the island.

Robert Peary first saw Eagle when he was a young boy camping on neighboring Haskell Island to the north. "I used to sit and look across at what seemed to me the most beautiful island in the world," he would later recall. "...it seemed to me like an island my mother used to tell me about in one of her fairy tales..."

And it still is magical. The Indians called the island Sawungun for the great blue heron that nested there. It also was once called Heron Island. Peary bought Eagle Island for $500 in 1881 while he was still an undergraduate at Bowdoin, but it wasn't until 1904 that he had enough money to build a cottage on the lonely 17-acre outpost. He envisioned the rocky bluff of Eagle as the prow of a great ship, steaming north and designed the cottage like a pilothouse, with a deck all around. When he wasn't away on one of his eight trips to the Arctic, he summered here. And when he was away, he always carried a photograph of what he called "The Promised Land."

Unfortunately for the driven and determined explorer, the North Pole was not such a promised land. When Admiral Peary announced his discovery of the North Pole on April 6, 1909, he learned that another explorer had made the identical claim five days earlier. Those claims proved to be a hoax, but as a result, Peary's evidence of reaching the Pole was meticulously scrutinized—and doubted—giving birth to a controversy that has never been completely resolved.

Hoping to put an end to the dispute, Congress officially recognized Peary's discovery of the North Pole in 1911 and awarded him a pension of $6,500 a year. The money helped him complete his house on Eagle Island, but the controversy about his claims to the pole continues. As recently as 1989, Peary's photographs were subjected to forensic photographic analysis to determine the angle of the shadows, the height of the sun, and the location's latitude. The question of whether Peary actually reached the North Pole continues to fascinate people, perhaps because the issues are as much those of character and obsession as those of fact and scientific proof.

Locals remember a different dispute. When Peary's ship, the *Roosevelt,* returned from her victorious arctic voyage, her first American port of call was Eagle Island. Local islanders were hired to put Peary's sled dogs on Upper Flag Island and tend to them and to help unload the arctic artifacts that Peary had brought back with him. There is a story that some of the helpers asked the explorer if they could have a few small trinkets, of which there seemed to be an abundance, but they were sternly refused. No one seemed to notice that after that the islanders all took to wearing high rubber boots, and somehow little souvenirs tended to fall into them.

Peary's descendants continued the tradition of summering on Eagle Island after the Admiral's death. Peary's daughter had been born aboard the *Roosevelt* during an arctic expedition, and she became known as the Snow Baby. In 1967, Mrs. William W. Kuhne of Brunswick, the famed Snow Baby, gave Eagle Island to the State of Maine.

152. Little Mark Island

From seaward, Little Mark Island is an obvious landmark—a tall, tapering white tower with a vertical black stripe and topped with a flashing white light. The island is technically owned by the U.S. government, but the gulls and the cormorants have staked the real claim to it. Small boats could land here, though it is difficult and the birds will make you feel most unwelcome, particularly during nesting season.

By sea. Brace yourself. This is one of those islands you can find with your eyes closed, as long as your nose works. Follow the rank, salty-briny smell of seabird guano and you will find treeless Little Mark. From Broad Sound, a delightful winding passage squiggles between Haskell Island to the north and Haddock Rock to the south. Even on the calmest of days, landing on Little Mark is difficult. The ocean swells surge around the shores, and there are no places to land other than on the slippery ledges.

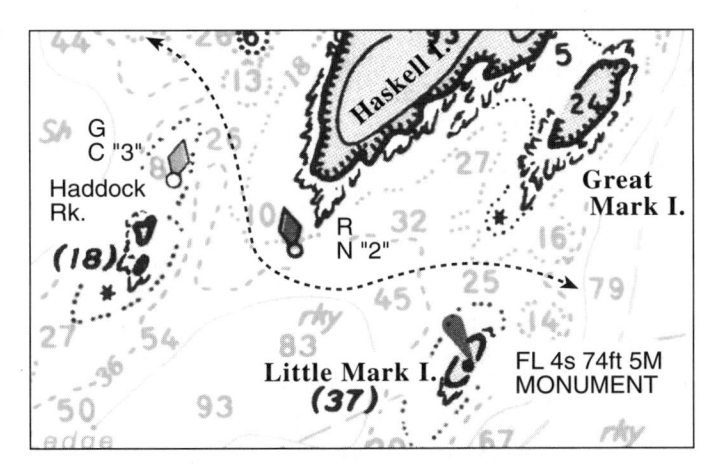

Ashore. Only land at the end of summer, when the bird nests are all empty.

The tall stone monument was erected by the U.S. government in 1827 both as a navigational aid and a memorial to sailors lost at sea. However, Capt. Samson of the U.S. Coast Guard wrote in his *History of New England Lights and Markers* that the tower was built by the British. A room was built into its base, presumably to store water and provisions and to shelter marooned seamen. The only record of the room ever being used, however, was for sheep. The beacon was installed just before World War II.

You will need to clear the cobwebs out of the entrance to the room at the base of the tower and peer into the gloom of the damp, dirt-floored chamber. One can't help but wonder if the builders of this monument were really thinking about shipwrecked sailors when they chose to make the tower hollow, or if they were just being practical and sparing themselves the task of hauling several additional and unnecessary tons of rock and rubble to this inaccessible outpost.

Robert Peary admired the monument from his house on Eagle Island, just to the west, and when a memorial to him was erected in the Arctic, the tower was used as a model.

153. Great Mark Island

Great Mark Island is an overstatement. It is only slightly greater in size than Little Mark Island, and its diminutive form seems like a small iceberg calved from the glacial face of Haskell.

163

The island is private, with a small cottage. Please do not land.

In addition to having been one of the New Damariscove Islands (see Haskell Island, p. 159), Great Mark has also been known as Woody Mark Island and Eastern Mark Island.

By sea. Like an iceberg, a fair amount of Great Mark is underwater. Ledges extend from the northeast and southwest ends, and a sand bar has formed between it and Haskell where the water is slowed by the constriction.

Boaters passing between Great and Little Mark should favor Little Mark to avoid the lone rock shown on the chart at the end of the ledge projecting southward from Great Mark Island.

HARPSWELL AND MERRICONEAG SOUNDS

Two wide sounds make up the deep slot between Harpswell Neck and the string of Sebascodegan, Orrs, and Bailey islands. Harpswell Sound begins at the fixed span bridge at Ewin Narrows. It broadens between wooded shores dotted with houses and sneaks into the diversions of Mill Cove, Long Cove, and Lumbos Hole. Once past Orrs Island and the cribstone bridge to Baileys Island, the Harpswell Sound becomes Merriconeag Sound and begins to take on the roll of the Atlantic.

By sea. Small boaters can launch at Ewin Narrows, Wills Gut, or Stover Point (see Ewin Narrows, p. 187, or entries below). The tide floods to the northeast and ebbs to the southwest. Both sounds are almost exactly aligned, lengthwise, with the summer southwesterlies, so generally the wind is either right on the stern or right on the nose. When the wind builds in the afternoon, it has enough fetch down the length of the sound to whip up a short chop, particularly during the ebb. And when the ocean swells are up, they will be felt in the lower portions of Merriconeag.

154. Strawberry Creek Island ▲

This woodsy little island is tucked against the head of Harpswell Sound, near the bridge at Ewin Narrows. It is state-owned and part of the Maine Island Trail, though being so far up Harpswell Sound, it gets less use than many other trail islands. Its sense of isolation is somewhat tarnished, however, by the whish of cars crossing the bridge and by a large contemporary house on the point to the north.

By sea. For a very short trip, you can use the launching ramp and put-in just north of the bridge in Ewin Narrows (see p. 187). Make careful note, however, of the extensive ledges that

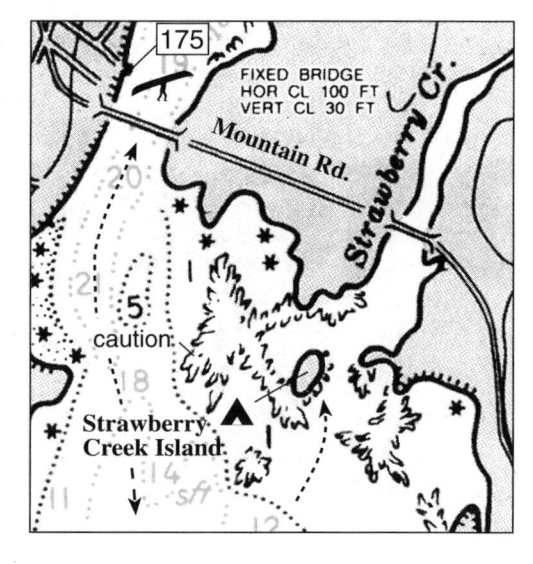

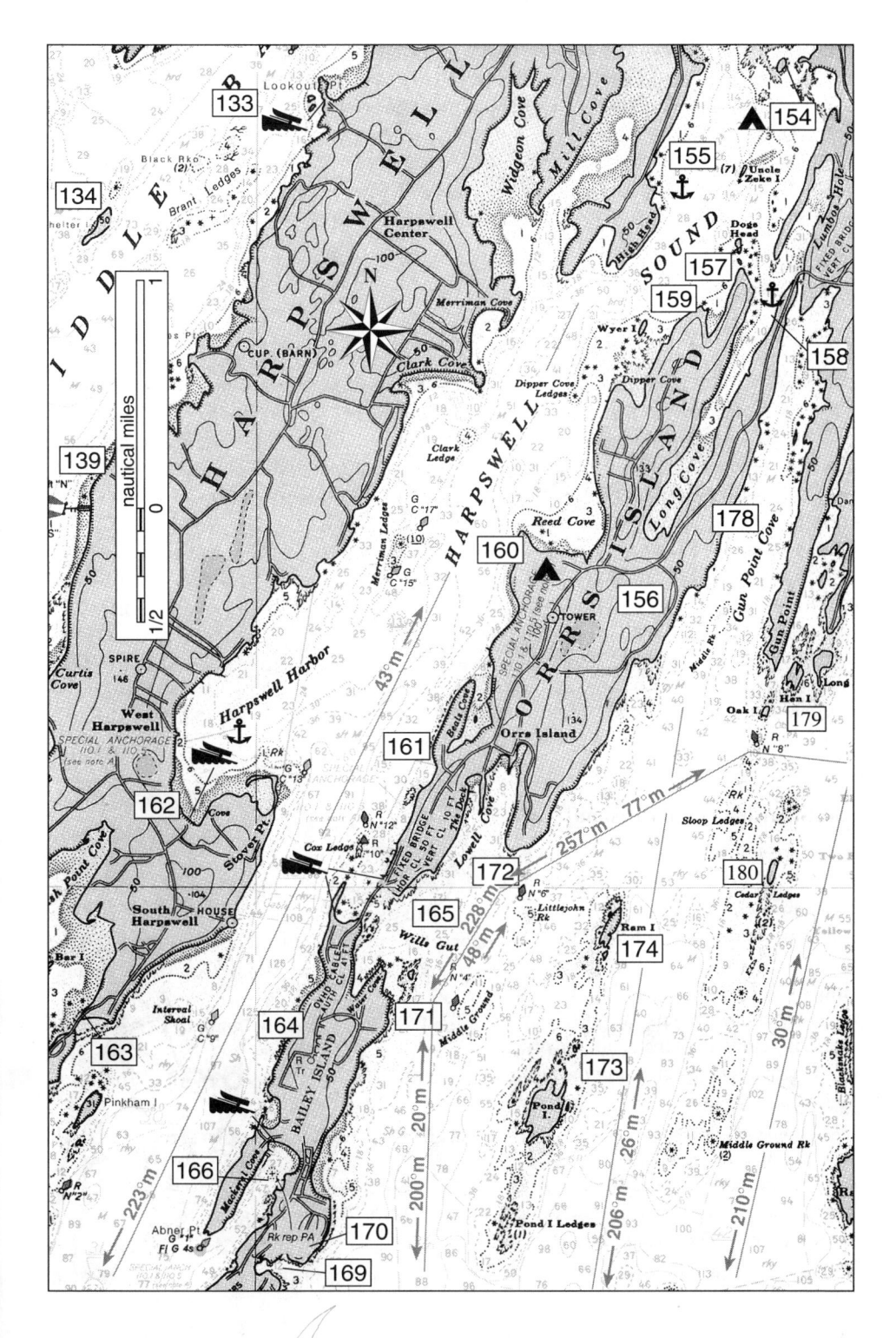

CASCO BAY

project far to the west and far to the south of this island. The water to the west and north is either shoal or mud flats, depending on the tide. The best approach is from the south, staying east of all of the ledges and landing on the rocky southeast shore.

Ashore. Small wooded campsites occupy the north end and the middle of the island. A third campsite is in the clearing at the southern tip. The southern campsite has a marvelous view down the length of Harpswell Sound, but it takes the full brunt of the afternoon sea breezes from the southwest.

155. High Head

High Head is the prominent end of a long peninsula which projects into Harpswell Sound off Harpswell Neck. To its inside, it forms the large but mostly shoal Mill Cove. The High Head Yacht Club (725-8440) occupies the little cove just north of High Head. This small club has no facilities for visitors, but you are sure to find kindred spirits.

By sea. High Head is bold with no obstructions except one rock to its north, shown on the chart. When coming from the south, be sure to favor the west side of Harpswell Sound to avoid Dipper Ledges. Club members may be able to direct you to a vacant mooring if you need one.

Ashore. High Head was settled by the Curtis family in 1744, and they farmed it continuously until their farmhouse burned in a disastrous fire 199 years later, in 1943. They dammed Mill Cove and for many years ran a grist mill, known as the Mill Cove Tide Mill. It was standing as late as 1904.

The High Head Yacht Club sits on land that was deeded to them by the last of the Curtis family.

156. Orrs Island

Orrs Island defines the eastern shore of the lower flank of Harpswell Sound. At either end, it is strung like a pearl on a necklace by bridges to other islands. Its north end is connected with Sebascodegan Island by a short bridge at Lumbos Hole, and its south end is connected to Bailey Island by the famous cribstone bridge.

Orrs offers small-craft boaters a convenient place to launch at the Gut (p. 172) or a convenient place to camp at the Orrs Island Campground on Reed Cove (p. 169). In addition, the tight passages at Lumbos Hole and under the cribstone bridge are exciting, protected-water passages into eastern Casco Bay.

By sea. Favor the west side of Harpswell Sound to avoid unmarked Dipper Cove Ledges off the island's northwest shore.

By land. Follow the Gurnet Road (Rt. 24) south from Cooks Corner in Brunswick and cross onto Orrs.

Ashore. Just after you have crossed the bridge onto Orrs, the pleasant Whaleback picnic area will be on your left, with picnic tables and short paths through the trees to the ledgy shore of Gun Point Cove.

Orrs was once called Little Sebascodegan, but it later took the names of two Irish brothers who had settled on Harpswell Neck, Clement and Joseph Orr. Both Orrs were weavers. In 1748, they bought the island for two shillings an acre. For the previous four years, Indians had been raiding the coast in what has been called King George's War, and settlers on the neck were uneasy. The Orrs built a garrison on the island for protection. In their preoccupation, Joseph had forgotten to get the signature of one of the heirs who were selling it, and this daughter was a hold-out. The affair wasn't resolved for twelve years, and Joseph was forced into giving this daughter one tenth of the island for a quit claim deed to the rest. In the meantime, Joseph built a 60-ton ship from island timber and used it in a successful enterprise of shipping cordwood to Boston.

Orrs was brought into the limelight in 1862 by author Harriet Beecher Stowe, already famous for writing *Uncle Tom's Cabin*. Her novel *Pearl of Orr's Island* celebrated life, mystery, and adventure on "this isle of enchantment with its blue-black spruces, its silver firs, and more varied and singular beauty than can ordinarily be found on any shore whatever."

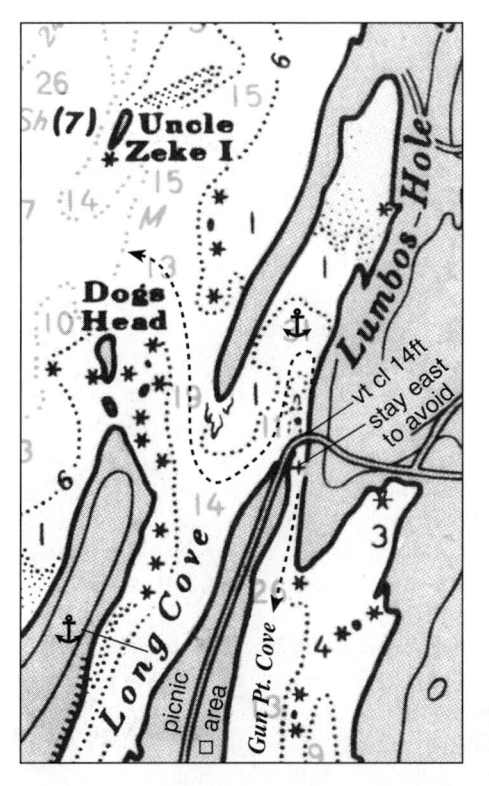

The reticent islanders were not universally pleased with the attention the novel brought to Orrs. So many curious readers descended on this quiet and otherwise unknown island that islanders refered to *Pearl* as "That Book." Stowe had boarded in the island home of Deacon Johnson, but after the book was published, he loudly proclaimed that he had not, nor would not, read a line of it, convinced as he was that most of the ills of the day could be traced to the evils of novel reading.

157. Dogs Head

Dogs Head is a small, private island. Its house, though, distinguished by a cupola, is a useful landmark for entering Long Cove. If you are still in doubt, there's even a sign that reads "Dog's Head."

158. Long Cove and Lumbos Hole

Long Cove is known among yachtsmen as an anchorage with almost complete protection. Small boats use it for the protected passage through its mouth and under the Orrs-Sebascodegan Bridge to Gun Point Cove and eastern Casco Bay. Long Cove's entrance is tricky, however, and the narrow slot beneath the bridge is even worse. Still, this makes a delightful exploration and a convenient way to head east or west in sheltered waters.

By sea. Long Cove is entered to the east of Dogs Head. Dogs Head is surrounded by a litter of rocks, visible at low. Head well to the east to avoid the rocks, then turn southward, aiming for a point off the narrow peninsula bordering Lumbos Hole. Note that ledges make out from its tip. Once inside, favor the east bank to avoid the rocks on the west.

The scale of the chart is inadequate for the passage beneath the bridge. Head south into Long Cove far enough to clear the ledges off Lumbos Hole's western tip, then snake north into the mouth of Lumbos Hole. The mouth is flanked by shoal water to the west and ledges to the east. Stay near the middle, slightly favoring the east, until you reach the actual hole, the 31-foot spot where there are some moorings. Now make a U-turn and head south, this time to the east of the ledges, closely hugging the bold flank of Sebascodegan. Proceed slowly beneath the bridge, still favoring the east side.

The bridge has a minimum vertical clearance of 14 feet at high tide and depths of 6 to 8 feet at low. Tides flood north under the bridge and ebb south. The rock shown as a cross on the chart south of the bridge is ledge off the private float on the west shore. Stay in the deep cleft near Sebascodegan to clear it. Beware, however, of the rock garden as you head into Gun Point Cove (see p. 190).

By land. Follow directions to Orrs Island, above. Route 24 runs along the length of Long Cove, to the east, but there is no access.

Ashore. If you plan to make this passage but want a look at it from land before you try, there is a turnout alongside several private fish houses and floats at the south end of the bridge on Orrs Island's west shore. You can park here for a moment and walk back over the bridge to have a look. Use caution on the busy road.

From the bridge, Orrs rises abruptly. Whaleback Picnic Area soon appears on the left, on the island's spine, with paths through the woods to the rocks at the edge of Gun Point Cove. The trees are too thick and the shores too steep for boat access.

159. Wyer Island and Thalheimer Preserve

Wyer Island and the peninsulas at the north end of Orrs and to the west of Long Cove are part of the 118-acre Thalheimer Preserve, which was recently donated to Bowdoin College for a marine sciences and natural history center. Bowdoin is building a science center on the property, and students will use the preserve for field work. While not actively encouraged because of possible disruption to the teaching or field work, the public is allowed to stroll this magnificent property and appreciate its natural beauty.

By sea. The preserve's shorefront lies on Harpswell Sound, between Wyer Island and Dogs Head, including the small cove shown on the chart with the one-foot sounding.

By land. Take Rt. 24 south onto Orrs Island. Once past the Orrs Island General Store on the right, take the next right, Bayview Road, and follow it to the end.

Ashore. Visitors are asked to use the property with great care, respect wildlife, and under no circumstances disturb plants, trees, or shrubs. Hunting, camping, and fires of any kind, including picnic grills, are not allowed.

CASCO BAY

160. Orr's Island Campground

Orr's Island Campground (833-5595) occupies the peninsula that defines Reed Cove, on the west side of Orrs Island, with beaches on both sides. The campground has wooded and private tent sites and all amenities, and it provides good access to Harpswell Sound. Both portable boats and lightweight trailered boats can be launched at most tides from their cobble beach. If you are boatless, the campground rents canoes.

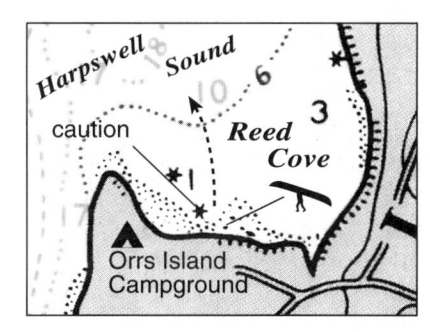

By sea. Land at the pebbly beach in Reed Cove or at the campground's float. The campground maintains a mooring here. Beware of the pair of rocks off the cove's western shore.

By land. The campground is on the west side of Rt. 24 about a mile south of the Orrs Island General Store.

Ashore. The campground has coin-op showers and laundry machines. A pay phone, snacks, and firewood are available at the office. A few short trails lead through the woods and open spaces. Each campsite is based on one vehicle. Reservations are recommended, particularly for off-site parking for boats and their tow vehicles. Credit cards are not accepted.

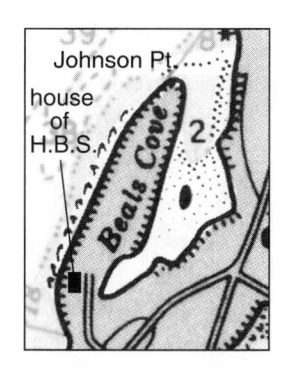

161. Johnson Point

Johnson Point is the last finger on the west side of Orrs Island. It forms Beals Cove to the east. On the west side of the isthmus, right where the road shown on the chart takes a bend, there is a white house with black shutters. This is the house where Harriet Beecher Stowe wrote the *Pearl of Orrs Island* (see Orrs Island entry, p. 166).

162. Harpswell Harbor and Stover Cove

Harpswell Harbor is a large bight on the west side of Harpswell Neck opposite Johnson Point. The houses and summer cottages of West Harpswell cluster along the shores, and some boats tug at their moorings. There is not much to explore here, but a small launching ramp at the harbor's very head, in what is called Stover Cove, makes this a possible staging point for a small-boat adventure either in Harpswell Sound to the north, through Wills Gut to east Casco Bay, or south to the mid-bay islands.

By sea. See chart next page. Once past green can "13" off Stover Point, the broad Harbor is obvious to the west. Despite how open the harbor is, Stover Cove is well protected from the prevailing southwesterlies. A small beach rings the cove, but at low it shoals to mud flats. The ramp is best at half-tide or above.

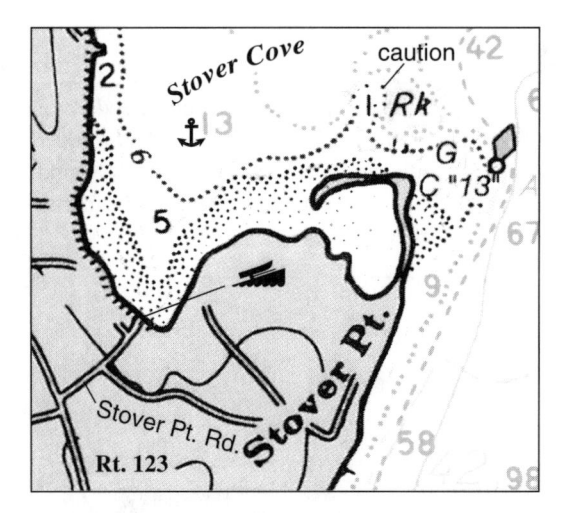

By land. Follow the Harpswell Road (Rt. 123) south. Pass through the village of West Harpswell, then turn left on Stover Point Road. When the road bends to the right, continue straight on a smaller road. The road becomes the ramp.

Ashore. This is a local ramp with limited space to park on the shoulder.

163. Estes Lobster House

Estes is a large restaurant at the northwest end of the causeway that leads from the tip of Harpswell Neck to what is nearly an island, called Potts Point.

By sea. Both sides of the causeway are obstructed, the west side by mud flats and the east by ledges. Conceivably, near high tide and with great care, portable boats could clear the ledges on the east side of the causeway and beach at the small sand beach by the large parking lot on the east side of the causeway. Or an easier, less tide-dependant landing can be made at either the dock or ramp on Potts Point a short distance away (see p. 157).

By land. Estes is directly on the Harpswell Road (Rt. 123).

164. Bailey Island

Bailey Island is the last of the islands in a chain connected by bridge from Brunswick south. Yet it still feels like an outer island, part of the spine of ledge that includes lonely Halfway Rock, stubbornly set in the full brunt of the Atlantic.

Bailey Island can provide shelter, fuel, or food at either its north or south ends, and boats can be launched near the cribstone bridge that arches across Wills Gut (see entries below).

By sea. Together Orrs Island and Baileys Island effectively divide Casco Bay into western and eastern halves, and Bailey is prominent from either side. Its southern end is distinguished by a couple of concrete observation towers above the trees. Narrow Wills Gut and the unique cribstone bridge define the northern end.

By land. Route 24 runs south from Cooks Corner in Brunswick to Bailey Island.

Ashore. Because you can drive to Bailey, it attracts more tourists than other less accessible islands. Still, Bailey retains a true island atmosphere, with shingled summer cottages, the cry of gulls, and an authentic fishing fleet in the harbor.

Bailey was first settled in the early 1700s, when many of the islands were settled by squatters who set up small fishing and fish-drying operations wherever geography provided a safe haven from the ocean and from the Indians. Will Black and his wife had left their troubles behind in Kittery and sailed eastward looking for some out-of-the-way place to settle where they could live in peace. They discovered Mackerel Cove. The island had rich woodlands, it was inhabited only by a few friendly Indians, and it had a deep and well-protected cove.

Will Black's father was Black Will, a former slave of mixed black, white, and Indian blood. When he was freed in 1700 by his owner Major Nicholas Shapleigh of Kittery, Black Will changed his name to Will Black. His son took the same name. In 1715, though, Will Black, Jr. was jailed for living with Elizabeth Turbot, a white woman. When he was released, they fled the town.

They settled by the cove, built a cabin, fished, farmed, and had children. They traded dried fish for supplies from passing ships, and they traded with the natives, who respected these settlers enough to never attack.

To encourage settlement, colonial law granted land titles to those who settled it for twenty years. Twenty years after dropping his anchor in Mackerel Cove, Will presented his claim to the Harpswell court, and they granted him ownership of the entire island, and he expected to live on what became known as Will's Island for the rest of his life.

Unfortunately for Will, his path crossed that of Hannah Curtis, an ardent Puritan. She moved from Hanover, Massachusetts and settled in Harpswell in 1731 as the second wife of Timothy Bailey. Despite the fact that Puritan influence was not nearly as strong in Maine as it was in Massachusetts, she had enough influential friends to managed to have her husband appointed as Deacon of the North Yarmouth Parish, which happened to include Will's Island. A deacon's pay was modest, but it carried with it great social standing and influence, and Hannah was determined to have a home to match. She began to covet Will's Island as the perfect place to settle.

Despite Will's legal title to the island, Hannah managed to apply enough social pressure and harassment on the Black family to finally force them to leave the island. Will retreated across the narrow gut that still bears his name and squatted on Orrs Island, while the righteous Baileys built a house and moved in, eventually managing somehow to purchase the island for a pound of tobacco and a gallon of rum from the North Yarmouth Land Proprietors.

Near the Bailey cabin, a spring bubbled forth from the sandy soil. Local Indians called it the Great Spirit Spring, and legend has it that in his old age, the Indian chief Mingo returned to the island so he could be buried near the spring, as had many of his ancestors before him. The Baileys took him in and nursed him in his final days, but before he died, he made them promise that they would never reveal the sacred Indian burial place. And, true to their word, they never did.

A small settlement grew up around the Bailey homestead, and, like everywhere along the coast, the relationship with the natives grew strained. Settlers on Bailey Island built a stone blockhouse for protection, and whenever Indians approached, a shot would be fired and settlers would hole up in the fort. A legend has it that Hannah's brother had a weakness for whiskey, and often when he was moved by that particular spirit, he would fire the Indian alarm and send the whole community scurrying to the blockhouse.

Bailey Island evolved as an agricultural and fishing community, and Casco Bay steamer service brought vacationers. The island's innovative fishermen are credited with being some of the first to set strings of multiple lobster traps in 1912, and with developing the sport of tuna fishing.

In the 1920s, after much debate, the islanders—at least a majority of them—decided to cast their fate with the mainland and voted to build the connecting bridge across Wills Gut. But they had little say in the matter when during World War II the army marched in convoy down Rt. 24 to create an observation outpost at the southern end of the island. Ferry service was suspended, because the ferries were commandeered for military use, and the submarine nets strung across the mouths of Portland Harbor prevented them from leaving anyway. And a long cable was strung out from Bailey toward Halfway Rock to detect the sounds of enemies lurking underwater.

After the war, the island saw renewed tourism, primarily via the car and the cribstone bridge. The center of the island's activity gradually shifted from the steamboat wharf in Mackerel Cove to the center of the island. Still, a Casco Bay Lines ferry makes the daily "mailboat run" from Portland to Bailey Island, now landing at Cooks Wharf in Garrison Cove.

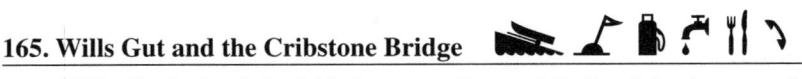

165. Wills Gut and the Cribstone Bridge

Wills Gut is the tight tickle between Orrs and Bailey Island, spanned by a unique cribstone bridge. Tides swirl between Harpswell Sound and Eastern Casco Bay through the bridge's granite cribbing.

Small boats can be launched on the west side of the bridge, either just north of it or in Garrison Cove to the south. Cooks Lobster House (833-2818) and wharf is on the narrow spit that defines Garrison Cove. Cooks pumps fuel and diesel and sells ice and raw lobsters, or you can have them served in the restaurant.

The Orrs/Bailey Yacht Club and Lester's Wharf (833-6702) lie to the north of Garrison Cove on Orrs Island's west shore. The yacht club pumps gas and dispenses plenty of camaraderie. Lester's has a few boats for rent and plenty of lobsters to sell.

Most small boats without masts can pass beneath the cribstone bridge to explore the exposed, outer reaches of eastern Casco Bay without the open-water trip around the southern end of Bailey Island.

By sea. The currents can run through the Gut and beneath the bridge at nearly a knot. On the east side, be sure to find the two stakes, privately maintained, that mark the channel between the tips of nearly overlapping ledges. The line between them is almost perpendicular to the bridge, forcing you to run nearly parallel to it to clear the ledges.

Cook's floats run along the west side of Garrison Cove. Please do not block the northern end of their float, since it is reserved for the Casco Bay Lines ferry. Gas and diesel pumps and ice are at the middle of the floats, and overnight dockage is available.

The Orrs/Bailey Yacht Club is located across the Gut on the west shore of Orrs, not far above the bridge. Their fuel float is beyond all the moored boats and has gas and water but not diesel. Lester's Wharf is the more commercial looking operation to the south. Both rent moorings.

Trailered boats can be launched either from a ramp at the southwest corner of

Garrison Cove or, for a small fee, from the gravel ramp run by S.J. Prince and Son (833-6210) just north of the bridge, on the west side. In Garrison, beware of the few rocks shown on the chart. A rock lies off Lowell's ramp, too, but it, or its rockweed, is usually visible. Portable boats can be launched at either location.

By land. Follow the Gurnet Road (Rt. 24) south from Cooks Corner in Brunswick.

Ashore. There is no public parking at the Garrison Cove town ramp. Be sure you aren't in the lot of Cooks Restaurant, or you will be towed. If you have doubts, ask at the restaurant. Pay phones are located at Cooks and at the yacht club.

Restaurants flank each end of the bridge. The Cribstone Bridge Restaurant (833-0600) is in the gray building on the Bailey Island end. The Orrs Island Chowder House, located in the red building on the Orrs end, combines a rustic restaurant with a general store lined with used books and fishing tackle.

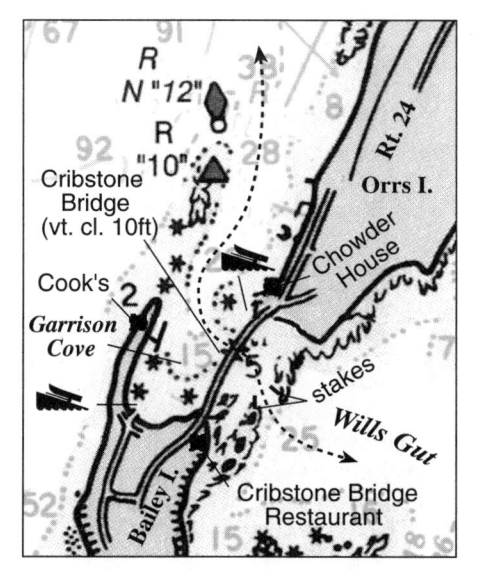

Long-term parking can be arranged at the Chowder House. H_2Outfitters (833-5257) and Paddleworks (833-5342) are located next to Prince's ramp, providing sea kayaking tours, instruction, and equipment for sale.

Wills Gut is named for Black Will, the unfortunate first settler of Bailey Island (see Bailey Island, p. 170). Garrison Cove is named for the garrison or blockhouse that was built here during the Indian Wars.

The decision of whether or not to build a bridge to Bailey Island almost split the town. The factions that formed were so strong that neighbors often wouldn't speak to each other or meet each other's eyes. By a narrow margin, the proponents won, and bridge construction began in 1926. Ten thousand tons of granite were cut at the Knight Brothers quarry in Pownal and floated by barge to the Gut. They were laid across the Gut in an open cribwork, so that tidal currents could still pass through. In a marvelous feat of engineering, the huge granite slabs are supported only by their own weight. The bridge was dedicated in 1928. It remains the only cribstone bridge in the world, declared a National Historic Civil Engineering Landmark and listed in the National Register of Historic Places.

Cooks Lobster House, across Garrison Cove from the bridge, is a full-scale lobster and fish restaurant. Each year during the last full week in July, they host the annual Casco Bay Tuna Tournament, a tradition since 1938. But since then, tuna fishing has become much more than sport. Many of the boats in Garrison Cove and Mackerel Cove are decked out with elaborate spotting towers and harpooning pulpits. The tuna have become increasingly rare and increasingly valuable. The largest tuna ever caught by the Casco Bay Tuna club weighed 1,009 pounds. Most of the commercial catch is bought for top dollar by dealers for the Japanese sushi market (see sidebar, p. 174).

Tuna

For many years, Atlantic bluefin tuna, *Thunnus thynnus*—or the horse mackerel as they were called—were considered a trash fish, or worse. They preyed on the mackerel and whiting that were the fishermen's livelihoods. So horse mackerel were hunted with harpoons from small punts and dragged ashore. The only commercial value was the oil drawn off the fishes' livers after they had been left standing in barrels in the sun. When it was refined, it was used for medicinal and lubricating purposes and as a medium for paints. Later, the canned tuna industry largely ignored bluefin because the color and texture of its meat was too variable. Instead they favored the smaller yellowfin, skipjack, or albacore tuna.

Undoubtedly, fishermen could not help but be awed by this fish, one of the ocean's biggest, fastest, and most powerful. Tuna can reach sizes up to 14 feet and weigh 1,500 pounds. They can swim at speeds of up to 50 knots, bursting to that speed from a standstill in less than 10 seconds. At top speeds, pelvic, pectoral and front dorsal fins retract into slots and the fish maintains its balance with horizontal stabilizers at the base of its tail. In fact, the tuna breathe by forcing water through their gills by their movement, so if they stop swimming, they will suffocate.

Tuna are able to dive to incredible depths and stay there for long periods. And their warmbloodedness has led to tales about fishermen saving their hands from frostbite by warming them in the body of a freshly caught tuna.

The sport of tuna fishing can be traced to a summer resident of Orrs Island, James Seymour of New Jersey, who began going after tuna with rod and reel out of a Hampton-type boat in 1910. The boat, *The Newark*, was built at Wilson's Boat Yard on Orrs, and her skipper was Henry Orr. Ashore, there were plenty of skeptics. However, Seymour persisted, and after five seasons in pursuit, he landed a bluefin with rod and reel. Even modern fishermen describe reeling in a tuna as "stopping a locomotive with a rope."

In the fall of 1938, three islanders organized the Tuna Fish Club and Tournament, based in Mackerel Cove. At this time whiting were abundant, and the big bluefins that chased them could be seen from the east side of Bailey Island. The first official tuna day was August 5, 1939. Prizes included a large silver trophy bowl for the largest tuna landed, as well as prizes for the yacht races. The first winner weighed 700 pounds, but that record climbed to a staggering 1,009 pounds. By 1977, more than 400 fishermen were competing, and at one point 55 bluefins were landed at the wharf to be weighed, and spectators had to leave for fear of the wharf collapsing. That same year, the Maine State rod and reel record was captured by Jerry Jamison for landing a 9 1/2-foot, 819-pound beauty.

Stan Johnson holds the record for the biggest fish story. He managed to hook a tuna while handlining from a dory. The tuna was so big that he couldn't lift it into his boat. Thinking quickly, he swamped the dory, rolled the fish into it, and swam his catch in.

The record for the largest numbers of tuna caught in a single day by rod and reel was set at a staggering 16 tuna. But by the late 1970s, there was growing concern about the tuna stocks. Some years the fish didn't show up at all, and when they did, there were few of them and they were more difficult to catch. New fishing regulations limited the catch to one fish per boat, and the tournament's popularity declined.

The sport changed dramatically again in the early 1990s when the price of fresh bluefin tuna soared to near $100 a pound at the fish auctions in Japan. The Japanese prize the raw tuna for *sushi* and *sashimi*. And the fish is supposed to bring good luck and good fortune. That is exactly what Atlantic fishermen hoped it would bring.

(continued on page 177)

166. Mackerel Cove

Mackerel Cove is the real harbor of Bailey Island. It is long and deep and surrounded by high sides. But the harbor faces the ocean from the island's southern end. When the sea is running, it funnels into the cove. Lobsterboats huddle together deep inside the cove, clinging to their mooring chains and snapping their steadying sails.

Mackerel Cove is a marvelous working harbor to explore, but don't get in the way of lobstermen in a hurry. The Lobster Village Restaurant and Marina (833-6656) makes a fun destination, with plenty of activity and fuel for you and the boat. Launching from the cove, though, is difficult. The head of Mackerel Cove is a sandy crescent with a town launching ramp in the western corner, but ashore there is, as one sign puts it, "No Pahkin."

By sea. The approach to Mackerel Cove is an easy, deep-water shot between Abner Point and the rest of Bailey to the east. Those in the know assert that the reported rock shown on the chart does not exist.

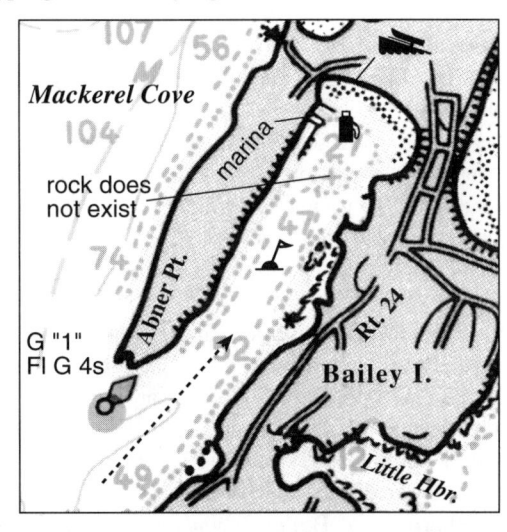

The Lobster Village Restaurant and Marina is on the west shore of the cove. The marina pumps gas and diesel, and the wharf has electricity, ice, and a pay phone. Dockage and moorings are available, but water is limited because it comes from a well.

By land. Follow Rt. 24 south to the cove. Abner Point Road runs to the right, down by the head of the cove and over to the marina.

Ashore. The Lobster Village Restaurant serves lunch and dinner and has plenty of good coffee in the morning. You can park along the narrow roads, but be very careful about where you leave your car. Even the marina posts a two-hour parking limit.

The field and the picnic area above the beach are public. The restaurant Jack Baker's Last Stand and the Bailey Island General Store and Deli are a short walk north on Rt. 24. The store sells snacks, limited groceries, and seemingly unlimited beer. Their deli serves breakfast and lunch. But be forewarned. A sign reads, "Prices subject to change according to customer's attitude."

167. Land's End and Jaquish Gut

Land's End is perfectly named. The southern tip of Bailey Island stabs into the Atlantic and abruptly stops. Jaquish Island and little Turnip hunker to the south, checking the swells. On one side, the islands of western Casco Bay pile together as if they have been washed up by the sea. On the other, the sparse islands of eastern Casco Bay taunt the openness around them. Jaquish Gut is the tight tickle between Jaquish Island

and the rocky shores of Bailey.

Turnip and Jaquish Island provide a little protection here, but not much. In fair weather, this can be an exciting place for a small boat; in bad, it is a dangerous lee shore with swells being compressed from the bottom by the shoaling water and from the sides by the tight passages. In 1948 it was the scene of a island tragedy when a lobsterboat was swamped by a wave and a father and son, both strong swimmers, drowned within a hundred feet of the shore.

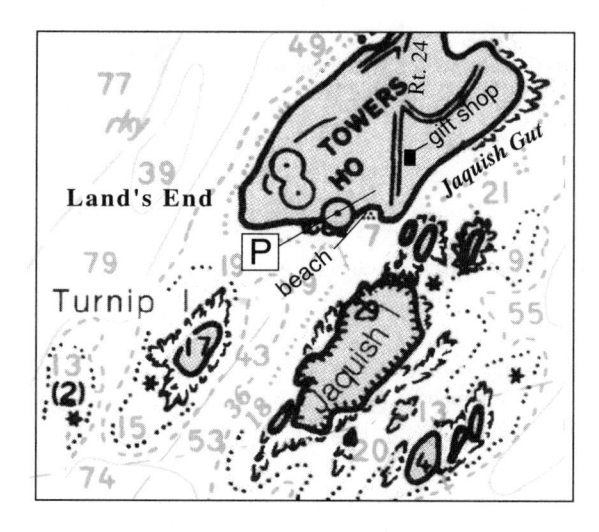

The waves have pounded the ledge into a small beach at the end of the road at Land's End. In fair weather portable boats can be launched here, though during the summer, parking is a problem. Also, you are bound to wind up on somebody's home video. Tour buses and sightseers in all shapes and sizes follow the road to its end where they discover not only the sweeping beauty of the ocean, but the huge Land's End Gift Shop.

By sea. The obvious large gray building to the east of the observation towers at the southern tip of Bailey Island houses the Land's End Gift Shop. The beach lies to its west, just north of the 7-foot sounding on the chart. The easiest approaches are from the south, between Turnip and Jaquish Island, or from the west, between Turnip and Bailey.

From Lands End, tight Jaquish Gut leads eastward to the open water of eastern Casco Bay. Jaquish Island includes several other islands and ledges to the north. Be sure to pass north of these island fragments, or you may end up fragmented yourself on the ledges that connect them. The scale of the chart is not detailed enough to show soundings through Jaquish Gut, so proceed cautiously. Depths are around six feet at low.

By land. Follow Rt. 24 south from Cooks Corner in Brunswick all the way to its end.

Ashore. The large parking lot across from the gift shop is for purchasers, not paddlers. In the off-season, though, the lot will be empty. In 1966, the State Highway Commission proposed a beautification project for Rt. 24 from Cooks Corner to Land's End. It included renaming the route the Shellfish Trail and taking land by eminent domain to create 23 paved turnouts and vistas, culminating in a massive 90-car parking lot with restrooms at Land's End. Bailey Islanders vehemently objected to the taking of private land just because it is beautiful, and they defeated the plan. As one fisherman put it, "We'd be just like monkeys at the zoo."

On the rocks near the beach, there is a small statue of a lobsterman. It was commissioned for the 1939 World's Fair and sculpted by Victor Kahill of Portland, with Elroy Johnson of Mackerel Cove as the model. Elroy, however, was never happy with the statue because it didn't include his faithful dog Bruin, who only missed five days of lobstering in his entire life. To make up for this oversight, when the statue was unveiled, Bruin was issued a lobsterman's license.

168. Jaquish and Turnip Island

Jaquish and Turnip Island are true ocean islands, windswept and treeless. Seabirds nest among what little scrub can get a toehold on the thin soil and survive the constant salt spray. These private islands have difficult landings. Please leave them to the birds. The many rocks and ledges around the islands, though, make promising striper territory.

By sea. Turnip Island Ledge claws the waves to the southwest of Turnip Island, in the mouth of Merriconeag Sound. It is marked by flashing red gong "8."

Tuna (continued from page 174)

The new prices set off a gold-rush mentality. Docks prices went from $10 to $20 and higher, with some single fish fetching prices in the neighborhood of $15,000. By the time the same fish reached Tokyo a day or two later, it would hit the market at about $80,000. Boat after boat refitted for the tuna chase. , The hunt, as one fisherman put it, became "a desperately serious business."

Scientists and regulators scrambled in their wake to collect data on the elusive stocks and to establish a quota system, both month-to-month and seasonally. In the early spring, the bluefin migrate north along the East Coast feeding on herring, mackerel, and squid. They reach Maine by mid-June, with the best fishing in July and August. Bluefin head south in September. The season ends for the month or the year when the quota is filled.

By 1994, 11,643 vessels had general tuna permits (which allow both harpoons and rod and reels). But the stocks had been depleted to the point where only 8% landed a salable fish. Harpoon-only boats, many employing spotter planes, have a success rate of about 34%. Still, of the 2000 or so tuna boats in the Gulf of Maine on a typical day, only 20 land fish. And as if that weren't enough of a gamble, the fear that the quota will be filled before a fish is caught can drive fishermen out in dangerous weather, risking their boats and their lives.

Scientists and regulators are worried. They estimate that in the last 22 years, 80% to 90% of the western Atlantic tuna stock has been caught, leaving only about 20,000 fish. Tuna are long-lived, not spawning until they are 10 or older and living up to 38 years, so depleted stocks will be slow to rebound. And they are highly migratory, so effective regulation must be international in scope.

An innovative new study involved placing small transmitters in the bodies of 160 tuna to record the location of the fish, its depth, its body temperature, and the temperature of the surrounding water *every two minutes*, with the data being relayed by satellite. The results may save the species.

Tuna navigate by the sun and the stars using a photoreceptive organ in their brains, and they can cover 5000 miles of open sea in as little as 50 days. Previously, it was thought that there were two basic breeding stocks of tuna in the Atlantic—one in the west and one in the east—and each is regulated differently. Now it is becoming apparent that the fish may all be of the same stock, spawning in the Gulf of Mexico and then fanning out across the North Atlantic. And the fish continue to surprise us. One fish descended to the excruciating pressures of 2400 feet, stayed there for two hours, and maintained its body temperature of 80 degrees in the near-freezing water.

In the fall of 1997, the economy of Japan stumbled. Ripples were felt in Maine as less demand or lower prices for the giant bluefins. This may not be good news for fishermen whose livelihoods depend on the tuna market. But for the tuna themselves, and perhaps for the fishermen in the long run, a little less fishing pressure, no matter how short, is much needed.

Jaquish Island includes several rocks and islands to its north, and an unnamed island to the east. Do not attempt to go between Jaquish and any of these smaller islands because of the ledges between them.

Ashore. Jaquish was named for Richard St. Jaques, who despite his French-sounding name, was British. He was an officer in the final attack on the Abenaki village at Norridgewock in 1728, the battle that shattered France's last toehold in the Maine frontier toward the end of the French and Indian Wars.

In 1908 the schooner *Race Horse*, carrying 175 tons of phosphate, went aground on the Jaquish Ledges in a thick fog. All crew members were rescued, and 15 tons of the phosphate was salvaged by Bailey Islanders.

The cribstone bridge to Bailey Island was completed in 1928, eight years after the Eighteenth Amendment was passed and prohibition became law. The connection by road to the mainland spurred an already active bootlegging business, and Jaquish Island, along with Turnip Island and Land's End nearby, became a hotbed of bootlegging activity. Foreign ships would stand offshore, and bootleggers and well-paid fishermen would make runs out to them and back under the cover of darkness or fog. A small cargo being landed on Harpswell Neck would be reported, and while the authorities rushed to confiscate it, a major shipment would be landed on remote Jaquish or ferried across to Bailey. If the Coast Guard dared to pursue them into this dangerous area, the bootleggers could sink their cargo in the shallow water around the islands and retrieve it later.

EASTERN CASCO BAY

Eastern Casco Bay lies to the east of the natural division formed by Orrs and Bailey Island, and of the two halves, it is much the more difficult to navigate. Casco Bay hooks to the east, so this side of it is wide open to the swells and winds of the southwest. The bedrock fragments into long, spiny peninsulas, extensive ledges, and scattered offshore islands.

Small-craft boaters should be extra careful in the open water here. The ledges, shoals, rocks, and "knobs" are so numerous that only a few are marked, and the wind that builds in the afternoon can push a lot of water ahead of it. Quahog Bay and the New Meadows River offer much more protected exploration, but the outer passages leading to them can be confusing.

By sea. Small boats can reach eastern Casco Bay in protected water either under the bridge at the north end of Gun Point Cove or under the cribstone bridge at Wills Gut. Or they can tackle the long way around, snaking around the north end of Sebascodegan and reaching the New Meadows River through the Gurnet.

From open water, eastern Casco Bay is reached from the west, by passing around Jaquish Island and Land's End off Bailey Island, or from the east, by rounding Cape Small.

Several main corridors run through the outer ledges and islands that are not immediately obvious on the chart, nor are they all marked. Most run in a northeast/southwest direction parallel to the grain of the ledge, but one runs across the grain, from the mouth of Gun Point Cove past Quahog Bay to the mouth of the New Meadows River. Beginning at Bailey Island, the northeast corridors are as follows:

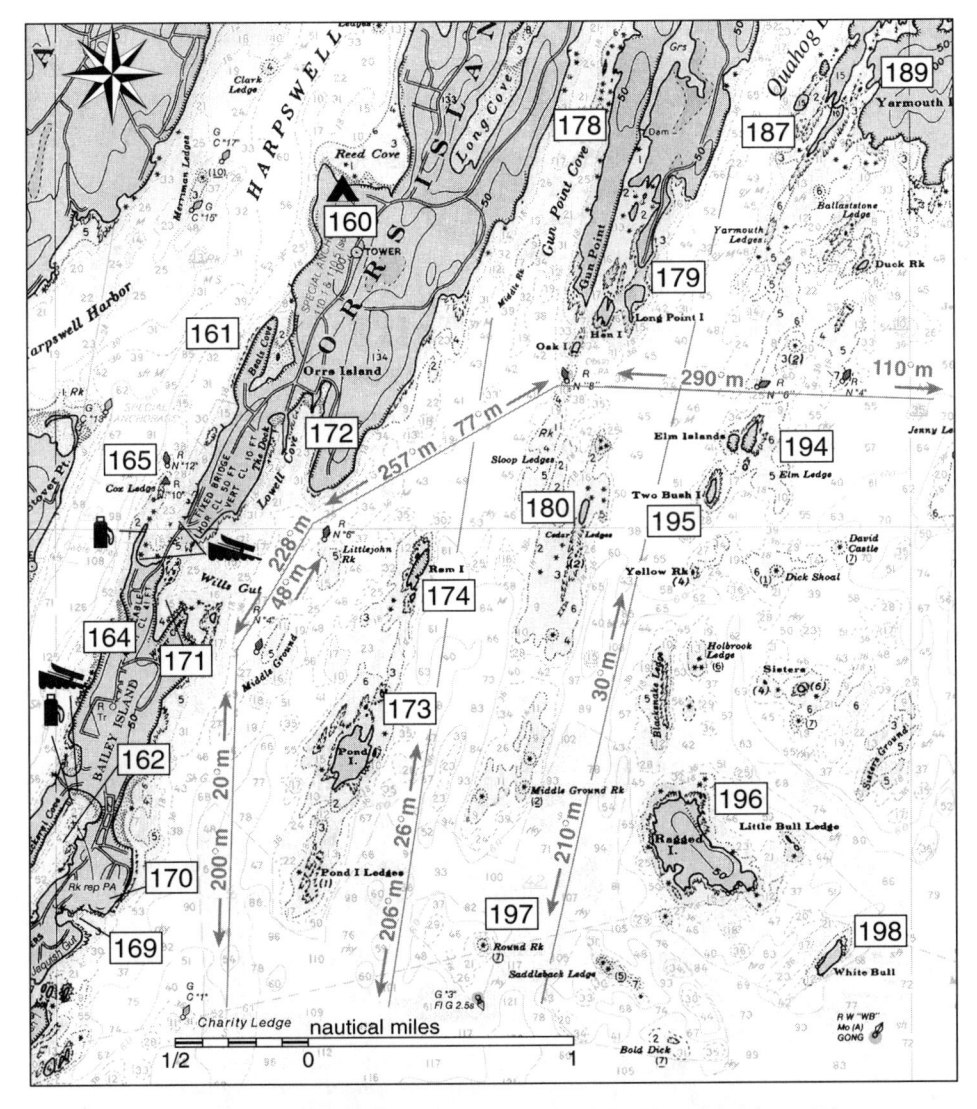

- between Bailey Island and Pond and Ram Island on either side of Middle Ground. The western side is marked.
- between Pond Island Ledges and Pond and Ram Island to the west and Middle Ground Rock and Cedar Ledges to the east. This route is unmarked.
- between Round Rock and Saddleback Ledge keeping Middle Ground Rock and Cedar Ledges to the west and Ragged Island, Blacksnake Ledge, and Two Bush and Elm Island to the east. Round Rock is marked, but the route is not.

• between White Bull and Mark Island Ledge, keeping Sisters Ground and Jenny Ledge to the west and Flag Island to the east and passing on either side of Long Ledge. The mouth of this corridor is marked with red and white gong "WB."

• between Mark Island and Wood Island, keeping Jamison Ledge to the west and Carrying Place Head and Harbor Island to the east. This route is marked.

The corridor across the grain of the ledge is strewn with obstacles, but it is well marked with a string of nuns. Beginning at the mouth of Gun Point Cove, keep nun "8" close aboard to port. Do the same for nun "6," nun "4," and nun "2," and you will arrive at the mouth of the New Meadows River.

169. Little Harbor

The name Little Harbor is stretching it a bit. Little, yes, but a harbor it isn't. Little Harbor is the deep indent on the east flank of Bailey Island, near its southern end. It is surrounded by high shores, but the protection they might offer is negated by its exposure to the ocean swells. This is not a place to spend the night, and the shoreline is private.

170. Giant's Steps

On the west side of Bailey Island, the high rocky shore is stratified, turned on edge, and lifts have broken away to form huge natural steps to the ocean. This formation is known as the Giant's Steps or Devil's Stairway. Each step is about 40 inches wide, and high tide reaches the lowest step. Legends abound that pirates used these very steps to unload treasure for burying nearby. Of course, the least likely place a pirate would bury his treasure is by a landmark as obvious as a giant set of stairs, and of course, the loot has never been found.

Still, some islanders maintain that an old iron crock was discovered in the vicinity of Giant's Steps, buried twenty feet deep. Instead of treasure, it held a poem on brittle parchment:

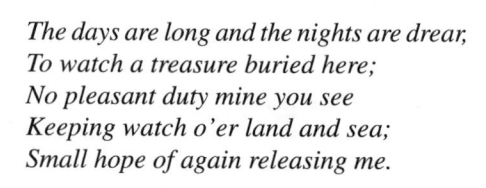

The days are long and the nights are drear,
To watch a treasure buried here;
No pleasant duty mine you see
Keeping watch o'er land and sea;
Small hope of again releasing me.

Nice poem. Some crock.

In 1910, Captain William Henry Sinnett and his wife Joanna gave the town of Bailey Island the real treasure—a public right-of-way along the cliff edge to Giant's Steps and the endless views beyond.

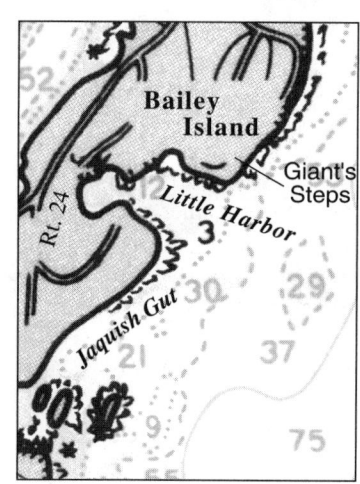

171. Water Cove, Cedar Island Beach

Water Cove, or Fresh Water Cove as it was once called, is the first cove to the south as you pass under the cribstone bridge from west to east. Coasting schooners used to fill their tanks from a fresh spring here, and it still makes a pleasant anchorage.

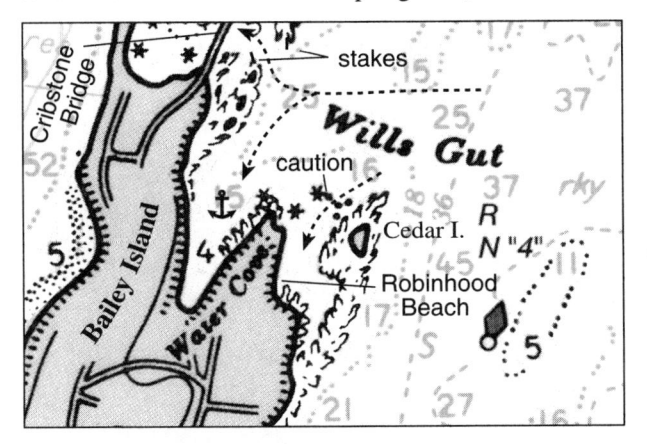

Just to the east of the cove is a small crescent of sand, packed between two spines of ledge. This is the only fine-sand beach on Bailey Island. The beach is owned by the town of Harpswell and open to the public, but ironically, all the property surrounding it is private. The only legal way to visit the beach is by boat, but it is tricky. At the top of the tide, small boats with very shallow draft can pick their way over the ledges and land on the beach.

By sea. The beach lies on the northeast shoulder of Bailey Island, behind a small island that is unnamed on the chart. It is actually known as Cedar Island. Ledges ring Cedar Island, and rocks stretch toward the point at Water Cove. At the top of the tide, enough water can be found around the rocks to get into the beach from the north, west of Cedar Island. Do not approach from the east, south of Cedar Island, because the island is connected to Bailey Island by a long arm of ledge. Outboarders should use particular care.

Ashore. Public access and even ownership of this beach has been contested for decades, but it has been gratefully used by islanders for generations.

Early settlers called it Robinhood Beach after Ragemin, the sachem of the Cannibas, a group within the Nequsset tribe that occupied the areas between Maquoit and Merrymeeting Bay. Other Cannibas lived in the Kennebec Valley. The English quickly slipped into calling Ragemin "Robinhood," and the nickname stuck. Robinhood Cove, off the Sheepscot River in Georgetown is also named for him.

More modern sentiment was expressed by one islander when she called Robinhood Beach "God's gift for pleasure."

172. Lowell Cove

The working harbor of Lowell Cove is nearly opposite Water Cove, to the north. It splits the southern end of Orrs Island and harbors the resident lobster fleet. But the cove is wide open to the south, and when the sea is up, the boats hang on to their moorings for dear life.

A narrow spine of ledge known as Little Island sticks into Lowell Cove near its western shore. This is the idyllic site of the Little Island Motel (833-2392), a nearly perfect base for small-boat exploration. The rooms literally hang out over the water, and boats can be docked at the motel's float.

Portable boats can be launched from the gravel beach at the head of the cove. Occasionally lightweight trailered boats are launched from the beach at the top of the tide, but parking is scarce. It is much easier to take them to the Gut (see p. 172).

By sea. Lowell Cove is east of the Cribstone Bridge, opposite Water Cove. The obvious brown buildings on Little Island are the motel. The motel's float hangs off the north end of the island, near its causeway. Use caution in approaching the float. A nasty ledge, visible at low, lurks just to the east.

By land. From Cooks Corner, follow Rt. 24 south onto Orrs. Take a left onto Lowell Cove Road, and then an immediate right onto Little Island Road, which leads to the motel.

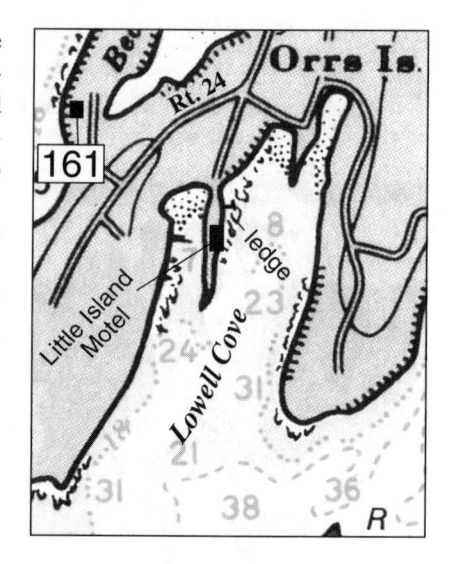

Ashore. Lowell Cove is the site of a study of juvenile lobsters started by marine biologist Diane Cowan. She counts and measures the young lobsters and inserts small magnetic tags into their legs in an effort to build a database on the size and health and life-cycles of Casco Bay's lobster population.

173. Pond Island

Due east of Bailey Island, a treeless hump of rock lies low in the water. Its bedrock forms a pocket that holds fresh water and gives the island its name, Pond Island.

Pond is owned by the State of Maine and managed by the Department of Inland Fisheries and Wildlife as a site for nesting sea birds. A cove at the island's north end makes landing possible, but the island should be avoided during the nesting season.

By sea. Pond Island, along with Ram Island to the north, is the visible portion of a long underwater ledge. The Pond Island Ledges extend more than a half mile south of the island itself. Portions of the ledge extending to the north are visible as little rocky fragments.

A small cove with a cobbly beach lies at the north end of Pond, but the northern ledge fragments must be cleared before approaching from the northeast.

Ashore. This is a windswept ocean island, with low bushes and scruff clinging to the rock. Near the north end, the pond has grown in and become a scrubby meadow. For generations, Bailey Islanders have used this island as a picnic getaway, and it has been the source of many legends that have originated more from gazing into the flames of a campfire than from delving into historical fact.

According to a sailor from the 18th-century Spanish treasure ship *Don Pedro del Montclova,* the *Don Pedro* was sailing in convoy with another ship from Mexico to Spain when a storm separated it from its escort. Alone, it fell prey to pirate Lowe off the coast of New York. The sailors of the *Don Pedro* were pressed into service as pirates, and they sailed northeastward. In the Gulf of Maine, they were spotted and chased by an English man of war, and to evade it, Lowe put in to eastern Casco Bay and anchored to the east of a small island. Three longboats were lowered and each was loaded with a bushel-sized kettle of silver bullion, coins, and jewels. The boats were rowed through a narrow channel between two ledges off the northern end of the island and into a cove which could not be seen from the open ocean. A pond lay at the head of the cove, about thirty feet deep, surrounded by rocks and trees. Two large kettles were lowered into the pond. To spread the risk of its complete discovery, the third kettle and two smaller ones were sunk in a long, narrow cove to the west, between a series of high ledges and the main island.

Lowe escaped the British, and the sailor eventually escaped from Lowe. Later, the sailor returned to Pond Island. He recognized the lay of the land and certain markings on the ledges, but he had no idea if the pirates had returned for their loot in the intervening years. He never found the treasure. Nor have the many treasure seekers who have scoured the island over the years, hopefully turning the earth of the meadow where the pond once stood.

In 1801, Pond was the site of the operations of a corporation formed to produce silver from morning dew. As far-fetched as this sounds, this type of scheme was not unique along the Maine coast. It may even have been the model for operations that were set up at Stage Island Harbor at Cape Porpoise and at Lubec for extracting gold from seawater almost a hundred years later. The real name of the man who showed up on Pond Island has been forgotten, and he probably never divulged it anyway. Instead he is remembered only as the "Acaraza Man," a man of technological smarts, vision, persuasion, and entrepreneurial spirit—a man, in short, who could make an investor rich. He convinced a group of backers that he could, in fact, produce silver from morning dew. They formed a corporation for this purpose and hired him as a consultant. The dew had to be gathered and treated just so. Dew was gathered from Freeport, brought to Pond Island, measured, heated, and stirred. It evaporated. The fault, the Acaraza Man explained, was that it was gathered incorrectly. So the next time it was gathered under tight quality control and again brought to Pond Island. This time Acaraza Man slipped in some silver coins, and his backers were so pleased with their success that they promptly paid the exorbitant fee for his services. Of course by the time they discovered they had been duped, the Acaraza Man had, like the dew, evaporated.

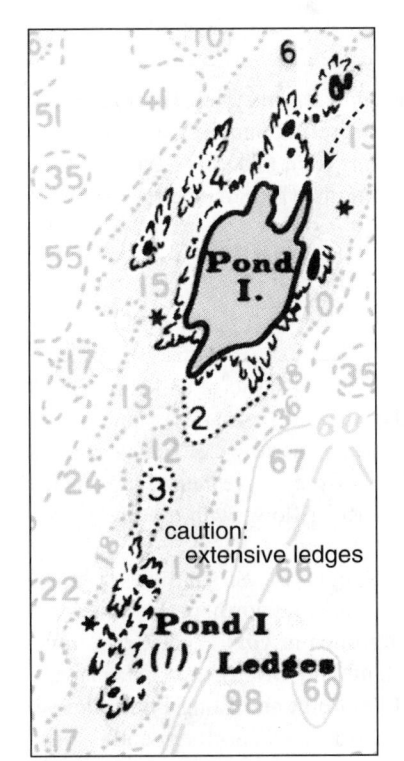

Pond Island was also the home of the infamous Hermit of Harpswell, who was said to have lived off the stagnant black water of the pond and decayed fish and putrid crustaceans that washed ashore. In truth, the Hermit was a fisherman named John Darling, who raised a family on Pond and rowed his children to Orrs for school. In later years, Pond was owned by the family of the poet Robert P. Tristram Coffin. His grandfather lived on the island for a brief period in a high wooden house that had to be held against the winds by chains to the rock. He later packed the house aboard a schooner and moved the family to Sebascodegan, near the Gurnet. After that, the family used the island for annual picnics, which was always an adventure and often dreaded. Peggy Coffin remembered it in *Yankee Coast*:

"The island picnic was an annual affair. No family, not even ours, could have taken more than one—and survived."*

174. Ram Island

Ram Island is the northern terminus of the ridge of the Pond Island Ledges. From the side, this high, bushy hump looks like the back of an enormous whale rolling back into the depths.

Ram Island is private, and its steep sides make landing difficult anyway.

By sea. Deep water surrounds Ram on all sides with two exceptions. To the south, the ridge of ledge stretching to Pond Island brings the depths to 14 feet or less. But the real danger lies to the southwest of Ram in the form of a 3-foot spot and two isolated rocks shown on the chart.

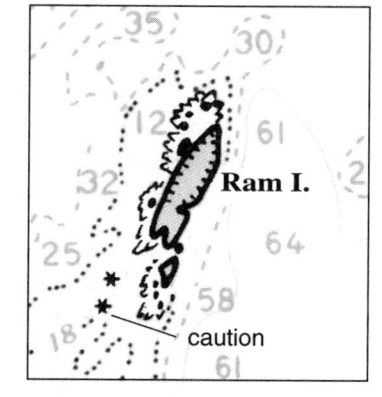

Ashore. The Maine coast has numerous Ram islands, a legacy left from the days when rams were kept on seperate islands from the ewes to prevent lambs from being born too early in the harsh spring weather. Even in summer, this Ram Island is a barren place exposed to open wind and waves. An area history written in 1878 had a better name for the place: Raw Island.

SEBASCODEGAN ISLAND

Sebascodegan is Casco Bay's biggest island, with miles of intricate and convoluted shoreline. It is a coast made for small boats. Creeks wind from pocket estuaries to landlocked coves ringed by granite and spruce. The tide sweeps in through narrow clefts, then sweeps out again. Shorebirds poke the edges of the rich mud flats. Osprey stake their claims in the trees of almost every headland. And the New Meadows River flows with the tide to the glistening Atlantic.

Sebascodegan consists of several of Casco Bay's long northeast-southwest ridges. Between them, long arms of water stab inland from the south and north, nearly touching their heads. On the west side of the island, the strong tides in Gun Point Cove have actually kept the little gut between Sebascodegan Island and Orrs open to Harpswell Sound (see Long Cove, p. 167). The cove between Gun Point and Long Point almost breaks through to the southern end of Card Cove, and Card Cove's northern end is only

* Reprinted with permission, see copyright page.

a few hundred yards from the headwaters of Long Reach. And the fist of Quahog Bay almost punches into the headwater estuary of Doughty Cove.

Each of these long arms is open to the prevailing winds coming from the southwest, but each is deep enough to quickly calm wind and seas and smooth the water for small boats. From Harpswell Sound, an inside passsage snakes around the north end of the island, through Ewin Narrows, Prince Gurnet, Long Reach, and Gurnet Strait all the way to the New Meadows River.

By sea. The route around Sebascodegan's west and north shores is detailed in the Inside Passage entry, p. 186. Though they are not actually on Sebascodegan, that passage has two possible launching sites, one at Ewin Narrows, the other at Buttermilk Cove. Two other ramps are located on Sebascodegan itself, one at Bethel Point (p. 196), between Quahog Bay and Ridley Cove, and another at Dingley Cove (p. 219) on the New Meadows River.

By land. Sebascodegan is southeast of Brunswick, and it is connected to the mainland in two places. Either follow Rt. 24 south from Brunswick's Cooks Corner and cross the Gurnet Bridge, or take the Harpswell Road, Rt. 123, from Brunswick Center to Harpswell Neck and take a left on Mountain Road, which crosses to Sebascodegan over Ewin Narrows.

Ashore. Sebascodegan Island, along with Harpswell Neck and Orrs and Bailey Island, makes up the town of Harpswell, but by virtue of geography, the town has always had two distinct halves, two different faces. Harpswell Neck was considered the more sophisticated side, with strong ties to education and commerce in Brunswick, while Sebascodegan was where the real people lived, hard working fishermen and farmers in isolated villages hard by the sea. Surprisingly for such a large island, there are no camping facilities on Sebascodegan, and no public lands.

Sebascodegan is an Indian word meaning "low marshy place." It refers either to the many possible portages between the arms and bays or to the abundant wild and waterfowl that congregated here. The Enlish simply called it Great Island.

Captain Martin Pring was one of the first Europeans to explore the island. He was commissioned by a group of apothecaries in Bristol, England to explore the New World for medicinal plants and herbs. In 1603, Pring's expedition anchored in the mouth of the New Meadows River and explored Sebascodegan in search of sassafras, used for the relief of rheumatism and many other ailments.

Early ownership of Sebascodegan, in part and in whole, changed hands numerous times and often with incomplete or inadequate deeds. At one time Harvard University claimed it through an old title, but the claim was denied.

The narrowness of the Gurnet at the island's north end made connection to the mainland inevitable. The first of many bridges was built there in 1839, but the strong currents required constant rebuilding or replacement. Now, the span has been shortened even more by strong abutments, and when you cross it by car you are hardly aware that you have arrived on an island. Still, the island's convoluted geography isolates many pockets, leaving them as remote and untouched as any island in Casco Bay.

INSIDE PASSAGE

Sebascodegan Island is separated from the mainland by a marvelous inside passage from the head of Harpswell Sound all the way to the Gurnet and the New Meadows River. This is a quiet, wild place, with tight tickles, surging currents, the screech of ospreys, and utter stillness. In places it is so narrow that it feels more like an inland river than a part of the ocean. Still, it carries that unmistakable briny tinge on the rise and fall of the tides. The water is peppered with lobster buoys, and rockweed trails from the ledges.

The Indians used the Inside Passage as a main canoe route between western portions of Casco Bay and the upper New Meadows and Kennebec River (see Middle Bay Cove, p. 146 and Brighams Cove, p. 216). Little has changed. Pines and spruce crowd the shores and the thump of an oar or paddle echoes between them. At low, mud flats ooze ripe, salty muck, and clammers rake their furrows. Egrets and blue heron stalk the shorelines, and ospreys stand sentinel from their lofty nests.

By sea. See chart next page. Exploring the inside passage is a marvelous small-boat adventure. It can be approached from either Harpswell Sound or the New Meadows River, or boats can be launched in Ewin Narrows or Buttermilk Cove (see following entries).

The inside passage around Sebascodegan Island is completely tidal, with strong currents in its narrowest sections, and moderate ones everywhere else. Often, though, small boats can avoid the current by finding eddies close to shore. The following description runs from the southwest to the northeast:

Ewin Narrows runs north from the bridge at the head of Harpswell Sound in a straight, deep-water shot. Houses line the shores of the lower portion, but soon the Narrows are well off the beaten path. The current at this end of the inside passage floods to the north and ebbs to the south with a maximum strength of several knots.

The top of the Narrows widens into broad, shallow estuaries to the west and north, the north being Harpswell Cove. The west shore of Harpswell Cove is the site of the ways of the famous Skolfield shipyard (see Middle Bay Cove, p. 146).

At Prince Point, the main channel squeezes through a narrow slot called Prince Gurnet and then swirls east in an S-curve around Doughty Point into Long Reach.

This is a wild place, with only one or two cottages visible from the water and current that races with the tide. Long Reach yearns toward the south, almost kissing the head of Card Cove off Quahog Bay at an old Indian portage. A mile of the eastern shore was once slated for condominium development, but its owners recently granted conservation easements to the Harpswell Heritage Trust to keep it "forever wild."

The main channel narrows in the northern half of Long Reach. Deceptively broad water disguises it at high tide, but at low it snakes between extensive mud flats. The channel is marked by sticks driven into the mud, which should be kept to port when heading north.

Depending on the state of the tide, the tides will meet somewhere in Long Reach along Prince Point. If you are in a self-propelled craft and were prudent enough to catch the flood up Ewin Narrows, you will now find that the same tide has flooded in from the east and will now oppose you. Or, if you struggled against the ebb up Ewin Narrows, your battle will be won, and it will be downhill from here.

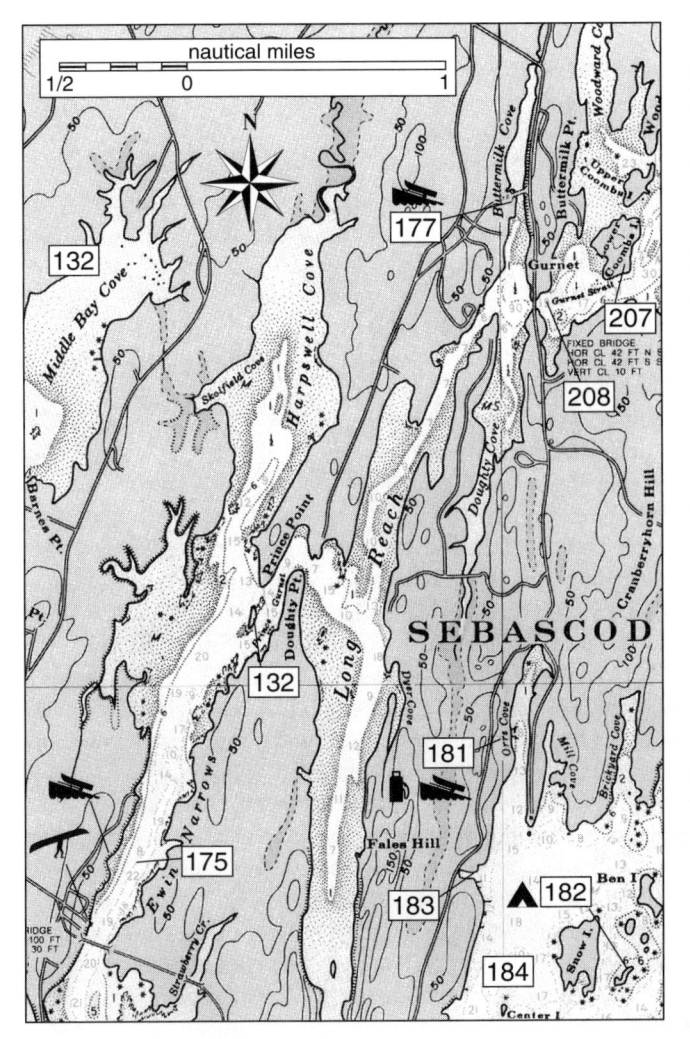

Finally, Long Reach splits into Doughty and Buttermilk Cove, etching to the south and north, while the main channel surges under the narrow span of Gurnet Bridge (see p. 211). Use caution here. The current beneath the bridge can be fierce, easily reaching four knots or more on any given tide, with an obvious drop in water level and eddies and boils. Just to the west of the bridge, the force of the current has bored a hole in the channel ninety feet deep.

If paddlers can't make headway against a contrary current under the bridge, they can tow their kayaks or canoes by clambering over the large boulders of the embankment. Otherwise, if the current is with you, enjoy the ride.

Once through the bridge, you will be in the New Meadows River, many sea miles and a world away from Harpswell Sound.

175. Ewin Narrows

Ewin Narrows begins where the head of Harpswell Sound is squeezed beneath a fixed green bridge. Somehow, in the years of mapping this squeeze, the cartographers popped the "g" right off the name "Ewing." It's labeled "Ewin" on the chart, but it is still pronounced and often spelled "Ewing."

Despite adequate depths as far as Prince Point, the Narrows is effectively sealed off to larger sailboats by the bridge's minimum vertical clearance of 30 feet. But for small boats, the bridge marks the gateway to a marvelous inland adventure of wending around the top of Sebascodegan Island, the largest island in Casco Bay.

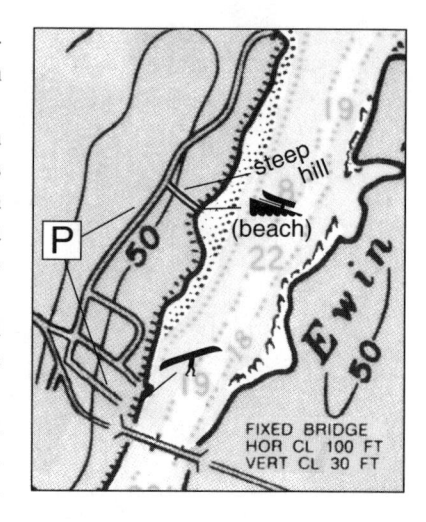

Depending on the tide, small boats have another advantage—a put-in and launching site on the west bank, though both are difficult.

By sea. Both sites are north of the bridge, on the west bank of Ewin Narrows. Portable boats can be put in at the end of Wharf Street, just north of the bridge, but they must be carried down a steep embankment and around the old wharf cribbing.

Lightweight trailered boats can be launched from a firm gravel bar that is also on the west shore slightly farther north, but this is also a challenge. The road leading down to the bar is steep enough to require four-wheel drive, or at least four-wheel brakes. The only turn-around is on the bar, so high tide forces you to back all the way down the road. The clammers who use this site are usually out only when the tide is down, so they park right on the bar. Following their example is not recommended. Things would get interesting if you didn't make it back before high.

By land. To reach the ramp and put-in on Ewin Narrows, follow Rt. 123, the Harpswell Road, south out of Brunswick and out Harpswell Neck. In North Harpswell, turn left on Mountain Road, then left again on Wharf Street, just before the Ewin Narrows Bridge. The put-in lies at the foot of Wharf Street. You will need to carry your boat down the steep bank and park your car on the narrow shoulder.

To reach the launching site, take the first left off Wharf Street. At exactly 2/10ths of a mile, the small, unmarked road leading to the bar will be on your right. It looks like one of the several driveways in the area, but it lies just before telephone pole number 7 and just after a drive on the opposite side of the street.

Ashore. If you have any doubts about the Ewin Narrows launching site—and you should—walk down the hill before you drive it. If it is high tide, you may have to back all the way down. If it looks too intimidating, or if the tides aren't cooperating, use the much-easier Buttermilk Cove ramp instead. Parking at both the put-in and the bar is limited to the shoulder of the road. Please do not park on the access the road or block nearby driveways.

176. Doughty Island

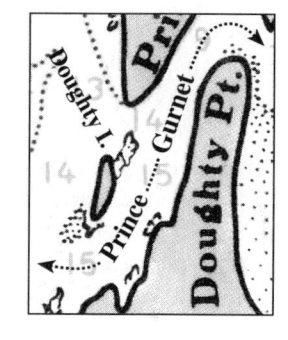

Little Doughty Island is owned by the Nature Conservancy. Landing is permitted for careful day use.

By sea. Doughty Island lies just off Prince Point in the slipstream of Prince Gurnet. Landing is easiest on the gradually sloping east shore.

Ashore. Ospreys nest in a tree near the northwest shore, so please try to avoid that area. As on all Nature Conservancy properties, fires and camping are not permitted.

177. Buttermilk Cove

A state-maintained, concrete launching ramp slopes into Buttermilk Cove, near the Gurnet bridge connecting Sebascodegan to the mainland. Buttermilk Cove becomes mud flats at low, so the ramp must be used at the top half of the tide. Otherwise it is an easy place to launch most trailered boats.

By sea. If you plan to pass beneath the bridge at the Gurnet to the New Meadows River, beware of the strong currents (see the Gurnet, p. 211).

By land. From Cooks Corner, head south on Rt. 24, the Gurnet Road. Turn right on Prince's Point Road and cross over the headwaters of Buttermilk Cove. The launching ramp is on the left.

Ashore. Park at the dirt turnout at the head of the ramp or along the shoulder. Do not crowd the ramp.

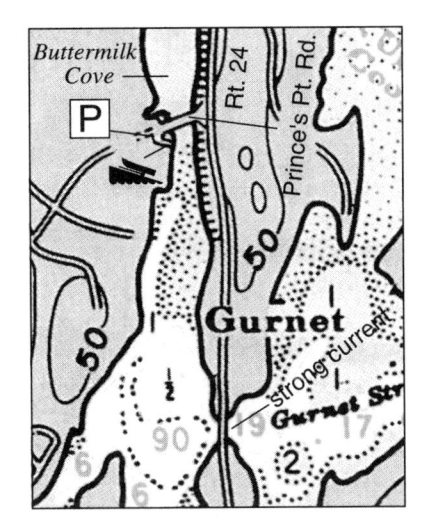

Pogies

If you know anything about pogies, you know they stink. Pogies are Atlantic menhaden, *Brevoortia tyrannus*, a small coastal fish that travels in great schools along the Atlantic seaboard. But they are pursued by voracious bluefish, which herd the pogies *en masse* into the cul-de-sacs of bays and coves to devour them in apocalyptic feeding frenzies.

From the perspective of the bluefish, the long and narrow coves in eastern Casco Bay are perfect corrals for trapping pogies. Still, many of the pogies would escape were it not for their number. So many fish in such constricted water deplete the water of oxygen, and the fish suffocate. And when they suffocate, humans suffocate. The tides wash thousands of dead and dying fish ashore, where they rot and stink.

Pogies are plankton eaters, filtering about 25 liters (almost seven gallons!) per minute. A typical school takes up an area about 100 feet by 85 feet, comprising about 140,000 fish weighing 64 tons! Together, a school is filtering 980,000 (7x140,000) gallons of seawater every minute! When a school of pogies is driven up rivers or into coves, crabs and even lobsters have been seen crawling up out of the water for air or keeled over on their backs from lack of it.

For centuries, pogies have been fished for their oil, which has been used for, among other things, oil-based house paint. In fact, menhaden oil is still one of the secret ingredients in Rustoleum brand paints. Menhaden are about 50% oil by weight, and rendering them is a relatively simple, if stinky, process. In 1875, there were 22 fish-rendering plants along the coast.

Yet no one fully understands the life cycle of the pogies and what causes their cyclical populations or inconsistent runs to Maine. Some years there are so many pogies that their corpses create a putrid mess along the shores of Casco Bay's creeks and coves. In other years there are enough to keep local purse seiners in business supplying the fish to Russian factory ships offshore, which grind the fish into meal and fertilizer. And some years, like the recent ones, there have been virtually no pogies at all.

178. Gun Point Cove

Gun Point Cove is the wide tongue of water between Orrs Island and Gun Point on Sebascodegan Island. It offers no protection as an anchorage, and its head is studded with unmarked rocks and ledges. But both shores are only sparsely developed and still have a certain wild beauty.

With care, small boats can work their way to the head of the cove and pass beneath the bridge and through the narrow cleft between Sebascodegan and Bailey Island.

By sea. The northern half of the cove becomes rockbound. Stay in the middle until you are abreast of what the chart shows as a small islet on the east shore. It actually is a large ledge, visible at all tides and often frequented by basking seals. Once past the ledge, favor the western shore until a point on Sebascodegan pinches the head down to a narrow gut leading to the bridge.

In the gut, cross over to the east shore and keep close by it through the gut, under the bridge, and all the way into Lumbos Hole. The bridge has a minimum vertical clearance of 14 feet. (see Long Cove, Lumbos Hole, p. 167).

By land. From Cooks Corner in Brunswick, follow Rt. 24 south onto Sebascodegan and over the head of Gun Point Cove where it crosses to Orrs Island.

Ashore. The passage beneath the bridge can be scoped out from land at the bridge to Orrs Island. A turnout near some fishing shacks on the Orrs Island side can provide temporary parking while you walk back to the bridge to have a look.

The middle reaches of Gun Point Cove can be seen from the Whaleback Picnic area farther down Rt. 24 on Orrs. Walk through the woods to the shore.

Gun Point, on the Sebascodegan shore, is a private association with no public access to the water.

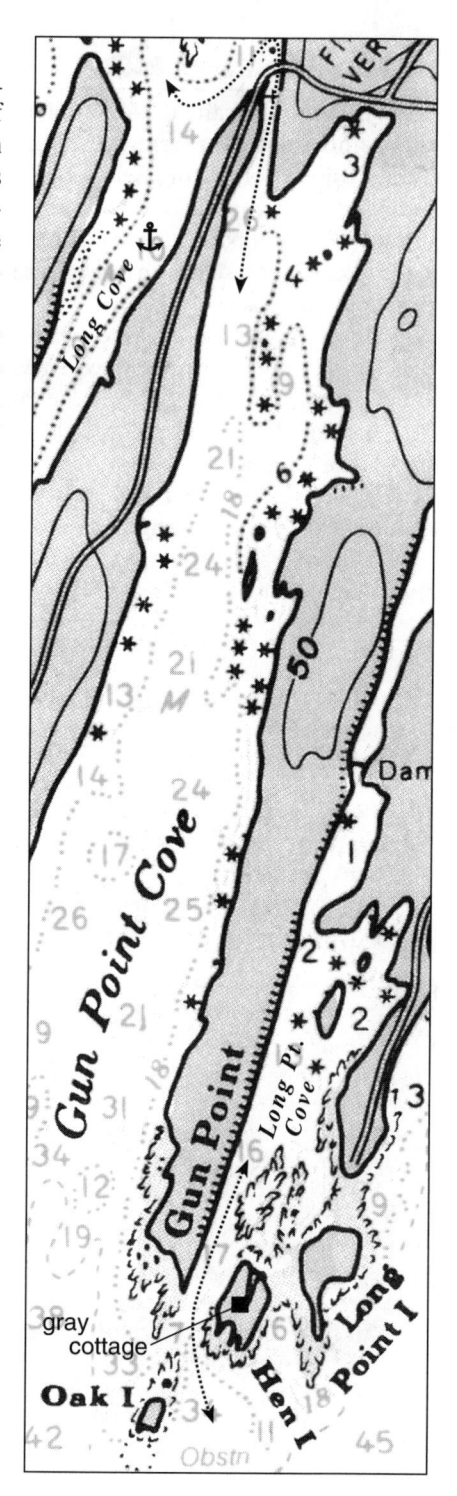

179. Long Point Cove ⚓

Between Gun Point and Long Point to the east, there is another finger of water, unnamed on the chart, called Long Point Cove. This is a surprising place. Three islands—Oak Island, Hen Island, and Long Point Island—and their almost connected and overlapping ledges form a nearly perfect baffle, providing this outer harbor remarkable protection.

There is no public shoreline here, but the cove makes a perfect gunkhole or refuge for small boats caught out in sudden foul weather. The lower, deep-water half of the harbor is filled with moored boats and floats from the surrounding houses. The cove's shallow head was once dammed for an old tide mill, and a small island with a cottage sits among the rocks at its waist.

By sea. This is small-boat-only territory with a tricky entrance and extensive ledges. Look carefully at the chart. Ledges connect Long Point, Long Point Island, and Hen Island. They run north from Hen, north from Oak, and south from Gun Point. The entrance to the cove is between Hen Island and Gun Point, with careful approaches from either side of Oak Island.

The safest slot lies east of Oak Island. Despite its name, Oak only has a few low trees on it. Identify Hen Island by its small but conspicuous gray cottage and approach from the south, east of Oak. Steer for deep water about two thirds of the way across from Oak to Hen, favoring Hen. Once abreast of Hen, hug Gun Point to clear the inner ledges.

180. Cedar Ledges

Cedar Ledges lie off Gun Point, halfway between Ram Island and the Elm Islands. Curiously, the chart omits naming the small island at the north end of the ledges. It is known as Cedar Island, but any Cedars that were on it long gone. The island is an abrupt, treeless rock—and a private one at that.

By sea. Cedar Island is an important landmark when approaching Quahog Bay from the open water between Middle Ground and Ragged Island. It and the small rock to its south are the only visible indication of the long spine of ledge that includes Cedar Ledges and Middle Ground Rock to the south and Sloop Ledges and a constellation of rocks to the north. The least obstructed water is due west of the island and, to a lesser extent, southeast.

Ashore. Few people gave Cedar Island a second thought until after the death of John Wilson of Bailey Island. Wilson was a man of modest means living on Bailey Island around 1840 when he took an uncharacteristic trip to Boston carrying a heavy suitcase. He returned in a brand new sloop and bought one of the finest farms on the island. For the rest of his life, he was tight-lipped about the strange trip to Boston. It wasn't until he died that his papers describing his trip to Cedar

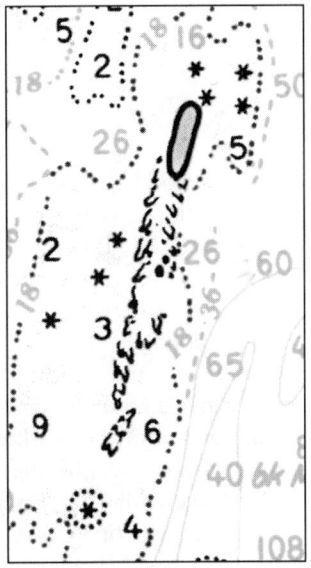

Island came to light. Wilson had been duck hunting here when his foot slipped into a crevice. When he extracted his foot, he discovered an old copper kettle full of pieces of Spanish gold. In Boston, he cashed the gold in for $15,000, a substantial fortune in those days.

This legend differs from many in Casco Bay in that the loot is said to have actually been found. But like many others, it may have grown up in the fertile loam of oral tradition. Bailey Islanders held summer clambakes on Cedar Island for generations, and low tide reveals a natural hole in the ledges that they named Pirates' Gold Pot. Inevitably, the two became bound together by storytelling. Or was it truth?

QUAHOG BAY

Quahog Bay is the largest of the flooded valleys between the ridges of Sebascodegan Island. Its shores are wooded and quietly populated with homes and summer cottages. Its narrow neck runs straight and true to the northeast, but its shores break away into the working harbor of Card Cove, the fingers of Orrs Cove, Mill Cove, Brickyard Cove, and Rich Cove, as well as the island fragments of Ben, Snow, Little Snow, Center, Pole, Raspberry, and tiny Mouse.

Quahog is easily accessible from the open water to the south or from ramps at Great Island Boat Yard in Orrs Cove or at Bethel Point. Limtied camping is allowed on state-owned Little Snow Island or, if you are a member of the Maine Island Trail Association, on private Raspberry Island (see individual entries below).

CASCO BAY

By sea. The offshore approaches are detailed in the Eastern Casco Bay entry on page 178.

The east side of the mouth of Quahog Bay is cluttered with the unmarked Yarmouth Ledges, so you need to favor the Long Point Island side to avoid them. Deep water passes to either side of large, wooded Pole Island, but a long line of ledge extends both north and south from it. Note that nun "4" on the South Ledges is not at its southern terminus, but part way up the ledge, marking the west channel. Do not cut tightly around this buoy to get from one channel to the other.

To avoid the North Ledges past Pole, favor the Sebascodegan shores until they broaden into the basin holding Snow and the other islands (see p. 194).

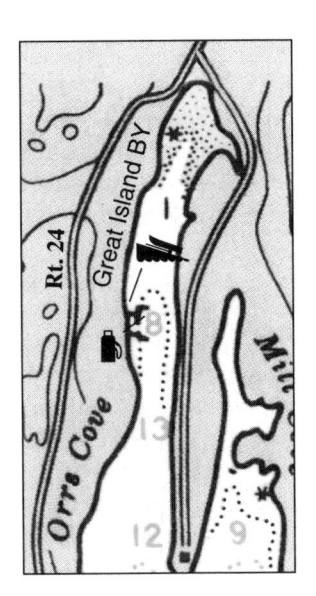

181. Great Island Boat Yard

Great Island Boat Yard (729-1639, Ch. 09) is an unpretentious marina and boat yard on the beautiful shores of little Orrs Cove, at the head of Quahog Bay. This full-service facility is a perfect spot for launching and parking for an extended exploration of Quahog Bay and vicinity.

By sea. See approaches to Quahog Bay, above. The floats have 7 feet of water at low, and gas, diesel, electricity, and water. Trailered boats can be launched on the paved ramp or by Travellift. Overnight dockage and moorings are available, but reservations are recommended.

By Land. Follow Rt. 24 south from Cooks Corner in Brunswick. The boat yard runs right to the edge of the road on the left.

Ashore. Great Island Boat Yard has a pay phone, showers, ice, and a small marine store. They can perform all types of hull and engine repairs.

182. Little Snow Island

Snow Island, the largest of the islands in the basin at the head of Quahog Bay, is the private retreat of world-famous sailor Dodge Morgan. A red cottage sits at its southeast tip, and landing is not allowed. The smaller island to the southeast, however, is owned by the Maine Bureau of Parks and Lands and managed by the Maine Island Trail Association.

Little Snow is beautiful, easy to get to, and completely protected—a combination that makes it busy. Its few campsites are often occupied.

By sea. See chart next page. Rocks lie off Little Snow's south and west shores, but the slot between Snow and Little Snow is remarkably free of obstructions. Land on the island's northwest shore.

At high tide, you can explore the little inlets on the mainland shore where you are bound to discover ospreys and blue heron.

Ashore. The three campsites are in constant use, so low-impact camping is essential here. So is respect for thy neighbors. Even if you happen to find yourself on the island alone, all of the abutting water is a popular cruising anchorage, with sound carrying far across the still water.

In the 1980s, Dodge Morgan broke set a new world record for a non-stop, single-handed sail around the world in his boat *American Promise*. You may see his latest vessel nearby, the stunning fantail steamer *Quiet Presence*, designed and built by Michael Porter on Chebeague Island.

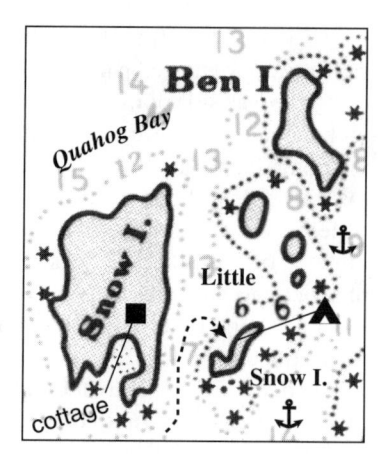

183. Dyers Cove

On the western shore of Quahog Bay, south of Orrs Cove, there is a small bight, hard by the road. The cove is unnamed on the charts, but locally, it is known as Dyers Cove. This tranquil spot holds several lobsterboats on moorings, and private wharves line the shores. It was from one of these wharves that the *Don*, a chartered passenger boat, departed on the morning of June 29, 1941, fully-loaded with passengers for a day trip to Monhegan. They never returned. See sidebar, p. 203, for more details.

184. Center Island

The little bump of Center Island and the two rocks north and south of it lie exactly on the longitude line of W070° 55'. Center has a few sprigs of trees. It makes a good reference point for clearing the unmarked North Ledges extending from Pole. You need to be at least halfway beyond Pole toward Center before you can safely cross Quahog Bay from west to east or east to west.

185. Pole Island

Pole Island is the most obvious landmark in Quahog Bay, sitting smack dab in the middle of its narrow waist. The island is long, narrow, and surprisingly high, with deep dark spruce making it seem higher still. A seasonal cottage is located on its southern end. Pole is private.

By sea. In addition to being a landmark, Pole is the summit of a range of ledges north and south of it. Deep channels run on either side of the island. Nun "4" on the South Ledges marks the western channel, where the local lobster fleet moors off the wharf of Webber's Lobster. North Ledges are unmarked and have to be avoided by favoring the Sebascodegan shores and using Center Island as a reference for your position (see above).

CASCO BAY

186. Card Cove ⚓

On the chart, Card Cove appears like an appendix to Quahog Bay, formed to the west of it by a breach in the spine of ledge at Pinkham Point. The cove makes a well-protected anchorage ringed by a mixture of summer residences and fishermen's homes and bejeweled with lobster buoys. Both the southern and northern reaches of the cove dry out at low, and well-traveled Rt. 24 to Orrs and Bailey Island hugs the northwest shore.

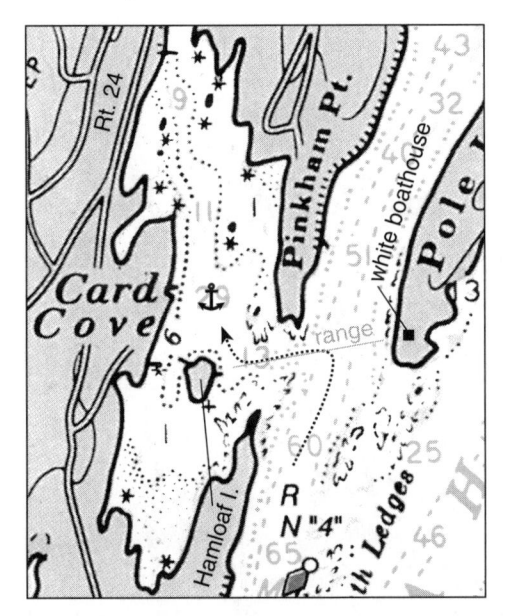

By sea. Notice that there is a lot of ledge across the entrance to the cove, extending from each point and overlapping slightly. Line up the white boathouse on the southern tip of Pole Island with the middle of the small, unnamed island in Card Cove, and run in on that line...slowly.

Ashore. The unnamed island is known locally as Hamloaf Island, and it was the treasured retreat of the late author Caskie Stinnett, familiar to anyone who read his "Room with a View" column for Down East Magazine. This is the view. As he put it, owning an island is "perhaps the most romantic concept left to mankind in the twentieth century."

Stinnett wrote that the entrance "...is so narrow that at low tide a chain could cut it off from the rest of Casco Bay."

187. Raspberry Island ▲

From seaward, Quahog Bay looks magical and somehow other-worldly. With just a trace of fog, the high islands and overlapping nubbits on the east side could almost be mistaken for somewhere in the South China Seas. The most western of these, too small to be named on the chart but marked with an elevation of 15 feet, is Raspberry Island.

Raspberry is private, but at the time of this writing the owners have graciously allowed it to be part of the Maine Island Trail, with a small wooded campsite near its north end for members. *Be sure to consult your current MITA guidebook to confirm that this island is still on the trail before you visit.*

By sea. Raspberry Island is barely two paddlestrokes from the ramp at Bethel Point (see below). It is thickly wooded and connected by ledge to the next island to the northeast. Land on the island's

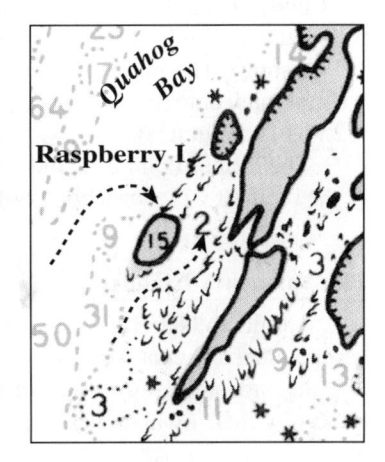

195

rocky northwest shoulder to avoid the ledge, or, if you have very shallow draft, work your way between the ledges south of the island and land on the east shore.

Ashore. Again, *membership in the Maine Island Trail is required for permission to use this island.* For information on joining, see Appendix C on conservation organizations.

The campsite is near the north end the island. No fires are allowed, so camp stoves should be used below the tide line.

188. Bethel Point

Bethel Point separates Quahog Bay from Ridley and Hen Cove. At its tip, a paved town launching ramp leads into the protected water behind Yarmouth Island. A small boat yard and a bed-and-breakfast to either side of the ramp make this a perfect place to launch a small-boat expedition.

By sea. The launching ramp lies at the southern end of Bethel Point, due north of Yarmouth Island, in the narrow gut between Ridley Cove and Quahog Bay. Depths are adequate at all tides.

The approach from Quahog is tricky. Favor the Bethel Point side to avoid the three-foot spot north of Yarmouth but beware that the ledges project way out from the point, as indicated by the five-foot sounding. From Ridley Cove, favor the Yarmouth and Bush Island side to avoid the large ledge east of the point.

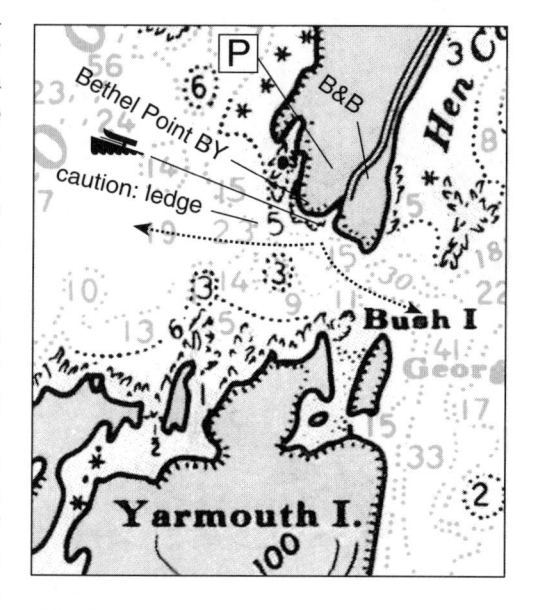

By land. From Cooks Corner in Brunswick, follow Rt. 24 south, then turn left onto the Cundys Harbor Road. After several miles, take Bethel Point Road to the right and follow it to the end.

Ashore. The ramp is town-owned. Parking adjacent to it is reserved for residents with permits, but paid parking can be arranged through the small Bethel Point Boat Yard (725-8145) right next door.

The Bethel Point Bed and Breakfast (725-1115, 888-238-8262) is just to the east of the ramp. It welcomes boaters, both in the warm beds and outdoor hot tub.

189. Yarmouth Islands

Yarmouth Island is the largest of the islands in Ridley Cove, and it nearly includes several other adjacent islands—Raspberry Island and Little Yarmouth Island on the Quahog Bay side and Bush Island in Ridley Cove. All of these islands are private and accessed by their owners from the ramp on Bethel Point. Bush Island was at one time called Pine Island, and it could certainly revert to its old name today. The woods on Yarmouth are so thick that they almost completely obscure the cottage there. Further development on this group of islands is precluded by conservation easements held by the Harpswell Heritage Trust.

By sea. The owners of Yarmouth have their dock in the miniature cove formed between Yarmouth and Bush Island. Use particular care off the southern end of Yarmouth, where there is a Milky Way of trouble between Yarmouth Island and Ballaststone and Yarmouth Ledges.

Ashore. Please do not land. The town of Harpswell was originally part of North Yarmouth. When it was incorporated in 1758, the Act of Incorporation named all the islands that were to become part of the new town, but somehow, one was forgotten. For years that island was known as North Yarmouth Island. It was annexed to Harpswell years later, and it eventually became known simply as Yarmouth Island.

RIDLEY COVE

Ridley Cove is separated from Quahog Bay by large Yarmouth Island, and it is peppered with Bush, George, and Big Hen Island. The outer cove, south of George Island, is broad and exposed to the southwest winds and swells, and all of the shoreline and islands in Ridley Cove are private. Still, Ridley Cove is an intriguing gunkhole, with an easy launching ramp and lodging at Bethel Point, a protected anchorage, and mysterious wrecks to explore.

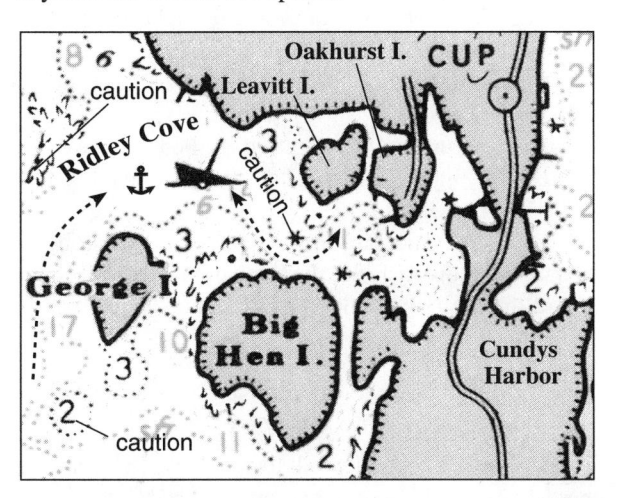

By sea. Ridley can be approached from the open water to the south or through the side entrance from Quahog Bay, between Yarmouth Island and Bethel Point. The southern entrance is straightforward except for the shoal areas south and southeast of George Island, shown on the chart with two and three-foot soundings. Favor the Yarmouth Island shore to avoid them.

Use caution in the side entrance. A couple of three-foot soundings lurk just to the north of Yarmouth Island, and a ledge extends from Bethel Point (see p. 196).

Once inside, be sure to keep close by Bush and George Island to avoid the extensive ledge at the mouth of Hen Cove. Also be sure to avoid the mast of the sunken schooner that lies northeast of George Island, visible at all tides.

If you anchor here, be sure to use a tripline on your anchor. The bottom may be fouled.

It is possible to work your way east and hoof it into the village of Cundys Harbor. Ledges lie off both the northwest shoulder of Big Hen Island and for a long way south of Leavitt Island, and the curving path between them is obscured on the chart by the wreck symbol. From the middle of the cove near the first wreck's mast, head for the middle of Big Hen's north shore and hug it until you are east of the southern point of Leavitt.

Oakhurst Island lies due east of Leavitt. You may be able to land at the southernmost of the four docks at the Oakhurst lobster station, or at the northernmost dock for the Oakhurst Island Boatshop. On higher tides, you might be able to work your way farther east past a second rusting wreck and land nearer to the village.

Ashore. The Oakhurst Island Boatshop (729-6025), run by Bob Flynn, specializes in small-boat repair and restoration and carries several lines of small craft.

From Oakhurst Island, a long but pleasant walk leads to Cundys Harbor Road. Head south into Cundys or north to the Block and Tackle Restaurant. If you land near the small dam farther east, Holbrook's General Store is just across the road.

Ridley Cove is named after Frank Ridley, who owned several schooners and had a fish station here. He eventually moved his operation to Sebasco (see p. 225).

The mast in the middle of the cove rises from the wreck of the *Philip E. Lake*, an old Grand Banks schooner. In 1986, two idealistic partners bought the old schooner at a Boston auction and rented a mooring in Ridley Cove. They had the schooner towed here from Boston and planned to restore it and sail it up the Kennebec. But apparently neither the new owners nor the owner of the mooring had any idea what they were getting into. The boat soon sank on its mooring, becoming the latest in a string of wrecked ships that have left their bones here, and its two owners disappeared.

The mooring was rented from Bud Darling of Cundys Harbor who had had similar experiences in the past. In 1973, he bought two retired steel trawlers, the *Storm* and the *Surf*, from the Rockland fishing fleet and brought them to Ridley Cove. Four years later, he turned around and sold them to a businessman from Florida, who in turn hired Bud to repair and refit the boats.

The man from Florida, however, came under investigation by Federal drug enforcement agencies, and he disappeared, leaving the *Storm* out in the cove and the mammoth *Surf* beached on the backside of Big Hen Island.

For years, that is where they sat, rusting and gurgling with every tide. Nobody would accept responsibility for the hulks. Finally in 1980, the State pumped the fuel out of their tanks to prevent a spill, and in the mid 1990s, the *Surf* was patched, refloated, towed out to sea, and scuttled.

190. George Island

George Island is also private and landing is not allowed. Its lee, however, makes a good anchorage to the north, in inner Ridley Cove. George was once called Birch Island.

191. Big Hen Island

Like the other islands in Ridley Cove, Big Hen is private and landing is not allowed. At high tide, the tight passages on either side of it can be fun to squeeze through, but beware of the ledges between Big Hen and George Island. One historical mystery still haunts Big Hen. At one time, Dan Wilson lived in a small cabin on the island. And that is where he was found, shot dead. The questions of who and why have never been answered.

CASCO BAY

192. Flash Island

Flash Island sits in the mouth of the outer portion of Ridley Cove, just off the southwest shoulder of Yarmouth Island. It belongs to the Town of Harpswell, but you should not land. Flash, along with nearby Jenny Island, supports populations of terns struggling to make a comeback despite the ever-present danger of gulls. Disruptive humans don't help.

193. Jenny Island

Jenny Island is larger and farther offshore than Flash, due south of Ridley Cove. It is also owned by the Town of Harpswell. On the east-west passage from the Orrs Island area to the mouth of the New Meadows River, you will pass close by, but don't land.

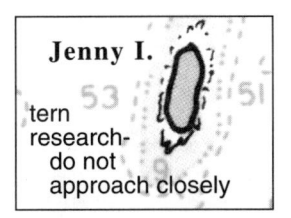

This bush-covered rock is the nesting site of common terns, least terns, and a few rare roseate terns. It is also the site of a tern study and reintroduction effort. During the nesting season, amid more than 350 pairs of terns, a caretaker camps on the island to ward off predatory gulls. The project is working. In 1994, the Jenny Island terns bred 700 chicks (see sidebar next page).

By sea. The water surrounding Jenny Island is free of obstructions, but please do not approach too closely or you will disturb the birds. North Jenny Ledge lies to the east, well marked by nun "2."

194. Elm Islands

The Elm Islands are the first offshore islands out the mouth of Quahog Bay, and, like nearby Cedar and Two Bush Island, the Elm Islands have outlived their names. They are treeless, with just low, windswept bushes.

The Elm Islands are owned by the Town of Harpswell and used, primarily, by the birds. For boaters, they make a convenient rest stop when exploring eastern Casco Bay.

By sea. The Elm Islands lie south of the east-west passage across eastern Casco Bay, at nun "6." Boats in the passage should pass between the nun and the Elm Islands. In settled summer southwesterlies, the slot between the islands makes a good landing spot when approached from the north.

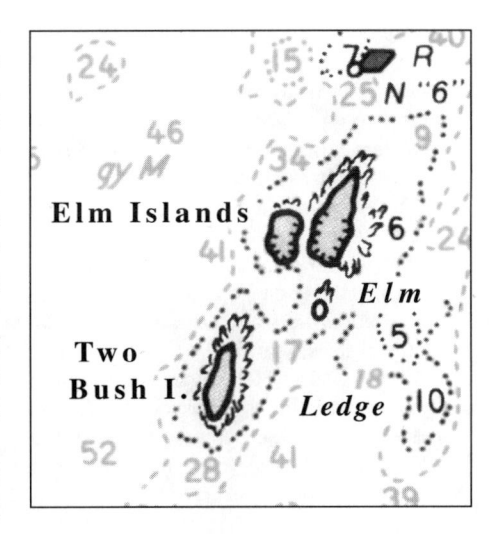

Ashore. Please do not land during nesting season.

195. Two Bush Island

Two Bush is southeast of the Elm Islands, and like the elm, the bushes didn't make it either. Now it should be called "No Bush." This island is a rocky bird-nesting island, and though it is owned by the state, landing is not recommended.

By sea. The shores of Two Bush Island are bold, with deep unobstructed water on all sides. The island is a good reference for the offshore channel leading to Quahog Bay, between Two Bush and Cedar Island. The water to the south and southeast of Two Bush is a minefield from visible Yellow Rock to David Castle, which is awash at halftide or lower.

Terns: Acrobats of the Sky

Along the coast of Maine, terns are the undisputed acrobats of the sky, wheeling and dodging on their lithe wings, then strumming the air to hover above their fish, then diving to the sea like an arrow from heaven. With another flick of their wings, they ascend again, their delicate bodies and long tapered wings a nearly perfect embodiment of flight.

Terns, or sea swallows, have white bodies with a long, forked tail. Their wings are swept back and gray on top, and their heads are capped in black. In Maine, the most prevalent tern is the common tern, which breeds from Labrador to the Caribbean. The arctic tern is rarer, breeding from the Arctic to as far south as Massachusetts, then crossing the Atlantic and flying down the coasts of Europe and Africa, an extraordinary annual migration of about 22,000 miles. Rarest of all is the endangered roseate tern, distinguished by its black beak and two long white tail streamers.

In the late 1800s, terns were hunted nearly to extinction for their feathers for the millinery trade. One hunter reported killing 1,200 birds in a single day, and as many as 100,000 birds were killed in a season. In 1885, common and arctic terns were nesting on 75 Maine islands. By 1900 they were found on only 16.

The tern slaughter was so swift and shocking that the Audubon movement was born to try to help threatened birds. In 1916, the terns were protected under the Migratory Bird Treaty Act, but the population was slow to rebound. The culled tern population gave seagulls, the terns' natural enemies, a chance to establish themselves on tern nesting grounds, eating the tern eggs and chicks and driving them away. By the 1950s, the developing coastal fishery—and fish scraps—gave the scavenging gull population an even bigger boost.

Tern populations continued to slide, until, in the early 1980s, the controversial Maine tern restoration program was begun. The U.S. Fish and Wildlife Service, with the resigned help of Audubon, began the systematic poisoning of herring and black-backed gulls on certain islands so terns could regain their nesting habitat.

The terns returned and their populations have rebounded. Today, 88 percent of Maine's terns live on managed islands.

Jenny Island (see page 199) is one of only four Maine Islands where the roseate tern nests. In 1997, of 94 pairs of roseates nesting in Maine, ten of them were on Jenny. Please keep well away from this fragile colony.

CASCO BAY

THE OUTER ISLANDS OF EASTERN CASCO BAY

196. Ragged Island

Ragged Island is a large offshore island in the middle of eastern Casco Bay and its treacherous ledges. This island is particularly beguiling, seemingly forever on the horizon, sometimes doubling its size by melting into a mirage.

Ragged Island was once known as Rugged Island, and that it is. The northeast shore is shear cliff. Ghost Cliff is on the Devil's Wall on the west shore, and the south shore is strewn with huge boulders beaten by the waves. Deep dark forests mount a ridge only to be split apart by a spine of ledge. And unlike most islands in Casco Bay, this one presents its long flank to the incessant wind and swells.

Ragged is private with a cottage ashore. Please do not land. However, Ragged's height and the shear drop to its northwest shore form a prodigious lee that makes a pleasant lunch stop on the anchor in fair weather. If there is any chance that foul weather is on the way, this is no place to be.

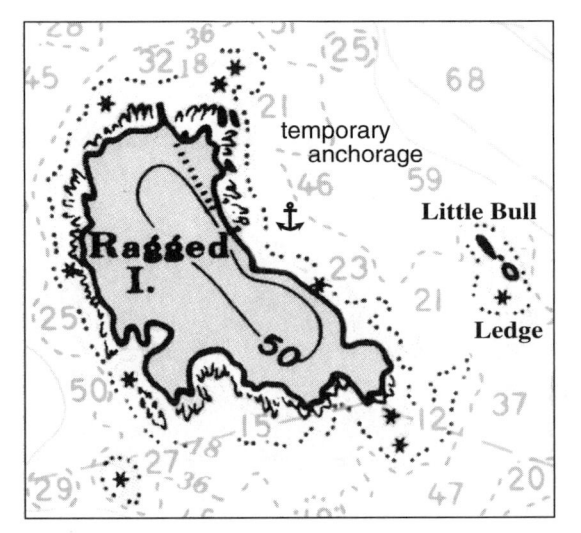

By sea. The easiest approach to Ragged's northeast shore is from the east, to either side of Little Bull Ledge, which is visible at all tides. Note that there is an additional rock south of the ledge.

From the west, pass north of Ragged and well east of its northeastern shoulder and the two rocks lying off of it. Then run south to shallower water in the lee.

A small cleft in the southwest shore forms a small pocket, but it is best avoided. Outlying ledges give it some protection from the ocean swells. But it faces both the ocean and the prevailing southwesterlies, so it is usually a dangerous lee shore.

Ashore. There are no records of the earliest settlement of Ragged, though undoubtedly it was used as a fishing station for landing and drying fish. With 50 acres, its timber was probably harvested too.

Tom Skolfield, one of the Skolfields of Harpswell (see Middle Bay Cove, p. 146), was one of early residents on Ragged. He built his house and a wharf at the head of the small harbor on the southwest shore and settled there with his wife. But she was very religious. Every Sunday Tom had to row her all the way to Elijah Kellogg's Parish on Harpswell Neck and back—a round trip of at least 10 miles, much of it in open water. Tom, understandably under the circumstances, was somewhat indifferent toward religion.

Reverend Kellogg was himself an ardent boater, regularly sailing his small catboat among the islands, often as far out as Ragged. One day, Tom hailed the Reverend's boat *Sky-Pilot* and asked if he would come preach on Ragged. He would, and did, and he became a frequent visitor to Ragged.

Tom Skolfield managed to build two sizable schooners on Ragged by himself, the *Patriot* and the *Satellite*. He cut the timber on Mark Island, to the east, and worked seven days a week now that he didn't have to row to church. When she was launched, the *Satellite* could carry 100,000 pounds of fish.

From his visits to the Skolfields, Reverend Kellogg came to love Ragged Island. He eventually bought a large portion of it and retired there. He wrote a successful series of boys' books, in which the island was refered to as Elm Island.

One of Maine's most famous poets, Edna St. Vincent Millay, first saw Ragged when she came from Paris to visit a friend on Bailey Island, and she was immediately captivated by it. In 1933 she bought it and used the island as a summer studio through the 1940s. She is said to have spent endless hours in quiet contemplation, sunbathing and swimming nude in the icy water.

197. Round Rock

This is no place to land and no place to be near in any kind of weather. Round Rock lies about two thirds of the way between Jaquish and Ram Island, directly on the purple COLREGS line on the chart. It is marked offshore by flashing G "3." Its equally treacherous neighbors are Saddleback Ledge and Bold Dick Rock, though neither of these are marked.

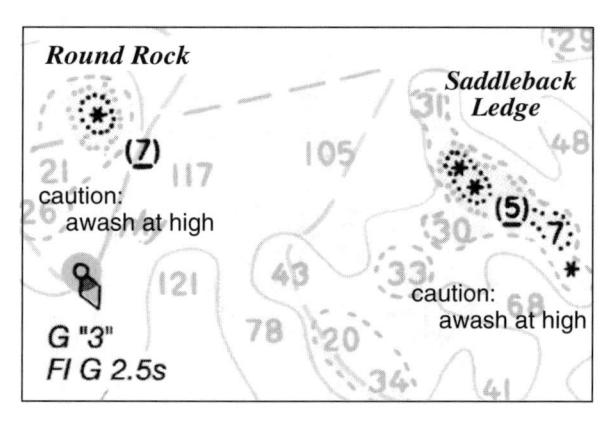

Together, Round Rock and Saddleback Ledge act as gateposts at the offshore entrance to the long, unmarked slot of deep water leading to the safety of Quahog Bay. But they will also be forever remembered as part of the mystery of one of Casco Bay's most tragic maritime disasters, the wreck of the *Don* (see sidebar).

198. White Bull Island

White Bull Island is a bald rock to the southeast of Ragged Island. It is state-owned and shag-claimed. White Bull, however, is a significant landmark for the approach to the New Meadows River between White Bull and Mark Island to the east.

Historically, White Bull is noted in the winter of 1780, which was so cold that eastern Casco Bay froze solid as far out as White Bull Island, and people trekked across the ice from Harpswell Neck to Portland. No thanks.

By sea. The passage between White Bull Island and Mark Island is marked by red-and-white gong "WB."

The *Don*

On the morning of June 29, 1941, 35 daytrippers boarded the 44-foot, ex-rumrunner *Don* in Dyer's Cove off Quahog Bay. The passengers were from the mill towns of Rumford and Mexico and were on a company outing to Monhegan for the day, sponsored by the local bank.

En route they disembarked at the small town of West Point. Captain Paul Johnson bought potatoes and onions at Reed's General Store for a chowder, and before casting off again, some of the passengers sent postcards back home.

The assistant lightkeeper on Seguin saw the *Don* pass to the south at about 11:20 AM and disappear in building fog as she headed for Monhegan. It was the last time she or her passengers were ever seen.

The *Don* was due back by 7:30 that night, but when night fell and the *Don* had not returned, no one was particularly alarmed. Captain Johnson had sailed these waters his whole life, and the *Don* had recently been overhauled. But as the night grew darker, the weather began to deteriorate. Calls to Monhegan confirmed the worst—the *Don* had never arrived. At midnight, the Damariscove Lifesaving Station was notified, and they began an unsuccessful search. By the following morning the shore was locked in thick fog.

Several fishing boats crept out from Bailey Island but couldn't go far, and it was much too thick for an aerial search. The next day, the fog lifted briefly and revealed a grim sight—two bodies afloat, both women. Then the fog shut down again. For the next six days and nights bodies were recovered all the way from Small Point to Biddeford Pool and landed in Mackerel Cove.

Yet the tragedy remained mysterious. Out of the 36 on board, only 14 bodies were recovered, and of those, all but the captain were women. And the Captain washed ashore on Bailey Island tied to a keg with his arms crossed over his chest and clothed in only his boots and his underwear. A watch on one of the victims had stopped at 11:42.

Investigations revealed that the *Don* had been iced in at her mooring that winter, that she had gone down on two other occasions when she wasn't carrying passengers, and that many of the locals considered her gear unsafe. Her high cabins, some claimed, made her top-heavy and prone to capsize. Damning evidence came from testimony that the *Don*'s gas tanks had developed a slight leak that morning, suggesting that she could have blown up instantly. Others thought the *Don* could have struck a German mine or been sunk by a U-boat. Yet the victims showed no definitive burn marks. The crew from a sardiner claimed they heard a racing engine in the fog that night, which supported the theory that the *Don* could have hit a ledge and the Captain was trying to back her off.

The official report concluded that the top-heavy *Don*, loaded with the weight of her passengers, simply capsized in the ground swell that had made up in the afternoon east of Seguin and had sunk in those deep waters sometime after 11:00 that morning. Yet the conclusion lacked concrete evidence of any kind, other than the watch perhaps, to confirm it, and for years the demise of the *Don* remained shrouded in a mystery as thick as the fog.

On a foggy August day in 1963, some of the answers came up in a trawl net. Bernard Johnson and John Lazarou were dragging in limited visibility when the tide set them dangerously close to Round Rock. The net snagged something heavy, and they hauled up wreckage of the stern section of a boat which appeared to be the *Don*. Round Rock, however, is far from the last sighting of the *Don* and in the opposite direction of the *Don*'s intended course. But under the circumstances, there is a fitting logic to the place.

(continued on page 204)

> The *Don* (continued from page 203)
>
> As Captain Johnson passed Seguin Island, the weather was deteriorating and visibility was shutting down. He probably realized that it would be difficult to make it to Monhegan and back and that it would be more prudent to put into someplace like Damariscove to cook his chowder and wait it out. But by evening, realizing that the fog was here to stay, he probably set out to feel his way back to Dyer's Cove, putting his navigational skills from his old rum-running days to the test. He probably found the bell off White Bull Island, but then he would have had to feel his way between Saddleback Ledge to starboard and Round Rock to port to find the straight slot of clean water leading to Quahog Bay. By then, night would have fallen, and the fog was thick. Neither of the treacherous hazards was marked, so the Captain would have been creeping along, listening hard for the wash of swells on rock.
>
> Suddenly, the boat hits hard and jolts to a stop. The groundswell picks her up again and drops her higher. Quickly, the Captain puts her full astern to try to back her off, hoping that the next wave will be just enough to lift her off. And it does, for a brief second, before dropping her harder on the rocks.
>
> The crew on a nearby sardine carrier hears the faint sound of a revving engine somewhere in the night, but two or three waves later, the *Don* floods quickly and settles on the ledge, eventually slipping in to deeper water. The watch of a passenger stops at 11:42 at *night*, not in the morning.
>
> The epilogue to this tragedy is that divers have never been able to find the wreck in the deep, murky waters just off Round Rock. The wreck of the *Don* and the mystery which surrounds it is the basis for a recent novel by Peter Landesman called The Raven. "At the heart of the novel," he says, "is the terror of loss and how we fill the vacuum with our imaginations."

199. Mark Island

Mark Island is a sudden pinnacle in a fairly deep portion of eastern Casco Bay, rising from depths of more than fifty feet to heights of more than fifty. Its steep banks are forested, and its perfectly round perimeter offers not even the slightest suggestion of a harbor or cove.

Mark Island is owned by the state and managed by the Department of Inland Fisheries and Wildlife. Visiting it, however, can be difficult or dangerous. Mark is in a very exposed position, and it offers little or no protection if the weather blows up.

By sea. If you are determined to go to Mark, time your trip carefully. The nearest real protection is over two miles away in West Point. There are no off-lying dangers other than the shallow spots at Chiver Ledge to the northeast and at Wyman Ledge due west. Landing is best in the lee of the island on the northeast shore.

200. East Brown Cow

East Brown Cow is the southernmost of the outer islands in eastern Casco Bay, exposed to the full brunt of the Atlantic. Wind and swells have kept this low rock washed clean of any soil or trees. Except for the birds and the occasional fishermen who work the surrounding ledges, East Brown Cow is seldom visited. It's known instead as a place to avoid, particularly in low visibility.

THE NEW MEADOWS RIVER

The New Meadows River is the only river draining into eastern Casco Bay. It is relatively short, but of all the Casco Bay rivers its the widest, deepest, and most navigable. In fact, the term river is almost a misnomer. It drains only a small area, saltwater reaches almost to the river's headwaters, and practically all of the water passing in and out of the river is tidal. The river is more like a long, splintered cove, part of the sea, but a world unto itself, made, it seems, for poking around in small boats.

Each part of the river is distinct. It begins as a slight drainage creek through cattails, but it quickly flows into a brackish pond formed by natural bedrock and the damming of the river at the Bath Road. Beneath the road's culvert, the tide falls downriver on the ebb and upriver on the flood, forming a modest reversing falls. From there, the river runs south between tight and rocky banks.

At its midsection it widens, the water slows, and silt sprawls in rich mud flats and eel ruts along the banks and between the river islands. Ospreys nest in trees on almost every island and point, comprising one of the most dense populations of the birds on the coast (see sidebar, p. 218).

In its lower reaches, the river is joined by several long and narrow coves and by the Gurnet, which carries seawater in from as far away as Harpswell Sound. It flows past the nearly land-locked pool of the Basin and by the working harbors of Cundys and Sebasco and then through a narrow mouth between Bear Island and Fort Point.

By sea. The New Meadows, despite its short length, has a large tidal volume by the time it reaches Casco Bay, with correspondingly strong currents. They can reach several knots in the narrow sections and be felt out in the bay as far as Wood Island. The ebb runs against the southwest winds, so when it is blowing from that quarter, the river becomes choppy, and so does much of eastern Casco Bay.

Boats can be launched from the town ramp in the upper reaches of the river, at the New Meadows Marina, or at the gravel ramp on the upper pond, known as New Meadows Lake.

By land. See the specific entries below.

201. New Meadows Lake

Near the head of the New Meadows River, ledges and partial damming have formed a wide, still body of water known as New Meadows Lake. Despite its name, the lake is still tidal, though its range is limited, and quite salty, with abundant clams and quahogs in the shallows.

The best way to explore New Meadows Lake is by launching at the gravel ramp off the Old Brunswick Road. From here, small boats can pass under Haydens Bridge and explore the short stretch of river to the headwater, or explore New Meadows Lake to the south.

The body of the lake to the south is split by the bridge of the busy new US Rt. 1 at its midsection, then by the high Central Maine Railroad trestle. The southern end of the lake is connected to the rest of the river by a large culvert under the Bath Road, the old

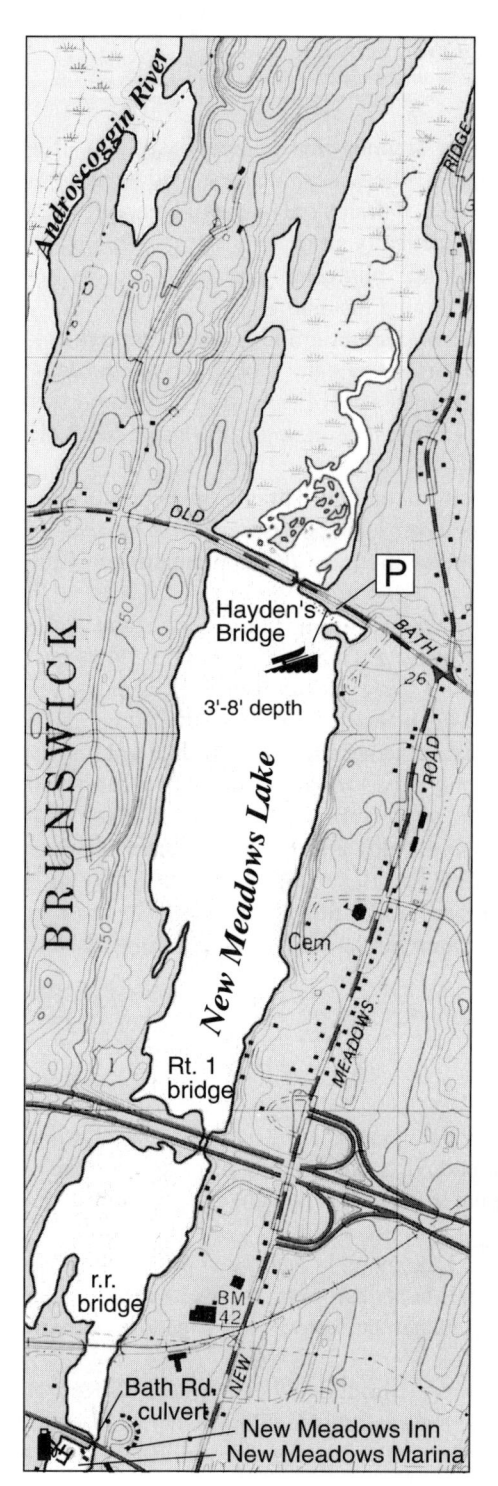

US Rt. 1. But the narrowness of the culvert and the swift current running through it effectively prohibit heading farther downriver (see Bath Road, p. 208).

By sea. New Meadows Lake is a cartographic enigma. The BBA Chart Kit omits most of the upper New Meadows above the Middle Ground Bar. NOAA chart 13290 takes you three miles farther north, but omits New Meadows Lake. NOAA chart 13293 shows the lake, but with no soundings, as does the USGS topo. So if you want to really feel like an explorer, here's your chance.

Getting to these upper reaches from farther down river, while not impossible, is impractical. Water, however, makes the trip with every tide, so New Meadows Lake is tidal. The gravel launching ramp is only good during the top half of the tide. Depths are predominantly shallow and consistent, in the 3 to 8-foot range and averaging about 5 feet. One clammer actually digs quahogs by wading throughout the lake and feeling for them with his hands.

Minimum vertical clearance for passing under Haydens Bridge and the Old Brunswick (Bath) Road is about 4 feet. The Rt. 1 spans are about 15 feet wide with minimum vertical clearances of about 8 feet. At the south end of the lake, there is plenty of room beneath the railroad trestle.

Because it is partially land-locked, New Meadows Lake has had a history of pollution. It is, however, rebounding, and the lower portion of the lake has recently been opened to shellfish harvesters who are licensed and equipped to further purify the mollusks before they go to market.

By Land. From US Rt. 1, take the New Meadows Road exit and take the road north. At the stop sign, turn left onto the Old Brunswick(Bath) Road. A wide, dirt shoulder and the gravel ramp will be on the left.

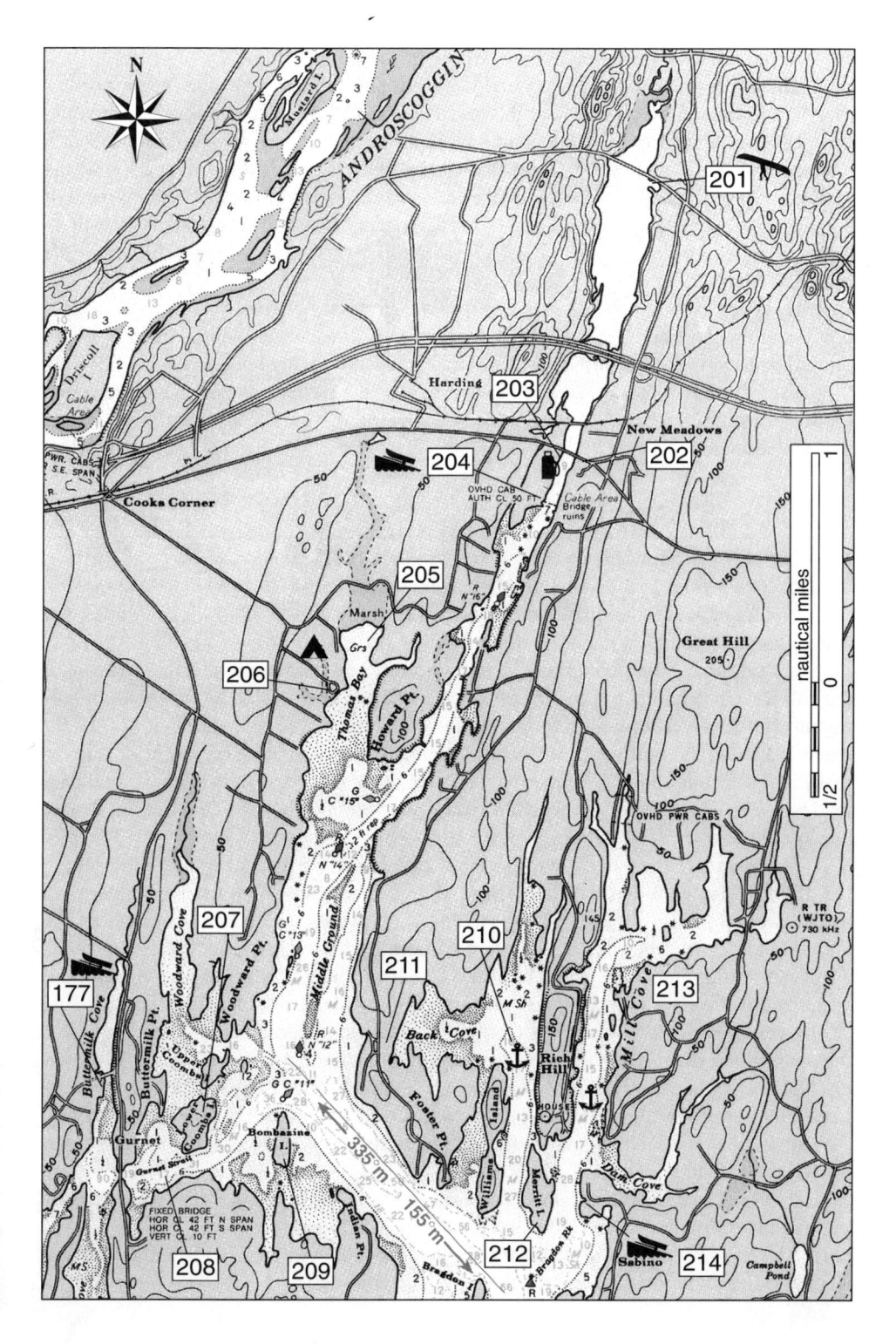

CASCO BAY

Ashore. The wide shoulder has plenty of room for parking.

The upper creek of the New Meadows tends almost due north, coming within less than half a mile of the point where the Androscoggin River widens into Merrymeeting Bay. This was an important Indian portage and strategic trading spot. Thomas Purchase, a successful trader and one of Brunswick's first settlers, built his cabin nearby. At the outbreak of the Indian Wars, however, the Indians remembered him for cheating them of some furs on Harpswell Neck. He had promised to pay with whisky. Instead he gave them well water (see Middle Bay, p. 143). In retaliation, his house was one of the first to be raided and burned.

In 1755, early entrepreneurs thought the portage between the New Meadows River and the Androscoggin would make a perfect shortcut for floating logs down to the Casco Bay mills and shipyards. But when a canal was dug between the two rivers, they discovered that the difference in the levels of the rivers was not enough to move the logs through the canal. With inadequate current, the logs would jam. The project was abandoned.

202. Bath Road

The New Meadows River flows beneath the Bath Road through a large culvert. At the same place, it flows over a natural ledge and partial dam built in 1938. When the tide is low, water cascades downriver through the culvert like a waterfall. At high tides, the water charges through in the other direction, upriver.

It is possible, though impractical, to take a small boat through the falls and through the culvert. One clammer in the upper reaches claims he has taken a fourteen-foot aluminum skiff upriver through the falls, but it was a tight squeeze and his motor barely made it against the outflowing current. A sixteen-footer, he guesses, might be able to make it, if you don't mind scratching up the sides a bit. Of course, any attempt should be made as near slack water as possible, when the tide matches the level of the upper portion of the river.

In addition to the narrow width of the culvert and the fast water through it, there is a third obstacle. When the tide is low, the water rushes down the dam with such force that it churns itself into a long-lasting foam. As John Fitzpatrick, owner of the New Meadows Marina puts it, "It's like something out of a science fiction movie." The foam builds into large piles before it is carried downstream by the current and wind, and it travels a long way downriver before it finally dissipates.

Even though the foam forms from quite clean salt water, it fouls the topsides of the boats along the river and is considered an eyesore to many river residents. The town has had a new sluiceway designed to produce less foam. But for now, the foam is controlled by a series of floats, tied end to end and strung across the outflow of the culvert. Any small boat making the passage through the falls will need to pass through, or over, the string of floats.

By sea. The culvert and falls are obvious at the point where the Bath Road crosses the river, hard by the New Meadows Marina.

By Land. From US Rt. 1, take the Cooks Corner exit in Brunswick and follow the Bath Road eastward until it crosses the New Meadows River.

Ashore. New Meadows Marina (see below) is on the west side of the crossing, and the New Meadows Inn (443-3921) is on the east. The Inn has rooms or self-contained cabins and frontage for possibly launching portable boats on either the upper or lower side of the culvert. Their restaurant, with a pay phone, is right on the river.

203. New Meadows Marina

The New Meadows Marina (443-6277) is a full-service marina on the river's west bank at the Bath Road crossing. They can launch, haul, fix, or store your boat, or they can sell you a new one. Their chandlery and outboard parts department can fill almost any small-boat need.

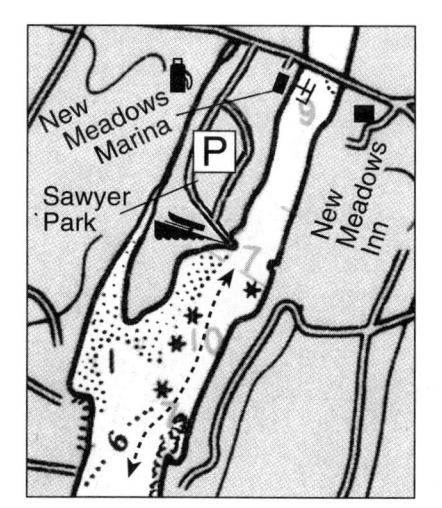

By sea. Follow the channel all the way up the New Meadows River. Chart Kit charts do not cover the upper portions of the river, so you will need to use NOAA chart 13290. When you can go no farther, the marina will be on your left.

By land. See Bath Road, above.

Ashore. Dockage can be arranged on the marina floats. They pump gas and water and have ice.

Seaspray Kayaking (1-888-349-7772) is also at New Meadows Marina. They rent kayaks and canoes, conduct sea kayaking tours, and offer full-moon kayak trips.

The Maine branch of H & H Propeller (442-7595) is next door to the Marina. These propeller and drive specialists can fix your propeller if you happen to have been exploring the coast a little too intimately.

204. Sawyer Park

Sawyer Park could be a model for a perfect public launching ramp. In additon to a new concrete ramp, this town park includes picnic tables and short paths in a beautiful woodsy setting on the west bank of the New Meadows River. Its design incorporates one-way traffic flow, specific areas for staging your launch or haul so you don't tie up the ramp, and plenty of easy parking, even for vehicles towing trailers. If you have a yen to explore the upper reaches of the New Meadows, this is an ideal departure point.

By sea. The ramp is obvious on the west bank of the river, about where the chart shows a cable area, opposite the label "bridge ruins." The ramp slopes fairly steeply, but it is made of ribbed concrete with good grip. Floats line the ramp, and depths are adequate for launching at all tides. There is no fee for parking or using the ramp. Follow the channel carefully here, since several rocks lurk near the shores.

By land. From Cooks Corner, take the Bath Road east. Turn right onto the park's drive just before the New Meadows Marina. A gate can cross the drive, but it is rarely closed. The park is open 24 hours a day.

Ashore. The parking is not limited, but we recommend contacting the Brunswick police (725-5521) if you plan on leaving your vehicle for an extended period. Several picnic tables are located in the woods near the river's edge, and trash cans and a clean and modern and handicapped accessible outhouse are near the parking lot.

205. Thomas Bay

Thomas Bay hooks to the west and north of the New Meadows behind Howard Point. Calling it a bay is a bit of an overstatement. The entire bay becomes mud flats at low, and at high it isn't very deep. Still, it makes a nice little adventure. Thomas Point Beach and campground is on the west bank of the bay, and a small marsh fills its head.

Small portable boats could conceivably be launched into the creek at the head of the bay, but they would need to be carried for some distance across the marsh.

By sea. Enter the bay near high tide, south of green can "15" off Howard Point. Once again, you will be just off the Chart Kit chart and will need NOAA chart 13290. The creek through the marsh begins near the east side of the bay, then curves to the west.

By land. There is a wide dirt shoulder at the head of the bay, with a beautiful view of the marsh. From Cooks Corner, take the Thomas Point Road to the right and then go left on Adams Road. The turnout will be on your right, just before a wooded knoll.

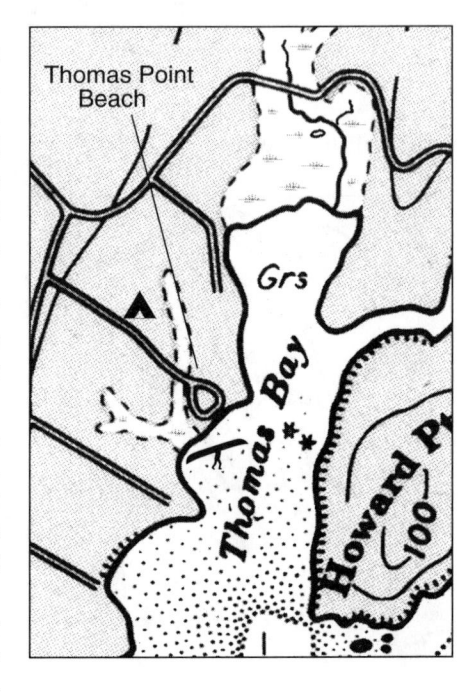

Ashore. A beautiful old cemetery occupies a peaceful knoll overlooking the marsh and a small marsh island.

206. Thomas Point Beach

Thomas Point Beach (725-6009) is a privately run bathing beach, recreational area, and campground on the west bank of Thomas Bay. The spacious grounds include fields and woods, a sandy beach with lifeguards, a snack bar, recreation hall, and outdoor games such as volleyball and horseshoes. Spacious campsites hide in the woods. Every summer the Maine Bluegrass Festival is held here, and each autumn, it hosts the Maine Festival to celebrate the creativity of Maine's artists, musicians, and craftsmen.

Thomas Point Beach is open from Memorial Day to Labor Day.

By sea. Thomas Point is easily recognized on the chart by a road with a circle at its end. Portable boats can be launched by the beach at high tide. There is no ramp.

CASCO BAY

By land. From Cooks Corner in Brunswick, take the Thomas Point Road. Thomas Point Beach will be on the left.

Ashore. Thomas Point Beach takes offers all the basics, including restrooms, showers, ice, laundry, a playground for the kids, and even an ice cream parlor. Your pets, however, are not invited.

207. Coombs Islands

Upper and Lower Coombs Island and a third island, unnamed on the chart but which might as well be called Outer Coombs Island, are all connected to each other and to Buttermilk Point by clam flats at low tide. At high, though, they make up an unspoiled mini-archipelago well worth drifting around in a small boat. All the islands are heavily wooded. The two big islands are commanded by large osprey nests at their north ends. Upper Coombs is private and posted.

By sea. The Coombs islands sit at the intersection of the New Meadows River, the Gurnet, and Woodward Cove. The extensive mud flats and a stray rock that sits northwest of Upper Coombs pose the only hazards. Be careful that the tide doesn't strand you.

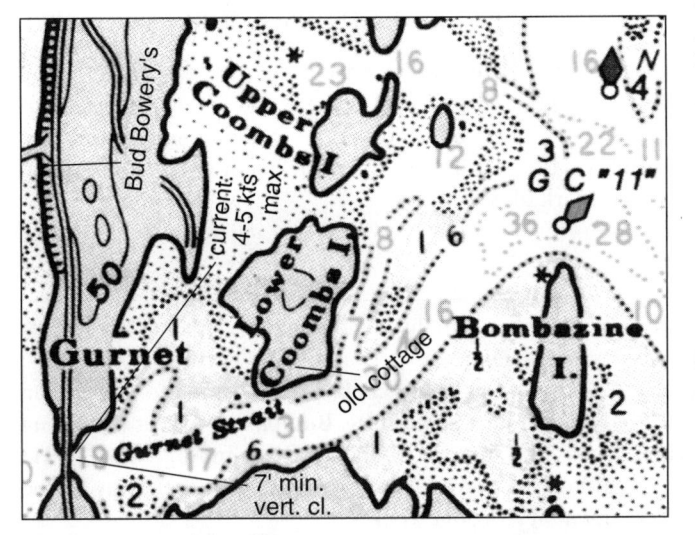

Ashore. Please do not land on Upper Coombs. Outer Coombs is so small that you'll disturb the ospreys if you land. Lower Coombs has recently been acquired by the Brunswick-Topsham Land Trust. A derelict cottage perches on its southern flank.

208. The Gurnet

Gurnet Strait veers to the west at Bombazine Island, around the north end of Sebascodegan Island, and under Gurnet Bridge. Together with Long Reach and Ewin Narrows, it defines Sebascodegan as an island (see Inside Passage, p. 186). The Strait also connects the launching ramp at Buttermilk Cove (p. 189) with the New Meadows River.

By sea. Gurnet Strait has shoaled considerably since the soundings were taken for the chart. At low tide, do not expect to find much water and proceed cautiously.

The passage beneath Gurnet Bridge is notorious for its current. Near slack, this is a deceptively calm passage. But at the maximum flood or ebb, the current can be fierce. The water surface slopes downward and accelerates between the embankments to four knots or more, with eddies and boils. Just to the west of the bridge, its force has bored a hole in the channel 90 feet deep.

The bridge has a fixed minimum vertical clearance of seven feet. Its embankments are made up of fairly large boulders which make good footing for towing your canoes or kayaks under the bridge if the current happens to be against you. Otherwise, if the current is with you, enjoy the ride.

By land. Rt. 24 leads south from Brunswick's Cooks Corner to Gurnet Bridge.

Ashore. The Gurnet was named, it is guessed, for its resemblance to several headlands along the English Channel, which in turn were named for the gurnet fish there. The term is used where the shore squeezes the currents and speeds them up.

Maine's famous poet Robert Tristram Coffin grew up right on the bridge, living above his father's shop. He describes it in *Yankee Coast*:

> "It was good bold water there in under us. I caught cunners and eels from the kitchen window, just a step from the stove and fry-pan waiting, all sizzling with salt-pork scraps, for them. One red-letter day I pulled up a lobster from the window-sill of the bedroom upstairs. I was perched on the bed I had slept in. It is not given to every little boy, even in Maine, to cast his line from his bed and bring in a lobster!" *

Live lobsters can still be bought from the pound at the bridge.

Just to the north of the bridge is the shop of Bud Bowery and his marvelous "museum" of antique outboard motors. Here is brute testament to the evolution of these cantankerous beasts and to Bud's passion at taming them. It is not everyday that you meet a man who makes his own spark plugs.

209. Bombazine Island

Bombazine Island is a thickly treed oval in the New Meadows River at the eastern end of Gurnet Strait. This is a private island with a float off the northwest end and a cottage ashore. These residents were not the first. Bombazine is named for the Indian sagamore Bombazine who lived here in the early 1700s. Bombazine was at the wrong place at the wrong time when he was crossing the Kennebec River in August, 1724. He was spotted and killed by a band of settlers hungry for revenge on their way to the famous raid on the Indian settlement at Norridgewock.

The island that bears his name, however, is equally famous for the legendary character Granny Young. In 1775, Granny Young poled her canoe out to Bombazine on a berry-picking expedition. In those days, settlers shared the islands and points with bears and wolves and other wild creatures. After having picked her fill, Granny Young pushed off in her canoe, but a bear who was on the island for a berry-picking expedition of his own spotted Granny Young. He plunged into the water in pursuit of her canoe.

When the bear tried to capsize Granny Young's frail canoe, she fended him off with the pole she was using to push the canoe. She hit the bear on the head until he was so stunned that she could hold him underwater and drown him. Unfazed, she tied the beast to the canoe and towed him to shore. No doubt she had bear and berries for dinner that night.

Reprinted with permission, see copyright page.

210. Back Cove

Back Cove is tucked into the elbow of Foster Point, to the west of Rich Hill. This is a lovely, tranquil spot, preserved from development by the steep slopes of Rich Hill, the private ownership the rest of the way around, and the Hamilton Sanctuary on Foster Point.

By sea. A long, narrow approach runs between Williams Island and Rich Hill. Head straight north between Merritt Island and Williams Island. The chart shows no obstructions, but the first cottage on the east shore of Williams has a sign on shore which reads in bold letters "ROCK," and there is a tell-tale cluster of lobster buoys just offshore, so favor the Merritt Island side at the entrance. The rock shown along the Rich Hill shore is just beyond the last wooden dock, and its rockweed is visible even at high. Once past the north end of Williams, most of the cove is shoal.

211. Hamilton Sanctuary

Hamilton Sanctuary is a 75-acre farm located at the narrow neck of Foster Point, on the east side. The sanctuary is owned by the Maine Audubon Society, which has recently begun to develop a few trails on the property. They lead from the old Hamilton Farmhouse through a field down to the marshy estuary and mud flats of Back Cove and through the woods out a small peninsula. The peace and tranquillity here is only disturbed by the low planes occasionally flying overhead from the Brunswick Naval Air Station.

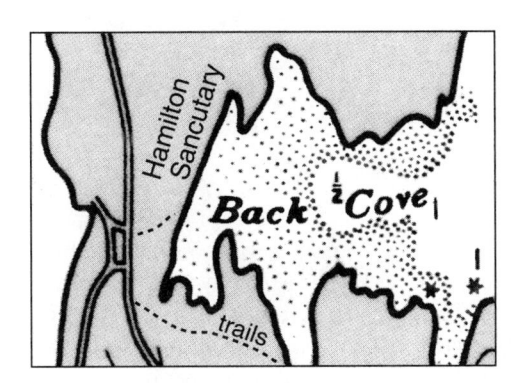

By sea. Hamilton Sanctuary is easily identified by its large open field on the west shore of Back Cove. At high tides it is possible to land at the foot of the field and stroll the path through the field or land along the wooded shore and find the trail marked by blue blazes. Time your visit carefully though. Low tide uncovers extensive mud flats.

By land. From Rt. 1, take the New Meadows Road exit and head south. Cross directly over the Bath Road onto Foster Point Road and follow it to the sanctuary. The white farmhouse will be on your right, close to the road, and the field will be on your left. Park on the grass across from the farmhouse, but leave room for the clammers who park here at low tide.

Ashore. A short trail leaves from the parking area and cuts through the field to the water. Another trail leaves from farther down the road, on the left. Follow the blue blazes through the woods and out the finger peninsulas. For more information, contact the Maine Audubon Society (781-2330). See Gilsland Farm, p. 72).

212. Merritt Island

Merritt is the southern geological extension of Rich Hill. It was settled in the 1820s and connected to Rich Hill at lower tides by a causeway known as "Jacob's Gate." Landing is not allowed on this private island.

213. Mill Cove

The high spine of Rich Hill and Merritt Island divides the water north of the river bend at Three Islands into two long and narrow coves. The easternmost, Mill Cove, is flanked by handsome cottages and summer camps. Its north end broadens into a shallow basin with fingers of fields and woods dipping to the water's edge. There is no public shore access, but at higher tides it makes for pleasant exploration.

By sea. Pass to either side of Bragdon Rock, which is marked by a daybeacon. There are no obstructions in the cove except the rocks off the little island on the east shore. The basin at the head of the cove and Dam Cove at its southern end can only be explored at higher tides. Boats can be launched at the mouth of the cove at the Sabino Ramp.

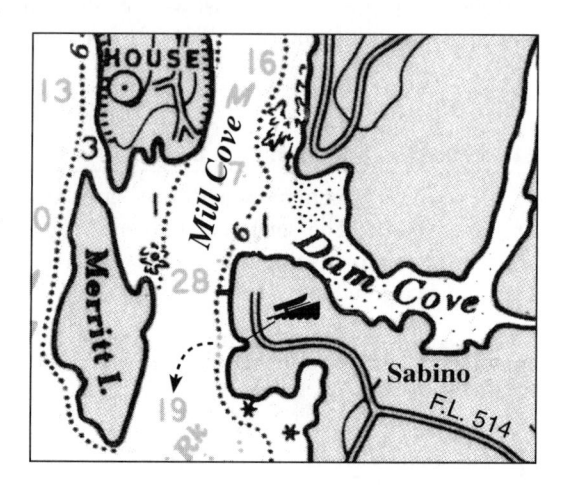

214. Sabino Ramp

The town of Phippsburg maintains a launching ramp in Sabino, at the end of the peninsula that defines the mouth of Mill Cove. The ramp is roughly paved, narrow, and very steep, but despite that, it is occasionally used by the largest hydraulic trailers. It is best near the top of the tide, but portable boats or even very light trailerables can use it when there's less water. The small gravely beach at its foot is quite solid, and there is limited parking at its head.

By sea. The ramp is tucked in a miniature cove on the right as you enter Mill Cove, just south of Dam Cove.

By Land. From Bath, take Rt. 209 south. Take a right onto Meadowbrook Road just before the road crosses Winnegance Creek. The Winnegance General Store will be on the right. When the road tees, take a right and then the first left onto Sabino Road. At the obvious, brown Sabino Hall on the right, take a right onto Fire Lane 514. Stop at the stop sign or you will drive into the water.

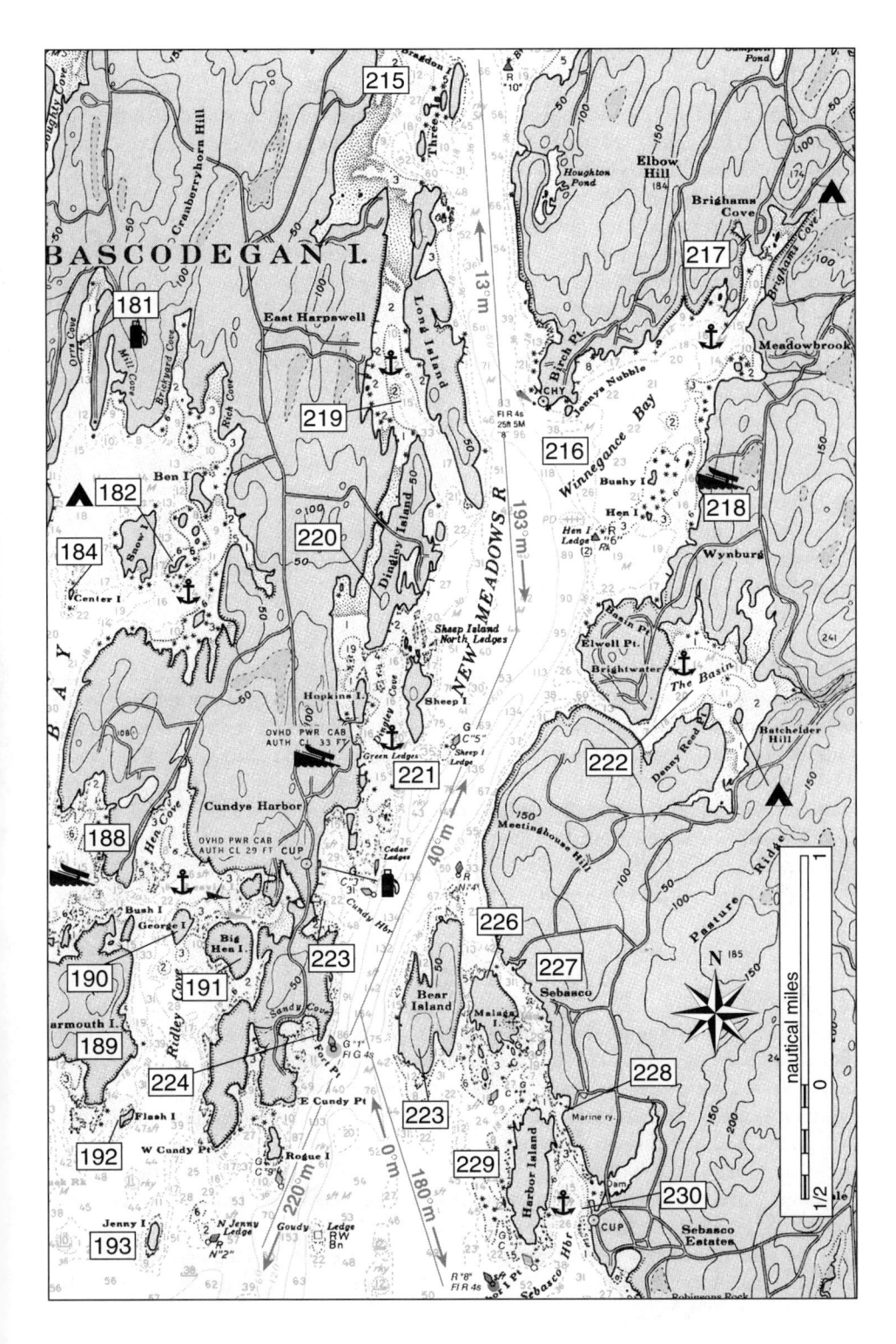

CASCO BAY

215. Three Islands

Well, actually there are four islands. They sit north of Long Island, and the New Meadows River bends around them. From north to south they are Bragdon Island, Cleaveland Island, Berry Island, and Hammond Island. Together, they make an idyllic little island paradise, each connected to the other by sandy bars and each crowned by pines and spruce. Yet they belong to someone else, with small camps on two of them and beach chairs on the bars. Please do not land.

It is possible, even for deep-draft boats, to anchor for a lunch stop to the west of the southernmost of the three islands, but the vista is marred by the homes that crowd the shore opposite the north end of Long Island.

By sea. To get inside of the islands, approach them from the south. Steer to the west dead center between the north tip of Long Island and the southernmost of the three islands, then bear northward. At the top of the tide, you can enter from the north, though there has been considerable silting here since the soundings were taken for the chart.

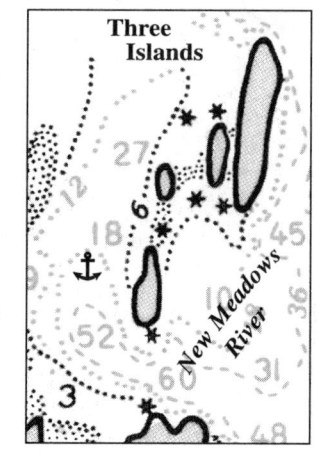

216. Winnegance Bay

Winnegance Bay is a broad widening of the New Meadows River, tending to the northeast and culminating in the tight little harbor of Brighams Cove. Its shores are lined with summer homes, and its western portion is studded with rocks and two small islands—Bushy, which is bushy, and Hen Island. The town of Phippsburg has a new launching ramp into the bay just south of Meadowbrook, on the east side (see entries below).

By sea. This is a pleasant, tranquil piece of water that would be easy to mistake for a lake were it not for the gentle ocean swells rolling in from the sea and the briny tinge to the air. It is, however, exposed to the full brunt of the southwesterlies that blow up the river.

217. Brighams Cove

This is a charming pocket, lined with cottages but remarkably tranquil. The high shores still seem woodsy, and fishing and pleasure boats anchor tightly together in the snug harbor. Cruising boats may find room to anchor at the outer end of the harbor, though it is more exposed there. Boaters in small craft will have to content themselves with a look-see; there are no public lands here.

The Meadowbrook Camping Area (800-370-2267) is perched in a field above Brighams Cove. Although it has no water frontage of its own, by land it is close to the ramps at Sabino, Painted Point, and on the Kennebec's Fiddler's Reach in Phippsburg.

By sea. The entrance to Brighams Cove lies between two deep and bold shores, with only one outlying rock off the west point. Once inside, there is another rock on the west side to avoid, but you are safe if you are in among the moored boats. The water shoals rapidly past the little island in the cove's head.

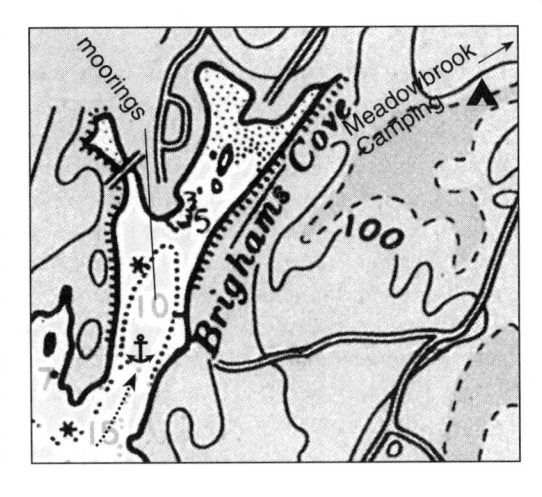

By Land. From Bath, take Rt. 209 south. By a brick house on the right, go right onto Stony Brook Road and follow it to the west. When it tees with Meadowbrook Road, go right. The campground will be on the left.

Ashore. Meadowbrook Camping is a large facility, with RV and tent sites, a pool, laundry facilities, and a small store. A pleasant nature trail borders the campsites.

The divisions of the nautical charts do not depict the lay of the land here very well. The head of Brighams Cove is within half a mile of the headwaters of Winnegance Creek, which flows into Fiddler Reach on the Kennebec River. This was a very important Indian portage, saving them days of paddling in the exposed, open water out to and around Small Point and through the dangerous currents at the mouth of the Kennebec. Winnegance, loosely translated, means "A River Boundary Place."

218. Painted Point Ramp

A new, concrete launching ramp lies on the east side of Winnegance Bay, south of the enclave of Meadowbrook. It is useable at all tides, the pitch is excellent, and there is plenty of parking.

By sea. The ramp lies in line with Bushy Island and the low, treeless rock to the northeast. From the New Meadows River, shallow-draft boats can run to either side of Bushy and Hen Island, though care must be taken to keep clear of the bevy of rocks surrounding them.

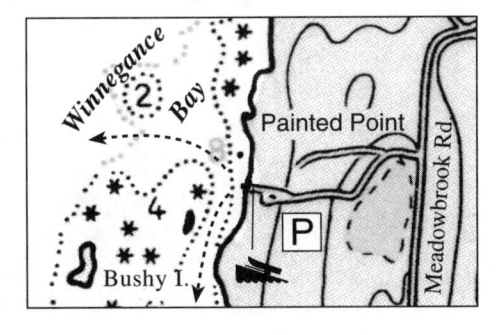

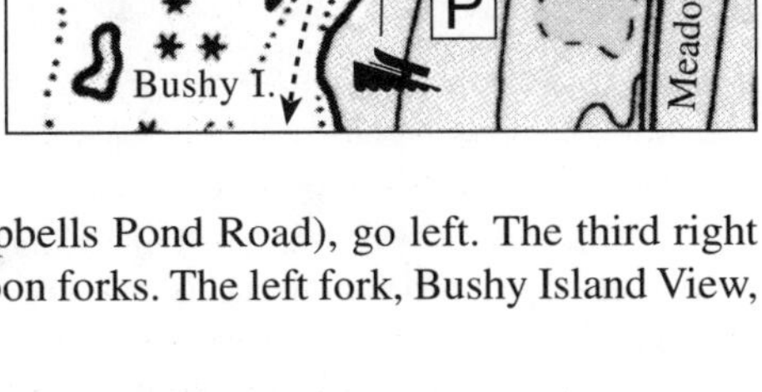

By land. Follow Rt. 209 south from Bath toward Phippsburg. At a brick house on the right, take Stony Brook Road to the right and follow it to the west. When it tees with Meadowbrook Road (also called Campbells Pond Road), go left. The third right will be the dirt Painted Point Road, which soon forks. The left fork, Bushy Island View, leads to the water.

219. Long Island Harbor ⚓

Long Island, north of Dingley, forms a large harbor that makes a fair anchorage. The southern entrance, between the high north end of Dingley Island and the high southern end of Long Island, is heavily wooded and beautiful, but the harbor itself has little to explore by small boat. Cottages line the mainland shore. A small landing belongs to the Long Island community for mainland access.

By sea. Approach from the south, steering clear of the ledges that make out from the southwest shore of Long Island. At high water, it is possible to cross the mud flat at the northern end of the harbor.

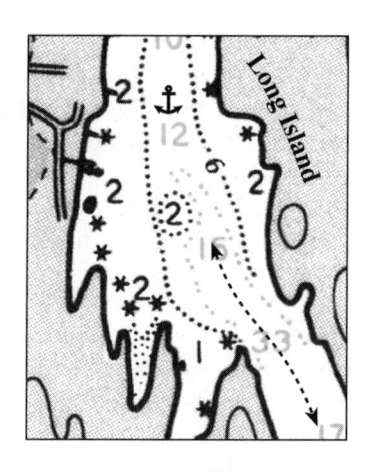

Ashore. Long Island is private, with most of the cottages on the east shore.

Ospreys

Few experiences are as moving as witnessing an osprey swoop to the sea and scoop out a live fish in its talons. This fish hawk has a wingspan of five or six feet, a sharp, curved beak, and talons as strong as an eagle's. It is camouflaged with a white underbelly, a brown backside, and beautiful brown-and-white patterning under its wings and tail.

Ospreys are almost exclusively fish eaters. They build large, disheveled nests of sticks near bodies of good aerated water, either fresh of salt, and they use the nests year after year. One nest on Sutton Island is over 100 years old. Ospreys return to Maine from their southern migration around mid-May to mate and lay two to four eggs. They incubate the eggs for abut 35 days and then fish tirelessly all day to feed the nest full of noisy, insatiable young. The chicks fledge in 48 to 59 days.

But despite the osprey's apparent strength and fortitude, the life of the osprey is fraught with danger. They are often harassed or preyed upon by opportunistic birds such as crows, ravens, starlings, and others. The chicks' long incubation period is followed by an even longer growth period. By the time young birds begin to fly in mid-August, Maine is sometimes already beset by fierce fall-like weather. Not only must they learn to fly, they must develop their fishing skills and stamina. In only two months, they must begin their first migration. Often the young birds are found dead from starvation or exhaustion or lack of defensive strength. On average, only about one of three osprey chicks survive to reach maturity.

Man almost irreversibly tipped the odds against the osprey's survival with the use of the pesticide DDT after World War II. The poison moved through the food chain, accumulating in large concentrations in fish, which in turn were eaten by ospreys. The DDT weakened the bird's egg shells, and whole generations of chicks never hatched or were deformed. Rachel Carson's book *Silent Spring* raised the alarm in 1962 and led to the banning of the life-threatening pesticides.

Humans can still negatively impact ospreys, often inadvertently. Disturbance of ospreys during the incubation or before the fledgling of their chicks can be stressful enough to cause abandonment or even chick death. When disturbed, an osprey will defend its nest vociferously and unmistakably, often diving at intruders and screaming "kee, kee, kee." If you find yourself near a nervous or irate osprey, move slowly and silently away and admire this majestic giant of the air from a respectful distance.

220. Dingley Island

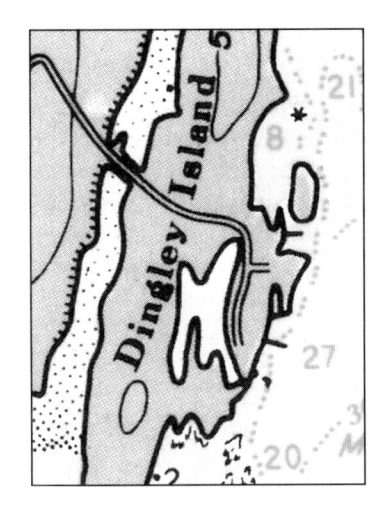

Dingley Island, south of Long Island, is connected to Sebascodegan by a causeway across a sliver of water. All of Dingley is private, with large estates on the south and southeast shores.

Ashore. The chart shows a large pond on Dingley that looks like spilled milk. This was the ice pond for Goddard's Icehouse, one of the major icehouses of Casco Bay. Another pond and icehouse was at Sebasco Harbor (see p. 228). Schooners docked on the east side of Dingley, and 10 to 30 tons of ice were slid into their holds and packed with insulating hay for their voyages to Boston and New York and even the West Indies.

Even the Indians are said to have used Dingley for refrigeration. Caves on Dingley are thought to have been used to cache their sturgeon, bear, and deer.

221. Dingley Cove

Dingley Cove lies on the west side of the New Meadows River. It is defined by Cedar Ledges to the south, Sheep Island to the east, and Dingley Island and a group of small islets to the north. As an anchorage, it is exposed to the south. Fishing boats that moor here huddle behind the ledges in the southwest corner, where there is a public ramp, used mostly by the fishermen. Sheep Island, Dingley Island, and Hopkins Island are all private, but together with the little islets and ledges, they form an intriguing mini-archipelago to explore by water.

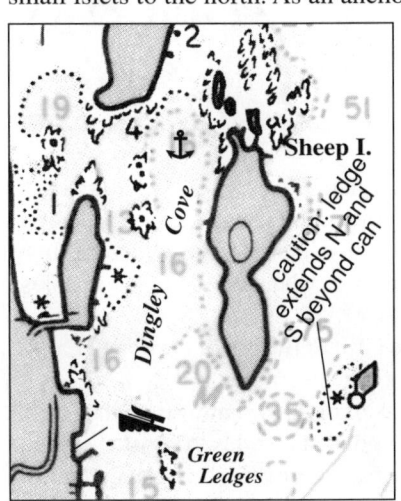

By sea. Approach from the south, favoring Sheep Island to avoid the Cedar and Green ledges. Notice Sheep Island Ledge, marked by can "5." Entering from the north is not good idea unless you are at the top of the tide or in a kayak.

The launching ramp is tucked behind the fishing wharf on the west shore. It is paved to a firm beach.

By land. From Brunswick's Cooks Corner, follow Rt. 24 south to a left on Cundys Harbor Road. As you drop into Cundys Harbor, Holbrook Street is on the left. Follow it to the end.

Ashore. There are a few parking spaces in the turnout opposite the ramp, but be careful that you don't bottom out on the rugged terrain.

222. The Basin and Basin Island ⚓ ⛺

Few places are as special as the Basin. A small cut of water opens up on the east bank of the New Meadows River, opposite Sheep Island, and tends to the southeast between thickly treed shores. Suddenly, it swings to the north and opens up into the broad expanse of what could easily be mistaken for an inland wilderness lake. Wooded points project into the still water, and a little treed nubbit of an island seems to float on the reflection of the sky. Ospreys screech from their perches, and heron dabble in the shallows.

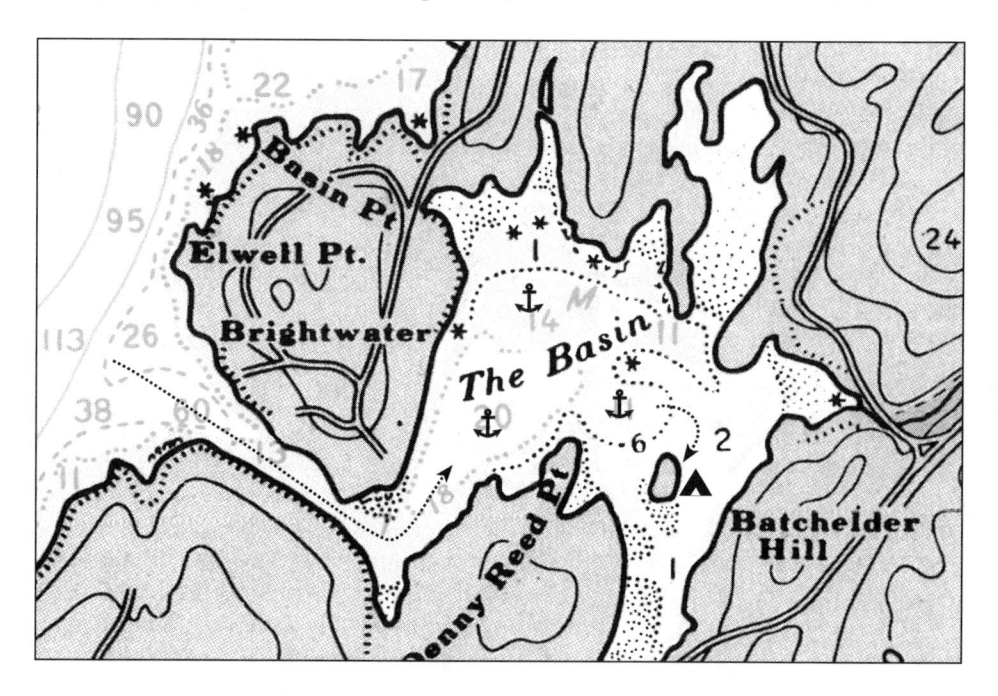

You'll probably have to share this place with cruising boats, who find it an ideal, virtually landlocked harbor, particularly in heavy blows. And sometimes jetskiers roar over its glassy surface, oblivious to the peace they're shattering. But when the light stretches, when you find your voices reduced to whispers, when you float on breathless water, the sense of discovery is almost palpable.

Basin Island is owned by the State and managed by the Bureau of Parks and Lands. It is part of the Maine Island Trail, and careful camping is permitted.

By sea. The current can run to a couple of knots through the entrance to the Basin. It may be choked with lobster buoys, but its depth is good at all tides. Almost anywhere in the Basin makes an ideal anchorage, except in the narrow coves which flat out at low. Beware, however of the one danger—the submerged rock just below the "i" in the word "Basin" on the chart.

Ashore. Land on Basin Island on its northeast side and walk lightly up the steep and easily eroded bank. Tent sites are located on the north end of the island. Avoid the island's south end and its northwest shoulder, where ospreys nest in the trees.

CASCO BAY

An archeological dig on the shore here has unearthed evidence of a year-round native settlement of 20 to 30 people from around 2000 B.C.. In the 1700s, settlers discovered tidal power and set up sawmills and saltwater farms along the its shores. A map of 1795 shows one sawmill on the southern shore at the mouth of the Basin.

The peninsula on the opposite shore is known locally as Brightwater. It consists of a narrow isthmus and a much wider head, which includes Basin Point and Elwell Point on the New Meadows River. In the late 1800s, when steamship service made "rusticating" popular on the Maine coast, a syndicate bought the peninsula and renamed it "New Venice." They planned a colony of summer cottages but got no farther than building a circular road through the property before the advent of the automobile and the excitement of travel lured away their potential customers. They had several offers to buy the whole project, but they refused them until the tax burden forced them to sell cheaply. In 1925, the Brightwater Cooperative Club was formed, and they, in turn, sold individual lots strictly to "professional men." Descendants of those same families continue to summer here.

223. Cundys Harbor

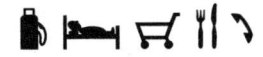

Cundys Harbor is the only real village on the New Meadows, stretched along a couple of miles of the Cundys Harbor Road. And it is real. Wharves and floats and fish buyers ring the harbor. Trawlers and gillnetters and tuna boats and lobsterboats fill the harbor. A church is perched on a hill. The post office is in one of the two general stores. Rubber boots are in the other. And the small restaurant is named the Block and Tackle.

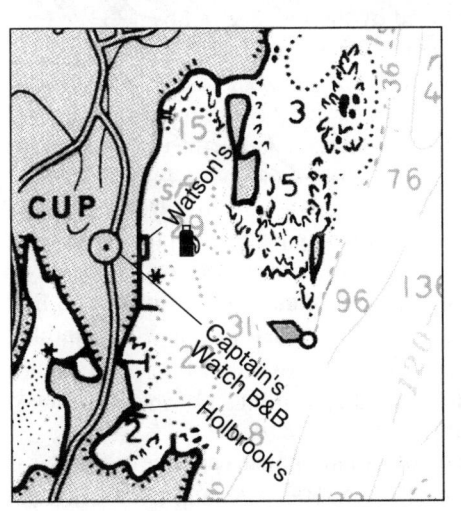

The harbor itself ("Cundy," with no "s") is a broad bight on the river's west side, near the mouth. Protection is adequate in fair weather, but in foul, offshore swells roll up the river and straight into the harbor, and the only thing that keeps the boats here are massive blocks of granite used for moorings.

This is a fun place to explore by small boat, with two possible docking spots, fuel, a seafood takeout, and even an elegant bed and breakfast. Don't, however, expect pleasure-boat amenities. This is a working harbor where boats put to sea for one reason only—fish.

By sea. There are no tricks to Cundy Harbor once you've located can "3" marking the southern extremity of Cedar Ledges. Keep the can to starboard, and you're in.

This is an exposed place. It would make a poor choice for an anchorage, and there are no moorings available for transients.

The fuel float of Watson's General Store (725-7794) pumps gas and diesel. It is located in the middle of the harbor, shown on the chart by a small rectangular protrusion on the west shore.

221

At the southern end of the harbor, Holbrook's Wharf has a float where you can tie up for a meal at their takeout or for a quick trip to the town's other general store, Holbrook's.

By land. Follow Rt. 24 south from Cooks Corner in Brunswick. Take a left onto Cundys Harbor Road, and follow it to its end.

Ashore. The Watson family started their store in 1819, making it the oldest family-operated general store in Maine. Here are all the basics of life right next to each other—milk and galvanized chain, candy bars and boots, bread and potwarp. Surprisingly, it doesn't sell lobsters retail.

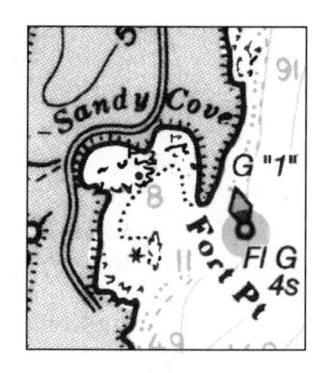

Holbrook's Wharf is a true Maine takeout, where you can dive into freshly boiled lobsters or clams at picnic tables on the wharf or buy live ones to go. If you will be eating at dusk, BYOBR (Bring Your Own Bug Repellent).

Holbrook's General Store (725-7794) has a basic groceries, beer, and ice. A cubby in the front corner houses the post office, and a pay phone is just outside.

Hawkes Lobster is next to Holbrook's Wharf, and in addition to live lobster, they sell clams and smoked salmon and other fish in season.

The cupola shown on the chart is that of the Captain's Watch Bed and Breakfast (725-0979). This elegant building was originally built as the Union Hotel, and it sits high above the harbor with views of the fleet. The hosts are happy to help you with your boats.

The land around Cundys Harbor was first bought by Colonel Shapleigh of Kittery in 1659. Early settlement was actively discouraged by the Indians, but by 1733, a Mr. Cundy, sometimes spelled Condy, had settled here. The harbor took his name, and a village began to grow.

A tavern and one of the first boarding houses in Casco Bay was built on the east side of Cundy's Point in 1762, just in time to play an important part in the Revolutionary War. It was called the Green House on account of its color, and it was run by a Tory named Eastman. A small British privateer, the *Picaroon*, had been raiding Yankee shipping just off the coast and occasionally they were brazen enough to slip into the harbor and pay the Green House a hearty visit.

The boldness of the *Picaroon's* crew, however, was too much for the men of Sebascodegan. A Scotsman by the name of Linnacum rounded up a band of volunteers, and they made plans to capture the *Picaroon*. A watch was posted for the return of the privateer, and before long, she drew near. At two in the morning, 17 vigilantes gave chase in their small, 14-ton schooner *America*.

The *Picaroon* high-tailed it back out to sea, but *America* managed to overtake her off Seguin. The *Picaroon* had longer-range guns than the *America*, but, by a series of well-timed gun volleys, the Yankees managed to overpower her. The *Picaroon's* helmsman stood fast at the wheel. Just as he shouted "I'll be damned if I'll dodge the flash of a Yankee Gun!" a bullet pierced his heart. He was buried on a small point of land in Cundys Harbor that bears his name—Shepard's Point.

224. Fort Point

Fort Point guards the western flank of the mouth of the New Meadows River, just opposite Bear Island. An earthwork fort with log foundations was built here to defend the New Meadows River during the War of 1812 and intercept boats carrying supplies to English vessels outside. Every vessel was required to hail the fort on its way in or out of the river. One stubborn fisherman, a Mr. Dingley (of Dingley Island, p. 219) refused, and his boat was fired upon and nearly sank before he could get her to shore. After the incident, there was still plenty of grumbling, but there was plenty of hailing too.

225. Bear Island

Opposite Fort Point, seemingly impenetrable stands of dark spruce fortify Bear Island. They crowd the ledgy shore, and the caw of crows and screech of ospreys linger in their shadows.

Bear is a large island, but it is private. A nearly invisible rustic-style cottage and boathouse hide among the trees on the small private cove at the northwest end of the island. The whole island is posted "no trespassing."

By sea. Ledges make out from both ends of Bear. The northern ledges are marked by nun "4." The pocket formed to the east of Bear Island and north of Malaga Island makes a secure harbor, used mostly by lobsterboats and draggers. Note that a cable crosses to Bear from the Sebasco shore, right through the small harbor north of Malaga. The cable crossing is marked by signs on both shores, but it is not shown on the charts. If you anchor, be sure to use a trip line in case you snag the cable.

It is possible for small boats to pass between Bear and Malaga at high tide. Steep wooded shores on both sides echo the slightest noise and sigh with the wind.

226. Malaga Island

Like Bear Island, Malaga is also private, though there is no cottage on it. The north end has a small beach, but otherwise the shores are steep-to, piled high with the traps of lobstermen who bring their boats in against the rocks at high tide to load their traps.

The lee of Malaga forms a relatively protected harbor to the north, where draggers and lobsterboats moor and where ospreys nest in the mast of a sunken fishing boat.

By sea. See chart next page. Anchoring is possible in the harbor, but a cable area, unmarked on the chart, runs right through the harbor to Bear Island. See Bear Island, above for more information.

It is possible to circumnavigate Malaga, squeezing through the slot between Malaga and Bear Island and then through the Tide Hole, the gut between Malaga and Sebasco on the mainland. (see Sebasco, p. 225).

Ashore. Some say Malaga's name comes from a Spanish port. Others say its the Abenaki word for cedars. Locally it is pronounced "Malago," but for many years it was known as Maine's "Scandal Island" (see sidebar, page 224).

The Sad Tale of Malaga Island

Malaga Island's tranquillity belies a sad history of hope and desperation. Malaga was settled sometime during the Civil War by Benjamin Darling, a black man. He had a wife, who may have been white, and two sons. Soon he was joined by a group of blacks, Indians, and other mixed breeds who built a community of driftwood shacks. The squatters and their descendants fished and scratch-farmed the rocky soil. They dug clams and caught lobsters and heated with whatever washed ashore. Occasionally they would work as laborers for mainland farmers.

But rumors began to grow. It was said that the social order of the Malagoites was loose and that incest was rampant. Ben Darling was said to have been an escaped slave, and the women were thought to have been concubines of local sea captains in the West Indian trade who were put ashore before the captains returned to their wives. Others were reported to have escaped from a slave-trading ship headed to the south. Some claimed that the children grew horns and lived like beasts in tunnels.

One of the group was James McKinney who was born in Phippsburg into a family of Scots. He became known as the "King of Malaga," but by the time he became the leader of this desperate outpost, his kingdom was a shambles. The natural bounty of clams had been depleted, the topsoil had eroded, and much of the population suffered from malnourishment and lack of education.

By 1903, the Malagoites were so desperate that they sought help from the town of Phippsburg, which at the time was being discovered as a place for summer cottage development. Not wanting the problems or the embarrassment of Malaga, Phippsburg was quick to argue that the island belonged to the town of Harpswell. For better or worse, the dispute publicized the islanders' plight. State legislators finally settled the dispute by granting Malaga to Phippsburg, but then, at the urging of Phippsburg, reversing their decision, leaving the Malagoites, by default, wards of the state. Locals called Malaga No Man's Land.

Malaga's plight caught the attention of Captain George Lane, who had a summer house on what was then called Horse Island to the south (see Harbor Island, p. 226). George was a descendant of the Lanes of Lanes Island at the mouth of the Royal and Cousins River (see p. 121) and Malden, Massachusetts. He used to sail into isolated coves and preach the Good Word. Concerned for the Malagoites, he approached the Superintendent of Schools only to discover that there was no money to build a school on the island. At Lane's insistence though, he conceded to providing a teacher if there was a suitable building.

In the spring of 1908, James McKenny, the King, allowed Lane to set up a temporary school in his house, taught by Lane's daughter. She would row across from Horse Island for classes. The Lanes raised food, clothes, and money, and by July, they broke ground on a new school building. When it was completed in October, the Superintendent, true to his word, supplied Malaga with a teacher.

In the summer of 1911, Governor Fredrick Plaisted visited Malaga to observe the progress. Instead, he saw only the squalor. Appalled, he suggested burning the shacks down, drilling a well, and rebuilding. But by this time, Malaga had become a highly publicized scandal and a political liability. Newspapers dubbed it "Maine's Scandal Island" and a "salt-water skid row."

The politically safer and more expedient alternative was eviction. The next year the State evicted the 56 residents, dug up the remains of the dead, and burned down the hovels. For lack of any other expeditious solution, many of the Malagoites were committed to the Maine School for the Feeble-Mined in Pownel. Others were left to fend for themselves.

Sadly, Malaga's stigma still haunts descendants of Malaga's exiled in the form of local taunts and jeers and name-calling.

CASCO BAY

THE EASTERN SHORE

227. Sebasco 🍴

The remote hamlet of Sebasco is on the mainland shore opposite Malaga, along a narrow gut called the Tide Hole. Several wharves and bait houses line the shore, and a quiet seriousness pervades the gearing-up and off-loading of the boats.

The Tide Hole itself is a fascinating passage, with plenty of depth for deep-draft boats. At the southern end, the Water's Edge takeout and restaurant is a nice reward.

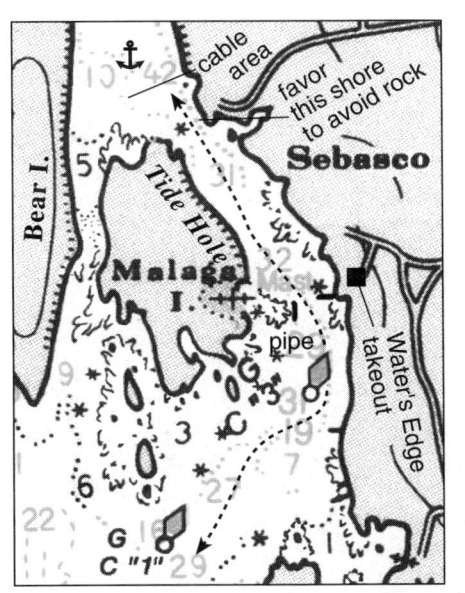

By sea. This is an easy passage, but it has some obstacles. From the north, favor the wharves on the mainland side to avoid the rock off the north end of Malaga, then stick to the Malaga side of the channel to clear the ledges jutting from the mainland side, shown west of the word "Sebasco" on the chart. The masts shown in the marshy pocket of Malaga are no longer there, but the rock to the right of the word "Mast" on the chart hasn't moved. It is marked by a pipe. Stay in mid channel, but to the west of the pipe. Can "3" is a long distance off the southeast flank of Malaga, but be sure to observe it, keeping to the east of it.

By land. From Bath, take Rt. 209 south, and then turn right on Rt. 217. Follow it to its end to reach the Sebasco Wharves. To reach the Water's Edge restaurant, take the next-to-last left.

Ashore. The northern wharf was bought in 1899 by Frank Ridley, of Ridley Cove on Sebascodegan Island. He owned several schooners and operated a fish buying and drying station, along with a general store.

Halfway through the Tide Hole, there is a large fish-freezing plant where a flash-freezing process was developed for lobsters.

The wharf and brown buildings at the southern end belong to the Water's Edge takeout and restaurant. If you are a patron, you can land at the float while you eat, but do not block it if lobsterboats are unloading.

In the process of helping the Malagoites, Captain Lane founded the Maine Sea Coast Mission. They saved the little red schoolhouse by dismantling it and moving it to Louds Island in Muscongus Bay, where it was reassembled to be used as a church. The Sea Coast Mission still operates today from its headquarters in Bar Harbor. Their *Sunbeam V* sails from its homeport of Northeast Harbor to bring religious services, practical help, and good cheer to the few remaining island communities along the coast.

228. Brewer's Boat Yard

Brewer's Boat Yard (389-1388) is located in the little ledgy indent northeast of Harbor Island, where the chart indicates a marine railway. It's still there. This is a true Maine yard where most of the clientele use their boats for a living. In addition to the railway, Brewer's hauls and launches with a hydraulic trailer, which is often hooked up to a tractor or old truck. Trailered boats can be launched on their ramp.

By sea. If you don't know this area, approach near the top of the tide, preferably as it's rising, from north of Harbor Island. The large red metal building on the mainland is a major bait dealer. The boat yard lies farther south.

Favor the mainland shore as you run south, steering toward the little cove on the north end of Harbor Island. At the mouth of the cove, turn due east, and pass between the tight ledges between Harbor Island and the point on the mainland, favoring the island side slightly. Once inside, the boat yard is dead ahead.

Do not attempt to pass through the ledgy gut between Harbor Island and the mainland into Sebasco Harbor unless it is near the top of the tide.

By land. From Bath, follow Rt. 209 south. Turn right onto Rt. 217 and follow it past the golf course and pond at Sebasco Harbor Resort. Once past the small post office on the right, take a left and then a left again.

Ashore. Brewer's can haul, store, and repair your boat—or salvage it if it sinks. Launching and long-term parking can be arranged here. Calling ahead is recommended, but when asked if they monitor a VHF channel, they replied, "Half the time, we don't even monitor the phone."

229. Harbor Island

Harbor Island forms Sebasco Harbor to its east. Like Bear and Malaga Island to the north, Harbor is heavily wooded. Most of the island is owned by Sebasco Harbor Resort, on the mainland across the harbor.

By sea. See Sebasco Harbor, p. 228.

Ashore. Sebasco Harbor was a major ice port. When the pond near the head of the harbor froze, blocks of ice were cut by hand and sledded off to the icehouses by horses. The ice was packed in hay to insulate it, and loaded as needed into schooners.

In the summer, the horses were put out to pasture on the island. It became known as Horse Island, and the harbor was Horse Island Harbor. The ice pond was called Cornelius Pond or by its Indian or Maine dialect name, Watah Lake. Ayuh.

Benjamin Darling bought Horse Island in 1794 for 15 pounds, but during the Civil War, for unknown reasons, he became one of the origianl settlers on ill-fated Malaga Island (see p. 223-224). The cottage at the north end of the island belonged to Captain George Lane, who founded the Maine Seacoast Missionary Society to bring religion, food, clothes, and, most important of all, fresh company to isolated island communities along the coast. One of his first great works was to build a school on Malaga Island just to the north, where his daughter became the teacher. The Seacoast Missionary Society is still in operation, based in Bar Harbor and operating its boat, the *Sunbeam V*, out of Northeast Harbor.

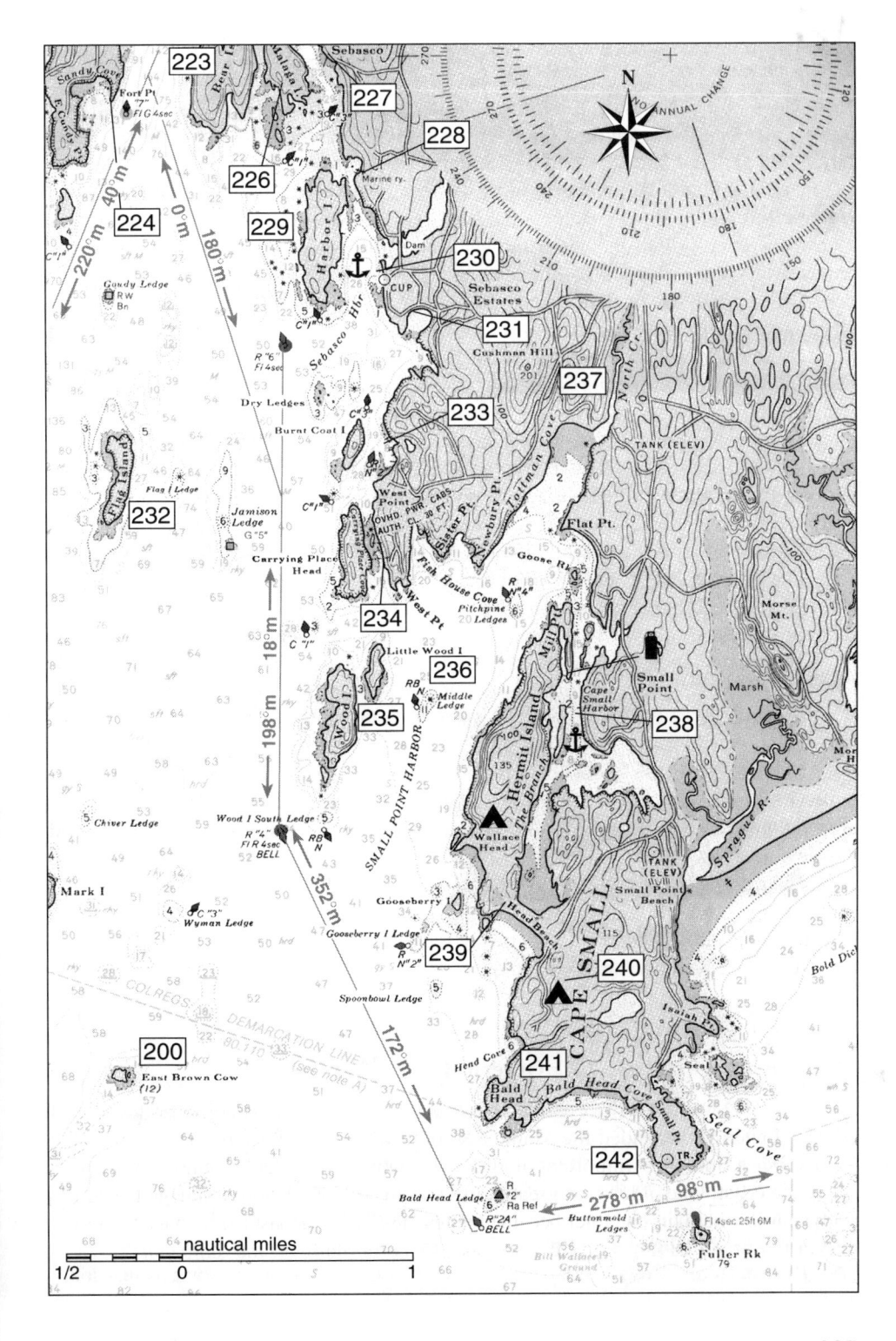

CASCO BAY

227

230. Sebasco Harbor

Sebasco Harbor is a broad pocket to the east of Harbor Island. On the chart it looks wide open to the south, though ledges at the harbor's mouth and the Dry Ledges farther out give it a fair degree of protection.

Cruising boats often anchor here or rent one of the heavy moorings set by Sebasco Harbor Resort (389-1161). Boaters are welcome to come ashore and use the Resort's many amenities, which include a saltwater swimming pool, a nine-hole golf course, tennis courts, and a restaurant and snack bar. The Resort or the Rock Gardens Inn next door make a good base for small-boat explorations. With permission, lightweight trailered or portable boats can be launched from the beach in Round Cove (see below).

By sea. Despite appearances on the chart, shallow draft boats can enter or leave Sebasco Harbor from the north during the top part of the tide, though this is best attempted after your courage has been fortified with a heavy dose of local knowledge.

The much more straightforward approach is from the south. Be sure to clear the unmarked but visible Dry Ledges before heading northeast into the harbor. Keep can "1," off the southern end of Harbor Island, to port, and continue well before turning north toward the harbor. At the harbor's mouth, stay in the middle as you enter to avoid the ledges on either side. A small pipe marks the ledge to starboard.

The moorings of Sebasco Harbor Resort are marked with dayglow polyballs. Reservations are recommended. During the day, a launch service operates from the resort float on the east shore, where they have regular gasoline, water, and ice.

The cupola marked on the chart is a multistoried octagonal building. It is called the Lighthouse, but it looks more like a wedding cake.

By land. From Bath, follow Rt. 209 south. Turn right onto Rt. 217, heading west. Sebasco Harbor Resort is on the left where Rt. 217 bends north.

Ashore. Sebasco Harbor Resort is a vacation spot with a long tradition of quiet, understated elegance. Its facilities, including a pool, showers, and laundry facilities, are available to visiting boaters. Guests may also rent kayaks to explore the harbor and the New Meadows River.

The resort's lodge was built in 1908 as a clubhouse by a New York contractor who sold it 17 years later to start the smaller Rock Gardens Inn next door (see below). It has recently been sold again, and the new owner is expanding the golf course, the spa, and the conference and banquet facilities and developing the resort as an exclusive getaway.

231. Round Cove and the Rock Gardens Inn

This elegant little inn (389-1339) was started by the founder of Sebasco Lodge, now the Sebasco Harbor Resort, on the next point south. There are only three rooms in the inn, but it includes ten cottages with several rooms apiece.

The round cove to the east of the point is—well—Round Cove. A sandy beach rings its head. At high tide it is possible to launch portable and even lightweight trailered boats from the small gravel ramp that slopes to the beach.

By sea. Round Cove is not named on the chart, but its shape is obvious just south of Sebasco Harbor. It is tidal, nearly landlocked, and without much depth, so it can only be used near the top of the tide. A visible rock connected by a not-so-visible ledge lies across half of the cove's mouth. They were probably part of a dam for a tide mill or to make the cove an ice pond or a swimming hole.

If you plan to launch trailered boats from the beach, please get permission from Sebasco Harbor Resort.

By land. See Sebasco Harbor Resort, above.

Ashore. At the height of the season, in July and August, the Rock Gardens Inn requires a minimum stay of five nights. Guests at Rock Gardens are allowed to use the facilities of Sebasco Harbor Resort. In fact, their grounds blend together along the quiet roads and golf cart paths, which are perfect for strolling.

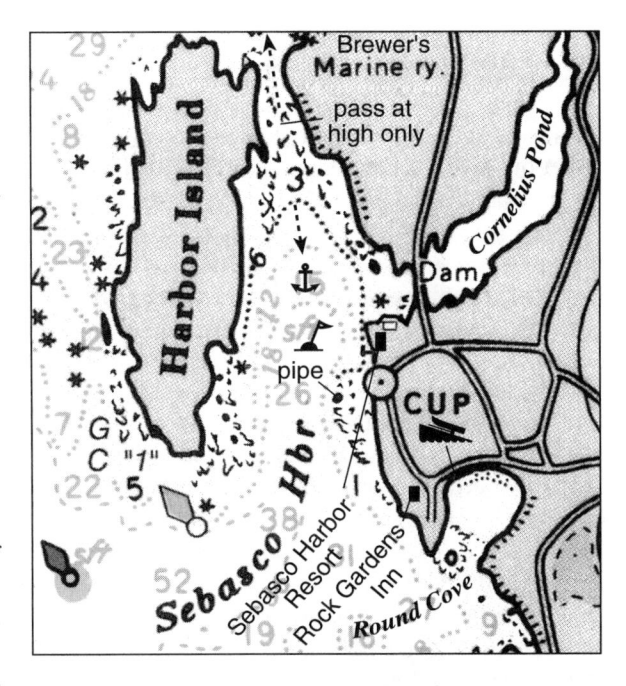

The Sebasco Harbor Resort and Rock Gardens Inn draw water from a spring northeast of Round Cove, which the Indians are said to have used.

232. Flag Island

Flag Island lies offshore to the southwest of Sebasco Harbor, straight upwind. It sits at the end of a spine of ledge that runs northward, then underwater, and then resurfaces again as the western half of Bear Island. Flag has a long and streamlined shape, crowned by trees. It is remote and exposed with no harbor of any kind. It is also private.

Flag, however, is an important visual landmark when approaching the New Meadows River from the south.

By sea. If you are passing to the west of Flag, favor Long Ledge to avoid the rocks and three-foot spot off Flag. If you are passing to the east of Flag and aren't thoroughly familiar with the area, honor can "7," marking Jamison Ledge, by keeping to the east of it.

233. Water Cove, Burnt Coat Island

Water Cove is not named on the chart. It is the ledgy bight behind Burnt Coat Island, just below a pond shown on the mainland. The deep and well-marked passage inside of Burnt is a fascinating working harbor, intriguing to explore by water. Burnt Coat Island itself is private.

By sea. Water Cove is not much of a harbor. The southern half of the gut inside of Burnt Coat Island runs right into the face of the prevailing southwesterlies and ocean swells, and ebbing currents add to the turmoil. Water Cove is practically filed with a ledge extending from its southern shore, but there is a narrow slip of water close by the private wharves.

Ashore. In summer, schooners used to fill their tanks here from the pond just uphill from the cove. In winter, they took on ice. The pond is named Water Cove Ice Pond.

234. West Point 🛒 🍴

West Point is a small fishing village clustered behind a high island, shown on the chart as Carrying Place Head. This is a real outport community, where small houses and fishing shacks crowd the shore and wharves wade tentatively on spindly legs.

Locally, Carrying Place Head is called West Point Island, and a small tight gut runs between it and the mainland. Smack dab in the middle of the gut is another island, tiny with an old cottage, and just to confuse things, this one is also called West Point Island. Most of the fishing fleet anchors in the north part of this gut, in the lee of the bigger West Point Island, in what is called Carrying Place Cove. The southern half is known as West Point Harbor, but it's not much of one.

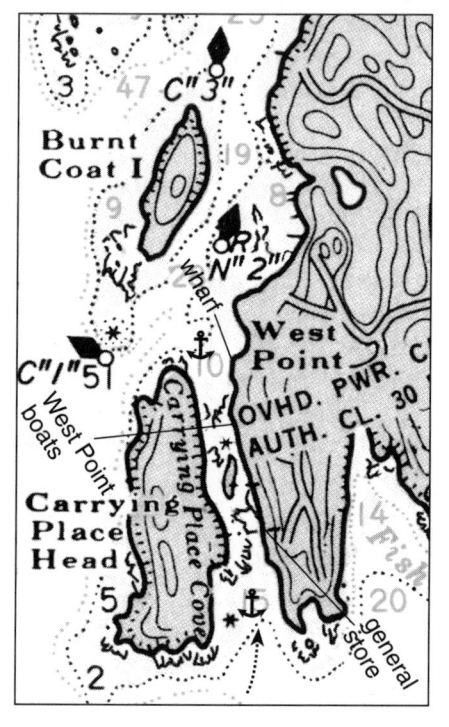

Small boats can anchor among the fleet or squeeze through the narrow gut or put in at the wharf of the West Point General Store, which perches over the water on pilings.

By sea. The easiest approach to Carrying Place Cove, where the fishing boats moor, is from the north. If you can find room among the moored boats, the holding ground opposite the Sea Horse lobster wharf on the mainland is good, thick mud, but it may be fouled with old gear. If you anchor, use a tripline.

Use caution passing through the gut. The scale of the chart is inadequate, without soundings, and powerlines (minimum vertical clearance of 30 feet) span the passage. At high there is enough depth for lobsterboats. From the north, favor the shore of the larger West Point Island to avoid the rock to the north of the smaller island. Stay to the west of the little West Point Island, but keep close. Once by the little West Point Island, you need to gradually cross over to the east side to avoid ledges projecting from the west. The West Point General Store is the red building in the southern part of the gut.

When approaching the West Point General Store from the south, favor the east shore.

By land. From Bath, follow Rt. 209 south. Turn right onto Rt. 217 and take the first left onto the West Point Road.

Ashore. Here, perhaps, is linguistic evidence that the sea is rising. At low tide, the reason for the Indian name of Carrying Place is obvious. Muddy ledges stretch between West Point, West Point Island and Carrying Place Head. The portage would have been slippery but short, and the effort would have spared them the extra distance and danger of paddling out around Carrying Place Head. They may have had to portage on the top half of the tide too, depending on the age of the name and the level of the sea. Now, high covers the ledges completely, and it is not a carrying place at all.

Carrying Place Head is the location of Carrying Place Boat Company where Jonathan Keyes builds what he calls West Pointers, a derivation of the traditional Casco Bay Hampton (see sidebar next page).

The West Point General Store acts as market, deli, restaurant, hangout, and virtual town hall for this small community. For several years this landmark was closed, but it has recently been taken over by new owners. They serve sandwiches and grilled items, with tables out on their wharf. On cool days, fishermen crowd around the table by the steamy window overlooking the harbor while the woodstove crackles.

235. Wood Island, Little Wood Island

A pair of substantial islands lies south of West Point Harbor, which when viewed from that vantage point look like dark ships on a blinding sea. Both are heavily wooded with dark spruce. The larger of the two, Wood Island, hunches its ragged flank to the sea, while Little Wood Island crouches in its lee. At low tide, a tight tickle barely separates the two.

Both islands are private with cottages. Please do not land.

236. Small Point Harbor

On the chart, Small Point Harbor is the wide-open body of water between the Wood islands and Hermit Island, but it is hardly a harbor. It is more than half a mile across and two miles deep, and it is directly in line with the prevailing winds and ocean swells from the southwest. In fact, it was originally called North Creek Bay, which is more fitting both geographically and semantically.

By sea. This can be a rough place for small boats when the wind is up, particularly near the head where it shoals dramatically and the waves become steeper.

The real Small Point Harbor, at least in the local vernacular, is what the chart calls Cape Small Harbor, the narrow pocket between Hermit Island and the mainland (see Cape Small Harbor, p. 234). The entrance is tricky, but once inside there is almost complete protection.

The Casco Bay Hampton

Early fishing in Casco Bay was done out of whaleboat type boats, lapstrake double-enders and dories. But in 1877 Captain David Perry Sinnett of Bailey Island tried a new design that was ideal for the conditions of the bay and the needs of its fishermen. Charles Gomez of Sebasco followed suit in 1903, builiding over his lifetime 250 of the type, refined for both power and sail.

The design drew on the lines of double-ended beach boats of New Hampshire, but the stern was squared off and the fullness of the hull brought aft. These boats were about 22.5 feet long, fitted with centerboards, and carried two sprit sails and one or two jibs in a miniature schooner rig, which would be unstepped when rowing. The type would become known as the Casco Bay Hampton, and it is heralded as a definitve step in the evolution of the modern lobsterboat.

Sinnett's first, with a smooth hull, was built for Tom Lubee of Bailey for about $100. Eventually around 1907 or 1908, the boats began to be equipped with small Hartford or Palmer engines, a setup that in the 1920s cost about $500.

Stunning Hamptons are still being crafted today by Richard S. Pulsifer on Merepoint (207-725-5457) and Jonathan Keyes at Carrying Place Boat Company in West Point (207-443-5171). For many, they still make the perfect small boat for exploring Casco Bay. Hard-core devotees of the Hamptons take an annual cruise, one year exploring as far afield as New York Harbor.

Robert Tristram Coffin describes the boat in 1947 in *Yankee Coast*:

"Now most of the lobstering is done in the Downeast, Novi-styled hulls of the typical lobsterboat, but the Hampton is still a favorite picnic boat or launch.

"...it is the Hampton boat, the reach-boat, the backbone of the profession of lobstering, which is the boat that now most means Maine. It goes by gas; but it is also potentially a sailing-boat, and a stout mast can be stepped in it forward. It is broad in the beam and carries a load handsomely; its rail swoops two ways with the life and beauty of a seagull's wing. It holds its nose high, for rough going. For storms and high seas and Winter's cold it wears a canvas spray-hood, slanted on a spar. It is a large boat, but one man can operate it easily, standing by the engine's housing and steering by the rudder-rope where it passes under the rail. It can go as fast as any aggregation of horsepower a man wants to put in it. It is boned with Maine red oak and fleshed with knotless Maine white pine. It is always heads-up and tail-over-the-dasher in the sea. The worst blow cannot rob it of its spunk and high spirits. It takes the waves just as a coot does, shakes them off, and smiles for more. This boat could go across the Atlantic safely, if a man could carry enough gas for the trip, and enough water and hard-tack for himself.

"This loveliest and usefullest of boats is still a home-made, a hand-made thing. In this day when ocean liners and destroyers are stamped out by the batch and plastered together with solder, it is good that there are some boats made by loving fingers and thumbs, their planking steamed by the kitchen teakettle, hands molding them as they grow from the first curve of the keel to the last curve of the sheer."*

A Bailey Island fisherman, as quoted by Beth Hill in her *Evolution of Bailey's Island*, is somewhat less romantic. "Winter fishing in a Casco Bay Hampton is known to sap vitality, crab boyish enthusiasm, put crow's feet around the eyes, seams in the face, and gray in the hair."

Reprinted with permission, see copyright page.

237. Tottman Cove, North Creek

The head of Small Point Harbor forms Tottman Cove. "Cove" is a misnomer for this place, since it is wide, shallow, and exposed, particularly to the southwest. The cove is actually the erosion and widening of the mouth of little North Creek. It is ringed by a broad sandy beach, but landing there can be difficult if the swells are up.

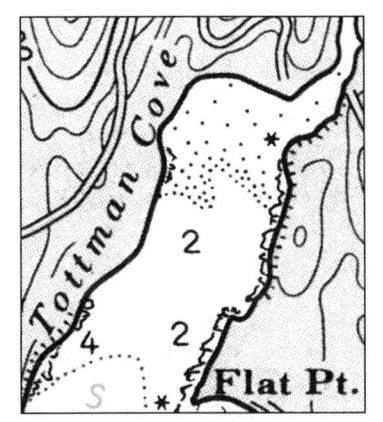

By sea. Despite its size, Tottman Cove is shallow. Shoaling begins as far out as Pitchpine Ledges, marked by nun "4." There is one rock just off Flat Point at the mouth of the cove, but otherwise it is free of obstructions.

Use caution. This is a dead-end lee shore where waves get funneled between the shores and pushed up by the shallow bottom to breaking heights. Their force is what made the beach in the first place and what carved Tottman Cove so far up the bed of North Creek. Only explore Tottman in the most stable, fair-weather conditions, and leave before it begins to blow.

Ashore. Tottman Cove is named after Henry Totman, of Devonshire, England, but somehow the charts added an extra "t" to his name. He arrived here in 1767 after being commissioned with the unpopular post of collecting Crown taxes for the town of Georgetown, which at the time encompassed all of Phippsburg. He built his cabin on the west end of the beach at the head of what would become known as Tottman Cove. Sheep were brought from Massachusetts, and he carved a large farm out of the wilds on the land running out to West Point. He and his wife raised 10 children here.

During the War of 1812, a field post operated a signal station at Robinson's Rock, on the high ridge that ran through the middle of the old Totman farm. If suspicious craft were seen entering Casco Bay from the east, two large black boards, 16 feet long by 30 inches (thirty inches!) wide were suspended in the form of a cross, and they could be seen through Captain Moody's Dollard telescope at the Portland Observatory (see Portland Observatory, p. 45). Robinson's Rock is still marked on the charts.

Around 1850, a schooner was built in an unlikely spot well back from the banks of North Creek by Captain George Washington Wildes. Neighbors said that his effort was a waste—that he would never get the ship to the sea. But on launch day they were all bribed with liquid refreshments, their oxen were harnessed, and the ship was inched on spruce rollers to Tottman Cove and then out to deeper waters. The process took a week.

The schooner was named the *Silvia O. Wildes* for Captain George's first wife, and she was put into the West Indian trade. Captain Wildes would again do the impossible when he moved a substantial building, chimney and all, from the steep hill over Tottman's Beach to a rugged site on Small Point where it became the Boston Gunning Club's clubhouse (see Small Point, p. 240). Captain Wildes died in 1890 and is buried in the North Creek Cemetery.

238. Cape Small Harbor

What the charts call Cape Small Harbor is what the locals actually call Small Point Harbor. It is a harbor, and nearly a perfect one, tucked between Hermit Island and the mainland. After a tricky entrance, a narrow slot affords almost complete, landlocked protection in a tranquil and scenic setting.

This harbor seems made for small boats. They can negotiate the double bars that lock the mouth of the harbor more easily than deeper-draft vessels. If the tide is high, they can explore the shallow cove to the east and stop at the Lobster House takeout for true downeast fare, or they can work their way up to the head of The Branch to the little general store at Hermit Island Campground or cross over to the beautiful, sandy Head Beach. Or, if they plan to stay, they may find anchoring room among the tightly packed lobsterboats in the narrow channel. For boaters staying at Hermit Island Campground (see p. 237), this is a perfect, protected departure point for small-boat exploration.

By sea. The approach to Cape Small Harbor depends on the state of the tide, and it is complicated by the inadequate scale of the chart.

From a distance, Goose Rock seems to blend with the mainland behind it, but as you approach, a narrow channel opens up behind it, known as The Guzzle. The Guzzle, however, is guarded by two overlapping bars southeast of Goose Rock, neither of which are usually marked. Near high tide, depending on your draft, you may be able to run a straight course over the two bars. Otherwise you will need to snake around them.

A long, sandy beach curves south from Flat Point and ends in an outcropping of white rocks. This is followed by a shorter sand beach and a second set of white rocks, which mark the beginning of the channel obstructions. The first bar is sand, extending from the rocks on the mainland. A short distance farther south, a rock ledge and mussel bed make out from the southeastern end of Goose Rock. Sometimes there is a stick with a lobster buoy at the end of the first bar, but don't count on it. The chart shows a red nun "2" marking the second ledge, but it, too, may not be there.

At Goose Rock, turn southward, keeping Goose Rock to starboard and favoring it to clear the first bar. About halfway down the length of Goose Rock, head well over to the mainland side to skirt the second bar, being careful that ebbing or flooding current doesn't set you onto either bar. The channel at low is about 60 feet wide and 5 or 6-feet deep.

Once past the bars, stay to the eastern side until you reach the first of two small islands. Keep the islands close aboard to port. Opposite the first island, a ledge extends halfway across the channel from the west side, so keep to the east, tight against the islands.

After this ledge, you have an almost clear shot to the anchorage. There is deep water near the lobster docks on the west side of the channel and among the moored lobsterboats.

Gas and diesel are available at the lobster dock. Several years ago the idyllic little boat yard of Robert Stevens Boatbuilder (389-1794) built and launched a replica of a Viking knarr, which completed a voyage from Greenland to Newfoundland. Even if you are not going that far, they can help you with repairs, or in a pinch you may be able to launch a trailered boat from their ramp.

The long and narrow island west of the moored boats is Tennants Island, and the deep water extends to its southern tip. After that, the channel narrows, bends to the west and shoals in The Branch. Halfway up the branch there is a small float for a charter boat running out of Hermit Island Campground. If you land here, please do not block the float.

At high tide you can explore the cove to the east by picking your way through the ledges. Stay to the north of the visible rocks but south of the ledges off the mainland. The Lobster House restaurant sits right by the water where the chart shows a "Y."

By land. Follow the directions to Hermit Island Campground, below.

Ashore. The first island inside the harbor is Webbers Island. It was once owned by turn-of-the-century artist John Marin, and long before that it was used as a fish-drying station. Lobstermen still pile its shores with traps, which they off-load directly from their boats by pulling up to the island's steep shores.

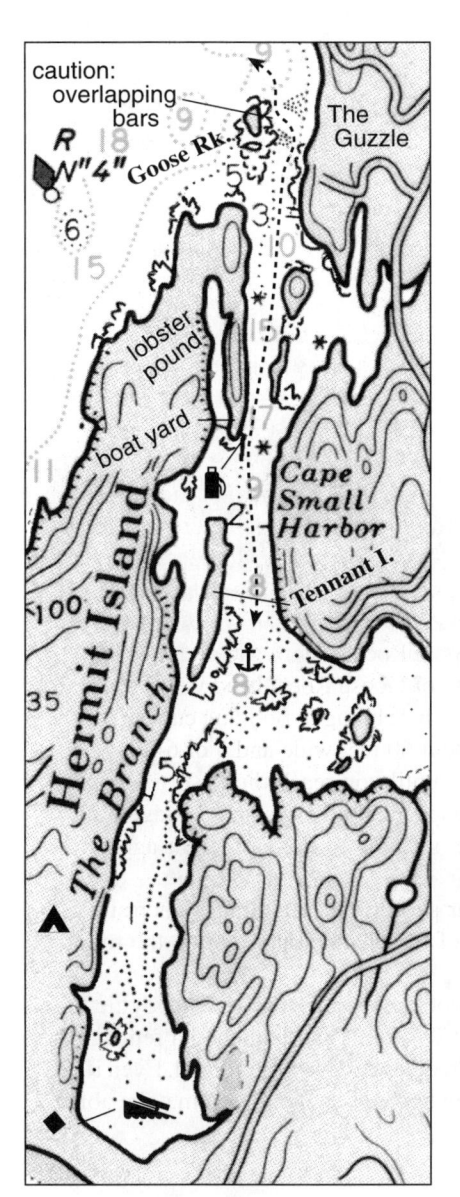

Please do not land on Tennants Island, home to an active rookery of great blue heron.

If you land at the lobster dock, you can walk across a narrow wooden footbridge over the mouth of a working lobster pound. Lobsters are stocked here in the fall to even out market fluctuations in late winter and early spring. The pound-keeper gambles that the "hoped for" price will be well above the "going in" price. This pound holds between 40,000 and 80,000 pounds of lobster, depending, as a small sign puts it, "on the state of the owner's ulcer."

From the lobster pound, trails for campground guests (see p. 237) lead all over Hermit Island, through the woods from one pocket beach to another and along stunning cliffs. Turn left and follow the road to the campground's general store for a trail map.

Small Point was named after Francis Small, one of the first settlers in the area. He operated a small trading house just east of The Guzzle in the 1680s. He was killed during an Indian raid in 1690. His predecessor was a fisherman named John Drake, who settled here around 1670 and married the daughter of the first settler in Phippsburg. The Drakes were only here for six years before their cabin was "consumed to ashes by ye enemy (Indians)" and the family fled.

In the early 1700s, there were more attempts at settlement. A group of Boston mer-

Lobsters and Lobstering

Of all the creatures along the Maine coast, few are tied to our imaginations as strongly as the humble lobster. We can't help but remember the biggest one or the sweetest one or even the next one. If Maine had a taste, undoubtedly it would be lobster.

James Rosier first chronicled the Maine lobster on Waymouth's expedition in 1605 when he wrote, "With a small net...very nigh the shore, we got about thirty very good and very great Lobsters."

Four-foot lobsters were not that uncommon. There were so many lobsters that storms would wash ashore whole windrows of lobsters, which were hauled away to be used as fertilizer. There were so many lobsters that there was no lobster industry—anybody could catch as many as he wanted.

In the mid 1800s, though, the French invention of canning changed everything. Suddenly, lobsters could be made into a worldwide commodity. The first cannery opened in Eastport in 1843. By 1880 there were 23 along the Maine coast. As demand increased, fishing techniques evolved from hoop-net traps set from sailboats and hauled by hand to multi-room "pots" set from boats with engines.

Immediately, the average size of the lobsters began to drop, and it has done so to this day. By 1887, about 2,000 lobstermen were hauling 109,000 traps for an annual catch of almost 22 million pounds. A century later, lobstermen fished two million traps and caught the same poundage.

Lobsters hatch from eggs and begin as tiny larvae floating near the ocean's surface. After several days they molt, shedding their old shell and developing a newer, larger one. A few weeks later, they molt again, and again, each time growing and becoming more complex. In the first year of life a lobster may molt seven times. In about seven years, the egg will have grown to a one-pound lobster, which will molt once a year, leaving its old shell intact, claws and all, on the sea floor. If it can manage to avoid a trap, it can live for 40 or 50 years.

When a lobsterman hauls his trap, he throws back "shorts." By law, "Keepers" must have a carapace length between 3 5/16" and 5 1/4." Any female with eggs on the underside of her tail, or "berried" as it's called, must also be thrown back, but first she is v-notched on her tail flipper. If she is caught again, the notch will tell other lobstermen that she is a breeding female and must be thrown back.

Several years ago, Maine imposed its first trap limit of 1200 traps. It will be reduced to 800 in the year 2000.

Size and trap regulation seems to be working. Recent years have seen landings at all-time high levels. In 1997, Maine's 7,000 licensed lobstermen landed 46.3 million pounds from 2.5-3 million traps, about half of all the lobsters caught in the nation.

But large landings may not indicate a healthy, sustainable lobster population. They may reflect a lack of predators—a situation that is fast changing with the increases in Maine stripers and seals. Or, more ominous, the landings could be the signs of a fishery on the verge of collapse. At the turn of the century, lobsters of up to 20 pounds were routinely caught, and anything less than 3 1/2 pounds was usually thrown back. Now, 90 percent of the lobsters caught have just reached the legal size at about 1 to 1 1/4 pounds, and only 10 percent of the females are sexually mature.

At the end of the day, a wholesaler weighs the lobsterman's catch and credits the lobsterman's account at the day's price. The lobsters are then sold to other wholesalers, like fish markets and restaurants, or sold to the public at retail, or, if the price of lobsters is down, held in large lobster pounds until there is an upturn in the price.

The price is determined by the economics of supply and demand, but in the case of lobsters, which hibernate in the mud in winter, it's the supply that fluctuates. The demand, as anyone who has been to the Maine coast knows, is insatiable.

chants formed a plan to establish settlements in what would become Maine. They called themselves the Pejepscot Proprietors, and in 1716 they sent the sloop *Pejepscot,* loaded with 4000 board feet of lumber, to start a fishing village at Small Point Harbor. A garrison was built up over the east side of The Guzzle, and roads were cleared across Small Point to the Sagadahoc (the Kennebec) River and the great expanses of salt marsh there.

One entrepreneur, Dr. Belcher Noyes, began a fishery which employed twenty boats at a time and was sustained by bounties paid for the fish by the King of England. The beach from which they operated, at the north end of what is now Hermit Island, got the name Bounty Cove.

Another settler had bounty of a different kind. John Blethen, despite the daily struggle for survival amid nearly constant Indian clashes, managed to have three wives, the first two bearing a total of 27 children. One wonders about that third wife!

The Pejepscot settlement was under frequent Indian attack, with little or no government protection. The settlers petitioned the General Court to formally designate this fishing settlement as a township called "Augusta." But that would have committed the government to helping defend the isolated outpost, so the petition was denied. The name, needless to say, was used elsewhere.

Indian clashes were nearly constant. Belcher Noyes built a stone fort for protection from the Indians, but it lacked one major necessity—water. Several years later the settlers fled to the fort when they were attacked by Indians, but they had no defense against the burning arrows. By 1724, Pejepscot was deserted, and resettlement was slow. By 1751, there were only five farms on the Casco Bay side of Phippsburg, most of them huddled around Small Point Harbor and a fort and a small sawmill there. The dam spanned The Guzzle and the mill was on the northern tip of Hermit Island, still labeled on the chart as Mill Point.

239. Hermit Island Campground and Head Beach

Hermit Island Campground (443-2101) is a marvelous family campground that occupies all of magnificent Hermit Island. It caters to tenters only, and some have been returning for generations to sites nestled in the woods, tucked behind dunes, or high atop bold cliffs. The rest of the 255-acre island is kept in a natural state, with extensive trails through the woods to remote pocket beaches and along the high cliffs to the west where the sunsets spill out of the sky.

Hermit Island rents canoes and sturdy rowboats, and you are welcome to bring along your own outboard. If you bring your own boat, you can launch it at high tide at their gravel beach into the head of The Branch or at the small boat yard on Hermit Island (see Cape Small Harbor, p. 234).

Hermit Island is not actually an island. An isthmus of sand and dune connect its southern end to the mainland. The southern side of this isthmus is a beautiful, fine-sand ocean beach, open to the public for a fee. In fair weather, portable boats can be launched or beached here, or you may just want to spread your towel and soak up the sun.

By sea. See detail chart, next page. Boats can approach from either side of the isthmus that connects Hermit Island to the mainland. The safest approach is from the north, through The Guzzle into Cape Small Harbor (see page 234).

Alternatively in calm weather, beachable boats can land at Head Beach or the beach south of Wallace Head, at the southern end of Hermit. Both are ocean landings subject to swells or even surf. Gooseberry Island Ledge, southwest of Gooseberry Island, is marked by nun "2," but the nun is well to the west of the ledge. Do not run a straight course from the nun to Head Beach or you will be on it. Beware, also, of the line of three rocks that extend a long way out from the head at the western end of Head Beach.

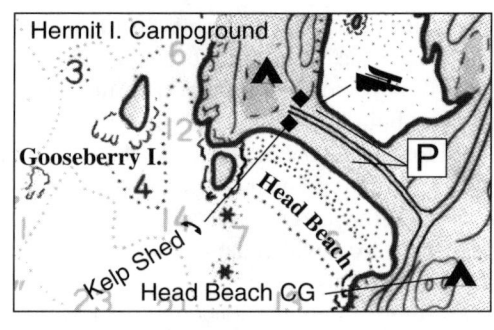

By land. From Bath, follow Rt. 209 south. When Rt. 209 veers to the left, continue straight on Rt. 216. Head Beach Road, which crosses behind the dunes to Hermit Island, will be close to the end, on the right, and well marked with signs. In season, there will be a fee for beach parking.

Ashore. Hermit Island Campground is open from mid-May to mid-October, and reservations are highly recommended. The small General Store and office for the campground is on the island side of the connecting isthmus, and their restaurant, the Kelp Shed, is on the other. Only one vehicle per tent site is allowed on the island, so extra cars or boats on trailers must be parked here.

The General Store has limited groceries, pay phones, and maps of the stunning island trails. If you are camping, the bold heads and cliffs on the west side make good surfcasting spots for stripers, and the pocket beaches on the north shore are perfect places to rest your weary bones. One of them, Spring Beach, on the northeast end of the island, is named for a spring of fresh water that bubbles to the surface just above the high water mark.

Hermit Island is named for Albert Morse, who lived there as a bachelor, fishing local waters, planting some crops, and raising some sheep and cattle. In addition to the island's name, his isolation inspired many stories and legends. In one, related by Stanwood and Margaret Gilman in *Small Point: Cape of Many Islands*, Albert is visited by his uncle, Percy Morse. Uncle Percy asks his unkempt nephew, "Why don't you get some new clothes, spunk up, look for a woman, get married, and be somebody?"

Albert replied, "Well, I am afraid I might find a woman, get to love her and then she would die. What would you do if the woman you loved died?"

"Well," said Uncle Percy, "I got one woman, so I guess I could get another."

Not long after this inspiring conversation, Albert hired a horse and carriage and took a young lady for a day's outing. She surprised him by paying for dinner and for the hired horse and carriage. And she also surprised him by telling him at the end of the day that she never wanted to see him again. It is said that from that day on, Albert never left Hermit Island except to buy food at a nearby store.

In 1950, Albert's descendents, William and Edward Morse, sold the island to former Governor Sewall who developed it into the campground with his sons, Nick and Dave, who still manage it.

240. Head Beach Campground

Head Beach Campground (389-1666) is almost at the end of Small Point, just opposite Head Beach Road, which leads behind the dunes to Hermit Island. It is ideal for campers in motorhomes or pulling trailers, since Hermit Island Campground only has tent sites.

By land. Follow directions to Hermit Island (p. 238).

Ashore. The campground has wooded sites with all hook-ups, and they also rent cottages. The small office and store sells limited groceries and ice. Beautiful Head Beach is within easy walking distance.

241. Bald Head

Bald Head is a high nub that forms the southwestern point of Cape Small. A lower sandy isthmus connects it to the mainland.

This is where historians guess that Giovanni da Verrazzano and his crew first encountered Maine natives, during their voyage of exploration in 1524. With difficulty, they traded with the fearful Indians by bringing their longboats to the rocks and waiting for the Indians to lower by cord whatever they had to offer in exchange for knives, fishhooks, and sharpened steel. "...when we had nothing left to exchange with them, the men at our departure made the most brutal signs of disdain and contempt possible for any brute creature to invent, such as exhibiting their bare behinds and laughing immoderately."

For this, Verrazzano named the coast *Terra Onde di Mala Gente*, or Land of the Bad People.

But the Indians had every reason to distrust Verrazzano, a hard-driving, ungenerous Captain, who referred to his crew as "the maritime mob." On this voyage they had already kidnapped an Indian infant from the arms of an old woman who was probably its grandmother, and when one brave Indian offered them what was probably a peace-pipe, they mistook it for "a burning stick" and they "..in turn fired off a blank shot from our musket at him and he trembled all over with fright and remained as if thunderstruck..."

Ashore. All the land of Cape Small is private, including Bald Head. In settled weather, the head creates a modest lee to the north, where, conceivably, Verrazzano's ship *La Dauphine* dropped anchor.

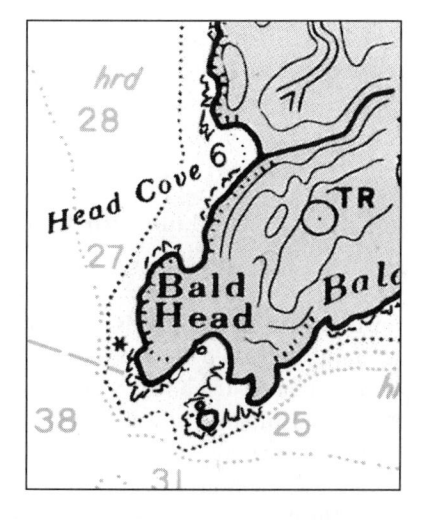

242. Small Point and Fuller Rock

Small Point is Casco Bay's eastern edge, its final frontier. This rocky arm reaches south from Cape Small into the open ocean and marks the division between Casco Bay and Maine's midcoast.

Small Point can be rounded in small boats, but the voyage should be timed carefully for settled weather and sea conditions. Good protection is not close by on either side of the point, and landing on the rocky shore is difficult if not impossible.

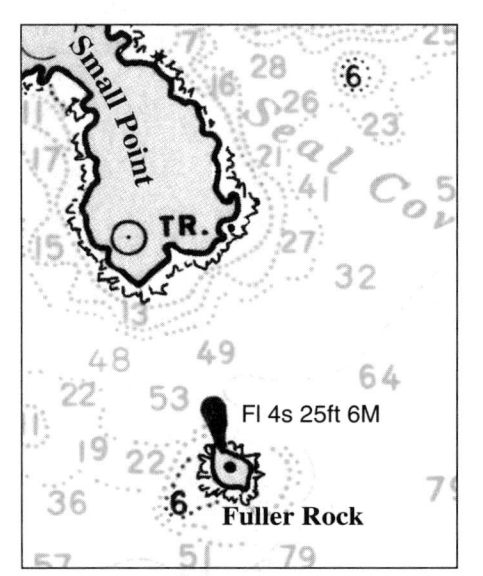

By sea. Small Point is easily distinguished from the water by a small white tower near its end and by Fuller Rock wallowing in the surge just offshore.

In addition to marking the eastern end of Casco Bay, Small Point marks the end of NOAA chart 13290. Be sure you have the next chart, number 13293, and that you have studied it before you attempt to round the point heading east. To make the rounding, pass between Small Point and Fuller Rock. The only danger is to the west, well-marked Bald Head Ledge.

High Seguin Island, one of Maine's most prominent coastal landmarks, lies to the east.

Ashore. The little white tower is maintained by the Coast Guard, but all of Small Point is private.

In the 1880s, an elite group of Boston businessmen formed the Boston Gunning Club and purchased a large tract of land extending from Bald Head to Small Point. The group also became known as the Small Point Gunning Club. They would arrive in the fall and spring to shoot coot, ducks, geese, and all kinds of waterfowl from blinds ashore and from duck boats. The daughter of the first caretaker of the property recalled seeing coot bones piled as high as the clubhouse's dining room window.

Despite their skepticism, the club hired Captain George Washington Wildes to move a substantial building from the steep banks above Tottman's Beach to Small Point to be their clubhouse (see Tottman Cove, p. 233). The Captain was already known for accomplishing the impossible. Somehow, he managed to get it down the steep hill and onto a scow and around the exposed waters of Small Point where he reversed the process and off-loaded the house over the rugged ledges just hours before a September hurricane.

The Gun Club developed lots near the clubhouse as a cottage community, and they even proposed building an electric railroad from Bath to Small Point. The trolley was never built, but the clubhouse and several cottages still stand near the point, though they are now privately owned.

In the 1940s, a Chicago company set up a moss-raking operation on the Point to harvest sea moss for processing into emulsifiers and stabilizing agents used in Jell-o, puddings, and ice cream. Rakers would bring small boats alongside the rocks, then stand in waders to fork the dark-red and purple sea moss into baskets. On a good day, a raker could land 500 to 1,000 pounds.

During World War II, a German sub was sighted off Small Point. Two planes were dispatched from the Brunswick Naval Air Station. They dropped depth charges and claimed to have sunk it, but German records discovered after the war revealed that the sub had actually escaped and was later sunk in the Mediterranean.

On June 22, 1942, observers in the towers on Bailey Island spotted a sub on the surface heading east. The destroyer *McCalla* was dispatched from Portland in pursuit. Then the observers in the towers at Sabino Head picked it up. When the *McCalla* caught up with it, the sub descended, but it was depth-charged off Small Point. An oil slick rose to the surface. Some reports claim that the next day the bodies of German sailors washed ashore on Small Point.

Underwater explorer Greg Brooks recently spearheaded a project attempting to locate the sunken submarine using side-scan sonars and magnetometers. They located an object that seems to fit the profile of a sub's underwater image. Unfortunately, the target sits on the bottom in water over 170 feet deep. Divers sent down to confirm the find discovered only dangerous currents and poor visibility, and they returned to the surface without positively identifying the sub.

APPENDIX A:
EMERGENCY NUMBERS

ORGANIZATION	VHF	PHONE	CELL
U.S. Coast Guard Search and Rescue	16	207-799-1680	* CG
Maine Marine Patrol		207-799-3380	
Maine State Police		1-800-482-0730	* 77
LOCATION		**POLICE, FIRE, AMBULANCE**	
Cape Elizabeth		207-799-8581	
Portland, South Portland		911	
Cushing Is., Peaks Is.		911	
Diamond Is., Cliff Is.		911	
Long Is.		207-775-3232	
Falmouth		207-781-4242	
Cumberland		207-829-3120 (police) 207-829-5211 (fire, ambulance)	
Chebeague		911	
Yarmouth		911	
South Freeport, Freeport		207-865-4800	
Brunswick		207-725-5521	
Harpswell		207-774-1444 (sheriff)	
Phippsburg		207-389-2141 (police) 207-443-9711 (fire, ambulance) 207-443-8201 (sheriff)	
OTHER SERVICES			
Poison Control Center		1-800-442-6305	
Maine Lyme Disease Project		207-761-9777	
Red Tide Hotline		1-800-232-4733	
Towing Service: Sea Tow	09, 16	207-772-6724	
Weather: NOAA forecast	wx01-wx10	207-688-3210	

APPENDIX B:
PUMP-OUT STATIONS

According to the Friends of Casco Bay, untreated waste from a single weekend boater contains the same bacteria count as the treated waste of a city of 100,000. By federal law, the discharge of untreated sewage is prohibited within three miles of the coast. Boats equipped with heads are required to have a Coast-Guard approved holding system. Holding tanks can be pumped out for free or for a nominal charge at the following locations:

LOCATION	MARINA, SERVICE	ENTRY	VHF	PHONE
South Portland	Spring Point Marina	8	09	767-3213
Portland Harbor, Islands	Baykeeper II (mobile)		09	776-0136
Falmouth Foreside	Handy Boat Service	62	09	781-5110
Royal River	Yarmouth Boat Yard	98	09	846-9050
	Yankee Marina	100	09	846-4326
Harraseeket River	Brewer's Marina	109	09	865-3181
Merepoint Bay	Paul's Marina	129	09	729-3067

APPENDIX C:
ENVIRONMENTAL ORGANIZATIONS

Casco Bay

Casco Bay Estuary Project 207-828-1043
312 Canco Rd.
Portland, ME 04103
   Coordinates research on the health of the Casco Bay watershed.

Friends of Casco Bay 207-799-8574
2 Fort Road
South Portland, ME 04106
   Dedicated to the improvement and protection of the environmental health of Casco Bay. Operates the *Baykeeper* pump-out boat.

Friends of the Presumpscot 207-892-4597
P.O. Box 223
South Windham, ME 04082

Friends of the Royal River 207-829-4602
John MacKinnon
1068 Sligo Rd.
North Yarmouth, ME 04097

Portland Trails 207-775-2411
1 India St.
Portland, ME 04101
http://www.trails.org
   Spearheads the effort to design and build an interconnected walking and bicycling trail system throughout greater Portland, including the trail from the Old Port to Back Cove.

State of Maine

Coastal Conservation Association-Maine 207-846-1015
40 Lafayette St.
Yarmouth, ME 04096
http://www.ccamaine.org
   The "Voice of the Saltwater Sport Fisherman" engaged in fish stock preservation and rebuilding, publisher *Maine Saltwater Angler*.

Gulf of Maine Council on the Marine Environment
20 Park Plaza, Suite 1112
Boston, MA 02116
http://gulfofmaine.org
    Fosters cooperation among scientific and political organizations and the general public to encourage understanding and sustainable resource use in the Gulf of Maine. Publishes *Gulf of Maine Times*.

Island Institute   207-594-9209
410 Main St.
Rockland, ME 04841
http://www.islandinstitute.org
    Dedicated to the stewardship and planning of Maine islands and island communities. Publishes *Island Journal* magazine.

Maine Audubon Society   207-781-2330
118 US Rt. 1
P.O. Box 6009
Falmouth, ME 04105-6009
http://www.maineaudubon.org/lin.htm
    Owns the Gilsland Farm on the Presumpscot River and Mast Landing Sanctuary on the Harraseeket River. Promotes ecological awareness, education, appreciation, and preservation. Publishes *Habitat* magazine.

Maine Bureau of Parks and Lands   207-287-3821
22 State House Stattion
Augusta, ME 04330-0022
(Wolf Neck Woods State Park: 207-865-4465)
http://www.state.me.us/doc/prkslnds/prkslnds.htm
    Manages the undeveloped islands owned by the state. Many BPL islands are open to the public, others are leased to towns or other managing organizations.

Maine Coast Heritage Trust   207-729-7366
167 Park Row
Brunswick, ME 04011
http://home.acadia.net/userpages/mchtme
    Pioneered coastal conservation through the use of conservation easements. Currently the largest land trust in Maine. Helps coordinate the efforts of smaller land trusts, which in Casco Bay include the Brunswick-Topsham Land Trust, Cumberland Mainland and Islands Trust, Freeport Conservation Trust, Harpswell Heritage Trust, and the Oceanside Conservation Trust.

Environmental organizations

Maine Department of Inland Fisheries and Wildlife   1-800-321-0184
328 Shaker Road   207-657-2345
Gray, ME 04039
http://wlm13.umenfa.maine.edu/randy/www/ifw
    Manages land and islands designated as primary sites for wildlife, particularly seabird and duck nesting. These islands are open for day use after August 15 when the nesting season is over. Camping is not allowed.

Maine Island Trail Association   207-596-6456
P.O. Box C
Rockland, ME 04841
Casco Bay office: 41A Union Wharf   207-761-8225
Portland, ME 04101
http://www.mita.org
    Promotes volunteer stewardship and careful use of publicly and privately owned islands. Publishes an annual *Maine Island Trail Guide*.

Maine State Museum   207-287-2301
88 State House Station
Augusta, ME 04332
    Museum of state history and archeology.

Marine Animal Lifeline   emergency hotline: 207-851-6625
P.O. Box 453   207-773-7377
Biddeford, ME 04005
http://www.stranding.org
    Committed to the rescue and rehabilitation of stranded marine mammals in the northeast.

The Nature Conservancy   207-729-5181
14 Maine Street, Suite 401
Brunswick, ME 04011
http://www.tnc.org/infield/State/Maine
    The Maine Chapter of the Nature Conservancy was formed in 1956 by famed ecologist-writer Rachel Carson to identify and protect Maine's most ecologically important sites, many of which are islands. This non-profit organization believes in preservation through ownership, and it is now the largest private landowner of Maine islands. Day stops are permitted on many, but no camping is allowed.

APPENDIX D:
BOAT RENTALS AND TOURS

The following is a list of small-boat rental and touring opportunities in Casco Bay, listed in geographical order, from southwest to northeast:

Portland Boat Rental   207-773-0014
390 Presumpscot St., Portland, ME 04104
     One bowrider type sport boat located at DiMillo's Marina.

Yacht Management Services   207-767-5611
Portland, ME 04101
     20'/120hp hard-bottom inflatable for full and half-day rentals

Maine Island Kayak Co.   1-800-766-2373
70 Luther St., Peaks Island, ME 04108
http://www.maineislandkayak.com
     Sea kayak tours, expeditions, and expert instruction.

Peaks Island Kayak   207-766-5004
 Army Dock Beach, Peaks Island, ME
     Hourly and daily rentals of sit-on-top kayaks, and instruction

Rings Marine Service   207-865-6143
Freeport, ME
     Canoe and kayak rentals.

Orr's Island Campground   207-833-5595
Rt 24, RR#1 Box 650, Orr's Island, ME 04066
     Canoe rentals.

H$_2$Outfitters   1-800-20-KAYAK
P.O. Box 72, Orr's Island, ME 04066   207-833-5257
http://www.H2Outfitters.com
     Kayak tours and instruction.

Seaspray Kayaking   1-888-349-7772
New Meadows Marina, Bath Rd., Brunswick, ME 04011
http://www.maineguides.com/members/seaspray
     Canoe and kayak rentals, tours, and instruction.

Hermit Island Campground   207-443-2101
Rt. 216, Small Point, ME
office: 42 Front Street Bath, ME 04530   207-443-2101
http://www.hermitisland.com
     Canoe, kayak, and rowboat rentals (you can bring your own outboard).

APPENDIX E: PUBLIC TRANSPORTATION

Bus Service

Greyhound	1-800-894-3355
Concord Trailways	1-800-639-5150
Portland Metro	207-774-0351

Air Service to Portland International Jetport

Business Express	1-800-345-3400
Continental	1-800-523-3273
Delta	1-800-221-1212
Pine State	1-800-353-6334
United	1-800-241-6522
USAir	1-800-428-4322

Ferry Service

Casco Bay Lines 207-774-7871	Portland, Peaks, Diamonds, Long, Chebeague, Cliff Bailey
Chebeague Island Transportation Co. 207-846-3700	Great Chebeague Is.

Water Taxi

Sea Tow Portland	207-772-6724 Ch. 09, 16

APPENDIX F:
SALTWATER FISHING

Maine waters are home to numerous saltwater fish that make excellent sport and delicious eating. Licenses are not required except for fishing Atlantic salmon. Size and bag limits apply to stripped bass, bluefish, and others as listed below. All restrictions are subject to change. For the most current information, contact the Maine Department of Marine Resources at 207-624-6550, or, for salmon regulations, contact Department of Inland Fisheries and Wildlife at 1-800-321-0184.

Responding to careful conservation measures along the entire eastern seaboard, stripped bass have made an astonishing recovery and have revived the nearly lost sport of surfcasting. Please practice careful catch-and-release techniques and respect the size and bag limits for stripers to ensure this continued success.

INSHORE FISH

BLUEFISH *(Pomatomus saltarix)*

in Maine:	July-September
restrictions:	no min. size, 10 fish/day
habitat:	surface schools
food:	wide variety of fish and invertebrates
size:	8-18 lbs.
state record:	19.68 lbs., 8/8/94

ATLANTIC MACKEREL *(Scomber scombrus)*

in Maine:	May-October
restrictions:	none
habitat:	swift-moving, schooling fish
food:	small fish, will hit almost any bait
size:	to 22"/2.5 lbs.
int. record:	2 lbs. 10 oz. Norway, 1992

ATLANTIC SALMON *(Salmo salar)*

restrictions:	*call for current regulations.* One fish annually, 14"-25" special license required: residents purchase through their town halls, non-residents through tackle shops.
habitat:	coastal bays where spawning rivers enter the sea, mostly in eastern Maine
food:	small fish, will hit most baits or lures
size:	sea run salmon, returning to spawn: 14"/5lb.-30"/20lb.
state record:	closed

Saltwater fishing

POLLOCK *(Pollochius virens)* ───────────────

restrictions:	none
habitat:	harbors in 1 to 5 fathoms, water temps 35-52 degrees F.
food:	krill, small fish
size:	3"-10", up to 3 lbs.
state record:	46 lbs.,10.9 oz., 10/24/90

STRIPED BASS *(Morone saxatilis)* ───────────────

in Maine:	May-October
restrictions:	Season: 6/10 through 10/15. Catch and release allowed outside of season.
	allowable sizes: 20"-26", 40" or greater
	bag limit: 1 fish/day from each slot
	selling of any Maine-caught striper prohibited
	gear: hook and line only, landing with gaff prohibitied
habitat:	schooling and solitary
	Feeds in current, hides among rocks and holes
food:	variety of small fish and bottom dwellers
size:	to 70 lbs.
state record:	67 lbs., 9/20/78

BOTTOM FISH

COD *(Gadus morthua)* ───────────────

restrictions:	20" min. size, 10 fish (cod and haddock combined)/day sale by recreational anglers prohibited
habitat:	near bottom, feeding near ledges and shoals
food:	fish, crabs, shrimp
size:	to 51"/77 lbs.. A 20" cod is about 4 years old.
state record:	80 lbs. 7 oz., 9/8/92

CUSK *(Brosme brosme)* ───────────────

restrictions:	none
habitat:	deep water, rocky, hard bottom
food:	fish, shrimp
size:	5-15 lbs. commonly to 32"/20 lbs..
state record:	30 lbs., 1 oz., 7/2/88

HADDOCK *(Melanogrammus aeglefinus)*

    restrictions: 20" min. size, 10 fish (cod and haddock combined)/day sale by recreational anglers prohibited.
    habitat: in depths from 25 to 75 fathoms in water temperatures of 36 to 50 degrees F.
    food: brittle stars, worms and shrimp.
    avg. size: 2-10 lbs. commonly to 32"/11 lbs.
    state record: 11 lbs. 11 oz. 9/12/91

WINTER FLOUNDER *(Pseudopleuronectes americanus)*

    restrictions: 20" min. size
    habitat: soft bottom
    food: worms, sea anemones and clams
    size: to 23"
        A 12" flounder is approximately 3 years old.
    state record: 4 lbs. 3 oz., 6/28/89

OTHER FISH

shad, eel, smelt, cunners (bergalls), menhaden (pogies), hake, wolf fish, sculpins, halibut

COMMON BAITS

sandworms, sand eels, clams, mussels, squid, mackerel, shrimp, pogies

CATCH AND RELEASE TECHNIQUES

    Gear: Use barbless hooks or hooks with crimped barbs to ease removal. Use artificial lures to reduce the possibility of the fish swallowing the hook, and replace the lure's treble hooks with single hooks to aid in removal. Use heavy tackle so the fish can be landed quickly with a minimum of exhaustion.

    Landing: Keep the fish in the water whenever possible, held close by the leader to avid thrashing. If the fish must be landed, handle it with wet gloves and avoid touching its gills or eyes or removing scales or mucus. Calm the fish by laying it on its back and/or covering its eyes.

    Hook removal: Back the hook out the way it went in. If fish is hooked irretrievably deep in its throat or gut, cut the leader, leaving a length about half as long as the fish hanging out of its mouth.

    Release: Gently lower the fish into the water, supporting its midsection until it swims away. If fish is exhausted, try resuscitating it by moving it through the water to force water through its gills. Bottom fish such as cod, pollock and haddock benefit from a belly rub to release air and help their descent. If the fish does not swim away, retrieve it and try resuscitation again.

Saltwater fishing

Stripers

In late April, a transformation takes place in Maine's inshore waters. Small striped bass, known as "schoolies," begin to arrive from their spawning grounds in the Cheaspeake Bay and Hudson River areas. They congregte in the warmer waters at the mouths of the coast's rivers, feeding on mackerel, herring, shad, perch, and eels, and even immmature lobster and crabs. Soon the schoolies are followed by the mature adults—strong, full-bodied fish that can grow to more than 70 pounds. As the ocean temperatures rise, the stripers move out of the rivers and along Maine's beaches and ledges. And following them, with increasing attention and excitement, are saltwater anglers.

Striped bass have made a miraculous recovery from near extinction. Over fishing by commercial fishermen in the 1960s and 70s whittled their landings from a peak of 15 million pounds in 1973 to only 1.7 million pounds ten years later. By the early 1980s, the threat of a federal fishing moratorium prompted most Atlantic states to impose severe regulations on the striped bass fishery. As a result, 1982 was a record spawning year for the fish. Ten year later, those fish were the 40-inch fighters that in one season practically reinvented the sport of striper fishing.

Striped bass are anadromous, returning from the sea to the river where they were born to spawn. Unlike many anadromous fish, such as salmon, stripers do not die after spawning. They return to the sea again to continue thier annual migrations along the coast. Typically, they can live up to 30 years and grow to more than 50 pounds. Maine's saltwater record stands at 67 pounds, taken in the Sheepscot River in 1978. The world record is 78.5 pounds, caught off Atlantic City, New Jersey in 1982.

Hot spots for striper action have a strong ebb current, like the mouths of rivers or narrows between islands, and by underwater obstacles that break the flow, such as rocks or ledges where the bait fish might hang in the eddies. Stripers hit mostly at dawn and dusk. Heavy rains with ample runoff may force the fish away from the rivers' mouths, and warmer ocean temperatures in later summer tend to disperse stripers among the islands.

Typical rod setups use 12-pound line for schoolies and 20 to 30-pound gear for the big stripers. Live bait can be mackerel, eel, herring, or sandworms. Small popper lures, Bucktails, or Castmasters work well for schoolies, and bigger rubber fish, swimming plugs, or bomber-type lures attract the big ones. Fly fishermen will use various decievers, Clousers, and teasers ahead of conventional lures. In all cases, try to match the baitfish in the area you are fishing. And when your fish hits, set the hook hard.

Maine's striper regulations are in a constant state of flux. For the most current information, please check the Maine Department of Marine Resources at 207-624-6550 or 207-633-9500. At the time of this writing, anglers are allowed to fish for striped bass all year round, but they can only keep fish between June 10 and October 15. In that period, they are allowed to keep one fish per day between 20" and 26" one fish per day 40" or longer. Under these rules, 90 percent of the catch is released. Hooks and lures should have no barbs to facilitate removal.

In the Casco Bay area, excellent advice, tackle, and guide services can be obatined at The Tackle Shop In Portland or L.L. Bean in Freeport. To support conservation efforts to protect the striped bass and to receive their newletter the Maine Saltwater Angler, join the Maine chapter of the Coastal Conservation Association by writing them at P.O. Box 239, Freeport, ME 04032 or calling 207-865-0396. Bruce Joule, of the Department of Marine Resources posts current striper information at http://www.state.me.us/dmr/recreational/homepage.html.

APPENDIX G: LAUNCHING RAMPS

Ramp	Entry	Type	Tides	Fee	Parking
S. Portland Boat Ramp	11	paved	all	●	●
East End Beach, Portland	32	paved	all		●
Falmouth Town Landing	64	paved	all		limited
Yarmouth Town Landing	97	paved	all	●	●
Winslow Memorial Park	104	paved	2/3-tide +	●	●
Dunning's Boat Yard	114	concrete	1/2-tide +		limited
Wharton Point	128	gravel	3/4-tide +		●
Simpson's Point	131	concrete	1/2-tide +		limited
Lookout Point	133	paved	all		●
Potts Point	145	to sand	2/3-tide +		
Stover Cove	162	paved	1/2-tide +		roadside
Wills Gut, Garrison Cove	165	paved	1/2-tide +		
Mackerel Cove	166	to sand	1/2-tide +		
Ewin Narrows	175	gravel	mid-tide		
Buttermilk Cove	177	paved	1/2-tide +		●
Bethel Point	188	paved	all		$
New Meadows Lake	201	grael	all		●
Sawyer Park	204	concrete	all		●
Sabino Ramp	214	gravel	1/2-tide +		limited
Painted Point Ramp	218	paved	all		●
Dingley Cove	221	to gravel	1/2-tide +		limited

APPENDIX H:
FUEL SERVICES

Location	Entry	Gas	Diesel	💧	🔧	⛽
Spring Point Marina, S. Portland	8	●	●	●	●	●
Sunset Marina, S. Portland	12	●	●	●		●
DiMillo's Marina, Portland	22	●	●	●		
Portland Yacht Services	29			●	●	
Peaks Island Marina	37	●	●			
Handy Boat, Falmouth Foreside	62	●	●	●	●	●
Chebeague Island Boat Yard	83	●		●	●	
Fishermen's Wharf, Cliff Island	85	●				
Yarmouth Boat Yard	98	●		●	●	●
Yankee Marina, Yarmouth	100			●	●	●
Royal River Boat Yard	101	●	●	●	●	
Brewer's South Freeport Marine	109	●	●	●	●	●
Strout's Point Wharf Company	110	●	●	●	●	
Paul's Marina, Merepoint	129	●		●	●	●
Dolphin Marine, Potts Harbor	155	●	●		●	
Cook's Lobster House, Bailey Island	165	●	●	●		
Lobster Village Restaurant, Bailey I.	166	●	●			
Great Island Boat Yard, Quahog Bay	181	●	●	●	●	
New Meadows Marina	203	●		●		
Watson's General Store, Cundys Hbr.	223	●	●			
Sebasco Harbor Resort	230	●		●		
Cape Small Harbor Lobster Dock	238	●	●		●	

254

APPENDIX I:
DINING BY BOAT

Location	Entry	Menu	Phone
Joe's Boathouse, South Portland	8	contemporary American	* 741-2780
Sea Dog Brewery, South Portland	12	seafood and tavern	* 799-6055
DiMillo's, Portland	22	surf and turf, Italian	* 772-2216
Jones' Landing, Peaks Island	37	seafood, American	766-5542
Diamond's Edge, Diamond Cove	45	American, seafood	* 766-5850
The Spar, Long Island	51	seafood, tavern	766-3310
Falmouth Sea Grill, Falmouth Foreside	62	contemporary seafood	* 781-5658
Chebeague Island Inn	74	fine American	* 846-5155
The Cannery, Royal River, Yarmouth	99	contemporary seafood	* 846-1226
The Muddy Rudder, Cousins River		seafood, American	846-3082
Haraseeket Lunch, South Freeport	108	seafood takeout	865-4888
Dolphin Marine Restaurant, Potts Harbor, Harpswell Neck	143	home cooking, lunch and dinner	833-6000
Estes Lobster House	163	seafood	
Orr's Island Chowder House	165	chowder, lunches	
Cribstone Bridge Restaurant	165	surf and turf	833-0600
Cook's Lobster House, Bailey Island	165	lobster, seafood	833-2818
Lobster Village Restaurant, Bailey I.	166	seafood, Amercian	833-6656
Holbrooks Wharf, Cundys Harbor	223	seafood takeout	
Water's Edge, Sebasco	227	seafood in or out	
Sebasco Harbor Resort	230	contemporary American	* 389-1161
Lobster House, Cape Small Harbor	238	seafood	
The Kelp Shed, Hermit Island	239	seafood and takeout	

reservations recommended

255

INDEX

Abenaki tribe 66, 69, 77, 91, 178
Abner Point 175
Absmeier 94
Acaraza Man 183
Active (schooner) 107
Ada Baker (3m schooner) 101
Adalaide (schooner) 81
Adams, Herbert 73
Addie Snow (stone sloop) 90
Allen, Commander William Henry 46
Allen's Lobster Wharf 148
America (schooner) 222
American Eagle (trimaran) 119
American Revolution 56, 133, 145, 222
American Promise 194
Anasabunticook tribe 144
Andarte 24
Andrews Island 53, 58
Androscoggin River 144, 148, 208
Annie C. Maguire (bark) 21, 22
Applegate, Jerimiah P. 36
Aqua Diving Academy 40
Aquarium Cove 65
archaeology 15. *See also* middens
Archangel 133
Archer (schooner) 109
Argus (sloop-of-war) 46
Ash Point 156, 158
Atlantic Improvement Company of Massachusetts 88
Atlantic Neptune 139
Atlantic Seal Bed and Breakfast 126
Atwood, Harry 93
Aucocisoco tribe 74
Audubon 72, 200. *See also* Maine Audubon

Back Beach 92
Back Cove (Portland) 38, 44, **47–49**
Back Cove (New Meadows River) 213
Bailey Island 42, 111, 155, 164, 166, **170-172,** 173, 175, 176, 178-181, 185, 190, 191, 195, 202, 203, 241
Bailey, Timothy 171
bait 251
Baker's Falls 115

bald eagles 14
Bald Head **239**, 240
Bald Head Ledge 240
Ballaststone Ledges 197
Bangs, Captain Joshua 53
Bangs Island 53, **112**
Bar Island 158
Barr, John 82
Basin Cove 155, **156–157**
Basin Island 220–221
Basin Point 143, 155, 156
Basin, The 205, **220–221**
Basket Island, Ledges 82, **83–84**, 92
bass. *See* striped bass
Batchelder and Skillins Shipyard 74
Bates Island 110, 112, **113–114**
Bates, Jane 113
Bath Iron Works 30, 33, 39, **44**
Bath Road 208–209
Battery Steele 57, 59
Baxter Boulevard 48
Baxter, Governor Percival 48, 76, 77
Baxter, Honorable James P. 77
Baxter School for the Deaf 77
Baykeeper 242
Beals Cove 169
Bear Island 205, 223, 226, 229
Becky's Restaurant 40
Ben Island 192
Benoit, Peter 106, 107
Berry Island 216
Bethel Point 185, 192, 195, **196**, 197
Bethel Point Bed and Breakfast 196
Bethel Point Boat Yard 196
Bibber, James 137
Biddeford Pool 203
Big and Little Moshier Island 120
Big Hen Island 197, 198
Big Sandy Beach (Long I.) 66, **67**
Birch Island 144, **145–146**, 149, 198
Birch Point 86
Black Rock 148
Black, Will 171
Blacksnake Ledge 179
Blake, Jacob 154

256

Blaney's Point 86
Blethen, John 237
Block and Tackle Restaurant 198, 221
Blue Hill Bay 4
bluefish 189, 249
boat
    equipment 11, float plan 10, rentals and tours 247, safety 9, seasons 4, types 9
boating in Maine xiv
Bold Dick Rock 202
Bombazine Island 211, **212**
Boston Gunning Club 233, 240
Bounty Cove 237
Bowdoin College 168
Bowery, Bud 212
Bowman Island 121
Brad's Bike Shop 56
Bragdon Island 216
Bragdon Rock 214
Branch, The 234, 235, 237
Brandy Pond 36
Brant Ledges 148
Breakwater Light 29
Brewer's Boat Yard **226**, 243
Brewer's South Freeport Marine 124, 125, **126**
Brickyard Cove 192
Bridgton 36
Brighams Cove 216–217
Brightwater 221
Broad Arrow Pines 115
Broad Cove 82–83
Broad Sound 110–113, 136, 138, 154, 155, **161**, 163
Broadicia (bark) 103
Broken Cove 110
Brooklyn (steamer) 51
Brooks, Greg 241
browntail moths 13, 68
Brunswick 140, 185
Brunswick Naval Air Station 102, 151, 213, 241
Brunswick-Topsham Land Trust 147, 211
Bug Light 26, 28, **29–30**, 31
Bunganuc, Bunganuc Brook 140
Burnham, Clara 157
Burnt Coat Island 230
bus service 248
Bush Island 196, 197
Bushy Island 216–218

Bustian, John 137
Bustins Island 134, **136–138**, 139
Bustins Ledge 136, 138
Buttermilk Cove, Point 185-188, **189**, 211

C adillac Mountain 4
Caleb Cushing (revenue cutter) 109
Californian (steamer) 23
Camden 4
Camp Berry 77
camping 12–15
Canada tribe 56
Canceaux (sloop) 159
Canibas tribe 144
cannery, canning 236
Cannery, The 117
Cape Cottage Casino. Park 24, 26
Cape Elizabeth 19, 22, 25, 31, 53, 111
    Lifesaving Station 23, 101
Cape Porpoise 183
Cape Shore Railroad Company 26
Cape Small 19, 178, 239, 240
Cape Small Harbor 231, **234–237**
Cape Standish 37
Captain's Watch Bed and Breakfast 222
Card Cove 184, 186, 192, **195**
Carrying Place Boat Company 232
Carrying Place Cove, Head 180, 230, 231
Carson, Rachel 218
Casco Bay Bridge 32, 33, 39
Casco Bay Estuary Project 244
Casco Bay Fort 71
Casco Bay Lines 27, 41, **42-43**, 53, 60, 62, 89, 94, 99, 137, 172
Casco Bay Rowing Center 117
Casco Bay Tuna Tournament 173
Casco Bay Yacht Exchange 130
Casco Castle 124, **127**
Casco Neck 69
Casino Beach **24–25**
Castine 4
catch and release techniques. *See* fishing, saltwater
Catnip Island 59
Cedar Island 199, 201
Cedar Island Beach 181
Cedar Ledges 179, **191–192**, 219
Center Island 192, **194**
Centerboard Yacht Club 31

Central Landing 91, 98
Central Maine Power 75
Chalons, Henry 50
Chandler Cove 92, **94**, 95
Chandlers Cove 43, 91, 93
charts, navigation 11
Chase, Capt. Jonathan 107, 108, 110, 114
Chase Leavitt 40
Chebeague Island 25, 42, 43, 47, 82–84, 86, **89–91**, 112, 194
Chebeague Island Boat Yard 97–98
Chebeague Island Golf Course 89
Chebeague Island Historical Society 91
Chebeague Island Inn 89, 91
Chebeague Island Transportation Company 86
Chebeague Orchard Inn 91
Chebeague Point 89
Chiver Ledge 204
City Point 61
Civil War 17, 21, 29, 49, 50, 59, 71, 77, 80, 93, 109, 138
Clapboard Island 77, 80, **81**, 83
Clark's Market 66, 67
Clean Water Act 70
Cleaveland Island 216
Cleeves, George 56, 86
Cliff Cottage 25
Cliff House 25
Cliff Island 42, 43, **99–100**, 103, 112, 113
Cliff/Jewell Island Passage 109
Coastal Conservation Association 244, 252
Cocawesco 51, 76
Cocktail Cove 62
codfish 250
Coffin, John 145
Coffin, Peggy 184
Coffin, Robert P. Tristram 145, 184, 212, 232
Cohauk 139
Colie 102
Congin 36
Cooks Lobster House 172, 173
Cooks Wharf 172
Coombs Islands 211
Coppersmith, Bill 24
Cora and Lillian (schooner) 23
Corineus (cutter) 151
Cornelia H. (steamer) 31
Cornelius Pond 226
Cornfield Point 86

Cottage Park 25
Cotton Mill Falls 115
Cousin Island 87
Cousin, John 88
Cousins Island 47, 83, 86, 87, 92, 115, 121
    town float 84–86
Cousins, John 86
Cousins River **118**, 119, 121
Cow Island 63–64
Cowan, Diane 182
Crab Island 124
Cribstone Bridge **172–173**, 181, 182
Cribstone Bridge Restaurant 173
Crooked River 36
Crotch Island 100
Crotch Island Pinky 100
Crow Island (Diamond Cove) 63
Crow Island (N of Long I.) 94
Crow Island (E of Chebeague I.) 97, **98**
Cumberland 86
Cumberland and Oxford Canal 29, 36, 37, 72, 74
Cumberland Foreside 82, 92
Cumberland Mainland and Islands Trust 83
Cumberland Mills 73
Cundys Harbor 197, 198, 205, **221–222**
currents: river 8, tidal 7, 8
Curtis, Hannah 171
Curtis, Joseph 149
Cushing, Colonel Eziekiel 66
Cushing, Eziekiel 53
Cushing Island 20, 22, 52, **53-55**, 58, 77, 111
Cushing Island Point 54, 103
Cushing, Lemuel 53, 54, 77
Cushing, Stanley 108
Cushing-Briggs 127, 128
cusk 250
Custom House Wharf 80

D.*W. Hammond* 22
Dam Cove 214
Damariscotta River 4
Damariscove 203, 204
Danford Cove 25
Darling, Bud 198
Darling, John 183
Dash (privateer) 125, **129**
David Castle 201
Davis Landing 118, 119

258

Days Lobster 118
DDT 218
Deer Point 82, 89
Deering, Captain James 48
Deering Oaks Park 48
Delorme's Map Store 118
DesBarres, Joseph F.W. 139
Devil's Stairway 180
Devil's Wall 201
Diamond Cove 61, **62–63**
Diamond Edge Restaurant 63
Diamond Island Association 61
Diamond Island Ledge 49, 51
Diamond Island Pass 25, 51, **60–61**
Diamond Island Roads 56
Diamond Islands 25, 27, 43, 52. *See also* Great, Little Diamond Island
DiMillo's Floating Marina, Restaurant 41
Dingley Cove, Island 185, 218, **219**, 223
Dipper Cove Ledges 166
diving, scuba 15
Division Point 88, 89, **91–92**
Dogs Head **167**, 168
Dollard telescope 45, 233
Dolphin Marine 155–156
dolphins 14
Don (power) 194, 202, **203-204**
Don Pedro del Montclova, 182
Doughty Cove 185, 187
Doughty Island 188
Doughty Point 186
Doughty's Island Market 91, 97
Douglas, Oliver 161
Doyle Point 84, 86
Drake, John 235
Drinkwater, John 87
Drinkwater, Perez 82
Drinkwater Point 83, 87
Dry Ledges 228
Dunning's Boat Yard 124, **128**, 129
Dyer Shipyard 37
Dyer's Cove **194**, 203, 204

Eagle Island 110, 126, 155, **161–162**
East Brown Cow 204
East Coast Yacht Sales 117
East End Beach 42, 44, **47**, 49, 71
East Yard 28
Eastern Argus 103

Eastern Mark Island 164
Eastern Promenade 42, 46, 47
Eastman 222
Eastport 236
Edward J. Lawrence (6m schooner) 51
Eliza Crowell (schooner) 54
Elkins, George 95
Elm Island (Ragged I.) 202
Elm Islands 179, 191, **199**, 200
Elwell Point 221
Embargo Act of 1807 71
EMERGENCY NUMBERS 242
environment, respect for 12
environmental organizations 244
erosion 12
Estes, Albion 149
Estes, Buster 110
Estes Lobster House 157, 158, **170**
Etnier, Stephen 154
Even Keel Boat Yard 119
Ewin Narrows 164, 185, 186, **187–188**, 211

Falls Point Marine 128
Falmouth, Falmouth Foreside 27, 65, **77–79**, 80, 81
Falmouth Sea Grill 79
Falmouth Town Landing 77, **80**, 81
ferry service 248
Ferry Village 31, 37
Fiddler's Reach 216, 217
Fifth Maine Regiment Memorial Hall 57, 59
Finney, Molly 142
fires 12. *See also* Great Portland Fire
Fisherman's Cove 99
Fishermen's Wharf (S. Portland) 31
fishing, saltwater 14, 249, 252
   regulations 252
Fitzpatrick, John 208
Flag Island 180, **229**
Flash Island 199
Flat Point 233, 234
flounder 251
Flying Point Campground 140–142
Flying Point Road Turnout 131–132
fog 7
Fogg Point 121–123
foraging 14
Fore River 17, 27, 28, 30, 31, **32–34**, 35–39, 72, 133

Fore River Sanctuary 37
Forest City Steamboat Company 26
Fort Allen, Fort Allen Park 46–47
Fort Christopher Levett 54
Fort Gorges 17, 27, **49–51**, 50, 60
Fort McKinley 61–63
Fort New Casco 71
Fort Point 205, **223**
Fort Preble 21, 25, 26, **27–28**
Fort Scammel 17, 52
Fort Williams **19**, 20, 21
Foster Point 213
Fountain of Youth 150
Fowler's Beach 65, 66
France, Captain John 23
Freeport **130**, 133, 140
Freeport Historical Society 130, 131
French and Indian Wars 28
French Island 138
Frenchman Bay 4
Fresh Water Cove 181
Fresnel lens 21
Friends of Casco Bay 27, 243, 244
Friends of the Presumpscot 244
Friends of the Royal River 244
Fuller Rock 240–241

Gales 7
Gallows Island 145
Gambo 36
garbage disposal 13
Garfield, James A. 128
Garrison Cove 172, 173
General Services Administration 50
George Felt, Jr. 58
George Island 197, **198**
George Washington 21
Gerald, Amos 127
Ghost Cliff 201
Giant's Steps 180
Gifte of God 50
Gilman, Stanwood and Margaret 238
Gilsland Farm 72
Glenrosa (3m schooner) 23
Goddard, John 21
Goddard Mansion 21, 25
Goddard's Icehouse 219
Gomez, Estevan 17
Gomez, Charles 232

Gooch's Falls 115
Googins Island 134
Googins Ledge 134
Goose Island. *See* Lower Goose I., Upper Goose I.
Goose Ledge 152
Goose Nest Ledge 112
Goose Rock 234
Gooseberry Island 238
Gooseberry Island Ledge 238
Gorges, Sir Ferdinando 50, 51, 56, 76, 81, 86, 91
Gorham 36
Goslings, The 149, **150–151**
Gowen Marine 40
GPS 3
Grand Trunk Railroad 39, 45, 48, 51, 75, wharf 23
granite 90
Grapeshot (clipper) 82
Grassy Ledge 151
Great Chebeague Golf Club 91
Great Chebeague Island. *See* Chebeague I.
Great Diamond Island 25, 42, 60, **61–62**, 63
Great Eastern (steamer-schooner) 46
Great Falls 36
Great Harbor Cove 160
Great Island *See* Sebascodegan Island
Great Island Bike Rentals 91
Great Island Boat Yard 192, **193**
Great Mark Island 163–164
Great Portland Fire of 1866 46, 80
Green House 222
Green Island Reef, Passage 101–102
Green Ledges 219
Greene Marine 118, **119**
Greene, Walter 119
Gritty McDuff's 38
Gulf of Maine Council on the Marine Environment 245
Gun Point 184, 190, 191
Gun Point Cove 167, 168, 178–180, 184, **190**
Guppy, Charles 137
Gurnet, The 146, 178, 184-186, 189, 205, **211–212**
Gurry Cove 26
Guzzle, The 234, 235, 237

H & H Propeller 209

260

H₂Outfitters 173
Hackett, Harold 42
haddock 251
Haddock Rock 163
Hadlock Cove 59
Halfway Rock 93, 104, **111**, 170, 172
Hamilton, Ambrose 90
Hamilton Marine 43
Hamilton Sanctuary 213
Hamilton Shipyard 74
Hamloaf Island 195
Hammond Island 216
Hampton, Casco Bay 144, **232**
Handy Boat 77, **79**, 243
Harbor de Grace 68
Harbor Island 103, 180, 224, 226, 228
Harpswell 143, 145, 185, 224
Harpswell Cove 148, 186
Harpswell Fuel Depot 151
Harpswell Harbor 169–170
Harpswell Heritage Trust 146, 149, 186, 197
Harpswell Inn 149
Harpswell Neck 143, 145-149, 151, 152, 155, 164, 166, 169, 178, 185
Harpswell Sound 169, 172, 184-187, 205
Harraseeket (steamer) 132
Harraseeket Inn 130
Harraseeket Lobster 126
Harraseeket Lunch 125, 126
Harraseeket River 56, 121, **124–125**, 130-134, 161
Harraseeket Yacht Club 124, **127**
Harriet S. Jackson 28
Harris, Abner 112
Haskell Island 155, **159–161**, 163
Hawkes Lobster 222
Haydens Bridge 205, 206
Head Beach 234, **237–238**, 238
Head Beach Campground 239
Helen Eliza 57
Hen Cove 196, 197
Hen Island 191, 216, 218
Hermit Island 231, 234, 235, 237, 239
Hermit Island Campground 234, 235, **237–238**, 247
High Head 166
High Head Yacht Club 166
Hill, Beth 232
Hockman (schooner) 54

Hog Island 61
Hog Island Ledge 51
Hoggiscand 61
Holbrook's General Store 198, 222
Holbrook's Wharf 222
Hope Island 95–97
Hopkins Island 219
Horse Beef 36
Horse Island 155, **159**, 224
Horse Island Harbor 226
Houdini, Harry 33
House Island 25, **51–52**, 53, 56
Houston, Henry 81
How to use this book xii, xiii
Howard Point 210
hurricanes 7
Hussey Anchorage 17, 65, 83, 93
Hussey Sound 60, 63, 64, **65**, 66, 100

Indian Point 92
Indian Wars 53, 56, 58, 76, 86, 106, 143, 145, 208
Inner (Little) Green Island 102–103
Innes, Richard 94
Inside Passage 185, **186–187**
International Ferry Terminal 39
Iowa (battleship) 65
Irony Island 151
Island Institute *vi*, 245
Isles of Shoals 66
Islesboro 4

Jack Baker's Last Stand 175
Jack Downing 37
Jackknife, The 152
Jacob's Gate 214
Jamison Ledge 180, 229
Jaquish Gut 175–178
Jaquish Island 175, 176, **177–178**, 202
Jaquish Ledges 178
Jefferson, Thomas 28
Jenny Island 199, 200
Jenny Ledge 180
Jericho Bay 4
Jetskis 43, 220
Jewell, George 105
Jewell Island 94, 100, **103–108**, 110, 123, 143, 144
Joe's Boathouse 28

261

John A. Briggs 128
Johnson, Bernard 203
Johnson, Captain Paul 203
Johnson, Elroy 176
Johnson, Fred 145
Johnson Point 169
Johnson, Stan 174
Johnson's Boat Yard 66
Johnson's Sporting Goods 40
Jones' Landing Marina, Restaurant 55-56
Jones Ledge 77
Jones, William 57
Joule, Bruce 252
Julie N. (tanker) 34
Junk of Pork 100–101

Kahill, Victor 176
Keller, Helen 137
Kellogg, Reverend Elijah 202
Kelp Shed Restaurant 238
Kennebec (steamer) 56
Kennebec River 4, 8, 45, 50, 129, 186, 217
Keyes, Jonathan 232
Kidd, Captain 107
King George's War 167
King Philip's War 76
King's Highway 132
Kittywink Islands 139
Knight Shipyard 74
Knight, Thomas E. 32
Knightsville 32

L.L. Bean 124, 130, 133
La Dauphine *239*
Lamson Cove 60
Landesman, Peter 204
Landing Boat Supply 117
Land's End 175–178
Land's End Gift Shop 176
Lane, Captain George 224, 226
Lane, Henry 123
Lane, James 106, 121, 123
Lane, Samuel 123
Lanes Island 115, 120, **121–123**, 224
Langzettel, Captain Ted 151
Lazarou, John 203
Leavitt Island 197, 198
Leona (schooner) 23
Lester's Wharf 172

Levett, Christopher 32, 51, 53, 69, 74
Liberty ships 21, 28, 30
lifesaving station 203
lighthouses 19–23, 27–30, 60, 111, 163
Lighthouse Board 21, 29
Lindbergh, Charles 102
Linnacum 222
Little Birch Island 155, **158**
Little Bull Ledge 103, 201
Little Bustins Island 138
Little Chebeague Island 92–94
Little Diamond Island 25, 29, 42, 49, 56, **60**, 61
Little Flying Point 140, 142
Little Fox Island 140
Little French Island 138
Little Green Island. *See* Inner Green Island
Little Harbor 180
Little Iron Island 151
Little Island 181
Little Island Motel 181
Little Jewell Island 103, **108–109**
Little Mark Island 163
Little Moshier 121
Little Moshier Island 123–124
Little River 121, **135**
Little Snow Island 192, **193–194**
Little Whaleboat Island 149, 152
Little Wood Island 231–237
Little Yarmouth Island 196
Littlejohn Island 84, **87–88**, 91
Lobstah Cafe 31
Lobster House 234, 235
Lobster Village Restaurant and Marina 175
lobsterboat 236
lobstering 8
lobsters and lobstering 8, **236**
Lochinvar (schooner) 22
Lohocla 103
L'Oiseau Blanc (plane) 102
Long Cove 164, **167–168**
Long Creek 34
Long Island 42, 43, 53, **65–67**, 68, 94, 216, 219
Long Island Civic Association 65, 66
Long Island Harbor 218
Long Lake 36
Long Ledge 180, 229
Long Point (Peaks I.) 59

Long Point (Sebascodegan I.), Long Point Cove 184, **191**
Long Point Island 191, 193
Long Pond 36
Long Reach 146, 185, 186, 187, 211
Longfellow, Henry Wadsworth 22, 57
Lookout Point 143, **148–149**
Louds Island (Muscongus Bay) 225
Lowell, Carroll 119
Lowell Cove 181–182
Lower Clapboard Island Ledge 77
Lower Falls. *See* Presumpscot Falls
Lower Falls Landing 116–117
Lower Goose Island **150**, 152
Lubec 183
Lumbos Hole 164, 166, **167–168**, 190
Lydia (schooner) 111
Lyme disease 13, 242

Mackerel 14, 249
Mackerel Cove 171–174, **175**, 176, 203
Mackworth, Arthur 76
Mackworth Island 48, 71, **75–77**, 79
Mackworth Point 75
MacMillan, Captain Donald 137
Madelon Point 86, **87**
Magout 139
Maiden Cove **24–25**, 26
Maine Audubon Society 72, 132, 213, 245
Maine Bluegrass Festival 210
Maine Boatbuilders Show 44
Maine Bureau of Parks and Lands 76, 92, 98, 103, 154, 158, 193, 220, 245
Maine Coast Heritage Trust 245
Maine Department of Inland Fisheries and Wildlife 112, 158, 182, 204, 246
Maine Department of Marine Resources 15, 252
Maine Festival 210
Maine Forest Service 12
Maine Island Kayak Company 56, 247
Maine Island Trail 164, 195, 196, 220
Maine Island Trail Association 10, 12, **40**, 98, 105, 158, 192, 193, 246
Maine Marine Patrol 242
Maine Narrow-Gauge Railway 44
Maine Sailing Partners 117
Maine Seacoast Missionary Society 225, 226
Maine Shipyard 31

Maine State Museum 15, 246
Maine State Police 242
Malaga Island 223, **224**, 225, 226
mammals, marine 14
Maquoit (ferry) 41, 43, 60
Maquoit Bay 139, **140**, 181
Maranbo II (ferry) 138
Marie L. (ferry) 138
Marin, John 235
Marine Animal Lifeline 246
Mariners Wharf 66
Mark Island 180, 202, **204**
Mark Island Ledge 180
Marsh Bridges 118, 119
Marsh Island 68
Martin Point, Bridge 69, 71, 73–76
Mary and John 50
Mary Ann 37
Mast Landing 124, 133
Mast Landing Sanctuary 132
masts and the broad arrow 35, 36, 69, 74, 125, 132, **133**
Matinicus Island 4
Maude M. Morey (4m schooner) 94
McCalla (destroyer) 241
McKeen family 108
McKinney, James 224
McLellan, Captain William 142
Meadowbrook 217
Meadowbrook Camping Area 216-217
Means, Thomas 140, 142
menhaden, Atlantic 189
Merchant Row 4
Merepoint 139, 140, **144–145**, 232
Merepoint Bay 145, 149
Merriconeag 143, 147
Merriconeag Sound 155, 158, 177
Merrill Marine Terminal 33
Merriman, Walter 145
Merritt Island 213, **214**
Merrucoonegan Farm 148
Merryman, Paul 154
Merrymeeting Bay 181, 208
Mexico 203
middens 15, 93
Middle Bay **143–144**, 148, 149, 151, 154
Middle Bay Cove 146–148
Middle Ground, 179, 191
Middle Ground Rock 191

263

Migratory Bird Treaty Act 14, 200
Mile Pond 72–74
Mill Cove 164, 166, 192, **214**
Mill Creek Shopping Center 32
Mill Point 237
Mill Stream 132
Millay, Edna St. Vincent 202
Miller, John 145
Million Dollar Bridge 33, 34
Ministerial Island 112, **113–114**
Mink Rocks 110
Mitchell, Jacob 154
Mitton, John 56
Monhegan Island 4, 203, 204
Montreal 29, 44, 45, 53
Moody, Captain 45, 233
Morgan, Dodge 38, 193, 194
Morse, Albert 238
Morse, Percy 238
Morse, Samuel 73
Morse, William and Edward 238
Moshier, Hugh 123
Moshier Island 121, **123–124**, 134
mosquitoes 12
Moulton, David 72
Mount Desert Island 4
Mouse Island 192
Mowatt, Capt. Henry 39, 159
Muddy Rudder Restaurant 118
Munjoy Hill 27, 39, 45
Muscongus Bay 4

N.*M. Haven* (brig) 82
Nancy 20
Nature Conservancy, The 83, 149, 188, 246
Nautical Camp Wychmere 137
navigation 10-11
Neck Island 144
Nequsset tribe 181
New Meadows Inn 209
New Meadows Lake 205–208
New Meadows Marina 205, 208, **209**
New Meadows River 146, 178-180, 184–187, 189, 199, 202, **205**, 208–212, 216, 217, 219, 220–223, 229
New Wharf 146
Newhall 36
Newport (ferry) 41
Norridgewock Tribe 56

North Atlantic Fleet 21, 65
North Creek 233
North Creek Bay 231
North Gorham 36
North Haven 4
North Ledges 193, 194
North Yarmouth 140
North Yarmouth Land Proprietors 171
Northwest Ledge 155
Norumbega 139
Norwood, John 52
Noyes, Dr. Belcher 237
Nubble, The 68, 136
Nungesser 102

Oak Island 191
Oakhurst Island 198
Oakhurst Island Boatshop 198
Obeds Rock 68
Oceanside Conservation Trust 66, 100
O'Donnell, Phil 45
Old Cove 66
Old Port 30, 39, 40, 44
Old Tide Mill 157
Olmstead, Frederick Law 53, 54
Olsen, Charles 112
O'Neil, Captain 21
Orr, Clement and Joseph 167
Orr, Henry 174
Orrs Cove 192, 193, 194
Orrs Island 164, **166–167**, 168–170, 172, 174, 178, 181, 184, 185, 190, 195, 199
Orrs Island Campground 166, **169**, 247
Orrs Island Chowder House 173
Orrs-Sebascodegan Bridge 167
Orrs/Bailey Yacht Club 172
ospreys 14, **218**
Ottawa House, Hotel 54, 55
Outer Green Island 100–101
Overset Island **65**, 67–241

Paddleworks 173
Painted Point 216, ramp 217
Palmer, John and Mary 56
Parker, James 86
Passamaquoddy Bay 4, 7
Patagonia 130
Patriot (schooner) 202
Paul's Marina 144, 145, 243

264

Peacock 36
Peaks Island 20, 25, 42, 43, 51–53, **55-57**, 56–61, 64, 65, 104, 111
Peaks Island House 56
Peaks Island Kayak 55, 247
Peaks Island Marina 55, 56
Peaks Island Merchantile 56
Peary, Admiral Robert E. 124, 159, 161–163
Peary-MacMillan Arctic Museum 162
Pejepscot, Pejepscot Proprietors 237
Pennellville 146
Penobscot Bay 4
Penobscot River 4
Penobscot tribe 56, 91
Pentecost Harbor 133
People's Ferry Company 31
Pettengill Farm 130–131
Pettengill, Mildred 130
Pettengill, Sam 107
Pettingill Island 139
Phantom (steamer) 137
Philip E. Lake (schooner) 198
Phippsburg 224
Phoenix (clipper) 32
Picaroon (privateer) 222
Picnic Point 58, **59**
Pigs Island 139
Pilgrim (steamer) 95
Pine Island 197
Pinkham Point 195
Pitchpine Ledges 233
Plaisted, Governor 224
Pleasant River 36
Plough 143
pogies 189
Poison Control Center 242
Pole Island 192, 193, 194
pollock 250
Ponce Landing 66
Pond Island 179, **182–184**
Pond Island Ledges 179, 182, 184
Popham Colony 50
Popham, Lord John 50
porpoises 14
Port Bake House 38
Port Harbor Marine 28
Porter, Michael 194
Porter, Captain Seward 129
Porter, Cole 137

Porter Landing 128
Porter, Samuel 129
Porter, Seward 129
Porter Shipyard 125, 126, 129
Porter's Landing 129
Portland, Portland Peninsula 4, 25, 30–32, 36, **38–39**, 45, 47, 49, 53, 55, 69, 71
Portland (steamer) 90, 118
Portland Boat Rental 247
Portland Bridge 33
Portland Channel 51
Portland Fish Pier 39
Portland Foundry 45
Portland Green Grocer 38
Portland Harbor 21, 24, 25, 26, 27, 28, 30, 33, 38, 41, 44, 45, 49, 51, 53, 54, 57, 60, 65, 104, 172
Portland Harbor Channel 20, **24**, 25, 53, 54
Portland Harbor Museum 27, 28
Portland Head **19–22**, 23, 24, 53, 55
Portland Head Light **19–22**, 28, 49, 53, 55
Portland International Jetport 33, 248
Portland Observatory 27, **45–46**, 69, 233
Portland Pilot 24
Portland Pipeline 28, **29**
Portland Public Market 38
Portland Town Floats **41–42**, 49
Portland Trails 244
Portland Yacht Club 77, **79–80**, 83
Portland Yacht Service 45
Portland Yacht Services 42, **44–45**
Pote, Captain Greenfield 134, 135
Potts Harbor 143, **155**, 156–159, 161
Potts Point 143, 155, **157–158**
Potts, Richard 106
Pound of Tea 124
Pratts Brook 119–120
Preface x, xi
Presumpscot estuary 71, 72, 75
Presumpscot Falls 69, 73–75
Presumpscot Falls Bridge 74
Presumpscot Land and Water Power Company 74
Presumpscot River 36, 37, **69–71**, 72, 73, 75, 76, 244
Presumpscot River Basin 71
Prince Gurnet 185, 186, 188
Prince, Lowell 173
Prince Point **83**, 146, 186, 187, 188

Prince Point Ledge 77
Pring, Captain Martin 185
private property 5
public transportation 248
Pulsifer, Richard S. 144, 232
Pumgustock Falls 115
pump-out stations 243
Pumpkin Knob **64**, 124
Punchbowl 104, 106, 110
Punkin Island 64
Purchase, Thomas 143, 144, 208
Purpooduck 27

Quahog Bay 139, 179, 185, 186, 191, **192–193**, 194–197, 199, 201–204
Quiet Presence 194

R. *M. Dobbin* (revenue cutter) 109
Race Horse (schooner) 178
Ragged Island 54, 103, 139, 179, 191, **201–202**
Railway Museum 44
Ram Island (E of Bailey) 179, 182, **184**, 191, 202
Ram Island (S of Cushing) **22–24**, 53, 100
Ram Island Ledge 22, 23, 54
Ram Island Ledge Light 20, 22, 53
Raspberry Island 192, **195–196**
Raven, The 204
Read, Charles W. 109
Recompence River 135
Recompence Shore Campsites 135–136
Red Star Lines 32
red tide 14, 242
Reed Cove 166, 169
Rennie, James 76
Reo Marine 30–31
Rhoda (schooner) 82, 83
Rich Cove 192
Rich Hill 213, 214
Rich, John 114
Richard of Plymouth 50
Richmond Island 69, 81, 106
Ridley Cove 185, 196, **197–198**, 199, 225
Ridley, Frank 198, 225
Ring, Captain Tom 126
Rings Marine 130, 247
Robinhood Beach 181
Robinson's Rock 233

rock, bedrock, composition of 90
Rock Gardens Inn 228–229
Roddings Creek, Island 121
Rodway, Frank 57
Rogues Island 95–97
Romer, Colonel W. 17
Roosevelt 162-163
Roosevelt, Eleanor 57
Rosier, James 236
Ross, Archie 138
Round Britain Race 119
Round Cove 228–229
Round Rock 179, **202**, 203
Route de Rhum 119
Royal River 86, **115**, 116, 118, 119, 121, 161, 244
Royal River Boat Yard 117
Royal River Provisioners 117
Royall, John 123
Royall, William 115, 121
Rugged Island 139, 201
Rule of Twelfths 8
Rumford 203

S.D. Warren 75
Sabbathday Lake 115
Sabino 216
Sabino Head 241
Sabino Ramp 214
Saccarappa 37
Saco River 45, 50
Saddleback Ledge 179, 202, 204
Sagadahoc River 237
salmon 15, 249
Samson, Capt. 163
Samuel (brig) 111
Sand Island 97
Sandy Beach (S. Freeport) 127–128
Sandy Point (Cousins I.) **86–87**, 121
Sandy Point Ledges 87
Sappi Company 75
Satellite (schooner) 202
Sawyer Farm 31
Sawyer Park, ramp 209–210
Scandal Island 223
Schoodic Point 4
Scotia Prince (int. ferry) 39
Scrag Island 146
Sea Dog Brewery Restaurant 30

266

Sea Horse lobster wharf 230
seagulls 200
seals 14, 236
Seaspray Kayaking 209, 247
Sebago 69
Sebago Lake 36, 61, 69, 76
Sebago Pond 37
Sebasco 4, 198, 223, **225–226**, 232
Sebasco Harbor 205, 219, 226, **228**, 229
Sebasco Harbor Resort 228, 229
Sebasco Lodge 228
Sebascodegan Island 143, 158, 164, 166, 168, 178, **184–185**, 186, 187, 189, 190, 192–194, 211, 219, 222, 225
Seguin Island 45, 203, 204, 240
Sewall, Governor 238
Seymour, James 174
Shapleigh, Colonel 143, 222
Shapleigh, Major Nicholas 171
Shark Cove 67
Sheep Island 219, 220
Sheep Island Ledge 219
Sheepscot River 4, 8
Shelter Island 144, 145, 148, **149**, 151
Shepard's Point 222
Shepherd, Thomas and Anne 134
Ship Cove 19, 24
shipbuilding 74, 82
Ship's Inn 137
Shipyard Ale 38
Silent Spring 218
Silver Islands 139
Silvia O. Wildes (schooner) 233
Simonton Cove 25, 26
Simonton, William 26
Simpson's Point 143, **146**
Sinnett, Captain David Perry 232
Sinnett, Captain William Henry 180
Sister Island 139
Sisters Ground 180
Skitterygusset 69, 74, 76
Skolfield Cove 146
Skolfield, George 148
Skolfield shipyard 186
Skolfield, Thomas 147, 201, 202
Sky-Pilot (catboat) 202
Sloop Ledges 191
Small, Frances 235
Small, Francis Neale 69

Small Point 111, 203, 217, 233, 235, 237, 239, **240–241**
Small Point Gunning Club 240
Small Point Harbor 231, 233, 237
Smelledge Shipyard 74
Smelt Hill Bridge, Dam 74–75
Smith, Captain John 66, 143
Smith, F.O.J. 37, 73-74
Smuggler's Cove 108
Smuttynose 63
Snodgrass, Ellis C. Memorial Bridge 87
Snow, Edward Rowe 102
Snow Island 192, 193
Snow Squall restaurant 32
Soldier Ledge 64, 65
Songo River, Lock 36, 37
Soule Brothers Shipyard 125, 126, 138
South Freeport 120, 121, 124, 125
South Freeport Town Dock 125–126
South Freeport Yacht Club 127
South Ledges 193, 194
South Port Marine 32
South Portland 25, 31, 32, 49, 53
South Portland Boat Ramp 27, **30**, 31
South Portland Shipbuilding Corporation 30
Southern Maine Coast 4
Southern Maine Technical College 27, 28
Sow Island 139
Spanish American War 50
Spar Restaurant 66
Speed, John J. 74
spills, fuel and oil 15, 34, 65, 242
Spring Beach 238
Spring Point 21, 24, **27–28**, 29, 30, 49, 51
Spring Point Ledge, Lighthouse 25, 26, 28, 47
Spring Point Marina 26, **28**, 29, 243
Spring Point Walkway 26, 27, 28, 30
Squando 76
St. George River 4, 133
St. Jaques, Richard 178
Stage Island Harbor 183
Standard Baking Company 38
Stanford Ledge 29
Staples Point, Staples Point Bridge 73, 74, 75
State Pier 42
Stave Island 81, **112**
Sterling, John 52, 58
Stevens II, John Calvin 48
Stevens, John Calvin 54

267

Stevens, Robert Boatbuilder 234
Stingy Hill 90
Stinnett, Caskie 195
Stockbridge Point 120, 121
Stockman Island 112
Stone Coast Brewing Company 38
stone sloops 90
Stone Wharf 89
Storm (trawler) 198
Stover Cove 169–170
Stover Point 164, 170
Stowe, Harriet Beecher 167, 169
Strawberry Creek Island 164–166
striped bass 14, 236, 250, **252**
Stroudwater 29, 32, 33, **34–40**, 35, 36, 133
Stroudwater Basin 35
Stroudwater Marsh 33, 34, 35
Stroudwater River 35
Strouts Point Marine 125
Strouts Point Village 125
Strouts Point Wharf Company 124, 125, 126
Sturdivant, Ephram 81
Sturdivant Island **81**, 82, 83
Sturdivant Island Ledge 77
Sturdivant, Joesph 114
Sunbeam V (missionary) 225, 226
Sunset House Bed and Breakfast Inn 91
Sunset Landing 91, **92**
Sunset Marina 30–31
Surf (trawler) 198
Surprise Beach (Jewell I.) 104, **106**
Susan's Fish 'n Chips 32
Sutton Island 218
symbols, key to *xiii*

Tackle Shop, The 43
Talbot and Bliss Brothers 125
Tamano (tanker) 65
Tarratine tribe 51
Tate, Captain George 35
Tate House 34, 35
Tennants Island 234, 235
terns, common, roseate 200
Thalheimer Preserve 168
The Brothers 79
The Newark (Hampton) 174
Thomas Bay 210
Thomas Point Beach 210–211
Thompson's Point 34

Thornton, Matthew 143
Three Islands 214, **216**
Thrumcap Island 155
ticks 13
tidal ranges 7
Tide Hole 223, 225
tide mills 121, 157, 166, 191, 229
tides 7, 8
Tiger (schooner) 54
Todds Corners 118, **119–120**
Torry Rock 155
Totman, Henry 233
Tottman Cove 233
Tottman's Beach 240
Towing Service 242
Town Landing Market 80
Trefethen, Henry 52
Trefethen, William S. 61
Trefethen-Evergreen Improvement Association 61
Trefethen's Landing 61
Trelawney, Richard 81
trespassing 5
Trotts 59
Trotts Rock 58
Tukey's Bridge 48
tuna, Atlantic bluefin **174**, 177
Turbot, Elizabeth 171
Turnip Island 175, 176, **177–178**
Turnip Island Ledge 177
Two Bush Island 179, 199, **200**
Two Lights 104
Tyng, Colonel John 107
Tyro (steamer) 132

U-boat 203
U.S. Coast Guard search and rescue 242
U.S. Navy 30
U.S.S. Portland (battleship) 46
University of Southern Maine 48
Upper Falls 115
Upper Flag Island 155, **159**, 162
Upper Goose Island 138, **149–150**, 152

Vaill Island 67, **68**
Valley View Hotel 61
Verrazzano, Giovanni da 17, 239
Vessel Services 40
Veterans Memorial Bridge 32, 34

268

Veterans' Taxi 91
VHF radio 3
Victory (ferry) 138
Vinalhaven 4
Vines, Richard 50, 76, 86
Virginia (pinnace) 50

W.*H. Jenkens* (bark) 54, 103, 111
Waite, Colonel 92
Waite's Landing Brickyard and Shipyard 74
Wakely, Thomas 74, 76
Waldo, Captain 90, 92
Waldo, Colonel Samuel 35, 74
Waldo Hotel 93
Waldo Point 92
Wallace Head 238
War of 1812 37, 52, 53, 129, 223, 233
waste disposal 13
Watah Lake 226
Water Cove (Bailey I.) **181**, 182
Water Cove (West Point) 230
water taxi 248
Water Witch (canal boat) 36, 37
Water's Edge Takeout and Restaurant 225
Watson's General Store 221
Waymouth, Captain George 50, 77, 133, 236
weather 6, forecasts 7, 9, 12, 242
Webbers Island 235
Webber's Lobster 194
Wengren, Ted 126
West Brown Cow 107, 110
West India, West Indian trade 90, 133
West Marine 43
West Point 4, 203, **230–237**, 232, 233
West Point General Store 230, 231
West Point Harbor, Island 230, 231
Westbrook 36
Westbrook, Colonel Thomas 35, 74, 91
Weston Point 127–128
Whaleback Picnic Area 168
Whaleboat Island 152, **154**
whales 14
Wharton Point 140, **142–143**
Wharton, Thomas 143
Wheeler, George 146
Whip and Spoon 38
White Bull 180
White Bull Island **202**, 204
White Head 53, 54

White Island 146
Whitehead Passage 20, 51, 53, **58**, 59, 100
Whites Point 37
Whitney, J.A. 71
Whitney, Jim's Boathouse 71–72
Whittier, John Greenleaf 129
Wildes, Capt. George Washington 233, 240
Willard Beach **25–26**, 30, 49
Willard, Captain B.J. 26
Willard Haven Hotel 26
William L. Elkins (schooner) 22
Williams Island 139, 213
Wills Gut 164, 169, 170, **172–173**, 178
Wilson, Dan 198
Wilson, John 191
Winnegance Bay **216**, 217
Winnegance Creek 217
Winslow Memorial Park, ramp **120–121**, 123
Wolf Neck, Wolfe Neck 121, 124, 134, 135
Wolfe, Henry 134
Wolfe's Neck Farm 134, 135, 136
Wolfe's Neck State Park 134–135
Wood Island 45, 180, **231–237**
Woodbury (revenue cutter) 101
Woodside (brig) 82
Woodward Cove 211
Woody Mark Island 164
World War II 17, 21, 28, 50, 57, 62, 65, 71, 72, 102, 104, 108, 137, 218, 241
Wreck Cove 67
wrecks 15
Wyer Island 168
Wyman Ledge 204
Wyman Power Station 84

Yacht Management Services 247
Yankee Coast vi, 232
Yankee Marina 117, 243
Yarmouth 82, 83, 86, 92, **115–116**, 118
Yarmouth Boat Yard **116**, 117, 243
Yarmouth Falls 115
Yarmouth Island **196–197**, 199
Yarmouth Ledges 193, 197
Yarmouth Town Landing 115–116
Yellow Rock 201
York Ledge 77
YWCA 38

Z*ebedee E. Cliff* (4m schooner) 94

Notes

CASCO BAY

Notes

Notes

CASCO BAY

Notes

MAINE COAST GUIDE

Curtis Rindlaub is a writer and photographer living on Peaks Island, Maine. He is co-author and publisher of *A Cruising Guide to the Maine Coast.*